Building the Customer-Centric Enterprise

Data Warehousing Techniques for Supporting Customer Relationship Management

Claudia Imhoff

Lisa Loftis

Jonathan G. Geiger

Wiley Computer Publishing

John Wiley & Sons, Inc.

NEW YORK · CHICHESTER · WEINHEIM · BRISBANE · SINGAPORE · TORONTO

To Judith Lynn

Publisher: Robert Ipsen
Editor: Robert M. Elliott
Assistant Editor: Emilie Herman
Managing Editor: John Atkins
Associate New Media Editor: Brian Snapp
Text Design & Composition: MacAllister Publishing Services

Library of Congress Cataloging-in-Publication Data:

ISBN: 0-471-31981-3

Printed in the United States of America.

10 9 8 7 6 5 4 3 2 1

Advance Praise for *Building the Customer-Centric Enterprise*

"When it comes time to get serious about CRM, all paths lead to the infrastructure that CRM processing is built on. And no one understands that architecture better than Claudia Imhoff and her co-authors."

W. H. Inmon, billinmon.com

"Alvin Toffler predicted this in Powershift 10 years ago. No one can say they weren't warned! Claudia Imhoff and her co-authors, Jonathan Geiger and Lisa Loftis, are giving you a roadmap to CRM ... This is a MUST READ for every serious manager."

John Zachman, Zachman International

"If your company wants to get closer to its customers, then read this book! It provides a practical guide for creating the technical infrastructure your company needs to effectively manage customer data and build lasting relationships with customers."

Wayne Eckerson, The Data Warehousing Institute

"Claudia Imhoff, along with her co-authors, has written another winner with Building the Customer-Centric Enterprise! Whether your company is just beginning to understand your customers' needs for personalized interaction, or has already made some inroads in providing a personalized customer experience, this book is for you. It describes not only what the move to CRM means, but also what frameworks, strategies, and structures will facilitate it."

Susan Osterfelt, Bank of America

"For years, customer-focused companies have tried to understand who their best customers are and how to best serve them. Getting the data and the tools was hard. Now with supermarket scanners, loyalty programs, and especially the Internet, we have the data. Now we need the tools. The Corporate Information Factory (CIF) is a valuable toolkit for customer-focused companies. The authors, all experts in the field, share their knowledge of CRM and CIF in chapters that build from the reasons to implement CRM to the data requirements and data management techniques for supporting CRM."

Bill Baker, Microsoft Corporation

CONTENTS

Acknowledgments   **xi**

Foreword   **xiii**

Introduction   **xv**

Part One   Introducing CRM   **1**

Chapter 1   The Customer Becomes the Center of the Business Universe   **3**

What Is True Customer Relationship Management?   6

Do We Have True CRM?   7
    How Many Customers?   8
    How Many Products?   8
    How Many Contacts?   9

The Customer in CRM   9

The Relationship in CRM   16
    Influence Value in the Contemporary Household   19
    Influence Value in the Extended Household   21

The Management in CRM   23

Summary: CRM Defined   28

Chapter 2   The Customer and the Corporate Information Factory (CIF)   **31**

The Need for a Corporate Information Factory Architecture   32
    Business Operations   32
    Business Intelligence   33
    Business Management   35

Why the Corporate Information Factory?   37

What a CRM Organization Wants   40
    "Give Me All The Data That I Need When I Need It!"   40
    "I'll Figure Out What I Want To Do With It."   41

Data Must Be Specific to My Functional Requirements   42

Data Must Be Reliable and Consistent   46

Data Must Be Delivered in a Timely Manner   50

Data Must Be Easily Accessible   52

It Must Be Flexible Enough to Support Multiple Functions   53

It Must Be Detailed Enough to Support All Queries   54

An Example of the Corporate Information Factory at Work   56
   Execute   57
   Monitor   58
   Optimize   58
Summary: The Need for Architecture   59

Chapter 3   Understanding the Customer Life Cycle   61

An Overview of the Customer Life Cycle   63
   The Enterprise, Products, and the Competition   66
   Consumers, Prospects, Customers, and You   72
   Trust and the Customer Touch Zone   76
Mapping Enterprise Processes to Customer Life Cycle Stages   80
   Intrude and Engage   80
   Acquire   82
   Retain and Expand   86
Summary   89

Part Two   Planning for CRM   91

Chapter 4   Are You Ready? Tuning the Organization for CRM   93

Critical Success Factors for CRM   95
   Implementing a Coordinated, Customer-Focused
     Business Strategy   96
   Creating a CRM-Friendly Organization Structure   101
   Establishing a CRM-Savvy Organization Culture   106
   Implementing an Integrated Customer Information
     Environment   108
   Ensuring Executive Commitment and Support   112
The Marketing, Service, and Sales CRM Roadmap   114
   Roadmap for Marketing   115
   Roadmap for Customer Service   119
Summary   125

Chapter 5   Getting Underway   127

Program Management   129
"Getting Data In" versus "Getting Information Out"   131
   Goals of the "Getting Data In" Team   132
   Goals of the "Getting Information Out" Team   135
Roles and Responsibilities of the Teams   138
   Program Management Team   138
   "Getting Data In" Team   146
   "Getting Information Out" Team   151
Summary   155

Chapter 6 Developing an Integrated CRM Technology Environment   157

Overview of the Zachman Framework   158
Zachman Framework Rules   161

Business Model Development Rules   171
Rule 1: Only One Business Model Exists   172
Rule 2: All Business Model Components Must Be Defined   175
Rule 3: An Item May Appear Only Once within the
Business Model   180

Models   182
Function Model   182
Subject Area Model   184
Business Data Model   187
System and Technology Data Model   193

Summary   199

Chapter 7 Capturing Customer Information   201

What Is Data Acquisition?   204

Mapping the Sources to the Targets   207
Creating Sustainable Identifiers   207
Choosing Appropriate Sources   209
Determining Refreshment Frequency   211
Determining Summarized, Derived, and Aggregated Fields   211

Creating the Extraction, Integration, Cleansing, and
Transformation Processes   212
Capturing Data   213
Data Cleansing   220
Integrating Data   221
Transforming the Integrated Data   222

Loading the Data Warehouse or Operational Data Store   223
Loading the Data Warehouse   223
Loading the ODS   226

Creating the Audit and Control Processes   228
Audit and Control Methodology   229
Define Processes and Data Attributes   231
Assess Process and Data Quality   232
Measure Process and Data Quality   232
Correct Errors   233
The Role of Audit and Control Meta Data   234

Meta Data Capture and Maintenance   236

Summary   236

Chapter 8 Quality Relationships Start with Quality Customer Data   239

Quality Defined   240
Myth 1: Quality Means Perfection   240

Myth 2: Quality Means Luxury   243
Myth 3: Quality Is Expensive   243
Myth 4: Quality Cannot Be Measured   244
Reality Check   245

The Foundations of a Quality Program: Deming's 14 Points   245
Point 1: Create Constancy of Purpose for the Improvement of
Products and Services   247
Point 2: Adopt the New Philosophy   248
Point 3: Cease Dependence on Mass Inspection   249
Point 4: End the Practice of Awarding Business on
Price Tag Alone   251
Point 5: Improve Constantly and Forever the System of
Production and Service   252
Point 6: Institute Training   255
Point 7: Institute Leadership   256
Point 8: Drive Out Fear   257
Point 9: Break Down Barriers between Staff Areas   258
Point 10: Eliminate Slogans, Exhortations, and Targets for the
Workforce   259
Point 11: Eliminate Numerical Quotas   259
Point 12: Remove Barriers to Pride of Workmanship   260
Point 13: Institute a Vigorous Program of Education and
Retraining   261
Point 14: Take Action to Accomplish the Transformation   262

Establishing Quality Customer Data   262
Capturing Data   263
Data Cleansing   266
Integrating Data   268
Transforming Data   269
Loading Data   270

Tools   270

Summary   271

Part Three Implementing CRM   **273**

**Chapter 9 Business Intelligence: Technologies for Understanding
Your Customers**   **275**

Defining the Strategic CRM Components   276

The Data Warehouse   279

Data Marts   281
Departmental versus Application-Specific Data Marts   283

Choosing the Best Data Mart Design   287
Determining Alternative Database Designs   290

Data Delivery   295

Decision Support Interface (DSI)   297

Summary   298

Chapter 10 Facilitating Customer Touches with the Customer ODS **303**

What Is an ODS? 306

What Is a Customer ODS . . . and Why Do I Need One? 309

Overview of an Ideal Customer ODS 313

A Detailed Look at the Ideal Customer ODS 315
Comprehensive Customer Definition 316
Customer Relationships 316
Extensive and Extensible Customer Models 320
Data Quality Tools 322
The Transaction Interface 323

Summary 327

Chapter 11 Automating the Sales and Service Process **329**

Why Automate? 331

Automating Customer Service and Sales 333
Automating Service 334
Automating Sales 346
Integrating Sales and Service Applications 353

Summary 358

Chapter 12 Interacting with Customers Online **361**

The Impact of E-Commerce on CRM 363
E-Commerce Models 365
E-Commerce Opportunities and Challenges 367
Permission Marketing and Personalization 371

Enabling E-Commerce 376
Customer Information for Click Stream Analysis 376
Technology Architecture for E-Commerce 381

Summary 386

Chapter 13 Putting It All Together with Enterprise Portals **389**

Enterprise Portals Defined 391
Why Enterprise Portals Are Needed 392
Toolbox 395
Library 396
Workbench 398

Developing Enterprise Portals 398
First Generation of Enterprise Portals 399
Second Generation of Enterprise Portals 400

Summary 402

Chapter 14 Preserving Customer Trust - The Role of Privacy **405**

The Importance of Protecting Privacy 406
Privacy before E-Commerce 409
Privacy with E-Commerce - Engendering Trust 411
Enforcement 412

Privacy Policy Components 414
Information Collected 415
Information Collectors and Users 417
Information Use 418
Customer Choice 419
Ownership 420
Access and Quality Control 420
Security 421

Privacy and the Customer Life Cycle 421
Building Trust during Intrude and Engage 422
Building Trust during Acquire 424
Building Trust during Retain and Expand 425

Privacy and the Corporate Information Factory 426

Summary 429

Chapter 15 The Future of CRM 431

The Evolving CRM Definition 433

Successful CRM Organizations of the Future 435

Challenges to CRM Implementation 436
Business Strategy Alignment 436
Loyalty 437
View of the Customer 440
Customer Selection 441
Acquisition Channel 442
Extended Enterprise 443
Commodity Business Environment 444
Organization Structure and Culture 445
Customer Information and Technology 447
Silver Bullet Syndrome 450
Closed Loop Approach 451

Weighing the Costs and Benefits 452

Summary 453

Glossary 457

Recommended Reading 471

Index 473

The authors wish to express their appreciation to the many personal and professional colleagues who have contributed to this book. We wish to thank the following people for providing us with their insight on the future of CRM and related privacy issues: Jim Kalustian, Steve Miller, Mike Evanisko, John Sievila, Larry Goldman, Tom Duvall, and Dave Mausner of Braun Consulting, Sue Osterfelt—Bank of America, Jack Sweeney—Sybase, Jack Garzella—NCR, Mike Griffiths—MatchLogic, Dick Hackathorn—Enterprise Management Associates, John A. Ladley—Knowledge InterSpace, Doug Laney—Meta Group, and Ron Shelby—XML Solutions Corporation.

We are also grateful for the support and contributions made by the following colleagues:

- Bill Baker—Microsoft
- Brian Burnett—Appsmart
- Lowell Fryman—CNET
- Stephen Gardner—NCR
- Jeff Gentry—Technology to Value, LLC
- David Imhoff—Intelligent Solutions
- Bob Lokken—Knosys
- Dave Marco—Enterprise Warehousing Solutions
- Joyce Norris-Montanari—Braun Consulting
- Steve Murchie—Microsoft
- Ron Powell—DM Review
- Bill Prentice—SAS Institute
- Dave Reinke—Braun Consulting
- Bob Terdeman—EMC2
- John A. Zachman—Zachman International

We owe a special debt of gratitude to Bill Inmon. Bill remains our staunchest supporter, mentor, visionary, and, most of all, friend. Thank you, Bill.

The authors also thank our editor, Bob Elliott, for his dedication to this project and his unwavering belief that we could actually finish this book! The book would not exist without the support of this superb editor and the help from his team.

Finally, Claudia Imhoff wishes to thank her family, Dave and Jessica, for their patience, encouragement, and steadfast support. Their tolerance of the late hours, missed meals, canceled events, and stressed wife and mother went above and beyond the call of duty.

The sweet fruits of customer relationship management are ample and ripe. Corporations view customer relationship management as the opportunity to achieve the following:

- Hold on to existing market share
- Grab more market share
- Exploit existing market share more fully

And corporations are correct. The key to being able to do all of these things—and more—is understanding the customer. Once you understand who your customers are, what their habits are, and what they represent, you are positioned to do a thousand positive things. The world opens up to you like a blossom.

In a word, the world of Customer Relationship Management (CRM) is attractive—compellingly attractive. Corporations simply can't wait to start exploiting their newfound knowledge of the customer.

In the rush to reap the rewards of CRM, businesses often forget that supporting CRM requires an infrastructure. Without the infrastructure, CRM just doesn't play. Yet the infrastructure needed to support CRM receives scant attention because it is, well, not as glamorous as CRM. To build the infrastructure requires work, investment, an understanding of architecture, dealing with complexity and time. Whatever the difficulties in the building of the infrastructure, it is nevertheless an absolute essential for successful CRM.

The elements of this CRM infrastructure are:

- Integration
- History
- Quality, detailed data

Without integration, one customer looks pretty much the same as any other customer. But once data is integrated, the business analyst can start to distinguish customers from each other and, in doing so, the business analyst is able to start to personalize the relationship with the customer. Integration adds color to a black-and-white picture.

History is vital because it is with history that the future can be predicted. History is the great predictor because customers are people, and people are creatures of habit. The habits we form early in our adulthood stick with us throughout our lives. Knowing what habits an individual has today enables us to predict what patterns of consumption and other activities the customer will engage in tomorrow. When it comes to customers, the secret to predicting the future is carefully understanding the past.

Another important aspect of the infrastructure is quality, detailed data. Detailed data is important because once an organization has a handle on its detail, it can reshape the data into any pattern desired. And to look at the customer in many different ways, flexible data is crucial.

These three elements—integration, history, and detailed data—are not automatically aligned upon entering the corporation. Some data comes in one way, whereas other data comes in other ways. Some data is time-constrained and other data is volume-constrained. Some data is structured and other data is unstructured. Some data is current and some data is time-variant. Some data is of good quality, whereas other data is questionable. To align this data, the infrastructure needs its own architecture. That architecture is called the Corporate Information Factory (CIF). The CIF is the ideal structure for the needs of the business that's serious about CRM. The CIF enables multiple touch points, where the information needed does the most good.

If anyone knows the CIF, it is the authors of this book. Applying the Corporate Information Factory to the world of Customer Relationship Management is merely a natural extension of their life work. When you read this book, you can be assured that you are on a solid foundation.

W.H. Inmon
November 23, 2000

If your company is one of the growing number of organizations making the transition from a product orientation to a customer focus, there is probably disagreement, or at the very least confusion, about how to get there. It's not uncommon to find contention and questions about the meaning of Customer Relationship Management (CRM), its value to the organization, and the technologies needed to support it. However, there is one issue upon which most business and technology executives agree: Accomplishing the transition to CRM requires a fundamental shift in business strategies and in organizational thought processes. It also requires a comprehensive infrastructure of integrated customer information technology to support these changes.

The Customer Should Be the Center of the Business Universe

Many CRM definitions focus on the importance of knowing your customer and acting on that knowledge. Putting this principle into practice is where the complexity lies. In Chapter 1, we introduce you to Bob, a sophisticated but demanding customer, and his bank, a CRM-savvy organization that has embraced the principles of Customer Relationship Management wholeheartedly. Throughout the book, we use the relationship between Bob and his current bank to highlight CRM success factors that can be readily applied across organizations and industries.

As you will see, Bob has not always been a customer of his current bank. As happens all too often today, Bob brought his business from a competitor when his initial bank would not, or could not, adapt its treatment of him to reflect his increasing value and changing banking requirements. The following true story chronicles Bob's experiences with his first bank, a bank that should have been his bank for life. Instead, the bank (it shall remain nameless!) lost a truly valuable customer, one who would have willingly assisted them in the transition to CRM. As you read about Bob's experiences, we encourage you to reflect on the stories of lost customers within your own organization. If you find similarities to the story below—and most readers will—read on to learn what your organization must do to correct these problems.

> When Bob was in high school, he opened a savings account with a local bank. In college he opened a checking account as well. During his senior year, the bank offered him his first credit card. He accepted—thrilled that any company would offer an unproven consumer such a wonderful thing, credit. (His credit limit was $500—we guess they didn't want to risk too much!)
>
> Through the years, Bob maintained a loyalty to that bank, slowly increasing his credit limit and monthly expenditures as his financial picture improved. He began using the card to charge all his travel expenses, racking up significant bills each month. All the while, he believed that his bank knew him and valued his continued loyalty. Ignoring the bombardment of other banks offering lower interest rates, no annual fee, and other enticements, he continued to use his original credit card.
>
> Even after the bank merged, acquired other banks, changed its name, and eventually lost all of that "local" bank flavor that attracted Bob to begin with, he still maintained his credit card account—until the following incident.
>
> During a particularly hectic travel month, he was several days late in making his monthly payment. Certainly he fully expected to get "dinged" with the interest charges stated in the application filled out so many years ago. What he did not expect was the impersonal and insulting treatment that he received from the bank. His next bill contained not only the expected finance charge (a hefty $321!) but also a number of other unexpected and disturbing charges. He had a $29 "late payment fee," a $29 "over-the-limit" fee (he managed to charge more than his credit limit allowed because his payment was late), and an annual fee of $50! Predictably, Bob's reaction was "Excuse me?" He was certainly willing to pay the finance charges— but the rest?
>
> He called the number on the back of the credit card to speak to his "personal" care representative. The first annoyance was typing his credit card number into the phone system ("so we can serve you better") and then having the customer service representative ask for the number again after she answered the call. OK, he let that one pass. He first requested that she remove the two $29 fees and was told that she was not authorized to do that; he would have to speak to her manager, who was out at the moment. Next he requested that she remove the $50 annual fee charge because she must know that he was a loyal and profitable customer, which should count for something—particularly since he could certainly get other credit cards for free. He was told that there was nothing she could do and that the annual fee was the same for all credit card holders.
>
> Finally, he requested that she increase the credit limit so that he would be less likely to go over the limit, should this happen again. He was told that she could not do that because it was not part of her job. He must call another 800 number if he wanted to do that. Bob hung up the phone, immediately paid his bill, cut up the credit card, and mailed the entire package to the president of the bank. He never heard a word back from them.

Increasingly sophisticated consumers like Bob are demanding that companies demonstrate that they understand their value as customers; this is in turn driving companies to CRM. Bob's first bank made many mistakes—the worst of which was not learning from prior dealings with him, anticipating his needs, and tailoring future interactions accordingly. Other mistakes include:

■ Not empowering the customer service representative to resolve Bob's issues (had she recognized them in the first place). As you will see in later chapters, effective CRM requires a holistic approach to managing interactions with customers (we call these customer "touches"). Service representatives must understand the objectives of the organization with respect to its customers. They must be educated about the importance of CRM to the organization. They must be judged and compensated on customer-oriented measures such as customer satisfaction. And they must understand the vital role they play in retaining good customers, imparting valuable information and product offers to these customers, and gaining permission to engage in a dialog that allows a continuous two-way flow of information between the customer and the organization.

■ Not implementing a customer service organization that facilitates the (apparently) seamless personalized service that sophisticated customers like Bob demand. While some organization structures facilitate CRM; others impede it. In Bob's eyes, the credit limit, the late fee, the finance charges, and the inability to talk to a single service representative are all features (or punishments!) associated with his credit card. In the bank's organization, the credit department handles credit limits, the collections area handles late fees and finance charges, and the call center interacts with customers. Problems like these are compounded when an organization has multiple call centers for different products, distinct channels such as the Internet and brick-and-mortar stores that are not fully integrated, or service, sales and marketing organizations that operate independently. Dramatic reorganization may be out of the question; however, your company can take steps to ensure that someone is responsible for the cross-functional coordination required in CRM.

■ Not developing the integrated technology environment required to understand Bob's true value as a customer and not distributing this information to the customer contact points. As the example indicates, CRM requires integrated customer information at the enterprise level. Without comprehensive customer information, the bank can't determine who its best customers are or what products these customers own, and business strategies (such as customer service activities) cannot be tailored to acknowledge the importance of the customer. In a company actively moving toward CRM, there will be an increasing demand to share customer information across business units. Satisfying this demand will require a technical architecture such as the Corporate Information Factory to facilitate the integration and distribution of customer information to all points of customer contact.

- Not ensuring the appropriate executive sponsorship for CRM. In the case of Bob's original bank, several factors point to a lack of executive support for CRM. First, a strong complaint directed at the office of the president received no response. Second, the service representative had no interest in preserving customer satisfaction. Third, the service organization was not set up to provide seamless customer service.

- Executive mandate is one of the most important factors in CRM success. Executive support facilitates the sweeping changes needed to achieve effective CRM. Without executive backing, it will be almost impossible to implement cross-functional business strategies, adopt a CRM-friendly structure and culture, and fund the integrated customer systems that support CRM.

The technology exists today to facilitate truly seamless global communications among customers, suppliers, geographically dispersed business units, and even competitors. Today's healthy economy and recent deregulations are combining to provide an increasingly level playing field in many industries, with competition in some instances coming from non-traditional sources. With so many options to choose from, consumers can afford to be demanding, and organizations must be in a position to profitably satisfy these demands.

As you will see in Chapter 1, the mantra for successful companies in the new millennium will be the following:

> Can we anticipate our customers' needs accurately enough to be in the right place, at the right time, with the right product for them?

Who Should Read This Book

This book should prove helpful to both technologists and business people who are tasked with making CRM happen. The book provides a roadmap for your company to follow as it transitions to a successful CRM environment. It explains the available CRM technology; identifies the cultural and organizational issues that must be managed; describes "best practices" for sales, marketing, and service; and provides practical examples and "starter-kits" to help you on your CRM journey.

How This Book Is Organized

The book contains three parts: Introducing CRM, Planning for CRM, and Implementing CRM.

Part 1: Introducing CRM

The first part of this book provides an overview of Customer Relationship Management (CRM) and its associated components. CRM is defined in terms designed to provide technical and business people with a common understanding of what CRM really means, why organizations are adopting CRM, and how the CRM transition could impact the organization. The Corporate Information Factory (CIF), the technology framework that provides the key to successful CRM, is also introduced. This part describes, in business terms, the basic building blocks required to construct a structured and integrated information systems architecture. The Customer Life Cycle is presented to provide a framework for understanding how a business and its customers interact, while also identifying and categorizing the various customer touch points that exist across the continuum of a customer's relationship with an organization.

Chapter 1: The Customer Becomes the Center of the Business Universe. This chapter provides a general introduction to enterprise CRM concepts. The chapter presents five basic questions businesses must be able to answer to be customer-oriented. It provides an initial definition of CRM and begins to answer the question of "Why adopt CRM?" It describes the product-to-customer shift, and it introduces the three key areas in a CRM environment: executive sponsorship, a customer-driven organizational structure, and an integrated CRM technology environment. The primary purpose of this chapter is to give both business and technology executives a common understanding of CRM. The sales, service, and marketing CRM concepts introduced here and detailed in Chapter 4 link directly to both the technology and Customer Life Cycle topics within the book. These core concepts provide continuity, bringing technology, customer life cycle, and business strategies together into a unified perspective on enterprise CRM.

Chapter 2: The Customer and the Corporate Information Factory. This chapter concisely introduces the Corporate Information Factory (CIF), which is a technical architecture that enables organizations to build an integrated technology environment. The CIF provides support for CRM through the application of customer-oriented technology. The primary purpose of this chapter is to present the architecture so that business and technology people can both understand and use the same terminology when communicating about customer-oriented information systems. Note that the technologies introduced here are described in more technical detail in Part 3 of the book, "Implementing CRM."

Chapter 3: Understanding the Customer Life Cycle. This chapter introduces the Customer Life Cycle as a structured mechanism for understanding all the potential interaction points between an organization and its customers. Representative touch points are described and categorized. The Life Cycle is presented pictorially, and the major phases of this Cycle are identified and described: Needs Identification, Awareness, Learning, Consideration, Evaluation, Customer Moment, Acquisition, Use, and Re-entry. The organization's role at each of the following customer stages is also described: Intrude and Engage, Acquire, and Retain and Expand.

Part 2: Planning for CRM

The second part of the book provides a roadmap for organizations undergoing the transformation to CRM. This part describes the organizational and cultural issues that must be addressed to obtain maximum benefit from customer technology. It covers team composition, project management, and the communications processes required for building the CIF to support CRM. It shows how to develop enterprise customer data models, capture, transform, and integrate customer information, and implement customer data quality standards and processes. These essential steps must be followed for building each new component of the CIF.

Chapter 4: Are You Ready? Tuning the Organization for CRM. Many organizations make the mistake of focusing all their time and effort on building CRM information systems without developing a complete understanding of the organizational structure, cultural environment, and business strategies that must also be in place to facilitate CRM. This chapter explains these nontechnical critical success factors, including: the executive mandate for CRM; enterprise CRM planning; CRM-oriented success measures; integration of CRM business strategy across the sales, service, and marketing management teams; and organizational culture. These factors must be understood in order to assess the organization's readiness to implement a CRM program.

Chapter 5: Getting Underway. Once priorities are set and the overall CRM program is defined, construction of the Corporate Information Factory to support CRM can begin. However, an integrated CRM environment is not built in a day (or even a year for that matter). Building the CIF requires attention from all levels within an organization. The necessary leadership and project teams must be defined. Effective teaming requires attention to the relationship between the information technology organization and the teams within the enterprise that are responsible for processes that directly interact with customers. The mission of these teams must be clearly defined and agreed upon. Formal communications lines must be implemented. The bridge between the business defining the informational requirements and the information technologists who are implementing the supporting technology are an additional critical success factor. This chapter outlines the requirements for these teams and provides a map for communicating between business and technology.

Chapter 6: Developing an Integrated CRM Technology Environment. In order to build information systems that fully support the organization's CRM strategies, it is necessary to understand customer information requirements across all phases of the Customer Life Cycle. This includes sales, service, marketing, and risk management. The best way to capture this is to define the requirements in the form of enterprise-oriented customer data models. These models are then used as the starting point for any system in the Corporate Information Factory that involves the customer. For the business reader, this chapter describes a framework for ensuring that all of these models work together to provide a cohesive view of the customer. For the technologist, the chapter provides sample models and describes the steps needed to develop the process models and the relational and dimensional data models.

Chapter 7: Capturing Customer Information. The first step to identifying your customers is to understand the information assets already available in operational systems and available from external sources. By mapping these data sources to target database schemas described in the previous chapter, an inventory of available data is created. You can then perform a gap analysis to identify what valuable data is not available. After the available customer data is identified and mapped to the CIF components, the data must be integrated. Customer information is usually scattered in many operational systems, and is often not in sync. External sources of data must be integrated with information from within the enterprise. Key data integration decisions are required to define how the enterprise will interact with customers. The process of capturing data from operational systems and external sources is one of the most intensive efforts in the creation of the CIF. This chapter discusses considerations for data extraction, cleansing, reformatting, scrubbing, reconciliation, de-duplication, transformation, categorization, and aggregation. Special consideration is given to customer contact and interaction data, management of events over time, and the support of meta data.

Chapter 8: Quality Relationships Start with Quality Customer Data The quality of customer data is key to successfully building mutually beneficial relationships. This chapter discusses the data quality issues that are key to effective CRM, including name and address hygiene, data quality scoring, and implementing business processes to ensure ongoing data quality.

Part 3: Implementing CRM

Part 3 describes how to implement the Corporate Information Factory to support CRM. This part maps the various components of the CIF to the sales, service, and marketing elements of the Customer Life Cycle, showing you how to simultaneously implement customer-oriented business processes and the underlying information technology. You will learn how to apply the CIF technology in order to do the following:

- Find out who your customers are
- Capture and store customer profile and behavior information
- Interact with customers more profitably based on this newfound understanding
- Capture information necessary to create customized products and services, and improved methods of distribution and delivery

Chapter 9: Business Intelligence-Technologies for Understanding Your Customers. A key factor in the success of any CRM strategy is the ability to utilize the available information about customers to influence the ways in which the customers and the organization interact. In order to accomplish this, data must be converted into information, and that information must be made available to decision makers within the organization. The primary systems and processes within the Corporate Information Factory that facilitate these capabilities are the Business Intelligence components. These components typically consist of the data warehouse, the data marts, the decision support interface, and the processes to get information in and out. This chapter details how the Business Intelligence portion of the Corporate Information Factory is used to support marketing and business analysis strategies within the Customer Life Cycle.

Chapter 10: The Customer ODS. An important result of improved CRM is that customers themselves become more aware of what is possible in a CRM-savvy organization. As this awareness grows, these same customers develop strong expectations about the treatment they receive when interacting with the organization. Sophisticated consumers now expect consistency of knowledge and treatment across all the points of contact within the Customer Life Cycle. They expect that, at every point of contact, the organization will understand: the breadth of products and services they own; the relationships they have with both the organization's employees and other customers (particularly with family members); the value they bring to the organization; and the past contacts they have had with the organization. The customer operational data store (ODS) is the primary vehicle to facilitate this type of customer knowledge. The customer ODS is described in relation to the business management capabilities it provides to the organization. The chapter also highlights the required interaction between business management and the other components of the Corporate Information Factory.

Chapter 11: Automating the Sales and Service Processes. This chapter expands on the concept of consistent customer knowledge that was introduced with the customer ODS in the previous chapter. If CRM business strategies are expected to integrate across all the functional areas in the customer touch zone, the systems that support these activities must also be capable of this integration. Increasingly, companies are implementing large-scale call center and sales force automation systems to assist in sales and service activities. To get the most from these systems, all types of customer interactions must be managed from a common knowledge base. Everyone in the enterprise must be aware of previous customer touches as well as those activities planned in the future to grow the relationship. In this chapter, these technologies are introduced and described in relation to the other components in the Corporate Information Factory.

Chapter 12: Interacting with Customers Online. There is no question that the Internet is affecting the way we do business. What started as an electronic method of selling products and services has changed into something much more complex, touching the way organizations relate to their customers, their employees, and their business partners. This chapter examines the role of e-commerce in CRM. We begin with an explanation of the impact of e-commerce. We then look at the three major e-commerce models that are employed today, along with the opportunities, as well as risks, they pose to effective CRM. The concepts of permission marketing (engaging the customer in the dialog) and personalization (customizing the way we deal with the customer) are covered. Additionally, none of this would be possible without a solid architecture. The chapter also explains how the Corporate Information Factory uses information obtained from the e-commerce activities to enable us to improve customer relationships.

Chapter 13: Putting It All Together. The introduction to this book begins with an experience between Bob and his prior bank that is decidedly not customer-focused. If the bank had adopted the principles of CRM, Bob's conversation with the service representative would have gone quite differently. She would have known from his incoming phone number exactly who he was and what value he brought to the organization. She would have been empowered to help him resolve his problems, and based on his profitability indicator, she would have had more leeway to react. She would have been prompted to ask him if he wanted to increase his credit limit based on his prior usage of the card and prompt payment history. And, she would have understood any past complaints that Bob had lodged with the organization, whether he lodged them with another service representative or with the president of the bank. Think about how the service representative would garner all this information. Some of it resides in the day-to-day operational systems, some in the analytical applications of the data warehouse and marts, and some in the integrated current data residing in the operational data store. For the service representative to converse with Bob rather than give him the impersonal response he received, she would have to have all this data ready, on the screen in a logical and easily accessible format. In order to present this type of picture, the development of a CRM technology infrastructure that fully leverages all of the enterprise's existing systems and available information assets, internal and external to the organization, is necessary. This chapter explores the emerging enterprise portal technologies that tie the components of the CIF together to provide a seamless, integrated view of the customer.

Chapter 14: Preserving Customer Trust—The Role of Privacy. A customer who trusts your company is much more likely to provide you with information and to continue doing business with you than is a customer who distrusts your company. This chapter examines contemporary privacy issues and their importance within the context of CRM. Modern computing capabilities and the Internet have provided a more efficient, and potentially more threatening, way of collecting and using personal information, but the principles of privacy have been with us for decades. People do not like to provide personal information, but are often willing to do so if they feel it will be beneficial for them. After exploring fundamental privacy issues, the chapter describes the challenges encountered in preserving privacy and identifies some of the external sources that are available to help companies maintain customer privacy and build customer trust. The chapter also relates these issues to the enterprise's activities within the Customer Life Cycle—intrude and engage, acquire, and retain and expand.

Chapter 15: The Future of CRM. CRM, as we know it today, may not be viewed in the same light a few years from now. Although our research shows that many companies excel at portions of CRM, few excel in all aspects of CRM. The successful CRM organization in the future will accomplish all aspects of CRM, aligning business strategy, organization structure, and culture with customer information and technology for mutually beneficial customer relationships. As we move into the future, the customer will be demanding greater and greater control over the relationship with our enterprise. This chapter describes the characteristics of the successful CRM organization of the future. It describes the challenges facing companies today, along with the actions these companies need to take now. The chapter brings together concepts introduced throughout the book, based on what leaders in the field told us would be important for future success.

PART ONE

Introducing CRM

Companies that want to succeed in the 21st century must act in a way that provides value to the customer and profit to the company. Part 1 introduces three fundamental concepts required to generate this value and profit: Customer Relationship Management (CRM), the Corporate Information Factory (CIF), and the Customer Life Cycle (CLC). Chapter 1 positions CRM as a business mandate and presents a definition of CRM that is used throughout the remainder of the book. Chapter 2, "The Customer and the Corporate Infomation Factory," introduces a structured conceptual architecture, the CIF, that your organization can use as a guide when building an integrated customer information environment. Comprehensive and integrated customer information is essential for achieving CRM strategies. To this end, the CIF establishes four data constructs—operational system databases, the data warehouse, the operational data store, and the data marts—and provides for the movement of information between each construct. With the CIF as a roadmap, your organization can ensure that all appropriate customer systems are in place and that customer information is available to anyone who needs it. Chapter 3, "Understanding the Customer Life Cycle," introduces the CLC as a structured mechanism for understanding all the potential interaction points between the organization and its customers. The CLC identifies the stages a customer moves through when making product purchase and use decisions. It also identifies the corresponding activities an organization undertakes based on the customer's life cycle position. Understanding the CLC will help determine where the customer is in the purchase cycle and what your organization must do to influence the customer to take steps that are beneficial to the organization.

CHAPTER 1

The Customer Becomes the Center of the Business Universe

Many Customer Relationship Management (CRM) definitions focus on the importance of knowing your customer and acting on that knowledge. Putting this principle into practice is where the complexity lies. The following example illustrates the type of dynamic CRM environment that thought-leading companies are aiming to provide. This story introduces you to two banking customers, Bob and his parents, and walks you through a "trip to the bank" with each one of them. (We'll explain later in this chapter why we view Bob's parents as one customer.) As you read through this example, keep in mind the following questions:

- Is one of these customers more profitable than the other?
- Do these two customers have different requirements when it comes to product or package features, services, and fees?
- Do these two customers have different expectations for how, where, and when they interact with their service providers?
- Will either customer go to a competitor if their current provider is unable or unwilling to satisfy these diverse requirements?

The first customer is Bob, a busy, young (late 30s) corporate executive with fairly typical banking requirements for someone in his circumstances. Bob has his paycheck automatically deposited into his checking account each month. He rarely writes checks because he has many of his standard monthly payments automatically deducted from his primary checking account, and those that cannot be paid by standing order, he pays over the Internet. He doesn't receive paper account statements or cancelled checks, preferring instead to track the activity in his accounts online as his busy schedule permits. His package of products and services provides him with no minimum balance requirements on his demand deposit accounts, no ATM fees, and a low interest rate on his credit card. His package also charges a standard fee for late credit card payments and includes fees for checks and for service interactions that require personal contact, such as calls involving a service center representative.

A well-managed banking interaction that satisfies Bob and profits the bank would go like this:

- Bob logs into the bank's Web site from his hotel room one evening after taking a group of clients out to dinner. In addition to the menu of available banking options, he sees a travel icon advertising discounted rates at several popular western ski destinations. He clicks on the icon and is taken to the site of a travel service associated with his bank credit card. Bob has enough interest in the subject that he requests electronic brochures from the travel service.

- Bob's encounter with the travel service is no accident. The bank understands that Bob has a high interest in active vacations because an analysis of his credit card usage has identified a consistent pattern of use at various resort hotels and ski facilities. Bob and others like him are considered to be likely candidates to take advantage of the new travel service and, as a result, they receive personalized notifications when they log onto the Web site.

- After the short detour to the travel site, Bob checks the balance in his travel-expense checking account, transfers funds from savings to checking, and pays his corporate credit card bill from this checking account.

- Before logging off the computer, Bob checks his personal email and finds an "info-mail" from his financial advisor who is associated with the bank's full service brokerage. The advisor recommends two stocks that fit the investment preference profile provided by Bob, and the info-mail contains links to the appropriate Web pages for each company. Bob makes a note to research these companies when he has the available time.

The second customer is Bob's parents—a busy, older (late 60s) retired couple who love to travel and who also have standard banking requirements. A point of interest here is that although Bob's parents are individual people, each with specific relationships to bank products, they function as an economic decision-making unit. This unit is recognized by the bank as a type of customer and is treated as such.

Bob's parents do not own a debit card and rarely, if ever, use the ATM service. They use the monthly account statements to balance their checkbook, and they open and read all the literature that comes to their home from the bank. Bob's parents frequently visit their local branch to perform banking transactions. If they have a banking question while they are on a trip, they call the bank's service center and speak to a phone service representative. Their package of products and services provides free checks, free credit protection on their credit cards, and branch and service center transaction support at no charge. They have a minimum balance requirement on their checking account, a relatively high interest rate on their credit card, and pay a fee for each non-bank ATM use.

A well-managed banking interaction that satisfies them and profits the bank would go like this:

- Bob's parents receive the monthly statement for their checking account. Included with the statement is a circular announcing an open house to introduce the new travel service associated with the bank's credit card. The statement also includes a letter from the branch manager personally inviting Bob's parents to attend the open house. The letter also details a discounted travel promotion for a Caribbean cruise that will be featured in the event.

- The letter from the branch manager is no accident. The bank understands that Bob's parents have a high level of interest in luxury travel because of the consistent usage patterns on their credit card. The branches hosting the open house have also been selected with care; they are typically located in communities containing large concentrations of wealthy retired people. Bob's parents, and others like them, have been identified as likely candidates to utilize the new travel service and have received the personalized invitations to the open house.

- Bob's parents time their next visit to the branch to coincide with the open house. When they walk into the branch, the tellers recognize them and greet them by name. They complete their normal banking transactions (cashing a check and transferring funds from savings to checking), stay for the open house, and ultimately sign up for the cruise promotion.

- Several weeks later, their investment advisor, who is associated with the bank's full-service brokerage, calls and makes an appointment to meet with them in their home to discuss options for rolling over an annuity that will be maturing in several months.

This story of Bob and his parents is a real-life example of a situation that is facing organizations in all industries on a daily basis. Some basic facts that all organizations will have to face are illustrated in the answers to the questions generated by this example:

Is one of these customers more profitable than the other?

Not necessarily.

Do these two customers have different requirements when it comes to product or package features, services, and fees?

Clearly.

Do these two customers have different expectations for how, where, and when they interact with their service providers?

Absolutely.

Will either customer go to a competitor if their current provider is unable or unwilling to satisfy these diverse requirements?

You better believe it.

A growing sophistication among consumers and the associated increased expectation for personalized service are the primary factors motivating companies to attempt the transition to CRM. The technology exists today to facilitate truly seamless, global communications among customers, suppliers, geographically dispersed business units, and even competitors. Today's healthy economy and recent deregulations are combining to provide an increasingly level playing field in many industries, with competition in some instances coming from nontraditional sources. With so many options to choose from, consumers can afford to be demanding, and organizations must be in a position to profitably satisfy these demands.

The mantra for successful companies in the new millennium must be as follows:

> Can we anticipate our customers' needs accurately enough to be in the right place, at the right time, with the right product for them?

What Is True Customer Relationship Management?

CRM is a very popular topic in the boardrooms of many corporations. As is often the case, its very popularity is also leading to confusion and misconceptions over just what CRM is. A common mistake is to consider CRM from the perspective of only one business function or technology. For example, an organization may be moving towards a customer focus if it is implementing "one-to-one" marketing strategies using a new marketing database complete with campaign management facilities. Another organization may also be moving in a

CRM direction when it implements a new call center and telephony package. After completing the CRM initiatives described previously, both of these organizations may call themselves CRM-ready; however, neither really is. It is only after an organization has implemented marketing, service, sales, and risk management technologies, can integrate all the parts, and can see a single view of the customer, that true CRM is realized. This type of cross-functional integration is what is required to facilitate the personalized customer contacts described in the story of Bob and his parents.

When determining a definition of CRM that is effective and can be agreed upon by both the business and technology folks in your organization, it is helpful to keep in mind the three words that make up the acronym CRM: the Customers, the Relationships, and the Management. The remainder of this chapter walks you through these terms, highlights their roles in CRM, and builds a comprehensive definition from which to construct your customer-related strategies. The chapter is useful for business and technology executives alike. In addition to a comprehensive CRM definition, the chapter provides a thorough discussion of all the factors that an organization must consider in order to achieve true CRM.

Do We Have True CRM?

Before you define CRM and build the plan for transitioning its processes, it is useful to determine how CRM savvy your organization is today. The starting point for this determination lies in the CRM mantra that was introduced earlier:

> Can we anticipate our customers' needs accurately enough to be in the Right place, at the Right time, with the Right product for them?

The three Rs to CRM are significantly different than the traditional reading, writing, and 'rithmetic that we learned in school. When your customers start answering yes to the "Right Place, Right Time, Right Product" test, then you will know that your organization has achieved CRM success.

Until then, an easy way to gauge the level of CRM accomplishment in your organization is to ask a few simple questions. You can consider these questions to be a "CRM readiness litmus test":

- How many customers do you have?
- How many products does each customer own?
- Can your customers contact you effectively and efficiently?

The answers you get to these questions, as well as the consistency of those answers across business and technology areas, will help you to understand how far your organization has progressed towards true CRM.

These questions provide the building blocks upon which the "Right Place, Right Time, Right Product" mantra is founded. Each question is important in and of itself. However, as with most issues relating to CRM, it is the sum of the parts that enables you to reach the whole. If you can't count your customers, it typically means you can't identify them. If you can't identify them, how can you determine what products and services they own? If you can't accurately determine what products they do own or who they really are, how can you ever hope to offer the right product, much less make any determination of the right time or right place? Given these considerations, let's examine each individual question in more detail:

How Many Customers?

The number of companies that cannot accurately determine how many customers they actually have is quite surprising. Even when an organization can determine this information, many times the actual customer count comes with various caveats. Telecommunications companies that operate from product-oriented billing systems often count customers based on the number of billing accounts that exist in their systems. To them, every account is counted as a customer. In many cases, the only reliable customer name on these accounts is the customer who pays the bill. If multiple users are associated with one billing account, these additional customers may not be included at all. If an individual or company has several billing accounts, they can be counted several times, once for each account.

Both situations have adverse consequences for a company attempting CRM. In the first case, the company has no knowledge of service users who don't pay the bill. In the second case, the company has no accurate way of understanding the number of products owned by a particular customer and thus no way of understanding that customer's true value. Either case can lead to missed opportunities to cross-sell other products and build customer loyalty.

How Many Products?

The number of products owned per customer can be another tough question. Multi-line insurance companies can often determine how many Property and Casualty (P&C) policies a customer has. (Most actually go so far as to offer multi-policy discounts within a business line.) However, many large organizations can't tell how many of their P&C policy owners also have life policies, and it is the rare company indeed that can determine how many customers with individual policies of any type also participate in employer-sponsored retirement products (401K), health insurance products, or supplemental life products. As illustrated in the prior bullet, it is difficult to understand the number of products owned when account- or product-based systems are the sole source of information. The examples given here also illustrate the most common difficulties faced by organizations trying to answer this question across independent business lines or subsidiaries. True customer value cannot be assessed without an accurate answer to this question. Effective action plans to maximize customer satisfaction are also difficult to develop if you don't understand the products owned.

How Many Contacts?

Effective and efficient customer contact across all possible touch points is another good indicator of CRM savvy in an organization. The ability to facilitate this advanced CRM concept transcends the more simplistic product and customer information issues highlighted by the first two questions. The management of customer contacts introduces an organization's structure and culture into the mix. A simple way to measure this is with the following question. How many phone calls does a good customer (one with multiple products) have to make to change his or her address across all the products that they own? Chances are that in any company with disparate products and multiple telephone service centers, the answer is more than one. Fixing customer contact issues like this one requires organizational policies that depend on CRM and an organizational structure that facilitates it.

In the Bob story, the bank is able to meet the CRM mantra and provide both Bob and his parents the right products in the right place at the right time. This is possible in part because the building blocks illustrated here are firmly in place. These questions are a good beginning to any CRM effort, because they provide both an assessment of the current CRM state as well as the knowledge of what should be addressed in order to succeed. True CRM requires a balance of organization, culture, strategy, and information. Any organization moving towards CRM should recognize the required balance and monitor all factors accordingly.

The Customer in CRM

The logical place to start when defining CRM is at the beginning: with the customer. To accurately answer the question posed in the prior section about how many customers exist, an organization must first decide what a customer is. In fact, this need to define "customer" goes beyond the requirement to determine how many of them your organization may have. A customer definition is necessary to determine which individuals and organizations you would like to keep information on. A customer definition is also necessary to identify the kinds of information you would like to capture about these individuals and organizations. A customer definition is mandatory if you are to design systems that provide this information to the people who need it to facilitate your business. A customer definition is essential to determine how you would like to interact with your customers, and how you would like them to interact with you. The definition of customer is the foundation upon which successful CRM strategies are built.

A very important consideration when deciding who is counted as a customer for your organization is to recognize that different business units have different requirements. The most common mistake made in defining a customer is to develop the definition from the perspective of a single business unit or information system. In the example of Bob and his parents, several business units representing numerous functions are involved in a cooperative effort to provide the personalized interactions described. The credit card product group is responsible for the analysis of card usage patterns, while the market research area determines who receives statement stuffers versus who views Web icons. The marketing group also profiles geographic regions and identifies the branches that should host the open houses. Marketing then works in conjunction with branch managers to plan the events and to bring customers in the door. This seemingly simple example involves sales, service, and marketing activities across multiple contact points or channels. Outside service providers, internal employees, and potential purchasers are all involved. To marketing, the customers include Bob, his parents, the travel service, the credit card product area, and the branch managers. To the travel service, the customer is anyone who is a likely candidate for the service and is not necessarily limited to current credit card owners. To the credit card division, the performance of the travel service has a direct impact on the card customer base, making this outside vendor an important party to understand and monitor. Additionally, different areas of the bank may even have opposing views on who they count as the customer. In the case of Bob's parents, marketing looks at the household (both parents) when deciding what to market next, while the Credit Department looks at each parent individually when assigning approved credit limits.

Given these complexities, it is easy to see why a comprehensive customer definition is important. The following provides a good starting point when defining customer as the foundation for a CRM strategy:

> **Customer:** A party who is involved with the acquisition of the company's goods and services and who is of interest to the organization

In this definition, customers can be either individuals or organizations. Customers can also be loose groups of individuals joined together as a membership organization, such as the American Association of Retired Persons (AARP) or the American Medical Association (AMA). Many banks and insurance companies offer special packages to these membership groups. To the banks and insurance companies, the AARP and AMA are clearly customers, as are the individual people who belong to these groups and purchase the specially offered packages.

A comprehensive definition of customer includes the simple customer types, those that own products and services. This definition should also include the more complex, extended customer types, such as the households and membership groups described earlier. In fact, the definition of customer proposed in this chapter is intended to cover a broad range of potential types of customers, including both simple and extended types. We use the words "of interest to the organization" and "involved in the acquisition" intentionally to ensure that you are not limited to only those organizations or individuals who actually own products or services.

A comprehensive customer definition will enable your organization to define customer as broadly as is required to facilitate the cross-functional CRM business strategies that are important to the organization. Establishing a broad customer definition like the previous one does not mean that all types of individuals and organizations are considered to have the same level of importance. In fact, certain types of customers, such as a referral source, may be used in far fewer business processes than other types, such as employees. The key to a comprehensive definition is simply to identify and include all potential customer types so that when a business strategy that requires a particular type of customer is developed, you have already defined those types and included them in your conceptual system designs.

The following list identifies and defines some customer types that are typically included in CRM customer definitions. (Note that some of the customer types on this list are individuals, some are organizations, and some can be either individuals or organizations).

Agent. Although agents do not purchase products and services, they control the relationships with those organizations and consumers who do purchase these products. In the insurance industry, the agent is often considered to be an important type of customer. Because independent agents are free to sell the products of any insurance company, each company must convince the agents of their particular product's value. These companies must make it attractive for the agents to do business with them. Captive agents sell only a single company's products or services, but the same concept applies. In order to retain the best agents and minimize the high agent turnover experienced by the insurance industry, companies must provide their independent agents with the tools to ensure success. Both the independent and captive agent situations necessitate that a company maximize the relationship by recognizing the agent as a customer, by making agent satisfaction a high priority, and by knowing as much about that agent as they would about their end customers. Additionally, you must understand the agent's relationship with his or her customers if you want to arrive at an accurate understanding of the profitability of your customers and the profitability of each individual product sale.

Beneficiary. Beneficiaries are found in many industries, such as insurance, banking, and investment to name a few. Although not all companies can collect and store enough information about beneficiaries to keep them as customers, most would like to. It is generally recognized that when a beneficiary is collecting benefits on a product, he or she has a high potential to become a profitable customer in his or her own right. Most organizations that deal with beneficiaries would like to maximize the value of these relationships and prepare for growth when the timing is appropriate.

Bill payer. This customer type is common in the telecommunications and utility industries, as well as in other environments where a bill is issued on a regular basis. In the case of the cellular telephone companies, the bill payer is the person responsible for the actual payment of all charges incurred. This responsible person is often different from the person who is actually using the service. In a company setting, the phone users may be the field sales staff, while the person responsible for paying the bill may be an accounting officer. Most cellular companies want to keep information about both the users and the bill payers, thus the importance of this customer type.

Customer. Many organizations that establish a comprehensive customer definition include a type that carries the actual label of customer. When a company includes a customer type or label, it typically defines this type as an individual or organization that actually owns or uses a product or service. When the customer type is included, the company acknowledges that an individual or organization can be a customer. This customer could actually own products and services while at the same time having the potential to also fit into some of the other explicitly defined types. For example, an individual who owns a product can also be an employee or a beneficiary on a product owned by someone else.

Several reasons exist for having multiple types and for allowing individuals and organizations to fit into more than one type at the same time. You may want to keep different kinds of information about your actual product owners than you keep about your referral sources or beneficiaries. In the case of a beneficiary, some fields that are mandatory for actual product owners, such as customer name, may not even be available for all beneficiaries (children of the marriage is a commonly allowed placeholder for beneficiaries on insurance policies). Also, you may want to keep information on a type, such as referral source, even when that individual does not own any products or services. If an estate planner consistently refers his or her clients to your investment company for a particular type of tax-sheltered annuity, you may be interested in maintaining a relationship with that estate planner, even if the planner never actually purchases a product for himself or herself. In this case, the estate planner fits into the extended customer definition as a referral source but does not fit into the simple 'customer' type.

Competitor. Organizations are taking a growing interest in including competitors in their customer definitions for several reasons. First, situations occur when competitors can truly be counted as customers. In the wireless communications industry, companies with broad satellite coverage sell the use of these facilities to their competitors. Thus, a small company that does not have the actual communications network can buy use of this commodity from a larger company and sell this use directly to its own customers. In this case, the large company considers the smaller one to be both a competitor and a customer. Second, many companies are incorporating the sale of competitive products into their standard business practices. The rationale for this is simple. You put an entire customer relationship at risk if you let that customer deal with a competitor, whereas you maintain control of that relationship if you agree to sell the competitive product yourself. The loss of revenue for a single product is preferable to the potential loss of revenue for all products.

Employee. An employee is a customer type that is somewhat similar to an agent. Most companies that develop a comprehensive customer definition include their own employees in this definition. Employees are included for several reasons. First, employees often have the ability to purchase company products and services at a discount. Most companies are interested in tracking the profitability of these special employee-discounted packages. They are also interested in understanding the characteristics of the employees who take advantage of these packages, as well as the ones who don't. Employees can be a tremendous source of feedback for product development, sales, and marketing. Second, and equally important, companies are interested in tracking the relationships that employees have with the end customer. The ability to link employees to the customers that they interact with is key for many CRM strategies, including customer satisfaction-oriented compensation, product cross-selling initiatives, and sales and deal team formation.

Guarantor. A guarantor is an individual or organization that submits a guarantee for the repayment of credit, such as a bank loan. Companies include a guarantor as a customer type for both cross-selling and risk management reasons. Although guarantors may or may not actually own products and services themselves, they are usually considered to be good prospects for the organization. In the course of accepting a guarantee, an organization collects quite a bit of information about the guarantor. This information can then be used to profile that guarantor and to identify potential cross-sales opportunities. From a risk management perspective, companies often want to understand if an individual or company is acting as a guarantor for multiple people or is using the same collateral to guarantee multiple loans. In these cases, the lending organization may want to limit the exposure it may have if a customer defaults, thus causing the guarantor to undertake repayment responsibility. In addition, if anything happens to the financial status of a multiple guarantor, the organization must be able to understand the potential consequences across all the products that fall under the guarantee.

Household. The household is a customer type that is increasing in importance as organizations look more closely at customers and their interactions. A household is an interesting concept because it is a group of individual or organizational customers, where the group or household is actually considered to be a customer. In the example of Bob and his parents, Bob's parents are considered to be one customer. In the comprehensive customer definition, Bob's parents fit into the household customer type. Each individual parent is also a customer in his or her own right, but the bank recognizes that they make decisions as a unit, thus the interest in the household. The traditional definition of household, as originated by marketing departments is "an economic decision-making unit."

Figure 1.1 illustrates the household concept in practical terms. In this case, the household is actually a family, and each member of that family owns products and services. When an organization takes a household view, it recognizes that decisions can and will be influenced by multiple members of the economic unit. It also recognizes the buying power and potential value of the unit. In Figure 1.1, the value of the household includes all the products owned by the household (depicted by the circle). This household value is much greater than the value of any one individual member.

Marketers understand the importance of identifying household groups and treating these groups as though they are one customer. Sending one direct mail solicitation per marketing campaign to a household rather than sending the same mailing to each product holder within the household can generate significant cost savings. Note that this also cuts down on the customer annoyance factor. Savvy CRM marketers also factor in household product ownership when determining what products to market next. An understanding that several members of a family own cell phones may highlight the propensity of a household to purchase an unlimited cell-to-cell calling feature.

Marketing is not the only area that benefits from household information. The story of Bob's parents provides a practical example of how a household can

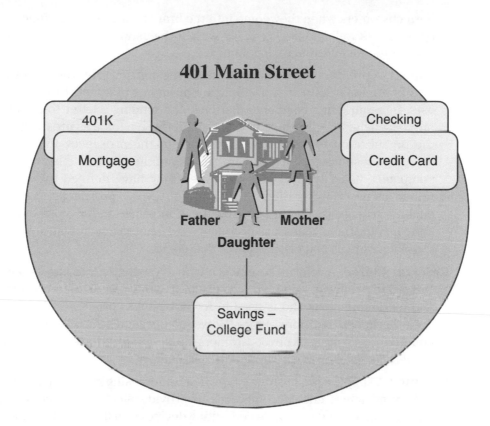

Figure 1.1 Traditional household.

be acknowledged and used by three distinct business functions: marketing, sales, and customer service. A more traditional view of customers would identify Bob's father and mother as two distinct customers. In this traditional view, Bob's father, who is the primary owner of the largest and most profitable account, the tax-sheltered pension account, would be labeled as a valuable customer and would receive special treatment. Bob's mother, who is a joint owner on all of the less profitable accounts but only a beneficiary on the pension account, would not get the same status or treatment. In this case, however, the bank recognizes that these two customers are also an economic decision-making unit, or household. Thus, it is the household that receives the high value status, allowing each member to be recognized as a VIP and treated accordingly. The marketing area recognizes this customer group and sends the household one solicitation for the travel promotion, rather than two. The customer service area recognizes it and provides VIP treatment to both customers when they come into the branch, and the sales function recognizes it as well and deals equally with both customers when attempting to sell additional investment accounts.

Prospect. A prospect is a useful customer type, particularly when an organization is tracking the use and efficiency of names obtained from purchased lists. In a marketing campaign that includes sending a letter to people on a purchased mailing list, the identification of these people as prospects allows the organization to track information about the prospects, the marketing campaign responses, and the overall quality of the purchased list itself. Many companies use a type of prospect when they have defined the type "customer" as described earlier. The use of both types, prospect and customer, enables an organization to keep one set of information for those individuals and organizations that own products, and another set of information on those individuals and organizations that do not.

Referral source. A referral source is a type of customer that is generally considered to be an extended type. As discussed, this type is of interest to sales and marketing areas and is used in fewer business processes than some of the other more traditional types. However, because referral sources can be an important source of new customers, most organizations include this type in their comprehensive definition of customer.

Supplier. A supplier is a customer type that is increasing in importance as technology advances enable companies to provide electronic access to more information through portable computing devices and the Internet. The ability of a supplier to meet the rapidly changing demands of innovative organizations can play a key role in the success of those organizations and in the satisfaction of the organization's ultimate customers. Many companies recognize the importance of a finely tuned supply chain and are managing their key suppliers much more closely. These companies are even going so far as to allow trusted suppliers to access inventory information and control shipments accordingly. This involvement of suppliers in the actual business processes of an organization makes the customer type of supplier key to CRM business strategies.

The Relationship in CRM

The prior section illustrates that successful CRM requires organizations to look beyond the obvious definition of customers as simply those who acquire products and services. This need to expand traditional thought processes is also present when looking at the importance of relationships in CRM. Relationship can be defined as follows:

Relationship: The type of involvement a party has with the organization or with other customers

Customer-focused strategies require an organization to consider several very different types of relationships. The first and most obvious relationship to consider is that between an organization and its customers. This relationship exists when:

A customer purchases a product or service from the organization. The most basic relationship is one in which a customer owns or uses products and services. As described earlier, many organizations find it difficult to identify exactly who these product owners are, while others can't determine the number of products owned by a single customer. Many of the CRM business strategies described throughout this book are designed to manage or influence this basic relationship. This type of relationship can be business-to-customer (B2C), where the customer is an individual or a household, or it can be business-to-business (B2B), where the customer is another business. An example of a B2B relationship is when an organization sells its products to another organization, such as the corporate banking division of a financial institution that sells cash management products to medium- or large-size corporations.

An organization assigns an employee or agent to manage a customer relationship. This is a key relationship between an organization and its customers. In this type of relationship, the organization assigns a specific employee to manage a customer or group of customers. Although most of these situations do not limit the customer from interacting with other employees when necessary or convenient, they do provide the customer with the ability to receive personalized service that results from having a single relationship manager within an organization who coordinates most interactions. Examples of this type of employee-to-customer relationship include the relationship between an insurance agent and his or her customers or the relationship between a private banker and his or her customers. The relationship between an organization and its customers is also prevalent in a B2B environment. Many organizations that sell products to other businesses assign an employee or team of employees to manage each business customer. The employees or teams involved in these B2B relationships are typically called account managers, sales teams, or deal teams.

The previous examples are all variations on the relationships that exist between an organization and its customers. A second relationship to consider is one that is slightly less obvious than the organization-to-customer relationship, but that is clearly gaining momentum and importance in the CRM world. This relationship involves the links between an organization and other businesses that do not own products or services. Many of the extended customer types that are introduced in the prior section of this chapter (supplier, competitor, and third-party vendor) exist in the customer definition because the organization wants to manage relationships with these companies. This type of relationship is always a B2B relationship and exists for several reasons:

An organization partners with a third-party vendor to provide additional value-added services to its customers. The travel service used in the banking example is a good illustration of this type of relationship. The travel service provides a non-banking product that is a natural fit to the credit card banking product. This service adds value to the bank by increasing customer satisfaction and loyalty. It also adds value to the customer base by providing the ability to earn discounted travel expenses through the use of the bank credit card product. Managing partner relationships such as the one between the bank and the travel service is something many CRM organizations are beginning to do.

An organization offers competitive products through its sales channels. As described in the customer definition section, many organizations are now allowing their sales representatives to sell competitive products in certain situations. Banking and insurance are two industries where this happens regularly. In both cases, a sales person can sell a competitive product when the company cannot meet the customer's needs with one of its own offerings. The rationale behind this philosophy is simple. If the customer is forced to go to a competitor to meet the need, a possibility exists that the customer will transfer all accounts to the competitor. Given this possibility, it is better to sell one competitive product than to risk the entire relationship by forcing the customer to go elsewhere. Implementing a CRM policy like this one requires an organization to manage relationships with its competitors.

An organization partners with its suppliers to more effectively manage inventory. This type of B2B relationship is also becoming more prevalent in CRM organizations. In this case, the organization recognizes that properly managed inventory can impact both the bottom line and customer satisfaction. Wal-Mart provides a good example of this type of relationship.

The Wal-Mart sidebar illustrates why these B2B supplier relationships can work to move an organization towards CRM. In this example, Wal-Mart has recognized that the level of inventory available in the stores has a direct impact on the satisfaction levels of the customers who shop there. In an effort to perfect the inventory management, Wal-Mart has developed a business process that actively involves the suppliers as well as the store managers. Wal-Mart will be collecting and maintaining information on its suppliers and, as a result, is operating on an expanded definition of "customer" along the lines of the one used in this book.

Wal-Mart: Managing Supplier Relationships

Wal-Mart has improved its suppliers' access to the retailer's sales and inventory data. In an effort to ensure uninterrupted flow of goods to its 3,400 stores worldwide, the chain has provided direct access to key data to its suppliers. These suppliers run customized applications that give them access to sales, inventory, and forecasting data about their specific products. The suppliers determine when and where to ship their products to ensure a "never out" situation. *Information Week*, Oct. 5, 1998.

The last type of relationship that exists in a CRM environment is the least obvious but can be quite important. It is known as a customer-to-customer (C2C) relationship. The household relationship that Bob's parents have is a good example of a C2C relationship. The first step in using C2C relationships is to understand that they exist. The bank discovered the household relationship of Bob's parents through a combination of joint account ownership and a shared mailing address. The organization must then understand how these types of relationships can influence the behavior of its customers. In the case of Bob's parents, the couple functions as a decision-making unit, which means that all key financial decisions for the household involve both parties. Last, the organization must make a determination as to how it will incorporate these relationships into its customer interactions. In the case of Bob's parents, both are treated as equal partners (mailings go to the household rather than to either member), and both have access to all appropriate bank products and service options.

The household example does more than introduce C2C relationships. It also serves to introduce an important relationship concept: influence value. Influence value is the understanding of how relationships within the customer base can affect both the customer's behavior and the organization's treatment of that customer. By choosing single household mailings and equal service status, the bank illustrates a clear incorporation of influence value into the customer contact interactions for Bob's parents.

Influence Value in the Contemporary Household

To get the true measure of influence value, let's look more closely at the household. Although many organizations view households as customers and include these groups in the overall definition of customer, it is actually the C2C relationships between the members of this group that produce the influence value. The concept of household relationship is not static; it is evolving to keep pace with our changing society. At one time, to be included in a traditional household, members were expected to have the same last name and the same address. A closer examination of influence value is causing CRM organizations to adopt a contemporary household view that eliminates these name and address limitations and looks instead at true economic links. Figure 1.2 portrays one version of a contemporary household.

In this example, the contemporary household includes not only the immediate family members, but also the elderly parents of the mother pictured in the traditional household. These elderly parents do not live at the same physical address and do not share the same last name as the traditional household members. However, the value of understanding contemporary household relationships like this one is clearly illustrated in the following true example.

The Marketing Department of a large regional U.S. bank performed an analysis of its customer base in order to understand the impact of raising service fees for customers in lower profitability categories. The bank first ran a traditional household analysis and categorized the resulting households according to value. The bank then decided to take a closer look at the households that fell into the lower profit categories to be sure it understood the influence value of these households before raising the fees. One of the techniques it employed in

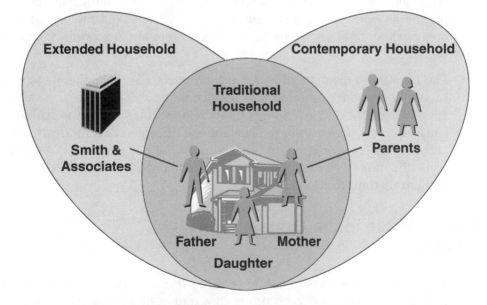

Figure 1.2 Contemporary household.

this additional analysis was to run matching software that looked not for name or address matches, but instead for links to common accounts and links to common phone numbers.

This analysis yielded an interesting and surprising result. One of the households that fell into the lower profit category (we'll call them the Smiths) matched on the account link to a different household (Mr. and Mrs. Johnson) that was in the highest profit category. Further investigation indicated that the Smith household did not use the bank as its primary financial institution; it had only a low-margin, high-volume checking account that was used to run the household expenses. However, Mrs. Smith also had non-ownership privileges on a highly profitable (multi-million dollar) investment account that was owned by her retired parents, the Johnsons. Because Mrs. Smith's parents did not live with her and did not share the same last name, this relationship was not identified in the traditional household analysis. If the bank had stopped after the first step, it would have completely missed the relationship that exists between Mrs. Smith and her parents. Because of this contemporary household relationship (not at all unusual in today's society), the Smith household has a true influence value that far exceeds the value of the accounts it actually owns. Any attempt to de-market the Smiths could result in the loss of the Johnsons' highly profitable account as well.

Although the contemporary household described here is clearly different than the traditional household represented by Bob's parents, a parallel can be drawn from the influence value of the contemporary household to the influence value inherent in Bob's relationship with his parents. The relationship between Bob and his parents is not directly recognized in the example cited in the introduction, but this relationship does exist. The potential for influence in this unrecognized relationship is the same as in the recognized relationship between the Smiths and the Johnsons. Other types of non-traditional household relationships like this also exist and have a potential influence value. Unmarried but attached couples or partners are one of a variety of examples. Therefore, it really does behoove an organization to understand both traditional and contemporary relationships between its customers.

Influence Value in the Extended Household

Figure 1.2 also illustrates another concept that is taking on more importance in the CRM world of today and tomorrow. This is the concept of the extended household. Sometimes called the social network or extended customer, this relationship goes beyond family relationships to look at other types of links. The most common type of extended relationship is one that exists between small- to medium-size businesses and the individuals who own these companies.

Although there is no question that the small business market segment is currently considered to be a high-potential growth area, the historic treatment of these small businesses tells another story. These small businesses do not typically have enough assets to be included in the corporate or business customer base, and they are different enough to cause an awkward fit when grouped with the retail or individual customer base. The banking industry illustrates this problem well. Businesses that have less than five to ten million dollars in revenue do not generate enough income to be handled by the corporate banking organization. Instead, these smaller businesses are typically handled in the retail bank. This can cause problems because the systems built to house retail customer information do not always provide the structures necessary to store more complex business customer information. Also, business policies designed to handle simple retail customer issues and relationships do not always work on more complex business customer situations. The following example from the telecommunications industry highlights the type of problem that can arise when an organization does not understand the extended relationships of its customer base, particularly those involving small businesses.

> A telecommunications company has a large established wireless business line offering cellular and paging services. It also owns a cable company that was recently purchased and now operates as a second business line. Because this merging of the cable and cellular companies was highly publicized, most customers are aware that the once-independent companies are now one entity. Shortly after the merger, a cable customer inadvertently skipped a bill payment. The cable organization let the allotted number of days pass and then sent the customer the standard "pay the bill or your services will be terminated" collection letter. Under normal circumstances, use of the standard collections policy is appropriate when a customer fails to pay the bill. However, this particular residential (retail) cable customer also happened to own a small construction business that purchased cell phones and calling plans from the wireless business line for each of its 25 mobile employees. Although this wireless relationship was an extremely profitable one, the company failed to recognize the link between the profitable small business owner and the individual cable customer. Had this link been understood, the company may have sent a milder letter or possibly tried a reminder phone call instead. It did none of these things, and in this case, the mistake was costly. The business owner was so irate over the company's failure to recognize his value and treat him accordingly that he moved his entire business account to another cellular provider.

Multiple solutions are available to assist in the identification of this type of relationship. One popular provider of information on the world's businesses, Dun & Bradstreet, has expanded the type of information it provides to include companies in this segment. Today some D&B products contain information on small businesses that includes, among other things, identification of the owners and principles of these organizations. Companies interested in understanding the extended relationships of their customers can match their retail customer names against the small business owner names in third party files like the one D&B provides. This process enables them to look at customers who already own individual or retail products to determine if these customers are also the owners of small businesses. Matches here highlight the overall relationship with the customer and the potential influence value of the customer. They can enable a company to tailor business processes to fit the true value of the customer and prevent a situation like the one described earlier. Also, if the small business owners in these files have individual or retail products with the company but obtain their business products elsewhere, the potential for high-margin cross sales is significant and likely. Either way, the understanding of these extended household relationships is key to CRM strategies.

The Management in CRM

When you understand who your customers are and can identify all the important relationships involving these customers, you are ready to take the next step to CRM and act on this customer knowledge. This step, management, is the ability to use the information you have gathered about your customers to start changing the way your organization interacts with these customers. The interactions that you should consider changing will range from simple interactions, such as those involving a single employee dealing with a single customer, to complex situations that cross departments and involve multiple customers. The banking vignette described in the introduction to this chapter provides many good examples of simple and complex interactions that are intentionally managed by the bank to provide Bob and his parents with a superior customer contact experience. In this example, the bank uses its extensive customer knowledge to influence each and every contact with both Bob and his parents. For Bob, the managed interactions include the following:

The info-mail from his full-service broker. This is a simple customer interaction involving only the broker and Bob. The broker understands Bob's contact preferences and has tailored the interactions accordingly. Rather than calling to request a meeting, the broker provides Bob with the level of service that best fits his busy lifestyle.

The Web-based marketing solicitation for discounted skiing vacations. This is a more complex customer interaction that requires the coordination of several departments within the bank. In order to facilitate this interaction, the Marketing Department must coordinate with customer service, the Credit Card Division, and an outside vendor—the travel service. The end result of this coordination is that Bob receives a solicitation for a service that has been tailored explicitly to him. In addition, Bob receives this solicitation over a channel, the Internet, where he is most likely to take the time to read the solicitation and respond to it. Had this offer come to Bob via direct mail, he would have probably thrown it away. By using the Internet, the bank is managing the method of contact as well as the contact itself.

The Internet direct-banking service channel. Although this example involves only one bank function, customer service, it is also quite complex because it requires that the bank recognize a subset of customers with unique service preferences. It also requires that the bank act on this knowledge to create new ways to satisfy these preferences. In this case, the Service Department at the bank understands that people like Bob do not have time to use the more traditional customer service options (such as the branch) and have developed alternative full-service channels including the Web and telephone banking facilities. Using these channels, Bob can satisfy all his banking requirements and never visit a physical bank location.

The situation with Bob's parents provides an additional example of CRM in practice. The bank understands the household relationship that exists between Bob's mother and father and treats the household unit as a single customer. Some of the interactions that are managed to the household level are as follows:

The phone call from their broker. This is a simple interaction between the broker and the household. In this case, the broker understands that Bob's parents prefer to discuss investment options in the comfort and privacy of their home. The broker reacts accordingly and phones to schedule an appointment when the investment portfolio requires attention.

The greeting from the branch teller. This is another example of a simple interaction, this time between the branch staff and their customers. In this case, the bank recognizes that when a customer visits a branch, a great opportunity arises to personalize the experience and build customer loyalty. Thus, the branch staff is trained to make the most of all the personal interactions that happen in this environment.

The open house to introduce the new travel service. In addition to the complex coordination between business units required to generate the travel service offer, this interaction introduces another aspect of interaction management. Here the bank has analyzed the demographics of its branches to determine which branches are located in areas where customers are likely to attend an open house. Customers who typically use the chosen branches, and who would be likely to take advantage of a travel offer, are personally invited by their branch manager to attend the subsequent open house. Thus, the bank is making an effort to understand its customers, both by their purchasing patterns and by where these customers live. The bank is then using this knowledge to manage service, sales, and marketing interactions.

The interactions listed previously provide a good example of the type and range of interactions that can be used to transition an organization towards CRM. Within this context, the management in CRM can be defined as follows:

> **Management:** The ability to facilitate interactions between a party and the organization that are valuable to both the party and the organization

Management is the glue that cements CRM concepts together into a cohesive vision that brings value to both the customers and the organization. This is worth repeating: Value must be brought to both the customers and the organization. If the move to CRM does not ultimately enhance this value, it is not worth doing. In the example of Bob and his parents, the bank is able to provide interactions with Bob that are very different from those provided to his parents. Bob uses the Internet banking services, communicates with his broker by email, and receives marketing solicitations over the Web, while his parents visit the branch, work with their broker from home, and receive marketing solicitations from the branch manager. Regardless of these differences, the bank is clearly able to facilitate interactions between itself, Bob, and Bob's parents to the satisfaction of all parties. Customer satisfaction leads to customer loyalty, to a propensity to buy more products, and ultimately to a higher customer value. This type of success and value enhancement is the essence of managing interactions in CRM and is the ultimate aim of CRM in general.

Although most interactions involving a customer or an extended customer are fair game for management, not all customer interactions require change or management. The issue is to identify which of the many interactions within your organization that should be managed to a customer focus. An effective process for targeting interactions for management is to first understand these interactions as they occur in your organization. Then prioritize them based on the impact on customer satisfaction and on the level of change required to move towards CRM. Most of the examples used thus far in this chapter contain customer interactions that should be managed. Examples of both good and bad CRM are illustrated in the following excerpts:

Good. The solicitations for new banking travel service to Bob and his parents; Web-based for Bob and personalized direct mail for his parents

Bad. A hasty collection letter to a valuable small business owner based on incomplete customer knowledge

Good. A complete analysis of contemporary household relationships and associated influence value prior to the de-marketing of a seemingly low-value household

Bad. Requiring the best customers (multiple product owners) to make multiple calls to accomplish a change of address when there are multiple product-oriented customer call centers and non-integrated service processes

Good. An identification of the disparity in product and service features preferred by Bob versus his parents, and the resulting offer of personalized product packages for each customer

Figure 1.3 introduces the CRM continuum and illustrates the inherent value to be gained from managing customer interactions to improve CRM focus and momentum. The steps within the CRM continuum are plotted on the grid, beginning with the product focus and progressing through the extended relationship. The Y-axis (vertical) illustrates an increasing value to both the organization and the customer as a company progresses up the continuum. The X-axis (horizontal) illustrates the increasing number of customer interactions that must meet CRM principles as the company progresses up the continuum. That these customer interactions are also increasing in complexity is not explicitly stated on the diagram but is understood upon contemplation of the type of interactions included with each move along the continuum. Following is an explanation of each point on the continuum:

Product Focus is the lowest point on the continuum. Organizations that are here have done little to adopt CRM. Few if any interactions are managed at a customer level, and little value is realized by the company or customer from CRM. Organizations that operate from product-based systems such as

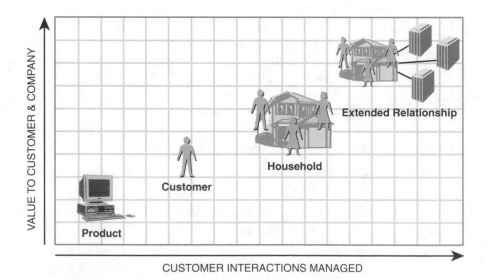

Figure 1.3 The value of managing interactions.

the billing system discussed earlier are typically at this point on the continuum. As discussed, these organizations find it difficult to count or identify all customers and tend to view the account and the customer synonymously. Organizations on the product focus point do not know how many products a single customer owns. Most of the interactions in a product-focused company are performed at a product level. Service is generally performed by product, with multiple interactions required for multiple products. Marketing activity may be present, but decisions on what to sell next cannot be made on the basis of full knowledge of a customer. Instead, these decisions are typically made based on the next best product for the company to sell rather than on the next best product for the customer to buy.

Customer Focus is next on the continuum. Companies on this point have made some significant steps towards CRM. A common customer definition has been established across all relevant business areas. Some ability to view a complete customer profile, including knowledge of most or all products owned, has been provided to points of customer contact. The company is identifying the interactions with the highest impact and is actively managing these. Other interactions are targeted for improvement as time and resources permit. The organization is moving towards the personalized service levels, such as those provided to Bob and his parents in the banking example. Marketing solicitations take into account the product ownership characteristics of the customer and actively determine what the customer might be most likely to purchase next. At this point, the customer is receiving increased value from his or her interactions with the organization, which is demonstrated by increased loyalty and increased propensity to purchase additional services. These demonstrated qualities also result in an increased value to the organization from its CRM efforts.

Household Focus is third on the continuum. Companies that are moving to this point are continuing to improve their focus on customers while also targeting some C2C relationships for inclusion. These organizations recognize the importance of influence value and are orienting their business processes to understand and react to it. Marketing, sales, service, and risk management decisions take into account influence value wherever possible. Value is high here for both the customer and the company.

Extended Relationship is the highest point on the CRM continuum. As with the household, this position indicates a continuing improvement based on the complete understanding of a customer and all the relevant relationships. Some included activities consist of single bills across all products if requested, a consistent service treatment regardless of the channel, one call or mouse click to change customer-level information across all products, and the dynamic allocation of product features for personalized product packaging. Much of the discussion of this part of the continuum is futuristic at this point because organizations are just beginning to realize the potential of these extended relationships. However, indications are that the value will be high. Look only as far as the Collections Department at the telecommunications company to understand some of the possible benefits.

Summary: CRM Defined

This chapter provides a comprehensive view of each of the individual components that make up the term Customer Relationship Management (CRM). Each is quite important in its own right. However, as the management section highlights, robust CRM requires a coordination of independent business units and a level of customer knowledge that goes beyond the adoption of the customer, relationship, and management components themselves. To achieve CRM, an organization must be able to integrate comprehensive knowledge of its customers with business strategies that span functional boundaries and that require extensive cooperation across the organization.

Given this premise of required integration, we would like to present a new definition of CRM. This definition identifies the CRM complexities but simplifies the CRM concept, and also promotes understanding by both business and technology:

> **Customer Relationship Management:** Aligning business strategy, organization structure and culture, and customer information and technology so that all customer interactions can be conducted to the long-term satisfaction of the customer and to the benefit and profit of the organization

This is the definition to which the remainder of the book will refer. We hope it is also the definition that your organization will adopt and rally around as you progress on the road to CRM nirvana. As you may have guessed while reading the prior section, managing interactions to the point of a household or an extended customer focus requires more than simply understanding your customers and their relationships. Business strategy, an organization's structure and culture, and customer information and technology become important considerations when aiming for true CRM. In order to achieve the successes illustrated in this chapter (and also to avoid the failures shown), an organization must align each of these. Managing the diverse interactions of both Bob and his parents required the cooperation of marketing, the credit card product group, the branch managers, the telephone service group, the Web banking group, and an outside vendor, the travel service.

To achieve this extensive cooperation across so many different departments, several components must be in place:

- Cross-functional business strategies that are understood throughout the organization, such as collection policies that can look across business lines and change based on customer value

- An overall organization structure that enables a cross-functional cooperation of this complexity, such as some facility to integrate or coordinate multiple independent call-centers or service channels

- An integrated technology that facilitates the information sharing required for this complex cooperation, such as a provision of a robust common customer profile for all customer contact points

- An executive-level support/mandate that facilitates the type of sweeping change required to attain the CRM reality, such as an executive management buy-in to ensure a change in the organization and in the business policies needed to implement enterprise cooperation

Because the changes required to achieve the highest point on the CRM continuum can be complex, we have devoted a chapter to explaining how you can begin to move your organization in this direction. Chapter 4, "Are You Ready? Tuning the Organization for CRM," delves into more detail about the types of cross-functional business strategies and organizational structures that are required to facilitate true CRM. This chapter also identifies some of the critical success factors that you should look for within your organization as you guide your company towards CRM.

Customer technology also plays a key role in the ability to achieve true CRM. The next chapter, Chapter 2, provides an overview of a recommended technology framework, the Corporate Information Factory (CIF). Developed by Bill Inmon, the CIF provides a structured method for understanding and implementing the integrated environment required to provide a common customer view throughout the organization. The systems required to facilitate CRM business strategies are introduced in this chapter and described in later in the book.

The Customer and the Corporate Information Factory (CIF)

For years, forward-thinking sales and marketing organizations, along with their counterparts in the customer care areas, have dreamed of a world in which they could develop creative marketing campaigns, execute and then track the progress of these campaigns, alter them when a negative trend is detected, and understand and respond quickly to each individual customer's needs. These organizations could thus demonstrate their value to the corporation by improving customer loyalty and retention while increasing overall revenue. This is the world of Customer Relationship Management (CRM), where different customers are treated differently and high-value customers get the most attention.

In this world, the marketers and sales personnel are not the only people that deal with the customers. From the example in Chapter 1, "The Customer Becomes the Center of the Business Universe," it can be seen that many different departments and personnel, from tellers to financial advisors, deal with Bob and his parents, all in significantly different ways. The entire enterprise has been reoriented from the product focus to the customer focus. Billing people, collections people, and customer service representatives (anyone that touches or has impact on the customer) also have access to all the information about that customer and can relate to that individual in a personal way.

Unfortunately, these organizations have also been frustrated by a lack of systems specific to their purposes, a lack of information technology (IT) support for their data needs, and the inability to access their own corporation's operational data. Consequently, they are turning to outside vendor solutions such as marketing databases to fill the void. These databases, while useful for some specific marketing functions, only address part of the problem and may, in fact, exacerbate the problem because they lack the ability to share information outside their immediate environments.

For the marketing, sales, and customer care managers, as well as their executives, the purpose of this chapter is to introduce a technological architecture that supports the constantly changing and demanding world in which these people live, and yet one that also fully supports the enterprise's move to true CRM as described in Chapter 1. If you read no more than just this chapter, you will at least have a good understanding of how the Corporate Information Factory architecture supports the specific requirements of each business unit and how it also provides a technology framework to fulfill the promise of CRM.

The Need for a Corporate Information Factory Architecture

Whenever a complex undertaking is begun, whether it is a building, an airplane, or a new set of applications to support your CRM initiative, the first step must be to create the high-level plan or architecture for what the ultimate product or environment will be. This architecture acts as a road map, guiding the developer in understanding how all the parts and components interact and cooperate.

Our high-level roadmap for CRM functionality is the Corporate Information Factory (CIF). The CIF is a logical architecture and its purpose is to deliver business intelligence and business management capabilities driven by data provided from business operations (see Figure 2.1). Let's look at each of the components of the CIF in the context of these business capabilities.

Business Operations

Business operations are the family of systems (e.g., operational, reporting, ERP) from which the rest of the Corporate Information Factory inherits its characteristics. These are the core operational systems that run the day-to-day business processes and that are accessed usually through application program interfaces (APIs). Examples of business operations are billing systems, product or policy systems, order entry systems, general ledgers and other accounting systems, lead-tracking software, and inventory reorder systems. Generally, these exist in older technology and consist of fragmented or disparate systems with manual interfaces that link them together.

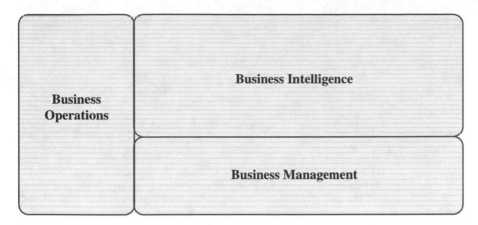

Figure 2.1 The three business functions supported by the Corporate Information Factory architecture.

Some systems built with newer technology also fall into the business operations category. Enterprise Resource Planning (ERP) systems are also considered business operations systems because of their focus on day-to-day activities. Call center and sales force automation systems have a single-function, day-to-day operational focus and can be included here as well. The operational environment represents a major source of data for the CIF. Other business operations sources may include external data, such as demographic information, competitor data, data purchased from credit companies, and informal data such as contract notes, emails, spreadsheets, and so on (see Figure 2.2).

The success or failure of the CIF depends heavily on these operational systems to supply the richness in data needed to understand customers and to provide the history needed to judge the health of the business.

Business Intelligence

Business intelligence consists of the ability to analyze data and information used in strategic decision support (see Figure 2.3). These systems are major consumers of data and are composed of the various business intelligence applications as well as the repository of historical data from which these applications are created (as detailed in the following sidebar). The components of business intelligence are the data warehouse, the data marts, the decision support interface (DSI), and the processes for "getting data in" and "getting

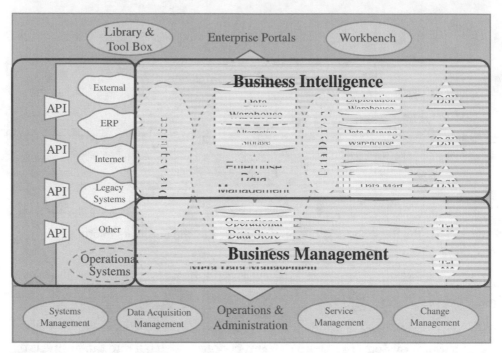

Figure 2.2 Business operations consist of the operational or legacy systems and their application programming interfaces.

information out." An in-depth discussion of these components is found in Chapter 9, "Business Intelligence: Technologies for Understanding Your Customers."

The data warehouse is the source of integrated, reengineered, detailed snapshots of historical data. From the operational systems, we can obtain the customer, product, contact, and usage data needed to analyze the lifetime value of a customer and then tailor our actions with that customer accordingly, such as Bob's value to the bank, the appropriate products to offer him, and the personalization of service that retains his loyalty. The data is extracted from the operational systems (or operational data store—see the next section on business management), cleaned up as much as possible, and then documented in terms of its sources, transformation rules, calculations, and so on. The data warehouse then serves as the historical repository of quality data for use in the construction of subsequent data marts.

The data mart, exploration warehouse, and data mining warehouse are subsets or derived collections of the data found in the data warehouse, formatted for

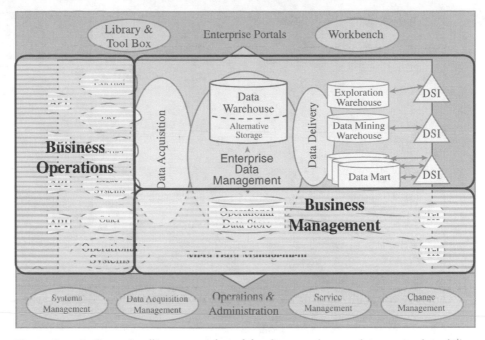

Figure 2.3 Business intelligence consists of the data warehouse, data marts, data delivery, and the decision support interface.

their particular function or department. These systems give us invaluable information about a customer's product usage patterns and enable us to determine the appropriate "next best" products to sell. For example, in Chapter 1, a study of Bob's parents' credit card usage pointed to the travel package for them. You can use these analytical tools to give your business insight into its customers, campaigns, and products. The data for these analyses may be aggregated or summarized, or you may take a statistical subset of data or an extract of transactional data. Usually, these analytical applications are built from a known set of requirements or existing reports.

Business Management

Business management enables corporations to act in a tactical fashion upon the intelligence obtained from the strategic decision support systems (see Figure 2.4). For example, from our study of Bob's parents and customers like them (business intelligence), we know that they are considered to be an economic

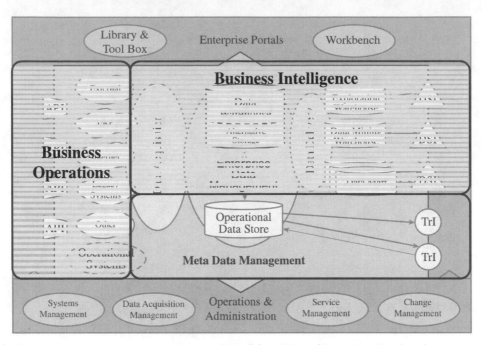

Figure 2.4 Business management consists of the ODS and its transaction interface.

decision-making unit as well as individual customers. To act on this intelligence, bank personnel must see this relationship stored in an integrated database, the operational data store (ODS), and change their behavior toward the couple accordingly.

The ODS is considered a major consumer of operational data. The sources are the same ones we use for business intelligence, except that in this case the data from the operational systems updates the ODS. That is, the old data in the ODS is overwritten by the new data and little or no history is retained (history is kept in the data warehouse). For example, Bob may move to a new address. When he informs the bank of this change, the change may be captured in one of the operational systems. That transaction is then sent to the ODS where Bob's old address is replaced with the new, current address. Now anyone who wants to contact Bob knows where to go to find the most current information, rather than hunting through all the non-integrated operational systems to find the address that was updated. Thus, the ODS is an integrated, cleansed, dynamic (or updateable), and current set of data for these tactical decision-making activities. To get to this data, the business community uses a transaction or online transaction processing (OLTP)-type interface similar to the ones they use for their operational systems. Generally, they access one record at a time and need very fast response times.

The ODS is accessible from anywhere in the organization and should not support any single operational application. As we saw in the example of Bob's address, many people throughout the bank need to access this integrated source of customer information.

Why the Corporate Information Factory?

To illustrate the need for the CIF architecture, let's look at what occurs in many organizations today, regardless of their size, in their marketing, sales, and customer care departments.

In the past, if marketers wanted to use a business intelligence application to determine product profitability or a strategic marketing application to determine which products to offer their customers, they had to look outside of their own company for help. This happened for a number of reasons:

- The internal IT department did not understand what the marketers wanted.
- The IT department had other priorities and would take too long to develop the needed technology.
- The marketers did not trust their own internal data, believing it to be of too poor a quality to be useful.
- The marketer did not understand the technology and thus could not explain what was needed, technologically, to his or her IT personnel.

When looking outside their own company for solutions, the marketers discovered the world of database marketing vendors. These highly specialized technologies seemed to perfectly fit the needs of the Marketing Department. A marketer could simply send his or her data off to the vendor and it would magically reappear at the right level of detail and be formatted to support the myriad requests coming from the marketer. The vendor understood the marketers' requirements, the models they used, and the types of data they needed. Now the marketer could study Bob and his parents to his or her heart's content. Sounds like nirvana!

And so it is for the enterprise that insists on doing business the old way. Traditional marketing departments isolated themselves from the rest of the company, technologically speaking, and performed their marketing tasks without truly understanding that the intelligence they were generating in their stand-alone databases would be extremely useful to the rest of the organization. The

Examples of Some CRM Analytical Applications

The following are examples of various analytical applications a CRM-focused enterprise would likely have:

Product/Service Profitability. This is used to study the historical performance of products, their costs, and revenues. The results are used to determine whether to change a product or service, or whether to continue to offer it.

Customer Demographic Profiling. This is used to consolidate and study customer demographic data (age, marital status, income level, number of children and their ages, home ownership, education level achieved, and so on). This information is used to target customers with the appropriate characteristics for particular products and services or campaigns.

Customer Lifetime Value Analysis. This is used to study the customer's historical interactions and purchases to determine their overall value (or profitability) to the corporation. A customer falls into one of several categories such as highly valuable, potentially valuable, and not valuable.

Campaign Analysis. This is used to compare the historical results of different campaigns. Determinations of the success of a campaign, which customers are likely to respond to specific campaigns, regional response differences, and so on are made from these applications.

Customer Buying Behavior. This is used to study the historical interactions and purchases of customers. The results determine which products and services customers are likely to buy or use in the future.

Sales Channel Analysis. This is used to study the historical activities of the various sales channels (Web, direct sales, or telemarketers). The results determine which sales channels are most effective for specific types of customers.

Sales Analysis. This is used to study the overall sales of products through all sales activities. The results give the enterprise a solid understanding of which products are selling best, in what regions, and through what sales efforts. This application can also determine if cannibalization (trading a profitable product for an unprofitable one) of a sales effort is occurring.

Call Center Analysis. This is used to study the workflow and statistics of call centers. The results are used to determine if new call centers are needed, if new personnel should be hired, and if the call centers and their personnel are performing efficiently.

Market Segment Analysis. This is used to determine appropriate market segments and to study customer behaviors within those segments. The results are used to better understand markets: which ones are profitable and which ones are not, which types of campaigns work well in different markets, and so on.

rest of the organization did not know who Bob and his parents were, whether these people were valuable to the organization, which products they bought, how many times they were contacted by the entire organization, and so on. No nirvana from their perspective (or from the customers)!

A second initiative comes from the sales function. Sales force automation has been very popular for years, and many companies have implemented sophisticated systems to support their mobile sales people. Again, the problem with these systems lies in their stovepipe or silo nature. The data generated in these systems is not available to others in the corporation. Thus, the customer call centers, for example, may not be aware of sales that have occurred, discounts that were offered, or a needed product customization. This makes the organization as a whole look rather inept to the customer. Note that some vendors are now linking sales force automation systems directly to call center systems. Although this linkage enables a partial sharing of data, the rest of the organization is still not in the information loop.

On the other hand, call centers have systems that may not be integrated with sales force automation or marketing systems, so sales and marketing people may not be aware that their customers are in the middle of a service complaint. Again, the corporation looks incompetent to the customer.

Finally, some customer care centers have homegrown or proprietary systems to track their activities. They garner a wealth of information about customers that would be invaluable to sales, marketing, and other business line call centers. Unfortunately, it is a rare event for contact information to be shared outside of the centers. Compare these situations to the interactions that Bob and his parents received from our CRM-savvy bank, and you realize the disadvantage of non-integrated, stovepipe information systems.

In the true CRM world, the marketing, sales or customer care people are not the only people with the invaluable customer information; the entire organization has it and uses it. But how do you manage to share this information throughout the corporation without negatively impacting any single department? This is where the CIF comes in. It is possible to do both: meet the needs of these specific business functions while also ensuring that the entire organization reaps the benefits of the intelligence generated from these systems. Read on to see how this is accomplished.

What a CRM Organization Wants

To the person functioning in a true CRM organization, how a corporation should implement the marketing strategy of CRM boils down to the following:

"Give me all the data I need when I need it! I'll figure out what I want to do with it."

This simple declaration should be the savvy CRM organization's mantra. In analyzing these two sentences though, we get to the real heart of the problem with the current technology. Using a Marketing Department as an example, let's look at what this really means (keep in mind that this must apply to all the functions of a corporation).

"Give Me All The Data That I Need When I Need It!"

This means:

Data must be specific to particular functional requirements. For a marketer, CRM consists of many different capabilities such as those mentioned in the sidebar. Generally, this does not require real-time data but rather data from some historical timeframe in a format that supports the particular function needed. For example, integrated customer data can be combined with purchased demographic data to yield the ability to target customers for products based on specific demographic profiles. The example in Chapter 1 where Bob's parents receive the invitation to the open house is an example of demographic profiling. They were selected (as was the branch office hosting the open house) based on their demographic profile: a wealthy retired couple with a propensity to travel.

Data must be reliable and consistent. CRM decisions are only as good as the data upon which they are based. The quality of the data should be analyzed, and consistent production methods should be used. This data must also be fully integrated from the operational sources into a single "version of the truth." Only when fully integrated data is available can the corporation's personnel truly understand their customers and the value of these customers to the corporation. For example, to determine the lifetime value of Bob and his parents, the bank had to have all of the customer information brought together. Leaving out an important fact such as the relationship between Bob's parents (that they are a single economic decision-making unit) could have disastrous results.

It must be delivered in a timely manner. Data that is stale or delivered late is of minimal value to a dynamic environment. Historical data is very useful for business intelligence, but then the corporation must be able to act upon that intelligence by having a current view of the customers, their products, and their usage of those products. For example, Bob would find little use of an info-mail about a stock that was several weeks old or worse, that was about one that he had just bought.

It must be delivered in a format that is intuitive and familiar to the user. The person trying to get answers to questions does not want to have to struggle with unfamiliar formats and access tool interfaces. The presentation of the data should be natural and similar in its usage as the person's other desktop tools.

"I'll Figure Out What I Want To Do With It."

Here's what this means:

Data must be easily accessed. For most business people, analyses should be intuitive, easily understood, and well documented. More than 80 percent of most queries are relatively straightforward and should require minimal technical expertise.

It must be flexible enough to support multiple purposes. A single source of good data can be reused over and over for various analysis capabilities, thereby reducing the overall cost through efficiency and reusability.

It must be detailed enough to support all queries. To support the myriad marketing capabilities as described, the data must be at a detailed level. Also, to understand a corporation's customers at the individual level, it is mandatory to maintain as much detail as possible about these customers.

Two approaches can solve these nirvana requirements: a piecemeal approach that generally leads to an unsustainable and chaotic environment, and an architected approach leading to a managed and adaptable environment. The first approach has appeal in that it is generally quick and relatively easy to create individual non-integrated marketing capabilities. However, these capabilities are also fractured, redundant, have questionable quality, cannot adapt as the business changes, and usually end up setting the marketing department back in terms of time, money, and delivered intelligence.

The second approach is to implement the Corporate Information Factory. The CIF architecture is a complete roadmap enabling the full CRM capabilities while producing a sustainable and adaptable environment. The full CIF environment will be demonstrated in the rest of the book. The architected approach will give marketing a fully functioning technology setting from which to perform all the analyses, trending, and statistical studies they desire, while also allowing the service and sales people to act upon all this garnered intelligence.

Those of you with little interest in the technological side of this story may choose to skip the rest of this chapter. Provide this book to your people who will be implementing this environment, supply them with business experts to help in the design, give them funding, and watch what develops. For those of you interested in knowing the specifics of the environment, read on! Let's look at the how the CIF will deliver on marketing needs.

Data Must Be Specific to My Functional Requirements

True CRM generates three distinct types of requirements: strategic analysis requirements like those used in marketing, tactical requirements such as those in customer service, and shareable data requirements to be used throughout the organization.

Requirements like these have generally been misunderstood by IT simply because they are not like "traditional" online transaction processing requirements. They do not fit neatly into the world so familiar to technologists—billing, order entry, General Ledger, and so on (static systems with limited flexibility and very structured usage). Some examples of analytical capabilities that flow from these requirements are as follows:

- Customer demographic profiling
- Market segment analysis
- Customer lifetime value analysis (segmentation and scoring)
- Purchasing behavior analysis
- Campaign management
- Sales channel analysis

Capabilities such as these require a lot of detailed, historical data. These historical snapshots of data are generally not updateable in the online transaction processing sense (you can't change them) and so they require minimal record-at-a-time processing. Once the snapshots are loaded into the data warehouse and data marts, they are not changed or altered except under unusual circumstances.

The capabilities do, however, require substantial analytical processing speed (it must be easy and fast to get the data specific to any one analysis). Furthermore, the results from one analysis are often used as the input for another capability.

For example, the high lifetime value customers identified in the customer value analysis may be fed directly into the purchasing behavior analysis to determine which products these valuable customers are actually buying and using. The results from that analysis in turn may be fed into the sales channel analysis to determine the best sales channel for reaching these customers.

A second set of capabilities is needed to give the organization the ability to *act* upon the intelligence garnered from their analyses. Once a trend has been spotted or a behavior analyzed, the marketer or customer care representative must be able to respond immediately and must be armed with data that shows the current situation. For example, a campaign may be launched based on the intelligence gained from the customer value, purchasing behavior, and sales channel analyses described earlier. This campaign is then monitored and tracked in a real-time mode to ensure its success according to expectations. Another example is lifetime value analysis. The results of this analysis can be fed into the ODS in the form of an indicator that is turned on for these valuable customers. Now if a VIP customer contacts the bank, everyone will know the customer's value and behave accordingly. These are examples of "closed-loop" processing where the analytical results acquired from one capability are fed into another for subsequent processing.

These characteristics were difficult to create up until recent times. The technology to support these types of systems was minimal and most IT personnel did not have an understanding of, or an architecture for, these systems (much less a methodology to use in building them). The results were myriad homegrown or purchased systems that were nonstandard, nonintegrated, point-solution applications that gave minimal relief to the frustration of the CRM personnel. Shareable data by the various customer contact points was impossible until now. The time (and technology) is ripe for the creation of very sophisticated enterprise-wide CRM capabilities. To achieve the closed-loop processing as previously mentioned, you must have a robust, planned, managed information architecture or the CIF (see Figure 2.5).

WARNING

A cautionary note is needed here. With so much new technology available, it is easy for both the IT and business communities to lose sight of the goal, get enamored with the technology, and see it as a means, not an end. It is for the purpose of preventing such problems that this book has been written. This book should be used as a guideline or roadmap to follow, customizing where needed, to fit into your particular environment. Keep in mind the ultimate CRM vision mapped out in the book will help all involved to see each aspect of CRM as the means to the ultimate goal: to manage to the customer.

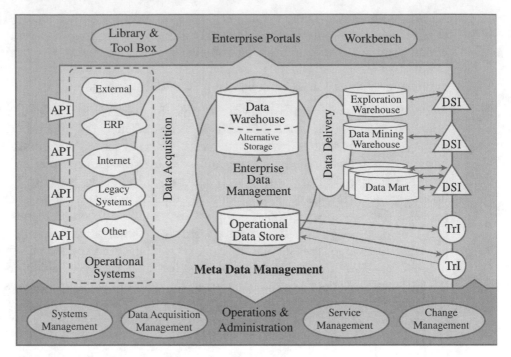

Figure 2.5 The Corporate Information Factory.

The CIF gives you the flexibility to bring in new technologies as they are developed, yet it enforces rigidity where it is absolutely mandatory. The CIF produces an adaptable yet stable and maintainable environment. Finally, it creates an environment that supports not only the analytical functions used to create corporate memory (who are your good customers, what have they purchased in the past, how have they responded to prior campaigns, and so on), but also those tactical functions used to maintain the relationship with the customer (the customization of a customer's purchase, allowing the customer to choose his or her sales channel, cross-selling or up-selling to the customer, and so on). See Figure 2.6 for an understanding of the strategic and tactical components of the CIF.

In the following paragraphs, each piece of the CIF will be examined, demonstrating how it supports the promised environment.

For the first requirement of your CRM organization—I need data specific to my functional capabilities; it should be obvious that a need exists for multiple forms of analysis and investigation that will require multiple technologies. Only by having databases set up for particular purposes—data marts, exploration warehouses, and data mining warehouses—can we achieve this first require-

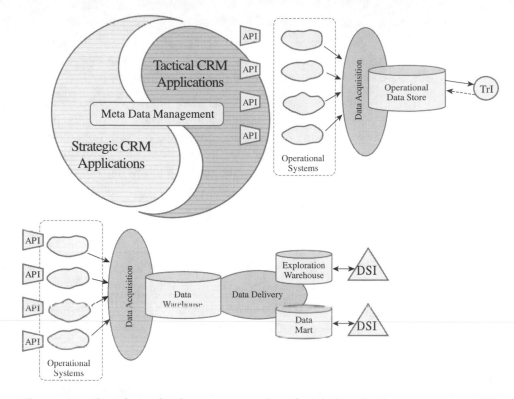

Figure 2.6 The relationship between strategic and tactical applications supporting CRM.

ment. These databases are important in that they provide business units with flexibility, control, and responsibility over their analytical capabilities.

Data marts are defined as:

- Databases that contain data tailored to support the specific multidimensional or online analytical requirements of a given business unit or business function utilizing a common view of strategic data. These structures permit business analysts to "slice and dice" their data, drilling down into more detail or around into different areas of interest. They are the most common form of business intelligence applications.

Exploration warehouses are defined as:

- Databases whose purpose is to provide a safe haven for exploratory and ad hoc processing. An exploration warehouse may utilize data compression, in-memory processing, parallel processing, specialized server platforms, and specialized database optimizers to provide fast response times with the ability to access the entire database.

Data mining warehouses are defined as:

- Databases created so analysts may test their hypotheses, assertions, and assumptions developed in the exploration warehouse. Specialized data mining tools containing intelligent agents are used to perform these tasks.

Data marts, exploration warehouses, and data mining warehouses are spawned from a central repository of data called a data warehouse (discussed in more detail in the next section). These three analytical components may be set up to perform simple querying and reporting, to enable trending and multidimensional analysis, to support sophisticated data mining such as pattern recognition, or to enable an unstructured exploration of the data. The beauty of these structures resides in their ability to match the technology to a particular capability.

The second set of capabilities, the ability to act upon the intelligence, comes from a different type of technology, the ODS. These capabilities are based, as mentioned earlier, on the need to have integrated and current data accessible from anywhere in the organization. The ODS is characterized as being:

- *Subject-oriented*   Oriented around major subjects of data like customer, product, transaction, and so on.

- *Integrated*   Containing one and only one version of the customer; it is a common view of enterprise-wide data.

- *Current*   As up-to-the-second as we can technologically make it.

- *Volatile*   Capable of receiving changes and updates to its data; most or all history is obliterated.

The ODS can be looked upon as a collection of integrated data used to support the tactical decision-making process for the enterprise. For CRM, this means the ODS generally has all of a customer's current information centrally available, such data as Bob's current address, phone number, product purchases, product utilization, and so on. It also mandates that full-blown referential integrity, such as that found in operational systems (cascading updates and deletes, or edit checks), be in place.

Data Must Be Reliable and Consistent

The difference between a good query and a bad one comes from the amount of thought and prior analysis done by the person asking the question. The difference between a good answer and a bad one is the quality of the data being queried. Data quality has become a major point of concern in CIF development whether for strategic analysis (such as customer demographic profiling) or tactical actions (contacting the customer for a cross-selling opportunity). The expression "garbage in, garbage out" is as relevant today as it was 15 years ago. Because we have so many operational systems —each doing its own bit of processing for the corporation, each with its own narrow slice of corporate data, each with its own way of doing business—it is no wonder that data quality problems exist. The wonder is that organizations seem to succeed in spite of these problems. Quality will be discussed in great detail in Chapter 8, "Quality Relationships Start with Quality Customer Data."

Of course, the quality of the data is greatly improved simply by extracting it from the operational environment, running it through the cleansing programs, integrating it with data from other systems, and transforming it into a corporate standard. All of these activities occur in the data acquisition process (see Figure 2.7).

Much of the effort in constructing the CIF (up to 80 percent of the overall effort) occurs in this process. The better this process is, the better the entire environment functions. The data acquisition process has the following definition:

> The processes necessary to capture, integrate, transform, cleanse, reengineer, and load source data into the data warehouse and operational data store.

Data reengineering is a significant part of the data acquisition process. It is defined to be the activities that investigate, standardize, and provide clean

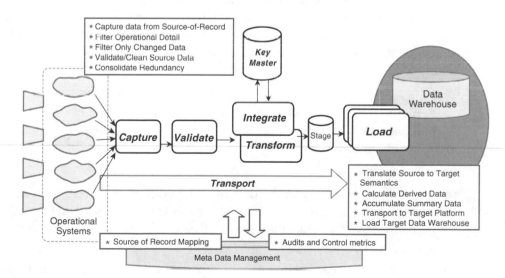

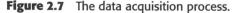

Figure 2.7 The data acquisition process.

consolidated data. Data acquisition is no accident; it takes a significant amount of data reengineering to accomplish the integration necessary for true CRM. As discussed in Chapter 1, just coming up with a solid, all-encompassing definition of customer can go a long way towards reengineering your data.

The data warehouse plays an important role in the delivery of the strategic data. It has some characteristics similar to the ODS; it too is subject-oriented and fully integrated. But it also has significant differences from the ODS in other areas:

- **It is a time-variant database.** It is a series of historical snapshots, each dated and accurate as of that point in time.

- **It is non-volatile.** It cannot accept transactional updates or changes; rather, it is appended or inserted with new additions.

- **It is a collection of static data.** It is used to support the strategic decision-making process for the enterprise and is the central point of data integration for business intelligence.

- **It is a source of data.** It feeds the data marts and delivers a common view of historical, enterprise data.

The roles of the data warehouse and ODS in improving data quality are undisputed. However, you should not abandon all plans for this environment because you think your data will never be perfect. Different levels of data quality are required throughout the environment. For example, data with a slightly lower level of quality can still be very useful, particularly for strategic analyses, if you can measure the quality and guarantee that it is consistently wrong. (Note: You may not be able to "fix" the source of the quality problem because it resides in an operational system over which you have no control.) Significant trends and patterns can be observed as long as the data has consistency, for example, it is consistently 10 percent low. The key is not to shoot the messenger, but to begin fixing data problems where they occur.

Of course, the CIF cannot guarantee the production of 100 percent accurate and complete data. However, by creating a central place to store integrated historical data (the data warehouse) and integrated current data (the operational data store), you can:

- Identify data problems, such as multiple instances of Bob.

- Enforce processes to fix the data in the operational sources, such as changing the business processes that enter transactional data (based on the *quality* of the data entered as well as the number of transactions entered).

- Identify those systems that cannot be fixed, such as aging systems that no longer support the new data capture requirements for CRM.

- Fix some of the data problems as they move through the data acquisition process, such as codes that are no longer being used.

Quality becomes exceptionally critical when you are dealing with current data for tactical decision-making, that is, when you are using the ODS. Getting Bob's email address wrong when you are contacting him with stock info-mail may be significantly worse than missing a single customer transaction out of 50 million for strategic analysis purposes.

Needless to say, it is important to have an environment that does the following:

- Establishes data quality baselines, such as service level agreements (SLAs) for quality baselines that include the percentage of errors accepted and types of errors corrected.

- Reports on data quality metrics within the CIF (the number of errors, corrections, rejected records, and so on).

- Reports on known sources of bad operational data.

- Establishes data quality procedures (when to reject a record, how to fix some problems, when to escalate a problem, when to stop processing, and so on).

Data quality that is quantifiable can be improved. If thought is given up front to data quality issues, the users of this environment will be far more confident in their analyses and will be more likely to use this system as opposed to one they have built themselves.

All of this information is useful, but only if it is accessible and understandable by both the IT developers and the business community using the environment. This means that you must have a collection point for the information that gives meaning to the data. That is the role of meta data, or the data about the environment. Meta data has the following definition:

> Meta data is data about data, activities, and knowledge. It provides the necessary details to promote data legibility, use, and administration.

Meta data is the glue that holds the entire CIF together. It supplies definitions for data, calculations used, information about where the data came from (which source systems), what was done to it (transformations, cleansing routines, and integration algorithms), who is using it, when they use it, and what the quality metrics are for various pieces of data. It provides you with the meanings of lifetime values and VIP indicators, and it may even tell you which behavior is appropriate in certain situations (such as the misuse of data or privacy standards). Meta data has become a very sophisticated element of the CIF, one that is equally needed for both the tactical and strategic sides. Table 2.1 outlines the various categories of meta data.

Table 2.1   Meta Data Categories

TECHNICAL META DATA	BUSINESS META DATA	ADMINISTRATIVE META DATA
Defines construction of the data warehouse • Sources • Targets • Transformation rules	Provides a business view of meta data • Definitions • Business rules • Calculations	Provides information about the health and well-being of the CIF • Usage patterns • Average response times • Content trends or problems • Load times • Quality of data
Used for ongoing upkeep • Maintenance • Distribution to data marts • Operations	Used to ensure that the business community understands the meaning of the information it is analyzing	Used to determine • Data quality • Infrequently used data • Inefficient ETL processing
Captured through extraction tools or via documentation of hand-coded programs	Generally must be manually captured and maintained	Captured through monitoring tools or via internally developed monitoring programs

Data Must Be Delivered in a Timely Manner

Just as different levels of data quality exist throughout the CIF, different levels of timely data delivery to the business community exist. It does no good to have access to data on Tuesday when the decision was made on Monday. The example of Bob's encounter with the travel service associated with his bank's Web site demonstrates this need for timely delivery. On the other hand, a monthly snapshot may be perfect to demonstrate a trend or pattern. For Bob's parents, their propensity to travel as identified in a monthly snapshot is sufficient to identify them as likely candidates for the open house. As you can see, the delivery of data for tactical decisions is significantly different than the delivery of data for strategic decisions.

The process of data delivery to the various data marts in support of strategic decisions is as critical as the data acquisition process. A stable, reliable, and consistent data delivery process is only possible if you have a solid CIF architecture that includes a robust data warehouse. Data delivery is defined as

A process that enables end users and their supporting IS group to build and manage views of the data warehouse within their data marts.

Data delivery consists of a three-step process:

1. **Filtering the data.** This consists of removing only the data that is needed for a particular capability. For example, we do not need Bob's demographic data to perform a buying behavior analysis on his activities.

2. **Formatting.** This step consists of putting the data into the proper format for the technology used. This entails determining whether the ultimate analytical functionality is multidimensional, statistical, or exploratory, and then selecting the right technology based on this determination.

3. **Delivering.** Here you ensure that the data extracted from the data warehouse is delivered to the data marts within the proper timeframe. SLAs may help assist in determining the required timeliness of data delivery.

The processes and the databases must work in concert with predictable and coordinated results. Scheduled delivery promotes consistency, efficiency, and confidence in the environment.

For the tactical part of the CIF (the ODS), timely data takes on a completely different meaning. Timely data acquisition means that the ODS should be updated with changes from the operational systems as quickly as it is technologically feasible and according to the business requirements. Ideally, this would happen instantaneously; a change occurring in the operational system would be reflected in the ODS a few seconds later. Unfortunately, because we are somewhat restricted by the technology available today, and because of the possible need for complex integration and data reengineering algorithms, we may not be able to have instantaneous updates. This forces us to make a difficult decision: What is the fastest that I can reasonably update the ODS versus what is the business need for the currency of the ODS data? For example, it may be fine to update the ODS with new customer value information once a day. However, any new product purchases must be brought into the ODS as soon as possible. This topic will be discussed further in a later chapter dealing specifically with the ODS.[1]

---

[1]Also see the book, *Building the Operational Data Store, Second Edition,* by W.H. Inmon, John Wiley & Sons, 1999.

Data Must Be Easily Accessible

Perhaps the most important aspect in any CIF is how the users of this environment interface with it. We caution you not to leave the design and implementation user interface until last. Time runs out, money runs out, patience runs out, and you end up with a suboptimal means of accessing the critical information contained in the databases.

For the strategic decision support side of the CIF (consisting of data marts predominantly and their variations), the interface should have the following characteristics:

It is intuitive. A person with insight and who is perceptive should be able to pick up the access tool and run with minimal training. For example, the business user of the campaign analysis data mart must be able to quickly develop analyses and get results without requiring significant tool training.

It is easy to use. The tool comes with built-in queries or algorithms, has simple menus, clear instructions, and helpful error messages. Many of the online analytical processing (OLAP) applications have standard queries that run periodically: total product sales by market segment, by sales channel, or by sales representative. These "canned" reports are easily created ahead of time and run on a regular schedule so that the user can simply view the results, rather than having to repeatedly create and run the report.

It interfaces to other tools. Most users of the CIF want to use their own desktop tools in addition to the one specified for the CIF. For example, the CIF tool must interface easily with word processing or spreadsheet tools.

This interface has been named the decision support interface (DSI) (refer to Figure 2.5) and is defined as follows:

> The DSI provides the end user with an easy-to-use, intuitively simple tool to distill information from data. It enables analytical activities and provides the flexibility to match the tool to the task.

DSI activities come in many flavors. They include data mining, OLAP, query and reporting, and statistical analysis or exploration. The most important criteria in choosing the proper tool is to ensure that you have matched the capability you want with the proper technology to support it. For example, if the capability is to simply report on campaign progress, then perhaps a simple reporting and querying tool is sufficient. However, if you are developing sophisticated and complicated models for predicting purchasing behavior, you will need the more advanced and possibly more difficult-to-use tools appropriate for data mining or exploration. In all cases, the tools should be able to handle massive amounts of data with ease and should be able to display this information in a comprehensible and manageable format.

The ODS has its own interface as well, the transaction interface (TrI), shown in Figure 2.5. In this case, though, it has a *transaction* orientation similar to the interfaces found in most OLTP applications. The TrI performs the following tasks:

- It provides an easy-to-use, intuitively simple interface to request and employ business management capabilities.

- It sources data from the ODS. The ODS serves as the repository of the current, integrated views of customers. All the information about Bob's parents is contained in the ODS, including the fact that they are an economic decision-making unit.

- It has a response time similar to that found in OLTP systems (in subseconds). For example, the ODS may contain the IDs of appropriate Web site messages for its Web customers. When Bob logs on, the ODS must supply that ID within a tenth of a second to the Web server for proper display.

- It handles record-at-a-time processing with ease. Anyone who interacts with Bob must be able to call up his specific customer record easily.

It Must Be Flexible Enough to Support Multiple Functions

If one constant holds true in your Corporate Information Factory environment, it is this: the environment will change. As marketers and others get more familiar with the capabilities and the tools, they will begin to use both in different ways than initially intended. For example, the capabilities may first be used in a rather tactical fashion, such as finding the answers to the results of the last campaign, who bought the most product last month, and which market segment was the most profitable. Slowly, the true strategic types of questions will emerge. Compare this quarter to last quarter and to the same quarter the year before. Which customers have consistently been our best ones? Which products sell best in which regions during which seasons? What is the pattern emerging from sales? Eventually, the need to act upon this intelligence will emerge as well and require the construction of the ODS.

As more strategic, longer-reaching questions begin to appear, usually the design of the data marts will also have to change in order to accommodate the new questions. These changes may be so severe that not only does the data mart design have to change, but also the underlying technology may no longer be appropriate.

These changes highlight the real beauty and effectiveness of the CIF. If the underpinning architecture of a data warehouse and the data delivery processes are in place, it is a simple thing to tear down and rebuild a data mart or swap out one tool for another. These changes are made efficiently and relatively seamlessly if we have taken the time up front to create the administrative functions for the CIF, have implemented streamlined processes to handle requests, and have the right resources to support and maintain the environment. We define these operations and administration functions (refer to Figure 2.1) as the set of activities that ensures

- Smooth daily operations
- The optimization of resources
- The management of growth

The operations and administration functions include the following processes:

Systems management. This guarantees that upgrades and new versions of hardware and software are installed with minimal impact on the CIF usage.

Data acquisition management. This certifies that data acquisition processes are working at peak efficiency and effectiveness.

Service management. This ensures that the business community requests and SLAs are handled properly.

Change management. This confirms that changes made to any part of the CIF are reflected in all appropriate documentation (models, programs, and meta data), structures (data warehouse, ODS, and data marts) and interfaces (DSI and TrI).

Enterprise data management. This performs backup and recovery processes as well as archival and retrieval procedures. It creates standard dimensions, calculations, and derivations (in the warehouse for use by data delivery), and it partitions data according to usage.

It Must Be Detailed Enough to Support All Queries

This last characteristic is what sets the CIF apart from the many imitators and data mart-only applications being developed today. The goal of the CIF is to have a single repository of historical data from which to build data marts and perform strategic analyses, and a single repository of current data from which to act upon these analytical findings to make tactical decisions.

Let's take the strategic side as an example of the power of the CIF. What would our environment look like if we did not have this single repository from which to build our marts? We would begin by building a single mart: extracting, integrating, cleansing, transforming our data, and then finally loading it into the data mart technology of choice. So far, so good. Then we would build our second data mart: extracting, integrating, cleansing, transforming our data, and then finally loading it into the data mart technology of choice. Then our third and our fourth and so on. Before long, the environment would resemble the chaos of Figure 2.8.

The problems become apparent after the second or third of these unarchitected databases:

- No consistency exists between the extractions. Customer information is fractured and inconsistent across the various marts.

- The same data from the same sources is extracted over and over. Inefficiency of extraction becomes readily apparent.

- No integration exists between the data marts (therefore, no method to interface results from one mart to another). Processes that require outputs from one mart to be fed into another (such as the demographic profiles

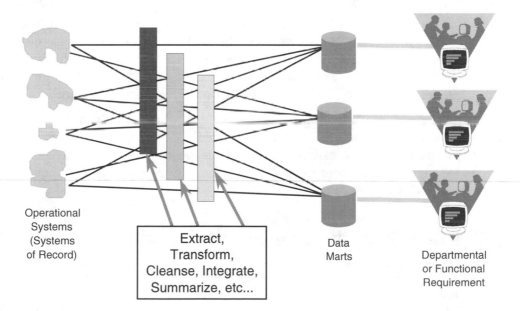

Operational Systems (Systems of Record)

Extract, Transform, Cleanse, Integrate, Summarize, etc...

Data Marts

Departmental or Functional Requirement

Figure 2.8   Data mart chaos.

into the sales channel mart) cannot be performed or can be performed only after a significant effort to integrate the data between the marts.

■ Minimal historical detail is available for analysis. No repository of all historical detail is available in this environment.

The result is a non-maintainable and non-adaptable environment that will eventually implode under its own weight. Other results would be that marketing intelligence capabilities are set back significantly and the goal of an integrated CRM enterprise is completely missed. In this environment, people contacting Bob and his parents would not know of other contacts, would not be aware of other efforts involving these customers, and would not use the same message when speaking to them.

If we look at the CIF, we see a very different environment, one that is much simpler to understand and therefore to build and maintain. The data warehouse becomes the center of data for the data marts. We liken the data warehouse to a large box of Legos, those wonderful plastic pieces from which you can build all kinds of structures: houses, rocket ships, robots, busses, and so on. You can build whatever you want and are only limited by your imagination and by the rectangular shape of the pieces.

The data warehouse is similar to the Legos, except that the data is reusable. You can build many different capabilities (the analytical applications as described in the sidebar) from the pieces of data. Only your technology and your level of sophistication with tools limit you.

A second benefit of the CIF is that you now have the ability to drill down to a lower level of detail than what may be found in your data mart. If you discover an anomaly or an exception to a trend, you can simply request the detailed data of that anomaly or exception from the data warehouse. It is easily obtained and you don't need to carry all that detail around in all the data marts.

Third, the data acquisition process, difficult as it is, is only performed once for each piece of data. You have an integrated and high-quality set of data on which to draw. Also, you can use the data warehouse as the starting point to analyze the quality of all your data. You can rationally approach any data quality problem with this single set of all data.

An Example of the Corporate Information Factory at Work

To illustrate the various components of the CIF at work, let's walk through a typical CRM function: campaign management. Campaign management is the process that marketers use to plan, execute, and monitor marketing campaigns. Throughout this process, measurements are taken to optimize the campaign (see Figure 2.9). These functions (plan, execute, monitor, and optimize) all use different parts of the CIF.

Planning a marketing campaign requires a variety of information found within the strategic marketing capabilities (data marts and their variants):

- Customer profiles
- Past customer behavior
- Marketing costs
- Budgetary information
- Historical promotion performance

The Corporate Information Factory provides the means to pull all of this information and data together with the means to:

- Access the information
- Analyze the information, such as segmentation
- Design the marketing campaign
- Cost the marketing campaign
- Socialize the design and projected results
- Prepare the campaign for execution

Execute

Campaign execution requires information on the status of the campaign as it progresses. This must be integrated, accurate, and high-quality data reflective of the current situation. An ODS is often the only place to find the following data:

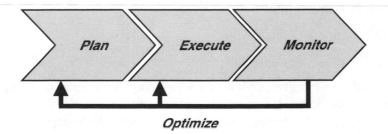

Figure 2.9 Campaign management and the CIF.

- Inventory levels
- Actual costs
- Actual revenues
- Key metrics
- Fulfillment statuses
- Promotional material release times
- Response rates and levels

Activities surrounding campaign execution vary based on the type and complexity of the campaign. The following activities generally involve the operational systems and ODS:

- Manage fulfillment
- Capture customer interaction metrics
- Track costs
- Track revenues
- Continual adjustment of interactive campaigns

Monitor

The information for campaign monitoring is vital for understanding the success or failure of campaigns. Current campaigns are constantly tracked and compared to previous ones in order to determine if the campaign is performing as expected, if it is above expectations, or if it should be halted due to negative trends. The process involves not only the operational systems and ODS, but it uses the history found in the data warehouse and data marts for comparisons. The measurements used to monitor campaigns include the following:

- The predicted outcome from campaign planning
- The budget and actual costs
- "Outside promotion" customer activity
- Customer interaction information

Optimize

The CIF provides an integrated view of a wide array of information in an easily manageable environment, thus permitting the continual optimization of campaigns. The integrated, current data used to optimize the campaign is found within the ODS and data marts. Measuring campaign performance includes the following tasks:

- Budget-to-actual analyses
- Response measurement
- Profitability analysis
- Market basket analysis
- Threshold detection

Optimization includes the following activities:

- Correction of negative trends
- Alteration of targeted audience
- Reduction of cost overruns
- Streamline the fulfillment process

Summary: The Need for Architecture

This chapter established the data requirements for a CRM organization: "give me what I need, when I need it." It also established the need for and the components of a solid architecture to support those requirements. The CIF supplies the CRM personnel with the following:

- An adaptable environment that is easily revamped and rebuilt as requirements change
- A stable environment supporting efficient and effective implementation processes
- A sustainable and maintainable environment reducing overall costs and promoting reusability
- A flexible environment that supports simple forms of reporting as well as complicated and sophisticated analyses
- An extensible environment that supports quick queries using highly aggregated data while preserving very detailed data for in-depth analyses

The next chapter introduces the Customer Life Cycle in detail. This is a structured mechanism for understanding all the potential interaction points between an organization and its customers. It is important to understand this life cycle before delving into the technology to support it.

CHAPTER 3

Understanding the Customer Life Cycle

H ave you ever experienced a situation in which a salesperson makes repeated suggestions or recommendations about a product before you are ready to make a purchase decision? Buying a car can be like that. You may not have completely decided the type of car you want, much less the dealer, but aggressive sales representatives have you seated in the manager's office talking financing and payment options before you know it. Anyone who has experienced these kinds of selling situations understands the distaste they can leave behind. Moving in for the sales close, or suggesting a solution prematurely, can do more than kill the sale; it can kill the relationship. Consider this:

> A Customer Relationship Management (CRM) consultant in a large systems integration company was recently asked to participate in an initial sales call with the marketing department of a potential customer. Although the consultant had not worked with the customer before, her company was currently working with this customer on several other projects. Prior to the call, the sales team planned its strategy: talk a little about the customer's situation (primarily for the benefit of the consultant, who did not know this customer), talk a little about the other projects with the organization in which they are involved, present the solution they have identified as appropriate for the customer, discuss the potential costs for this solution, and then send the formal proposal the next day.

> Things started out well, with a good discussion about the customer's environment and the CRM direction in which they were trying to move. The consultant got her first clue that something might be amiss when she asked the customer to talk about the problems they were trying to solve and they replied, "we can give you our initial thoughts, but we are still in the process of defining these."

At this point, the consultant called a break in the meeting and suggested to her team that they consider postponing the solution presentation until the next call and change the forum for this visit into an interactive discussion to help spell out potential problems the customer might resolve with a CRM package. The account manager denied the request, citing the difficulties involved in getting time from the product specialist who was to give the presentation. "Besides," he reasoned, "I know this customer and I am sure this is the right solution for them."

At the start of the presentation, the customer asked why they were presenting this particular product. The account manager explained that based on his extensive knowledge of the customer's environment, he thought this product was the appropriate solution and would help them move toward CRM. The customer crossed his arms, sat back, and let the presentation resume.

The end result: not only did the team lose the sale, but the customer also resented that the team had "tried to shove the solution down his throat using the strength of the existing relationship," and relations on the other projects became strained.

The most unfortunate part of this story is that the suggested product probably was the right solution for the customer, and the account manager truly did understand the customer's environment. He simply misread the customer's position in the buying cycle. If he had understood (as did the CRM consultant) that the customer had not yet reached the point of consideration, contemplating how a specific product might meet an identified need, and if he had changed his customer interaction strategy accordingly, the team could have helped to advance the customer through the buying cycle and presented the solution when the customer was ready to receive it.

As we stress throughout this book, CRM is about leveraging your knowledge of your customers to manage each interaction (sales, marketing, or service) so that it is satisfactory to the customer and profitable to you. Although CRM technology, cross-functional business strategies, and the appropriate organization structure and culture help you to achieve this, another key to managing customer interactions is understanding the Customer Life Cycle (CLC). The CLC is a means of defining and communicating the way in which an enterprise interacts with its customers and prospects.

This chapter introduces the CLC and presents a generic model from which to start when defining the CLC specific to your organization. The chapter begins with a general introduction to the CLC, which explains the environment in which the CLC functions and introduces the various CLC stages. Next, the chapter provides a detailed description of the CLC stages and maps enterprise processes to these stages. Both business executives and technologists will benefit from an understanding of the Customer Life Cycle.

An Overview of the Customer Life Cycle

The purpose of the Customer Life Cycle is to define the stages through which a customer progresses when considering, purchasing, and using products. Its purpose is also to define the associated business processes a company uses to move the customer through the CLC. Business managers need a detailed understanding of each CLC stage to identify and manage customer interactions taking place in each stage. In the preceding story, a better understanding of his customer's position in the CLC could have enabled the account manager to plan a more appropriate customer interaction and could have possibly saved the sale and preserved the relationship. Because they are not actively managing customer interactions, technologists don't require as much detail. The value of the CLC to a technology executive lies in its mapping to the Corporate Information Factory (CIF). However, in order to create this map of systems to processes, the technologist must have some understanding of the major stages in the CLC. The map of CRM technology to the CLC provides a mechanism for prioritizing systems projects and for understanding the information required by specific customer interactions. Details are presented in Chapter 9, "Business Intelligence: Technologies for Understanding Your Customers," Chapter 10, "Facilitating Customer Touches with the Customer ODS," and Chapter 11, "Automating the Sales and Service Process."

A generic Customer Life Cycle is pictured in Figure 3.1. The stages shown represent thought processes for typical customers and companies. Although these stages may or may not change, it is likely that the business processes that map to these stages will differ from company to company. The remainder of this chapter focuses on the generic model. We recommend that you start with this CLC, compare it to your organization's situation, and modify it accordingly.

The Customer Life Cycle is depicted as a circle (or ellipse) to represent the fact that this is truly a cycle, one that you want your best customers to move through again and again. Each stage will be explained in detail later in the chapter, but first let's start with a summary of the CLC that provides a high level understanding of the major pieces and how they complement each other.

When a customer (considered a prospect in the early stages of the CLC) is considering the purchase of a product or service, he or she goes through a series of thought processes (or stages). These stages, shown just inside the circle on the CLC diagram in Figure 3.1, are as follows:

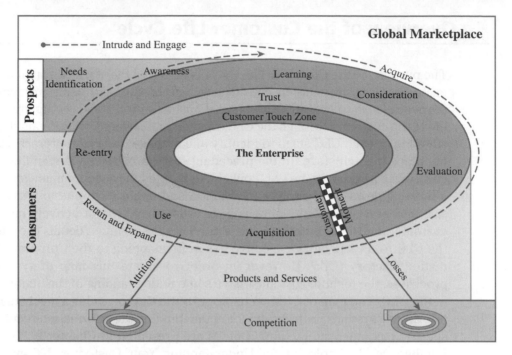

Figure 3.1 The Customer Life Cycle.

Identify needs that may be filled by a product or service available for purchase.

Develop an *awareness* that your organization exists and may be able to fulfill the identified need.

Learn more about your organization and the products and services that may fill the need.

Consider how the products and services offered by your organization do or don't satisfy the identified need.

Evaluate the suitability of your products and services against others (the competition) to fill the identified need.

Decide to purchase your product or service, go to a competitor, or to not fill the need. We refer to this stage as the *customer moment*.

Once the prospect reaches the customer moment and decides to purchase the product or service from you, he or she becomes an actual customer. At this point, the stages in the CLC transition from a focus on the customer's purchase decisions to a focus on customer satisfaction and relationship nurturing as the customer uses the products he or she has purchased. As the customer moves through these "product or service use" stages, your organization has an increasing ability to influence customer satisfaction. Unfortunately, this influence can be either negative or positive. Inaccurate or untimely fulfillment and poor service can result in a decision by the customer not to purchase additional products or services from you. On the other hand, satisfied customers can become customers for life, owning many products and services, and generating much profit. After the customer moment, the CLC stages include the following:

Acquisition of the product or service (delivering the product or service) is typically the first interaction the customer has with your organization after the purchase decision.

Use by the customer of the products and services is typically for the life of product ownership, and sometimes beyond.

Re-entry by the customer into the CLC represents a positive decision to do additional business with your organization.

The outermost circle (dotted lines) in Figure 3.1 represents the flip side of the customer stages described earlier. Here we illustrate the processes your organization undertakes to move a customer through the CLC. Once you determine the mindset, and thus the possible behaviors, of your customers as they move through the CLC, you can identify the interactions your organization has with these customers. If you map these interactions to the appropriate CLC stage, you are less likely to misread a situation (as did the account manager in the chapter introduction) and will be more confident that the action you take will indeed advance the customer to the next stage in the CLC. The business processes conducted by your organization fall into the following general categories:

- **Intrude and Engage.** This includes the efforts of your organization to get the attention of a prospect, have that prospect become aware of your company, and engage the prospect in a dialog designed to move him or her into the CLC.

- **Acquire.** Simply because prospects are aware of your organization does not guarantee that they will purchase products or services. You must work to educate the prospects about your company, and you must maintain the prospects' attention and interest as they continue with their buying decision.

- **Retain and Expand.** After a prospect buys your products or services and becomes a customer, the real work begins. Many of the cross-functional business strategies designed to increase customer satisfaction and foster customer loyalty are conducted in this section of the CLC.

In a properly defined Customer Life Cycle, the organization's processes map clearly to the customer stages, and a relationship that complements both the customer and the organization can be established.

Now that we have introduced the CLC, let's take a closer look at the interaction between the business and the competitive environment, as well as at the various stages described earlier.

The Enterprise, Products, and the Competition

The enterprise, your products and services, and the competitive environment all work together to shape the CLC.

The Extended Enterprise

The enterprise is at the center of the Customer Life Cycle. Although we often think of the enterprise as simply our organization, adopting the customer's perspective changes our thoughts dramatically. To the customer, the enterprise represents a combination of businesses, organizations, or governments that provide goods and services. Often called the extended enterprise, this point of view looks beyond our company and represents the complete value chain for goods and services. The extended enterprise concept ties directly back to the extended customer definition introduced in Chapter 1, "The Customer Becomes the Center of the Business Universe." This definition, "a party of interest to the organization who is involved in the acquisition of goods and services," includes suppliers, competitors, and other third parties.

Wal-Mart's inclusion of a supplier in its customer definition and in its business processes (also introduced in Chapter 1) provides a good example of the extended enterprise. To you and me, the ultimate customers of Wal-Mart, the most important consideration is this: Does Wal-Mart have the exact product of the brand name and type that we came into the store to purchase? If a store is out of the particular gardening tool that we wanted, we are not likely to think, "the supplier of this tool has not produced enough product to meet the demands of the gardening season. It is not Wal-Mart's fault." Instead, we are more likely to mutter, "Wal-Mart doesn't have what we need. We'll shop at Home Depot from now on."

Although the complete value chain for goods and services starts with the manufacturing of the product or service and continues through the ultimate sale of these by Wal-Mart, we as consumers do not recognize each discreet step in the chain. We see the extended enterprise only from the perspective of our interaction with the retail store. The good news here is that companies such as Wal-Mart do consider the extended enterprise when defining customer and designing the CLC. By providing suppliers with access to the information systems they need to manage store inventory, Wal-Mart is using its extended enterprise to facilitate sound CRM.

It is also interesting to consider the extended enterprise from the perspective of the manufacturer or distribution company. Consider the music industry. A large entertainment company may own several popular record labels. The value chain for this company is complex and includes the artists who actually perform the songs, the radio stations that play the songs and generate interest and billboard ratings, the music stores that carry the CDs, and the associations that develop awards such as the Grammys and the Country Music Awards. As you can imagine, this company has a complex definition of customer. Music stores are counted as primary customers, but they aren't the only customers. Customer interactions take into account the entire extended enterprise. As an example, marketing dollars and promotional activities are aimed in multiple directions along this value chain: to get airplay and award recognition for songs, to stimulate interest and purchases among end consumers (you and me), to convince music stores of the potential success of a song (thus ensuring that they stock enough CDs to meet demand), and to attract popular artists to the record label to ensure a steady stream of new songs.

The extended enterprise functions from a global venue as well. Your company may be a subsidiary of a corporation in another country, and it may also have subsidiaries in other countries. The CLC is therefore set in the global marketplace. Geography plays a decreasing role in defining the audience for your products and services, and the rapidly shrinking world plays an increasing role in pushing the boundaries of the extended enterprise. (Additional details on the forces shaping the extended enterprise will be covered later.)

A shoe company that was featured on National Public Radio portrays this point. The products of this company epitomize CRM and mass customization. The shoes are surprisingly affordable, but every pair of shoes is handmade to the customer's specifications. The premise is this: Each person's feet are different, so how can anyone be comfortable in mass-produced shoes? Here's how it works: You log onto the company's Web site, pick from a number of available shoe designs, provide your address and credit card information, draw the outline of each foot on a piece of paper, fax your feet to the specified number, and wait for your shoes, which come in the mail several months later. And guess where this company is located (actually it is a family-owned shoemaker)— Switzerland! You can order and receive custom-made shoes without ever leaving the house, and if you did not recognize that the fax was a Swiss phone number, you would not know that you were doing business internationally.

Although this may seem like a humorous example, it is real, and it does illustrate the CLC in the global marketplace.

Products and Services

The custom shoes offered by the Swiss shoemaker illustrate another point with regard to the CLC: The products and services you offer can influence your success as a CRM organization. Throughout this book, we emphasize that the successful CRM organizations are those that make the transition from a product focus to a customer focus. This does not mean that products become unimportant; it simply means that we build our products to satisfy our customers. More and more, companies are tailoring products to meet the needs of individual customers. The shoemaker is one example, while the bank that serves Bob and his parents is another. The package of products and services offered to Bob is very different than that offered to his parents, and each package is priced according to the features most likely to be used. For example, Bob pays no fees for ATM transactions but does pay to use the branch. His parents, on the other hand, pay for each use of the ATM but have unlimited branch visits. As Figure 3.1 illustrates, the CLC sits upon the foundation provided by the products and services offered to your customers.

Competition

Competition is another factor that influences the Customer Life Cycle. Although the CLC activities sit upon the foundation of products and services as indicated previously, the CLC itself is driven by the principle of competition. A competitor is any enterprise that offers customers products and services that rival your own. The need for (and value of) CRM is influenced by the amount of competition faced by an organization or industry.

Consider the utility industry in the southern U.S. prior to the recent deregulation. Before deregulation, little or no competition existed at all. In many areas, customers had no choice on where to purchase energy. You simply moved in and signed up with the established local provider. In the northern U.S., some competition took place. Although customers may not have been able to select their electricity provider, they could opt for an alternative form of energy (such as natural gas) to satisfy some of their needs. Most electric utility companies, if asked, would tell you that they did not know much (if anything) about their customers; they did not need to. The customer was the box on the side of the building. "Who is paying the bill?" was probably the most important question.

Now that competition exists, customers receive notices from their electric provider informing them of options. They also receive plenty of mail from alternate providers soliciting business. All these companies are now interested in the customer as an individual, not just as a bill payer.

Airline frequent flier programs provide another interesting and timely example of the role of competition in the CLC. At one point in the past, a school of thought believed that loyalty programs, such as those offered by the airlines to frequent travelers, did not lead to increased profit. This idea stemmed from the thought that once a company offered a loyalty program, competitors would jump to match it and all companies would simply end up giving away items without really generating additional revenue. This thinking is shortsighted and docs not take into account the premise of CRM, managing customer interactions to the satisfaction of the customer and to the *long-term* profit of the organization. Programs that increase customer satisfaction, and thus loyalty, are not about generating short-term revenue; they are about generating long-term profit through lasting customer relationships.

Consider what is happening now in the airline industry as international carriers are adding more routes to the U.S. and domestic carriers are breaking into the European markets. U.S. travelers have many options for transatlantic flights, both domestic and otherwise. To make it more attractive for customers to stay with their preferred carriers, the airlines are doing several things. First, they are forming alliances across multiple international carriers, which simplify the process of connecting to multiple destinations in other countries. These alliances provide the opportunity to share loyalty points and frequent flier status levels across multiple airlines. Some European airports have even rearranged the check-in facilities and departure gates to group alliance partner airlines in the same physical location. Second, the airlines are recognizing their frequent fliers as VIP customers and treating them as such. Several airlines are building customer databases for these fliers and providing service preferences (food and drink, seating, and past customer comments) to flight crews for use during the trip. The pilot of one United Airlines flight recently used these comments to identify the platinum-level frequent fliers on his trip and wrote them individual thank-you notes, which were then distributed to these passengers during flight. These databases will also be shared with reservations staff to enable more efficient service and provide options such as booking flights on partners and in some cases even with competitors.

Personalized traveler cards, containing profile information, to speed you through check-in and customs are next. Most of these initiatives are directly connected to the increasing number of choices provided to passengers because of increasing competition. The competitive environment as the driving factor in CRM is represented in the CLC by the position of competition in Figure 3.1 (underlying the entire structure).

Forces Shaping the Extended Enterprise

As Figure 3.2 indicates, four forces are helping to extend the enterprise. These forces are as follows:

The force of process. Business processes are extended in a number of ways: The supply chain is becoming flexible enough to provide more customized products and services, while partnering among product and service providers is increasing. The demand chains are reaching deeper into customer organizations to deliver products and services (for example, the customer has more say in the customization process). An increasing emphasis is being placed on information in all customer-facing business processes as knowledge management is transformed into knowledge sharing with an emphasis on the capture of customer information and the targeting of communications with customers. Knowledge sharing will shape business processes into a seamlessly integrated customer focus.

The force of people. How people relate to the enterprise is changing. The maturity of geographic markets places a greater demand for skilled team members, while the maturity of the global network increases the viability of a distributed work force. (For example, customer service representatives must become relationship managers rather than order takers, and many organizations are adopting work-at-home policies rather than requiring skilled employees to change locations). In this changing environment, the increasing number of companies in the value chain changes the emphasis from employee to team member as processes become more complex. Additionally, knowledge work is distributed from the "job of the few" to the "task of the many."

The force of business. Organizations are shifting from product to customer. Competition comes from non-traditional sectors (banks are selling insurance products) and competition is expanding into a global marketplace. Acceptance of the Internet as a marketplace changes the way products are acquired, and convergence of the Internet and "brick and mortar" provides more sales and service options as well as more sales and service complexities. These changes cause innovation to shift from a trait to be admired to a necessity for survival.

The force of technology. Customer knowledge can scale up to millions. Vast amounts of data can be leveraged for business intelligence, while business intelligence for the masses enables an unprecedented availability of strategic information. CRM systems extend the ability to share knowledge across the enterprise, and maturing tools improve implementation speed and ongoing flexibility, while emerging administration tools make the technology easier to manage.

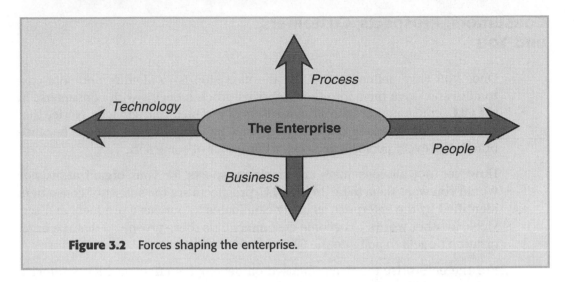

Figure 3.2 Forces shaping the enterprise.

One last point about competition has to do with the two ways a customer or prospect can drop out of the Customer Life Cycle. The first is termed loss, which is the capture of a prospect by a competitor at or before the customer moment. Losses are a fact of doing business. Although losses are not desirable, if the loss occurs on the prospect's first trip through the CLC, it is at least acceptable. Note that the longer (and more expensive) the sales cycle, and the higher the potential sale, the less true the prior statement becomes. Losses become a higher priority issue when they occur for customers who have been through the CLC before. The loss of the marketing project by the systems integration company, detailed at the start of this chapter, is more devastating because of an erosion of established trust with an established customer.

This second way for a customer to leave can be more severe than a simple loss; this is known as attrition. Attrition is the erosion of customer loyalty after the customer moment, leading to their capture by a competitor. These are customers, not prospects. Frequently, the company has made a significant investment in the relationship. A plumber who takes all his business to a competitor after a bad experience with the collections department is a good example of the consequences of attrition. The organization loses a valuable customer due to its inability to provide acceptable service. Not only will the organization have a hard time winning him back, it may also have to deal with questions of other disgruntled customers if he is vocal about his dissatisfaction in the local business community. Worse than that, he may influence others who are not yet customers not to even consider the company.

Consumers, Prospects, Customers, and You

Once you have defined your CLC, the next step is to identify potential customers and drive them into the CLC. This process begins with consumers. In the CLC, consumers are the ultimate users of products and services. Notice that consumers are pictured outside the actual CLC in Figure 3.1. This is because practically every person on earth is a consumer of some sort.

However, not all consumers are viable prospects for your organization, nor would you want them to be. In the CLC, prospects are the subset of consumers identified by the enterprise as likely candidates to purchase products and services, in other words, to become customers. It is these prospects that the organization targets to pull into the CLC.

For the enterprise to remain focused on developing effective CRM strategies and on building the customer base, a clear distinction must be developed between consumers at large and prospective customers. The more the enterprise can focus customer acquisition strategies on prospects, and only prospects, the more successful downstream CRM strategies are likely to be. When the reality diverges from the strategy (the organization spends dollars or conducts activities targeted towards consumers outside the defined prospect base), the enterprise should be reminded of its CRM acquisition strategies. Sometimes changes in the environment dictate that the enterprise rethinks that strategy.

The audience for pre-paid cell phone usage packages is a good example. A Canadian communications company initially targeted these products to the lower income, poor credit market. When the company analyzed the actual users of this service, it found that the actual users did not match its targeted market. Wealthier segments (families and small businesses) were using the service as a means to provide cell phones but control costs and usage. The company subsequently changed the profile of customers it targeted based on this analysis.

One effective method for identifying the prospects that may become profitable customers is to first determine the characteristics of your profitable customers and then look for consumers that share these characteristics. It is quite surprising how many successful salespeople can't tell you exactly what these characteristics are. A large mutual insurance company provides a good example of this:

> The company touted an image of its customer base, wealthy individuals, which most agents agreed with. When revenues became stagnant for several years running, the Marketing Department decided to look at new customers to see if they matched the accepted profile. (The marketers had a second, less obvious objective in this exercise:

to break down existing cultural barriers between the agents and the company and foster an environment where customer information was more readily shared.)

To kick off the initiative, marketing changed the new policy applications to include a set of questions designed to profile the new customers. When marketing analyzed the information, it uncovered a surprising result. Although some of the new customers did indeed fit the profile of wealthy professionals, a majority of these customers were actually in the next lower customer segment. Subsequent profitability analysis confirmed that both groups were equally profitable to the company.

Marketing took these results to the agents with a suggestion that they spend more time and money on prospecting for customers from the lower customer segment. Not only did sales increase (along with agent commissions), relations between the agents and marketing also improved because the agents received a first-hand demonstration of the value derived from sharing information.

In this instance, the insurance company needed to change its customer acquisition strategy to match the characteristics of its actual customers. Continuous effort is required to keep the business aligned with its customer strategies, and to ensure that the sales and marketing organization, and the enterprise as a whole, stays focused on its true prospects, rather than on all consumers. Figure 3.3 illustrates a process used by successful organizations to help maintain focus on the appropriate group of consumers and prospects.

Lead management is the process of identifying, qualifying, and informing prospective customers so that salespeople can efficiently convert these prospects into customers. In Figure 3.3, the process flow of lead management, as it relates to the CLC, is illustrated:

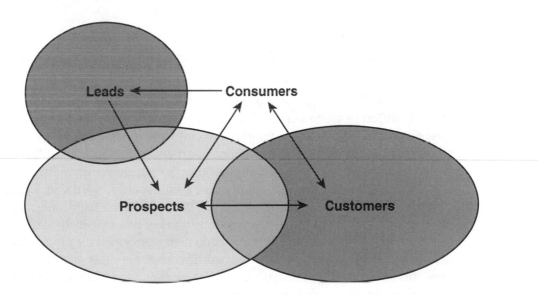

Figure 3.3 Lead management.

- Consumers with the appropriate characteristics are identified and targeted as leads.

- Until the leads have been qualified through some type of contact, they are no different than consumers as a whole.

- Leads must become prospects before becoming customers.

- The subset of leads that responds positively to qualification becomes prospects.

- Prospects are drawn through the CLC to become actual customers.

An important part of the lead management process involves closely tracking all contacts made throughout the sales process. These contacts, and the associated lead or prospect responses, are analyzed to achieve ongoing process improvement and gain a greater insight on prospects and customers. This analysis can identify the most responsive type of prospect or it can highlight differences between reality and perception (such as that described for the insurance company). Sales force automation systems play a key role in the lead management process and, in combination with call center systems, provide a vehicle to track and manage prospect and customer interactions throughout the CLC. Chapter 11 provides more detail on these vital CRM systems.

"Megamarkets" provide an additional point to consider when targeting your prospects and defining your CLC. Three major megamarkets exist in the current economy:

The individual consumer market. The individual consumers who buy products and services.

The business market. The organizations that buy products and services.

The government market. The government agencies that buy products and services.

Although the three megamarkets occasionally overlap, they differ in significant ways: in different customers, different expectations, different competitors, different sales and marketing approaches, and different customer interaction steps. Customers can reside in two megamarkets at the same time. An example would be someone in the consumer market who purchases an individual insurance policy from the same company that administers his 401K at work. Customer expectations for treatment can be very different from one market to another. Individuals in the consumer megamarket don't typically expect to be assigned long-lasting personal relationship managers when they purchase products (exceptions include high net worth financial services customers), while most organizations base large purchasing decisions in part around relationships with the companies from whom they are purchasing products.

Companies that deal with all three megamarkets recognize the distinctions and define a CLC for each one. Many times, different organizational units deal with each market. A common example can be found in the banking industry. A large bank usually has customers in all three markets. One segment that the bank focuses on is retail (the consumer megamarket). This is administered through an organization called a retail bank. Customers interact with the retail bank through branches, the telephone banking service center, and the Internet. Although these customers may have personal bankers assigned to them, this is the exception rather than the norm. Generally, only the high net worth customers have ongoing relationship managers monitoring their accounts. In addition, marketing conducts many targeted direct marketing campaigns, such as mailings and promotions designed to touch large numbers of consumers.

The bank also has a profitable customer base in the business megamarket. The number of customers in the business market is much smaller than in retail—several hundred thousand businesses versus ten million retail customers. These business customers are administered through the corporate bank, a distinctly different organization than a retail bank. Relationship managers and team selling practices are the norm, and marketing rarely does direct marketing, preferring instead to work with sales to interact with potential customers in a much more personal way.

The bank's last megamarket is the government market. Not only is this administered by a separate organization, but new products and services are tailored specifically for the government. The bank in our example has formed alliances and partnerships with outside parties to provide e-commerce solutions to government agencies in order to facilitate payments for government-to-consumer (G2C) and government-to-business (G2B) transactions. These include payments for items such as motor vehicle registrations and drivers license renewals, as well as corporate filings, building permits, and professional licenses.

One alarming issue can occur when the customer bases in the megamarkets overlap. Customers with small businesses and retail products, or those who interact with your organization both at work and at home, may not be easily viewed by the enterprise across both markets. (Remember the plumber in the communications company?) The previous examples are instances of the extended household concept that is introduced in Chapter 1.

As you may recall from the discussion in Chapter 1, understanding households and extended households is the key to leveraging the influence value that is associated with these households. A customer in the individual consumer megamarket who is also the CEO of a profitable business customer has tremendous influence over that business account. Unsatisfactory treatment of the

CEO in the consumer market can have severe consequences to the business market as well.

When defining the differences between megamarkets, you must guard against the tendency to move away from CRM into organizational silos that actually prevent customer focus. If your organization defines distinct business processes and requirements for each megamarket in a vacuum, you will establish organization silos. You must also identify the intersection points between megamarkets and build these into your business processes. It is necessary to recognize differences in customer interactions across these markets, but it is key to CRM to also recognize the similarities and position the organization to take an enterprise view.

Trust and the Customer Touch Zone

A customer touch is any interaction between the customer and the enterprise. Customer touches can be initiated by either the company or the customer. As Chapter 1 indicated, the management in CRM is the identification and management of all customer interactions to the satisfaction of the customer and the long-term profit of the organization. Typically, two channels are available for these customer interactions (for now!). The first channel contains groups of (sometimes independent) intermediaries who deliver products and services to the marketplace. These groups provide face-to-face human contact: retailers, brokers, agents, sales force employees, and bank tellers. Bob's parents prefer this type of customer touch and utilize the bank branch where they interact with a teller who handles all their banking requirements.

The second channel consists of the media used to interact directly with the customer. Although a human may participate somewhere in this process, the contact is not face-to-face. Instead, these channels include telephone calls, mail, Web sites, kiosks, automated teller machines (ATM), television, and so on.

An organization can sometimes have conflicting goals with regard to the management of these two channels. On one hand, CRM principles dictate that the organization must provide customers with the channel options of the customers' choice. Bob and his parents have significantly different preferences for how each interacts with their bank, and the bank facilitates both sets of preferences. On the other hand, in the interest of profit, organizations also want to shift interactions to the most efficient (lowest cost) channel. A large bank in a conservative Midwestern U.S. city recently caused significant controversy (and received lots of negative press) when it levied fees on most branch transactions in an effort to move customers toward the ATM and phone banking channels. Successful CRM organizations find a way to balance this channel conflict and manage customer touches appropriately. The Midwestern bank would have been well served to understand its customer base a little better and develop package and pricing options favoring one or the other channel, as did Bob's bank, rather than simply dictating an unpalatable solution.

Customer touches can be further classified into two distinct types: synchronous and asynchronous. Synchronous customer touches are highly interactive, taking place in real time or near real time. These include phone calls, Web site visits, personal delivery of a product to the customer, fax back services, and so on. Asynchronous touches are not interactive and usually require a day or more to complete. These include letters, bills, e-mails, thank-you notes, and mass media (billboards).

As you can imagine, facilitating the highly interactive, real-time synchronous customer touches utilizes more sophisticated CRM technology, such as the customer operational data store (ODS), which is detailed in Chapter 10. Although asynchronous touches require less sophisticated technology, they are not always less expensive. Consider what many computer manufacturers are doing with the warranty registration process for new equipment. Traditionally, warranty registration forms were sent out with the product and the customer completed the form and sent it back to the manufacturer. Today the process is quite different. The installation and setup process for the equipment includes an option to register the product online during setup. Customers choosing not to register at the time of setup have the option to log onto the Web site at another time to complete the warranty process. This process change (from asynchronous mail to synchronous Web) is based on convenience for the customer and cost for the company. It actually costs the company less on an ongoing basis to use the synchronous Web channel. Savings come in the form of lower labor costs, no postal fees for the return forms, and no forms or envelopes. The new process also lets the company leverage the existing Web infrastructure and provides greater flexibility for the customer.

Each customer touch, synchronous or asynchronous, face-to-face or through other media, is accounted for in the CLC. We illustrate this with the Customer Touch Zone. This Zone is portrayed in Figure 3.1 as a circle on the immediate outside of the enterprise and is where all interactions with the customer happen. When popular sports figures are doing well at their game, they are said to be "in the zone." Successful CRM companies should be in the zone as well, the Customer Touch Zone.

Once you have a customer in the Customer Life Cycle, every interaction occurring in the Customer Touch Zone is a tremendous opportunity to build trust and reinforce the relationship. Figure 3.4 depicts trust in the CLC and illustrates the key role it plays. Trust plays such a key role because it can be gained or lost anywhere in the CLC, and the loss of trust is detrimental to CRM strategies.

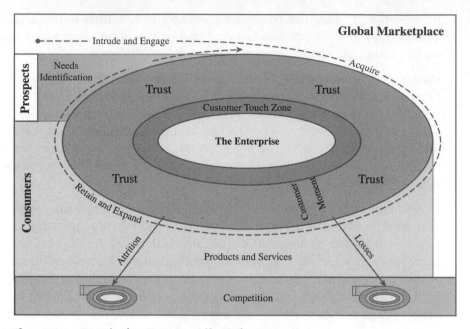

Figure 3.4 Trust in the Customer Life Cycle.

Consider the example that opens this chapter. The prospect for the marketing project had been through the CLC several times before and always made a positive decision at the customer moment. Trust, accumulated from prior experiences, motivated the prospect to share his ideas on a new marketing direction before these ideas were completely formed. When the account manager pushed with a solution, the customer was still in the earliest stage of the CLC, Needs Identification. Because the customer interpreted this action as a hard sell and felt that the systems integration firm was misusing the existing relationship, all the accumulated trust was instantly gone and replaced with suspicion.

As this example illustrates, it can take a long time to build trust, but only a moment to destroy it. The management section of Chapter 1 provides examples of interactions that have been managed well (customer oriented—good) versus interactions that have been managed poorly (non-customer oriented—bad). All these examples are within the Customer Touch Zone and each has an associated impact to the customer's level of trust in the organization. Applying trust to these examples yields the following:

Good. Solicitations of new banking travel services to Bob and his parents—Web-based for Bob and personalized direct mail for his parents. The bank has illustrated to both Bob and his parents that it understands their preferences, and that it actively looks for offers that match these preferences. This builds trust.

Bad. A hasty collection letter sent to a valuable small business owner based on incomplete customer knowledge. The communications company has demonstrated to the small business owner that it does not understand him and does not know which products and services he has purchased. The negative effects of this demonstration are magnified because relationship managers are assigned to businesses to provide high-touch treatment, and purchase decisions are frequently made on the strength of the relationship between the business owner and the organization. Trust is eroded here.

Good. A complete analysis of contemporary household relationships and associated influence value prior to the de-marketing of a seemingly low-value household. In this instance, the household in question owned only an unprofitable checking account, but a member of this household also managed an extremely profitable annuity for her elderly parents who resided at a different address. If the bank wanted to de-market this household, it could have done so by substantially raising fees. Although certain situations will occur when it is not bad to raise fees for unprofitable customers, this is not one of them. Putting the breaks on this potential service interaction avoids a situation where trust would have been eroded, with potentially drastic consequences (the loss of the annuity business).

Bad. A number of calls must be made by the best customers (multiple product owners) to provide change of address information due to problems in product-oriented customer call centers and non-integrated service processes. When customers with multiple products have to make several calls to change customer information that is common to all products, trust is eroded. In this case, it is trust that the organization cares enough about the customer to provide convenient service, and that the organization understands the customer's value.

Good. Identification of the disparity in product and service features preferred by Bob versus his parents, which results in the offer of personalized product packages for each customer. This builds the exact type of trust that is eroded in the previous example. Here the bank has demonstrated to Bob that it understands his value and cares enough about him as a customer to provide the convenient service options and optimum package pricing that he requires.

Several more examples of trust currently pertinent to CRM include the following:

Good. A reliable privacy policy (see Chapter 14, "Preserving Customer Trust—The Role of Privacy," for more on privacy) that provides verifiable evidence that the information provided by the customer is not being misused.

Bad. A company strategy that abuses the information provided by the customers, such as the listing of its customer list for sale as an asset by the bankrupt Toysmart.com.

Mapping Enterprise Processes to Customer Life Cycle Stages

We started this chapter with a high-level description of the stages that a prospect passes through when making purchase and use decisions. We also introduced you to the activities conducted by the enterprise through the Customer Life Cycle to turn prospects into customers and to build lasting and profitable relationships. In this section, we map these enterprise activities and processes to the appropriate CLC stages so that you can effectively tailor your own CRM strategies.

Intrude and Engage

Figure 3.5 highlights the enterprise processes of Intrude and Engage and maps these to the accompanying CLC stages, Needs Identification and Awareness.

Intrude and Engage deal primarily with consumers and qualified leads that have been targeted as potential prospects. In the CLC introduction, these two processes are described as the effort of your organization to get the attention of a prospect, have that prospect become aware of your company, and engage the prospect as a willing participant in a dialog designed to move him or her into the CLC. Mass marketing and advertising are examples of intrusions on consumers that are designed to capture their attention. These intrusions typically interrupt the consumer, diverting his or her attention from whatever it happened to be focused on prior to noticing the marketing piece or advertisement. A customer who is listening to the music on his or her favorite radio station only to be bombarded with a string of commercials is interrupted by these ads. The customer does not solicit these commercials, but the interruptions are a necessary part of capturing new customers. Unless they are already looking for a specific product and know of your organization (a later stage in the life cycle), they are not likely to come looking for you.

Much of what the advertising industry calls *branding* happens through these mass marketing and advertising campaigns. Branding develops public awareness of a company and its products, and sets expectations with respect to design, features, quality, price, or service levels. Consider the popular athletic

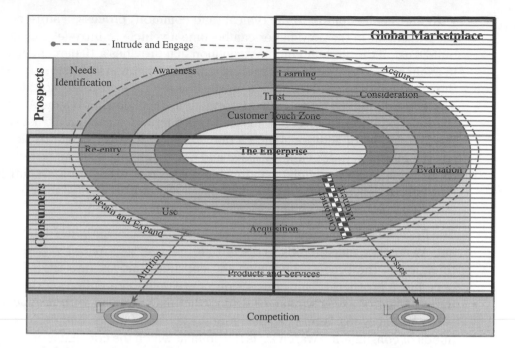

Figure 3.5 Intrude and Engage.

shoe company that once used the slogan "Just do it." The advertisements for this company typically pictured famous and successful professional athletes wearing the shoes and performing spectacular feats of athletic prowess. These ads promoted a brand that is associated with high performance and quality.

In the world of CRM, intruding on consumers with unsolicited messages, while necessary to pull them into the CLC, is not enough to keep them there. Once you have the attention of the consumer, the key to successful CRM is to use the momentary attention you have gained to begin a dialog with the consumer whereby you are gathering information about them as well as imparting information about you.

As we mentioned earlier in the chapter, every interaction with the customer or prospect is an opportunity to build trust. One way to build this trust is to accumulate knowledge about your customers, and to judiciously use this knowledge to tailor your subsequent interactions to better meet their needs. This postulate holds true whether you are interacting with a long-time customer or with a consumer that has yet to move into the CLC.

With one small addition to the typical (and common) process, a store circular advertisement in the newspaper can become a vehicle to intrude, engage, and build trust. If the circular contains a coupon that provides a 10 percent discount in exchange for a customer's name and email address, and if the store then uses the information to send thank-you emails that refer the customer to the store's Web site for future sales and other information, the dialog has begun. As long as the solicited information is not misused, this interaction can build trust and lay the foundation for additional interactions. The key to successful intrusion is to use the intrusion to solicit knowledge and understanding that can be leveraged to grow mutually beneficial relationships. With few exceptions, an intrusion that fails to deliver on the second half of the equation to engage the consumer into an interactive relationship is an intrusion that has failed.

The first two Customer Life Cycle stages for the consumer, Needs Identification and Awareness, map directly to the Intrude and Engage processes. Needs Identification is the process by which the consumer moves into the CLC (and becomes a prospect). This consists of a developing perception on the part of the prospect of needs, wants, or desires that may be filled with products and services. Savvy marketers can generate these needs, wants, and desires in the minds of consumers. Awareness is the point at which the consumer or prospect becomes cognizant of the enterprise and begins to understand that the enterprise may be somehow related to their needs. Many times the prospect experiences these two stages simultaneously. The prospect that sees the shoe commercial and thinks, "My tennis shoes are wearing out. Maybe it is time to get new ones," immediately followed by, "Those shoes are cool," has moved quickly from Needs Identification to Awareness that the company in the ad exists. In this case, the marketers for the shoe company did indeed generate the need for new shoes in the mind of the prospect.

In the example that opened this chapter, the marketing prospect became aware of a need to move towards CRM on its own, or through previous non-sales interactions with the systems integration company. Although it was aware that the systems integration company existed, it had not fully moved out of Needs Identification. According to the CLC, the account manager should have moved to engage the prospect in a dialog at this stage. An effective dialog would have included soliciting information from the prospect on current problems.

Acquire

Acquire starts when a prospect has entered the Customer Life Cycle and is aware of the enterprise or its agents or resellers. All the business processes that lead up to the decision point, the customer moment, are included in Acquire. This is where the enterprise begins to have increasingly meaningful dialog with the prospect. Careful attention should be paid to these communications, and all actions should be tailored to leverage the growing knowledge of the prospect to move him or her towards the customer moment. Figure 3.6 illustrates Acquire and the associated CLC stages.

In Acquire, the enterprise helps the prospect in a number of ways. It assists the prospect in refining his or her needs and in identifying possible solutions. It points the prospect in the direction of the appropriate products and services and highlights the most pertinent features. The enterprise also helps the prospect to become familiar with its company and understand the competitive advantages (if any) offered by the enterprise. The enterprise acts as a facilitator for the evaluation process, making that process as painless as possible.

Prior to CRM, the Acquire process was often considered more important than the rest of the CLC, because the emphasis in a product-focused organization is often on selling more products. Today this process is important, but no more so than the service-focused processes that come after the customer moment. Companies are learning that there may be a greater yield for marketing dollars spent on nurturing and expanding existing relationships than ones spent on finding new relationships.

The first stage the prospect goes through in this part of the CLC is learning. Learning occurs as the prospect associates the enterprise with the ability to

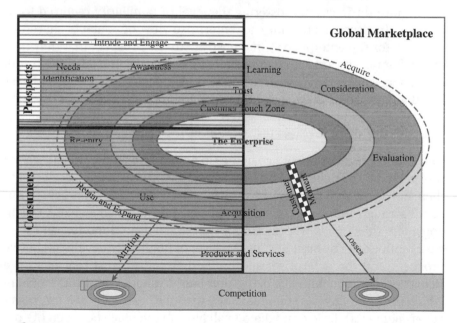

Figure 3.6 Acquire.

meet his or her needs through products and services. In order to consider the options available to meet these needs, prospects must first understand what is available and who offers it. Often, the prospect learns more about the need itself, and sometimes even refines the need identified in the earlier part of the CLC.

Learning would have been the logical next step for the marketing prospect in the example that opened the chapter. This prospect understood the need to move toward CRM but did not know enough to understand that a CRM system of the type proposed would help them get there. The consultant suggested an interactive discussion that would have allowed the systems integration company to learn more about exactly what the prospect did and did not know. The company could have used this discussion to advance the prospect through the learning process and at the same time refine his need.

While in the learning stage, the prospect should become familiar with the enterprise. The higher the level of familiarity between the prospect and the enterprise, the greater the opportunity for the enterprise to build trust. This is because building familiarity requires a dialog with the prospect, providing the enterprise takes the action we advocated earlier: Collect information about that prospect, turn it into understanding, and use it to manage all future customer touches. It is easier for the prospect to build this familiarity with the enterprise than it is for the enterprise to build it with the prospect. Why? Because the prospect is an individual with an easy recall of past interactions. The enterprise has a more difficult time fostering the level of familiarity required for trust to develop. Institutional memory, an enterprise view of contacts shared by all, is required for the enterprise to demonstrate to the prospect that they are understood. Familiarity, trust, and eventually loyalty are built by demonstrating, with each successive interaction, that you understand your prospects and customers and that you are willing to act on this understanding. Learning is often the stage in the CLC where the first strong two-way communication between the prospect and the enterprise is fostered.

Consideration is the next stage in the Customer Life Cycle. Consideration takes prospects to the point of contemplating how products and services will meet their needs, wants, and desires. Attitudes, feelings, and a perceived match-to-needs strongly influence consideration. Once the facts are at hand, the prospect considers these facts with a strong dose of emotion. Emotion and feeling are easily influenced by branding, by the level of familiarity developed between the prospect and the enterprise, and by the amount of trust that has developed. Because of the commodity being purchased (shoes), and the mechanism by which the company has communicated with the customer thus far (mass media advertisements), little or no dialog will have taken place between the prospect, who is now shopping for shoes, and the shoe manufacturer. Thus, although some level of familiarity may be established due to repeated marketing intrusions, the biggest considerations for the prospect walking into the store will be feelings and emotions about the shoes, the brand recognition, and perceptions about how those particular shoes match the prospect's needs at the moment.

Because those perceptions about a match-to-needs were likely put in the prospect's mind by the commercial he or she watched, there is a good chance that an equally strong in-store promotion for another brand of shoes can sway emotions and perceptions again, and the prospect could walk out of the store with a different brand of shoes. In a situation in which the prospect has a chance to develop familiarity and trust through dialog, the outcome could be a little different. The prospect that provides an email address to a clothing store in exchange for a discount, and then receives a thank-you note, may just click through to the Web site. This builds familiarity and provides the store with an opportunity to continue the dialog. Trust can be built in a situation like this, and the customer may be more likely to shop in that store again before going to its cross-town (or cross-mall) rival.

Evaluation is the last stage in the Customer Life Cycle before the customer moment. Evaluation is the point at which the prospect assesses the suitability of a product or service before making an acquisition. Evaluation varies greatly between products, markets, and customers. For example, a dealer may provide a good prospect with a new car to test-drive overnight, knowing that the prospect is likely to develop an emotional bond by having possession of the car. Software vendors provide a similar evaluation opportunity through trial periods. On the other hand, evaluating the produce in a grocery store is something that happens in a split second, if at all. A prospect is not going to take the bananas home for a few days prior to purchasing them. If a true evaluation period occurs, a strong dialog will likely take place between the prospect and the enterprise.

One software vendor offers a case study evaluation for its customer name and address data quality tools (see Chapter 8, "Quality Relationships Start with Quality Customer Data," for more information on the utility of these tools). In this evaluation, the vendor gets samples of the prospect's actual customer data and runs the samples through the tools. The results are analyzed, problems in the data are highlighted, areas of strength are determined, and the results are presented to the prospect in an interactive dialog. This evaluation gives the prospect the opportunity to see first-hand exactly what the tools will do for him or her. He or she has the additional opportunity to see just how bad or good the customer data is, and to understand the magnitude of the errors contained therein. In some cases, these errors come as quite a surprise. In addition to what the prospect learns about the benefits of these tools in his or her own environment, the prospect is also investing both time and emotion in the case study process. As you can imagine, these case studies, in combination with the associated dialog, are a great evaluation device to push the prospect toward the customer moment.

The customer moment is that point of decision, that split second, when a prospect decides to become a customer, go to a competitor, or not make an acquisition. The purpose of the CRM strategy is to positively influence the customer moment and to gain the ability to bring this influence to bear multiple times during the course of the relationship. The customer moment does not represent the actual transaction in a financial sense, the payment. Instead, it is the actual decision to acquire, or the moment of acquisition and approval in the case of financial services credit products. Some organizations look at this instant as a "magic moment" and try to leverage immediate opportunities for a cross-sale of additional products. One large Canadian bank viewed the notification of acceptance for a mortgage as a magic moment and created incentive programs tied around the cross-sale of credit cards and overdraft protection products to new mortgage customers. The thinking behind the magic moment concept is that this instant carries a high level of trust (enough to push the decision), and a high level of positive feeling and emotion (particularly in the case of a mortgage acceptance where the bank is actually granting the prospect the ability to buy a house). What better time to compress the CLC and solidify the relationship than now?

Retain and Expand

Once the prospect has made the decision to buy and has transitioned from prospect into customer, the enterprise must also transition from acquisition mode to retention and expansion mode. Retention is focused on keeping relationships with profitable customers once they have engaged the enterprise. Expansion is focused on increasing the share of wallet for profitable customers by helping them through the CLC again and again. Figure 3.7 illustrates retention and expansion.

Much emphasis is placed on this part of the CLC because the cost of attracting new customers can be many times higher than the cost of selling additional products to existing customers. The commonly quoted figure is that it costs, on average, eight times more to gain a new customer than to cross-sell a new product to an existing customer. In some industries, this figure can actually be much higher. Several online brokerages offer cash incentives of up to $100 to lure new customers. Because this is a one-time cost applied to the opening of an account, future transactions cost the company significantly less if the customer is retained.

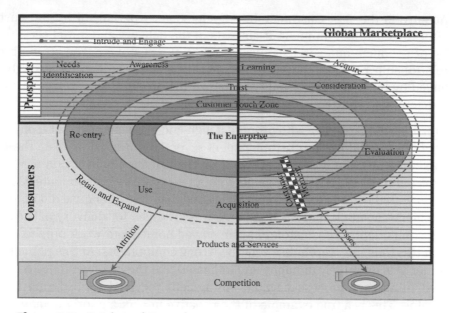

Figure 3.7 Retain and Expand.

The benefits of expanding the share of wallet are similar to the benefits of customer retention: additional sales without the cost of acquiring new customers. Many times the most profitable customers are those that spend a large percentage of their budget with the enterprise. For example, one bank identified three segments of customers: full-service customers, midrange customers, and incidental customers. Full-service customers were those that considered the bank to be their primary financial institution. These customers used the most products and did the least business elsewhere. Incidental customers did not consider the bank as their primary institution and typically had only one account there. Midrange customers were those that fell somewhere in the middle. They typically used more than one product, but not enough to earn the designation of a primary customer.

As you might expect, the profitability of these customers matched the segment to which they were assigned, with primary customers as the most profitable. The bank determined the characteristics of customers in each group that indicated a likelihood to move up from one segment to the next. Customers fitting these profiles were targeted for cross-sales, and incentive programs were established to shift customers into more profitable segments.

Acquire is the first Customer Life Cycle stage experienced by the customer after the customer moment. It consists of the delivery and initial service activity of products and services purchased by the customer. The strength of the relationship between the customer and the enterprise can be strongly influenced by the enterprise's ability to deliver the products or services in a timely, efficient, and courteous manner.

Consider the customer who ordered a high-end entertainment set from a major credit card catalog. The customer spent several thousand dollars on the set and stayed home from work to receive it on the arranged delivery date. When the entertainment set arrived, it came without several key components. Conversations with the credit card company clarified that the warehouse did not have all the pieces in stock, and a second date was arranged for delivery of the remaining components. The customer again stayed home from work only to discover that this time, the warehouse sent the wrong components. At this point, the customer was extremely unhappy and indicated that the inconvenience of the bungled fulfillment process negated any benefit received by ordering from the catalog. This is a true example of the negative impact a poorly managed fulfillment process can have on a customer relationship. However, in this case, the credit card company in question is a widely acknowledged leader in CRM, and the story had a happy ending. The company recognized both its mistake and the value of the customer and proposed to provide one of the components for free as well as to pay all shipping charges. The customer was happy with both the solution and the recognition of value and remains loyal and satisfied.

Use is the next stage in the Customer Life Cycle. Use is where the organization has the opportunity to build a trusting and mutually beneficial relationship between the customer and the enterprise, leading to repeat purchases, up-sells, and cross-sales. Every opportunity to deliver service, or to address a problem such as the acquisition issue described earlier, is an opportunity to strengthen a relationship. Many organizations find that their customers, and their customer service staff, are happier when service personnel are empowered to solve customer problems. In the previous example, the service representative had the authority to authorize a substantial discount to alleviate the customer's discontent. This clearly made the customer happy, but it also makes the employees happy. Establishing a culture within your organization that is conducive to CRM requires customer contact personnel who recognize the value in customer focus, who are empowered to make CRM happen, and who actively work in this direction. This culture benefits the organization, the employees, and the customers. Chapter 4, "Are You Ready? Tuning the Organization for CRM," details the cultural issues surrounding CRM.

Re-entry is the last stage in the Customer Life Cycle. Re-entry is actually the culmination of all the efforts of the enterprise to build trust, loyalty, and satisfaction. Re-entry occurs when the customer comes back through the CLC. It is usually easier and less costly for repeat trips, thus the numbers on the expense of attracting new customers versus cross-selling existing ones. Each trip through the CLC should build higher levels of trust and provide additional knowledge.

Summary

This chapter presented the CLC as a vehicle for defining and communicating the stages a customer goes through when purchasing and using products. This chapter also illustrated the associated business processes a company uses to move the customer through the CLC.

These customer stages, as summarized in the introduction to the Customer Life Cycle, are as follows:

Identify needs that may be filled by a product or service available for purchase.

Develop an *awareness* that your organization exists and may be able to fulfill the identified need.

Learn more about your organization and the products and services that may fill the need.

Consider how the products and services offered by your organization match (or do not match) the identified need.

Evaluate the suitability of your products and services against others (the competition) to fill the identified need.

Decide at the *customer moment* to purchase your product or service, go to a competitor, or not fill the need.

Acquire the product or service by the customer. This is typically the first interaction the customer has with your organization after the purchase decision.

Use of the product or service by the customer is typically for the life of product ownership, and sometimes beyond.

Re-entry by the customer into the CLC represents a positive decision to do additional business with your organization.

The processes a company uses to move the customer though the CLC, also summarized in the chapter introduction, are as follows:

Intrude and Engage. This includes the efforts of your organization to get the attention of a prospect, have that prospect become aware of your company, and engage the prospect in a dialog designed to move him or her into the CLC.

Acquire. Simply because a prospect is aware of your organization does not guarantee that he or she will purchase products or services. You must work to educate the prospect on your company, and you must maintain the prospect's attention and interest as he or she continues with buying decisions.

Retain and Expand. After a prospect buys your products or services, the real work begins. Many of the cross-functional business strategies designed to increase customer satisfaction and foster customer loyalty are conducted in this section of the CLC.

Chapter 4 provides details on the critical success factors that an organization must manage in order to successfully implement the business processes that are part of the CLC. Chapters 9, 10, and 11 will map the business intelligence, business management, and business operations components of the Corporate Information Factory to the Customer Life Cycle in order to illustrate the types of customer information that is generated and used at various points in the cycle.

PART TWO

Planning for CRM

The five chapters in this part of the book provide a roadmap to help organizations plan for CRM. The first step in the planning process is getting a realistic assessment of your organization's readiness for CRM. In Chapter 4, we begin by examining organizational structure, cultural environment, and business strategy and suggesting approaches that help align these to improve customer relationships and profit. The next step in the planning process is to ensure that the organization can build the integrated customer information environment required to support the move to CRM. The Corporate Information Factory (CIF) is the mechanism that your organization can apply to ensure a sound technical infrastructure. The roles and responsibilities for deploying the CIF are explored in Chapter 5, "Getting Underway," and the development process is described in Chapter 6, "Developing an Integrated CRM Technology Environment." The next step in planning for CRM involves ensuring that you have comprehensive and accurate customer information. To this end, data acquisition is one key to the success of the CRM effort. Data must be acquired using operational systems, and it must then be migrated into the data warehouse, operational data store, and data marts. Data quality is extremely important if we are to correctly segment our customers and provide them with the sales, service, and marketing that they expect. Chapter 7, "Capturing Customer Information," delves into the data acquisition issues, and Chapter 8, "Quality Relationships Start with Quality Customer Data," examines the data quality issues.

Are You Ready? Tuning the Organization for CRM

Picture this: The increasing momentum of and continuous press around Customer Relationship Management (CRM) has caught the attention of a high-spirited, forward-thinking executive in your organization. Intrigued, he or she asks you to determine what all the excitement is really about and to recommend a course of action. After reading *Building the Customer-Centric Enterprise*, you present the following:

CRM involves expanding your definition of customer to include more than just organizations and individuals who purchase products and services. It involves understanding the relationships within your customer base that yield the most influence value, and leveraging the knowledge of your customers and their relationships to manage each and every interaction they have with your organization.

The Corporate Information Factory (CIF) enables the support of CRM initiatives through the application of customer-oriented technology to support business intelligence, business operations, and business management. Business intelligence includes the data warehouse and data marts, and it provides the capability to analyze customers and their actions to make strategic decisions for the organization. Business operations include the systems that run your day-to-day processes, such as billing, customer service, and sales. Business operations also generate much of the customer information used throughout the organization. Business management provides systems, such as the operational data store (ODS), that house a collection of integrated data and provide a centrally available view of a customers profile.

The Customer Life Cycle (CLC) defines the stages that a customer moves through when considering the acquisition of products and services and when using these items after purchase. Understanding the Customer Life Cycle and mapping your current customer interactions to the appropriate Life Cycle stages will enhance your ability to successfully move customers through the cycle and build lasting, profitable customer relationships.

CRM represents a philosophy for interacting with your customers that promotes satisfied, loyal, and profitable customers and provides distinct advantage in an increasingly competitive environment.

In conclusion, you strongly recommend that the organization adopt CRM.

Your presentation is a resounding success, and the executive responds with great enthusiasm. You are given a sizable budget and told, "Get started." You think, "An enthusiastic champion with money to spend, and a mandate to move, what can stop us now?" More than you might initially recognize. Consider the following quote from Niccolo Machiavelli (*The Prince*, 1513) frequently cited by strategists and politicians:

> It must be considered that there is nothing more difficult to carry out, nor more doubtful of success, nor more dangerous to handle, than to initiate a new order of things.

When you think of CRM as the enterprise philosophy that it is, there is no question that its adoption means a new order of things for most organizations. Although the implementation of a CRM program may not call for Machiavellian tactics, it certainly does require careful planning, an understanding of CRM critical success factors, and an ability to manage these success factors while continuing to facilitate change. To better understand why money and a mandate alone may not be enough, let's review the definition of CRM that was introduced in Chapter 1. "CRM is aligning business strategy, organization structure and culture, customer information, and technology so that all customer interactions can be conducted to the long-term satisfaction of the customer and to the benefit and profit of the organization."

This definition highlights the importance of business strategy, organization structure, organization culture, customer information, and technology to the success of your CRM program. Not implicitly stated in this definition but also true, are the following:

- Certain business strategies advance CRM; others inhibit CRM.
- Certain organization structures facilitate CRM; others inhibit CRM.
- Certain organization cultures promote CRM; others inhibit CRM.

- Certain technical environments enable CRM; others inhibit CRM.
- Certain executive management teams support CRM; others inhibit CRM.

Most successful organizations that initiate CRM programs will find that some (usually most) aspects of their strategy, structure, culture, technology, and management support structures fall into the "inhibit" category. There is a perfectly logical reason for this. An organization that has been successfully focused on selling or servicing specific products will have created very efficient business strategies and supporting technologies that are geared around these products. Simply because a company realizes the benefit to be gained from a customer focus does not mean that it immediately realizes, and is willing to undertake, the magnitude of change required to bring this benefit to fruition. And make no mistake; these changes are far-reaching, encompassing structure, culture, strategy, and technology. Thus, a new order usually *is* in order. And it is always a good idea to ask, "Are we ready?" before diving in.

This chapter identifies the critical success factors imperative to CRM. The business and technology issues associated with each critical success factor are discussed, and the potential effects of not managing these issues are highlighted. The chapter also provides a roadmap of business policy and practice suggestions for areas strongly impacted by CRM, such as marketing, customer service, and sales. The highlighted best practices focus on developing CRM-specific business plans, adopting CRM-oriented goals and objectives, coordinating CRM activity both within and across business areas, and managing the cultural and people aspects of organizational change. Although many of these best practices originate in industries that are advanced in CRM (financial services, telecommunications, and hospitality) the practices are not the exclusive domain of these industries. Instead, the ideas are readily applied in organizations across numerous industries. Understanding these best practices, and adopting them in your organization will facilitate CRM success.

Information technology (IT) managers reading this chapter will gain an understanding of the organizational issues they must manage to ensure that customer components of the CIF, including the data warehouse, achieve maximum benefit. Business executives reading this chapter will gain insight into how to revamp their organizations to make the most of CRM programs.

Critical Success Factors for CRM

A critical success factor is something an organization must do exceedingly well to succeed in the short run and thrive in the long run. Many technology executives are familiar with the concept of critical success factors because project scope documents routinely prioritize these issues in terms of risk factors. These risk factors are often issues that may endanger a team's ability to perform a necessary project task exceedingly well (sound familiar?). Typical project risk factors may include the inability to obtain sufficient resources for the duration of a project due to other competing projects, or the lack of experience in a particular new technology, such as data warehouse expertise. Business executives also identify critical issues when setting corporate or product goals and objectives. These issues can endanger the organization's ability to achieve its objectives and typically qualify strategic goals as follows: the revenue goals for this product line are dependent on the organization's ability to be first to market with a new service, or the increase in corporate profit is dependent on a change in government regulations currently prohibiting expansion across geographic boundaries.

Dealing with CRM requires both business executives and technologists to change their perspectives on what constitutes a critical success factor. When technologists build customer-oriented systems, they can no longer look only at traditional concerns such as resource constraints or technical skill sets. Similarly, when business executives implement CRM corporate strategies, they must broaden their view to include more than external factors or specific technology constraints.

The factors that can impact the success of a CRM initiative typically center on cooperation, integration, and overall enterprise planning. These issues are most likely to surface in the four categories discussed at the beginning of this chapter: business strategy, organization structure, organization culture, and technology. Issues may also arise in a fifth category—executive commitment and support. An organization must manage the critical issues within all five of these areas when building technology to support CRM and when implementing CRM business strategies. The five critical success factors for CRM are as follows:

1. Implement a coordinated, customer-focused business strategy
2. Create a CRM-friendly organization structure
3. Establish a CRM-savvy organization culture
4. Implement an integrated customer information environment
5. Ensure executive commitment and support

Implementing a Coordinated, Customer-Focused Business Strategy

The owner of a large privately held communications and entertainment company was a strong proponent of converging the company's multiple business lines into a single, common "face to the customer." The owner talked repeatedly about leveraging the loyal customer relationships held within each of the business lines to become the sole communications provider for all the organization's best customers. He was most enthusiastic about possible offerings including free or discounted movie rentals for high levels of long-distance usage, single billing across all business lines, and VIP treatment for all multiple product owners. Although most business line executives acknowledged the owner's enthusiasm, they continued to run their individual organizations as they had always run them: without cross-product discounts, VIP statuses, or bills that included more than one product. Eventually, the owner hired an outside executive and assigned her to implement his CRM goals. Today the organization is successfully implementing all of the owner's original visions.

This example is an illustration of the first critical success factor: the organization must have business strategies that promote CRM across functional boundaries. To succeed, these strategies must be understood and accepted throughout the organization. As illustrated, a company can have an enterprise goal to become more customer-focused or to increase customer satisfaction. However, if no underlying strategies are in place that force a customer view across business functions, the organization is not likely to move far from the traditional product focus.

Webster's Dictionary defines strategy as follows: "A plan or method for achieving a specific goal." In the sidebar example of the communications company, the goals of the organization were to:

- Provide customized services
- Increase customer satisfaction and loyalty
- Retain valuable customers

The strategies or action steps to achieve these goals were to:

- Customize product packaging and pricing
- Make multiple billing options available
- Provide consistent service levels across multiple channels
- Support one-call or one-click services across all product lines

The key here is to avoid getting caught up in semantics: "Is this a goal or a strategy?" Instead, use the organization goals as a starting point in your assessment. Ask first, "Do we need cross-functional strategies or action plans to achieve these goals?" If the answer is yes, then begin looking for the supporting detail steps or strategies as well. If no formal action plans have been made, your organization has some work to do before it can successfully implement CRM initiatives.

CRM Strategy or CRM Systems, Which Comes First?

The question: Shouldn't business strategy be driving the move to CRM? The answer: Just because it should doesn't mean it does. The technology to support CRM business strategies should be in place in advance of the customer strategies that will use these technologies. However, building these enterprise-level CRM systems can be difficult, particularly if the organization has not achieved a buy-in across enough business areas to fully fund these expensive projects. It is not unusual for technology folks to anticipate time and cost implications associated with building CRM technology well in advance of when the company actually adopts the CRM strategy. Although the business may be considering the customer strategies, it is not a given that they will understand the systems challenges required to implement these strategies. If they know CRM is coming, forward-thinking IT executives are then challenged to obtain buy-in and funding for systems that the business is not yet asking for.

Consider this true example: The IT executives in a large Latin American insurance company were faced with a unique problem. The company consisted of several very powerful, independent business units that all worked with a central IT group for information support. Market conditions, including the impending encroachment of American companies into the area, indicated an immediate increase in both the number of and sophistication of potential competitors. Given the changing market conditions, the IT executives anticipated that the company would soon be adopting some customer-focused strategies to help maintain its number one market position. However, the information systems supporting the company were all structured along business unit lines, with no ability to easily provide customer information at an enterprise level. Supporting these changing information needs would require substantial technology investment.

For the IT executives, funding the construction of an enterprise customer system in advance of any stated business need posed an interesting problem. The money for the new systems had to come from the business units, yet those business units had no immediate pressing requirements for shared customer information. The solution employed by the technology group was both inventive and successful. They developed a series of seminars aimed at providing business-level education on CRM. These seminars identified customer-focused strategies already in place by successful competitors, defined potential benefits associated with CRM, and detailed the technology required to facilitate CRM. The seminars were conducted at all levels of the business community and coincided with a grass roots campaign for support aimed directly at the business executives. The end result: Executives developed an understanding of the technology requirements associated with CRM and funding was obtained.

Let's look next at the term cross-functional. Figure 4.1 illustrates the distinction between single-function strategies and those that cross functions or business areas.

The vertical rectangles with the labels Sales, Service, Marketing, Risk Management, and Profitability represent the various places within an organization where these functions are done. In a typical organization, many business functions are performed in multiple locations by different groups of employees. In Figure 4.1, the functions all have more than one rectangle, which indicates that they are done in multiple places. Marketing is a good example; campaigns can be designed and conducted by the branch or field offices, by the product managers, or by the central marketing group.

The horizontal that stretch across the business functions represent action plans or steps that move an organization towards customer-focused business strategies. In this illustration, multiple action plans and business strategies are represented:

Branch Marketing Campaign. The business strategy behind the marketing effort pictured here is to increase the share of wallet for profitable customers. The associated action step is labeled Branch Marketing Campaign and covers only one of the three marketing areas. This action step has the smallest degree of cross-functionality of any on the diagram. In an organization that has multiple levels of marketing activity, such as the organization in Figure 4.1, the lack of coordination mechanisms for marketing can have a negative impact on customer satisfaction and on customer purchases. If each marketing area is carrying out independent marketing campaigns designed to further its own

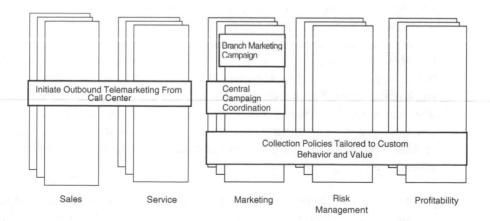

Figure 4.1   Cross-functional strategies.

departmental objectives, there is a high probability that the best customers are receiving multiple, and in some cases conflicting, offers.

Central Campaign Coordination. The share of wallet objective described earlier holds true for this example as well. Here the action step is labeled Central Campaign Coordination and covers the entire marketing function. This step ensures that when various groups within the organization are conducting campaigns, the campaign activity is prioritized and coordinated, which prevents over-solicitation of the customer base. Contrasting this action step with the first one highlights an important issue. In order to promote successful CRM, activities must be coordinated within business functions, even when different groups in the organization perform these activities.

Outbound Call Center Telemarketing. The objective pictured here is to more profitably utilize sales and service channels by shifting staff effort between channels when more traditional workloads are light. The action step is labeled Outbound Call Center Telemarketing and covers two independent business functions: sales and service. This is a cross-functional strategy because it combines direct sales activity with more traditional service activities. An organization can execute this action step in several ways. It can place sales personnel into the call center in an effort to start co-mingling staff. It can also provide sales training and qualified leads to the service representatives and change the business process to include telemarketing activities during slow periods. Either way, the action step requires cooperation across multiple business functions.

Collection Policies Tailored to Customer Behavior and Value. The strategy represented here focuses on increasing customer satisfaction. The action step is labeled Collection Policies Tailored to Customer Behavior and Value and covers the marketing, risk management, and profitability functions. This strategy requires coordination from multiple sources but can yield a highly positive outcome for the organization. Chapter 1 illustrates the negative impact that can occur when an organization cannot implement action plans like this one. In this example, a small business owner with a very profitable business account purchased consumer services from another business line in the organization. The retail business line did not realize that this customer also had a small business account and sent a hasty collection letter following late payment on the consumer account. This treatment angered the customer enough that he cancelled both his personal and business accounts and went elsewhere.

Again, the key issue here is simply that both business executives and technologists should pay careful attention to the presence or absence of customer-oriented business strategies and action plans. A lack of action steps like the ones discussed can be a strong indicator that the systems or business initiative you are about to begin may stall before completion. On the other hand, an abundance of strategies like these may dictate that you need to start immediately to build the customer components of the Corporate Information Factory, as these will be required to support the expanding CRM strategy base.

Creating a CRM-Friendly Organization Structure

In order to successfully implement CRM, the overall organizational structure must promote cross-functional cooperation. A decentralized organization makes it difficult to provide coordinated customer service. If each business unit has its own procedures for handling collections, it will be difficult to ensure that business units always check for the VIP indicator prior to sending a nasty letter. It can also be difficult to implement new CRM-friendly procedures to fix such problems. The inability to coordinate across multiple areas can, in turn, impact the quality and consistency of service that a customer receives from one product to another. For example, to change his billing information, a customer may be forced to make a separate call for each product he's purchased. What can be worse for satisfaction and loyalty than actually penalizing your best customers for owning multiple products? Consider the following example where the separation of the frequent flier service center from the reservations center costs a major airline a very profitable customer:

A consultant we know, who flies about 20,000 miles a month, recently had an experience with a major airline that antagonized him so much that he now refuses to fly this airline. As the consultant was making a reservation, the customer service representative tried to confirm his phone number. As it turns out, the phone number on the airline's record was a number that was cancelled 10 years ago, and the consultant had been providing the corrected number every time he made a reservation. The consultant provided the correct number (again) and requested that the airline update his permanent record and stop asking him this question. The customer service representative replied that she could only put the number in this particular reservation, and in order to change the number permanently, he would have to call the Frequent Flyer desk and update the information there. Understandably annoyed, the consultant informed her of his frequent flier status, and once again requested that the airline take care of this small matter. When the consultant was again told to call the Frequent Flier desk, his response was, "Not only do I not have to call the Frequent Flier desk, I don't have to call your airline ever again." In this case, the airline had the opportunity to gain the loyalty of a very profitable customer, but because of non-integrated systems, and because the service representative could not or would not step outside the normal business process to assist the customer, the airline lost him.

It can be hard to achieve CRM objectives like increased customer satisfaction if the organization doesn't support coordinated processes and quality across independent business lines. In the preceding example, several factors contributed to the problem experienced by the customer. First, the service representative did not have access to the appropriate systems to change the customer's profile. Second, the service center and the Frequent Flier desk were completely independent organizations with no coordination or cooperation facilitated. Third, no business processes were designed to deal with the situation when a customer might expect to cross between the two service organizations. The fact that the customer took all his business elsewhere can be the expected outcome if your organization's structure is one that actually inhibits cross-functional coordination.

Organization structure can also have a strong impact on technology. An enterprise customer system, which enables customer information across all products to be changed with a single call, will be much harder to fund if the organization structure forces each business unit to deal with customer service on an independent basis. In this organization structure, no driving reason may exist to share customer information across the call centers (note that customer desires may take a back seat to business unit objectives in this environment). No driving business reason to share customer information usually means no real need for enterprise customer systems. Although these issues can be overcome, as was the case with the Latin American insurance company described in the earlier sidebar, you should consider the organization structure when planning for CRM. Figure 4.2 illustrates all the points of coordination that must occur when an organization that is structured around product lines tries to implement CRM activities.

This sample organization is a communications company that has three lines of business: cellular, long distance, and cable. In this example, the cellular and long-distance products are administered as one business line sharing marketing, sales, service, and Information Technology departments. The cable product is run as an independent business line and has its own groups performing marketing, sales, service, and systems. The dotted arrows represent places where the two business lines must cooperate in order to do a cross-functional strategy, such as cellular marketing and cable marketing. This coordination must occur any time someone wants to do a business strategy that involves both groups. The coordination includes selling the concept to one or both business managers, identifying the resources to do the project, developing the business processes that link the two groups, and fixing the existing systems to support the changes in process.

If we apply the desire of the communications company executive to provide a "movies for minutes" cross-product discount to the organization structure pictured in Figure 4.2, the problems with this structure are clear. In this example,

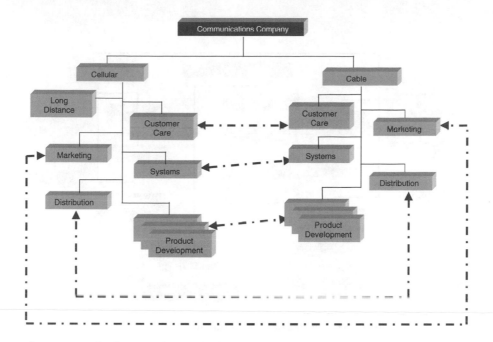

Figure 4.2 The impact of organization structure.

the executive would like to provide free movie rentals to customers who have both cable and cellular products. This customized promotion requires the coordination of product development groups to develop the pricing and packaging options for both products, the coordination of service groups to provide customized service to all customers who call about the free movies, and the coordination of systems groups to provide the common customer information to all the business areas. Add to this the required coordination of marketing and selling activities across business lines. The cross-product discounts become impossible to accomplish without the appropriate organization structure.

What is the ideal organization structure for CRM? Unfortunately, this question has no pat answer. Even if the perfect CRM structure could be described, it is not realistic to expect that all companies who want to adopt CRM can radically change their existing structures to match this nirvana. A better approach is to understand the qualities that a CRM-friendly organization structure should have and assess your organization against these qualities. One thing is clear— the most important quality to look for in a CRM organization is the ability to facilitate cross-functional cooperation.

Figures 4.3 and 4.4 illustrate two very different types of organizational structures, both of which facilitate cross-functional cooperation. In each case, the basic organization structure is quite common in today's world. Figure 4.3

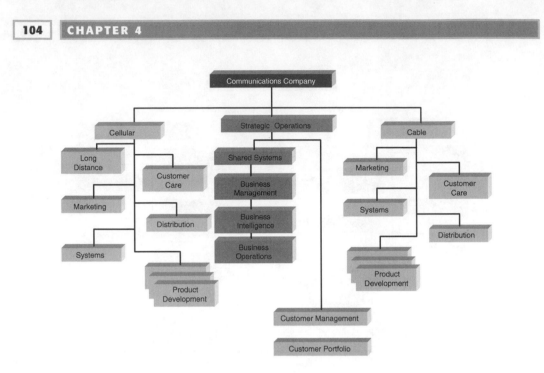

Figure 4.3 The decentralized CRM organization.

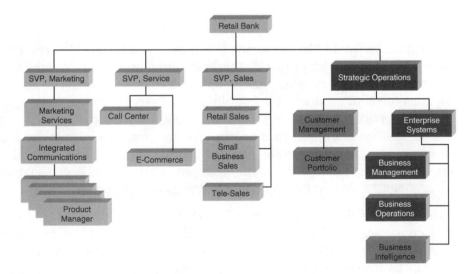

Figure 4.4 The centralized CRM organization.

represents the decentralized organization described earlier, while Figure 4.4 represents the opposite perspective, a centralized organization. Both structures have been modified to make them more CRM-friendly.

Figure 4.3 begins with the same premise as Figure 4.2: two independent business lines that perform their own marketing, sales, service, and systems development. However, in this example, the coordination activity described in Figure 4.2 has been formalized and added to the organization structure in the form of a strategic operations group. This group is responsible for all operations that cross business lines. Not only does this group provide the single coordination point that was missing in Figure 4.2, but it also provides resources, funds, and processes to enable CRM initiatives. In addition, because this unit reports directly to the CEO, the decisions made here will be impartial, designed for the good of the organization and the customer, and completely independent of the interests of any single group.

The shared systems area focuses on all enterprise-level systems including the data warehouse, the operational data store (customer database), and any other system that will be shared by cellular, long distance, and cable. The customer management area focuses on any business strategy that requires cooperation from multiple business lines. Collections policies that include both cable and cellular products are developed and implemented here, multi-product discounts such as those offered to Bob and his parents are developed and implemented here, and one-call service options to change customer-level information across all product lines are developed and implemented here. Note that while Figure 4.3 shows both the shared systems group and the customer management area reporting through a strategic operations group, there is also another equally viable organization structure. In the alternative organization (not pictured) each group exists on the same level as the independent business lines, and each group reports directly to the top level (the communications company), without the intermediate strategic operations group.

A centralized organization is not immune to the coordination problems described by Figure 4.2. The retail banking organization pictured in Figure 4.4 can have marketing campaigns developed and conducted within the marketing area as well as from the branch offices. Without coordination, the over-solicitation problems described in the business strategy section of this chapter are likely to surface in this organization.

Another good example of the need for coordination is illustrated via the product groups in Figure 4.4. It is true that these groups all report to a centralized marketing function. However, they also have individual objectives based on sales volume and profitability, which are specific to each product. Marketing also has objectives that center around the total number of products sold through campaign activity. In this case, all areas are focused on achieving specific objectives, and no group is focused on what is the true next best product or service for a particular customer.

Figure 4.4 also shows how the coordination of activity and information can be effectively done in a centralized organization. The solution is similar to that proposed in Figure 4.2. Here a strategic operations business unit reports to the same level in the organization as marketing and sales. The group includes business and systems coordination functions, and the objectives of the unit are the same as in Figure 4.2—to provide enterprise coordination and resolve conflicts when dealing with customers.

Establishing a CRM-Savvy Organization Culture

Earlier in this chapter, we introduced the owner of a communications and entertainment company who enthusiastically supported CRM long before his organization adopted it. The obvious lack of CRM business strategy hindered his company's efforts to adopt a customer focus. However, another more obscure factor contributed to the lack of CRM movement, the culture of this organization. In this case, the organization continued on its traditional course despite the owner's vocal desires to the contrary. Change did not occur until the owner brought in an effective change agent, a CRM expert from the outside. The change agent had to identify key employees at all levels within the company and work with these individuals to effect the change to CRM. Chances are that the culture for adopting change in this company is one of bottom-up, or middle-up-and-down change, rather than top-down change. It took the external change agent, actually in the ranks working with both lower-level staff and her peers, to effect this level of organizational change.

Organization culture, while intangible, can hinder the move to CRM, particularly if your organization has experienced a history of failures at implementing major changes, high employee dissatisfaction and turnover, or failed attempts at building complex computer systems. Speaking of computer systems and culture, the way that the rest of the organization views the systems area can impact CRM. A poor relationship between the business community and IT exponentially increases the difficulties involved in deploying the CIF. A lack of cooperation among independent applications groups also hampers CIF deployment.

Business executives face similar cultural concerns. Is the customer contact staff made up of proactive sellers or are they merely order takers? Is there an attitude of cooperation and sharing across business lines or is each line run autonomously? Autonomous business lines and order-taking sellers simply do not fit within the CRM philosophy of cooperation and customer orientation.

Two aspects of your organization's culture can significantly affect the outcome of CRM initiatives. The first is your ability to effect major change, and the second is the degree to which the business units work together, effect compromise, and facilitate shared strategies. These qualities are difficult to measure. Managing them requires that the organization honestly assess its weaknesses and develop a plan to address turn these into strengths. Let's look first at the organization's ability to change. A couple key questions can help predict change ability:

■ Does your organization have a successful history of implementing major changes? History is usually a good indicator of future success. Because CRM may require changes in organization structure, business strategy, and customer systems, the history of change in a company is particularly pertinent when assessing CRM readiness.

■ How is change effected within your organization? The communications company that opens this section is a good example of this question in action. This company affected change from the bottom-up, with key employees sold on the change and added to the change-planning process. The owner brought an outside change agent into the organization and established the authority to mandate the change. An equally viable alternative is to identify key change agents within the company and solicit their support for CRM change. Thought leaders in the organization are typically good drivers for change. These thought leaders are found at all levels within the organization; they should be identified and included in the planning process. If the change agents within an organization are not CRM experts, CRM expertise should be actively recruited in the form of consultants or new employees.

Once you understand how your organization deals with change, you must look closely at the second cultural issue: how the organization works together across business areas. As discussed earlier in this chapter, a CRM business strategy requires cross-functional cooperation. To assess your organization's cooperation ability, ask the following questions:

■ Does each business area have a positive view of other business area contributions to the organization?

■ Do any current processes require cooperation between business areas?

■ Do the business areas compete for customers, profits, or activities?

■ Is the sharing of information or resources done with any regularity?

In addition to the general questions listed here, it is important to understand how each business area feels about cooperation and sharing across the organization. This understanding will indicate the amount of hand-holding required by each business unit as the company transitions toward CRM. Marketing, sales,

Evaluating Past Change

Reorganizations, acquisitions, and mergers are good for evaluating change ability. Ask the following questions to assess past change: Did the acquisition or merger disrupt business and employee morale? Did the company clearly and frequently communicate intentions during the change process? Did the reorganization or merger live up to prechange expectations?

Note that past failure at organizational change does not always equate to future failure. Understanding why past efforts have failed and managing the reasons for the failure can ensure successful change efforts in the future.

and service are most impacted by CRM and thus should be assessed at the start of a drive to CRM. The last major section of this chapter, "The Marketing, Service, and Sales CRM Roadmap," examines the cultural issues in more detail for each of the impacted business functions.

Implementing an Integrated Customer Information Environment

A successful utility company determines that CRM is a necessity if it is to emerge from the current climate of competition and deregulation as a market leader. It decides that it is well positioned to become the full-service utility provider for its most profitable residential and commercial customers. The organization chooses to start with its customer service group. It provides the service representatives with extensive sales training and implements incentive programs designed to promote cross-sales of additional products from the service centers. It also conducts customer surveys and market research to determine the strengths and weaknesses of products relative to those of the competition. These results are then distributed to the service representatives to support their selling efforts.

When the company looks to the current customer billing system to provide the customer profiles required to support cross-sales, they discover a problem. This billing system is organized around the billing account, meaning that if a customer gets multiple bills, one record exists in the system for each bill. The customer information is repeated on each bill, maximizing the potential for duplicates or conflicting information about a single customer. Providing customer profiles from the billing system can be done, but not easily. It will require IT to extract customer information from the billing system, match the extracted records on the customer, reconcile any differences between duplicate records for the same customer, and somehow get this matched information to the service representatives. If current information is required, this extract and match process must done multiple times per day.

In isolation, the extract process described here may seem manageable, but when you consider the number of processes similar to this one that will have to be developed to facilitate multiple cross-functional CRM strategies, the support issues quickly become overwhelming. As the example indicates, CRM requires integrated customer information at the enterprise level. Without comprehensive customer information, CRM business processes are not enabled. The utility company can't determine who its best customers are or which products these customers own.

Business strategies cannot be tailored to acknowledge the importance or value of the customer. In a company actively moving toward CRM, the demand to share customer information across business units will increase. Satisfying this demand will require a technical architecture, such as the CIF (see Chapter 2, "The Customer and the Corporate Information Factory (CIF)," for details), to facilitate the integration.

The remainder of this section highlights the coordination, planning, and standards that must be present to provide sharable and integrated customer information. It poses three fundamental questions that must be answered:

- Can our technology area recognize duplicate, interdependent, or complementary systems projects and combine or coordinate these if necessary?

- Does my organization have a plan governing all CRM systems development?

- Do we have a standard set of customer definitions and customer information requirements that are used for all customer systems development?

Coordinating Technology Efforts

If you are about to embark on a CRM odyssey and want to ensure that your technology group is ready to support you, the first question you should ask is "Can the technology area recognize duplicate, interdependent, or complementary systems projects and combine or coordinate these if necessary?"

Reality dictates that multiple systems' development initiatives will be underway at the same time. Situations such as the following are not unusual:

The systems development organization within a large bank was in the middle of phase one of a multi-phased effort to implement a customer-oriented data warehouse. During the same time period, the credit card product line determined that to meet its profit objectives for the next year, it required a data mart containing customer and transaction information. This credit card data mart was labeled a high-priority requirement, funds to begin the project were made available, and the search for an appropriate vendor was initiated.

Fortunately, the bank in this example had an enterprise project management group whose involvement was mandated in all projects above a cost threshold. This group recognized the relationship between these two independent projects and initiated meetings to determine if they should be coordinated or combined. In this case, the immediate need and high potential benefit assigned to the card mart dictated that both projects should continue in parallel with some project activities, such as customer data design, coordinated between the two. In addition, plans to migrate the credit card mart into the warehouse were also developed and added as a future phase of the project plans for both projects.

Although the perfect CRM solution in this situation may have been to construct the mart after the warehouse, the agreed coordination is highly preferable to the alternative—pursuing two completely independent projects that would create separate databases and programs and make it difficult or impossible to integrate the databases later.

Planning for Integrated Customer Information

Question number two for your CRM odyssey is "Does my organization have a plan governing all CRM systems development?"

The Corporate Information Factory provides the foundation for the customer information development plan discussed here. The CIF performs the following tasks:

- Recognizes all pertinent systems within the organization
- Classifies these systems by use (business intelligence, business operations, and business management)
- Identifies points where integration among systems is required
- Identifies the required tools and management environment for each classification

A structured framework for systems development is essential because it identifies components that should be reused across multiple projects. It also illustrates conceptually where systems need to share information. Adopting the CIF framework eliminates unintentional duplicate systems development, such as the warehouse and data mart described in the bank example. However, simply ascribing to the CIF is not enough. You must also understand which customer systems are required to support specific CRM business strategies, how these systems will interact and share information, and how to maintain an acceptable level of customer data quality in these systems.

The systems that should be positioned within the CIF framework were introduced in Chapter 2. These include business operations systems such as product accounting systems, sales force and call center automation systems, business management systems such as the enterprise customer operational data store, and business intelligence systems such as the customer-oriented warehouse and associated data marts. (Systems that are key to the implementation of CRM business strategies are described in detail in Part 3.)

After the appropriate CRM systems have been identified, an effort should be made to prioritize individual development projects based on business benefits, the timing of needs, and technical feasibility. This prioritization exercise has several immediate benefits. First, the prioritized projects form the actual CRM development plan. Second, the prioritization exercise is a great forum for communicating the need for shared customer information to the executives in the organization. Third, the plan provides the ability to communicate a customer systems development schedule to the business community and to arbitrate conflicts such as the dueling bank projects described earlier. If the bank in the previous example had been using a CRM development plan, it would have discovered the duplication of project efforts during the scoping process for these projects, rather than having to rely on the project management organization to catch this after both projects were already underway.

Implementing Customer Information Standards

The third and extremely important question for the CRM odyssey is: "Do we have a standard set of customer definitions and customer information requirements that are used for all customer system development?"

A distinct possibility exists that each functional unit or business line within an organization may have a different view of what constitutes a customer. Account managers in the sales area may want to maintain information about individuals who typically refer customers to the organization. Because of the benefit to be gained by cultivating relationships with these individuals, the account manager may consider the referral sources to be a type of customer. On the other hand, billing departments in customer service may never deal directly with a referral source and thus may have little interest in this individual as a type of customer. In a case like this, it is key that the customer definition be developed to include the requirements from both sales and service, and that customer systems are built to incorporate all types of customers, regardless of which business area these systems are built to support.

The need to build customer systems from a comprehensive definition was introduced in Chapter 1 and is illustrated in the following example, which picks up from the previous example. The Marketing Department and account managers decide to improve relationships with key referral sources and target this group to receive special discounts or promotional offers based on the number of customers referred. The most effective way to implement this new promotion is to have the customer service reps begin to collect referral information directly from the customers. Customer service will also handle calls related to the promotion offer, which means dealing directly with the referral sources that reply to the marketing campaign. If the information systems that support customer service are built without considering sales and marketing requirements, chances are that support for the referral source is not included. The resulting lack of systems support will have a negative impact on the new CRM business strategy.

These information requirements and the customer definition typically take the form of enterprise customer models. A customer model is a way to document the information required to support customer-oriented business processes. These models document current and future business processes that involve customers, highlight the information required to support those processes, and provide a common point of communication between the technologists who build the customer systems and the business folks who use these systems to run the business. These models also contribute to the meta data (data about data) that informs users what information is available to them. A comprehensive set of customer information requirements includes the needs from sales, marketing, service, and risk management. All customer-oriented system developments look first to the models to identify any required information and eliminate the construction of systems that cannot share customer information. All business process initiatives also start with a review of these models to ensure that all appropriate areas are included. In conjunction with the CRM development plan described earlier, these enterprise models become the roadmap from which all CRM initiatives, both business and systems, are conducted. Chapter 6, "Developing an Integrated CRM Technology Environment," describes these models in detail and provides examples from which to begin.

Ensuring Executive Commitment and Support

After conducting several informal initiatives to help the top-producing agents in a large insurance company better understand their customers, the Marketing Department determined that the available customer information was inadequate and not well distributed. Agents had extensive information about their individual customers that, if shared with marketing, would dramatically improve the quality of marketing analyses, leading in turn to more effective marketing campaigns and more profitable customers. Marketing had analysis capabilities and customer segmentation models that could be applied to an agent's customer base to enable that agent to understand the characteristics of their profitable customers and apply these characteristics when looking for new prospects. Marketing and the agent base agreed that an enterprise customer file, shared between the two groups, would resolve the problem and provide significant additional benefits. Higher profitability, better cross sales, and improved rapport between the agents and the insurance company were among the identified benefits. Marketing obtained support from the agents, customer service, and product development; prepared a solid business case; and asked for funding at the quarterly meeting of the CEO and his executives. Despite the vocal and enthusiastic support from all the business units, the CEO determined that an infrastructure project did not warrant the expenditure and vetoed the project.

Contrast this disheartening but true example with this next one (also true):

> The Marketing Department of a large national bank maintained an extensive marketing database to support customer and household analysis. This marketing database had numerous deficiencies: little historical information, no ability for campaign tracking, and a time lag of six weeks between database updates. In addition, the structure and complexity of the database limited access to a few computer-savvy marketing analysts. Marketing determined that a customer-oriented data warehouse would yield great benefits and eliminate the information bottleneck caused by the current limited access. When approached with the proposal to build the data warehouse, the managing director, a strong CRM proponent, was in full agreement. Not only did he agree to fund the endeavor, but he also gently but clearly mandated that all business areas provide funding and resources for the project. This organization went on to build one of the early banking data warehouses and is a CRM leader today.

When you consider both of the previous examples, it becomes clear that an executive mandate is one of the most important factors in CRM success. Executive support facilitates the sweeping change required to attain CRM reality. Without executive backing, it is almost impossible to implement cross-functional business strategies, adopt a CRM-friendly structure and culture, and fund the integrated customer systems that support CRM.

Effective executive support requires more than executives who know the CRM buzz words. First, an organization must have an active and knowledgeable executive sponsor for CRM. Active is the key word here. Active sponsorship can be guaranteed if the sponsor has a vested interest in CRM. Sponsors measured on CRM initiatives and held accountable for CRM successes and failures are likely to actively monitor the efforts. The sponsor must also have a thorough understanding of all aspects of CRM. Understanding CRM drivers, expected business results, and what it will take to move the organization to CRM is key. What it will take includes an understanding of what constitutes CRM-friendly organization structures, organization cultures, business strategies, and technology, as well as an understanding of the shortcomings of the current organization in these areas.

Second, the sponsor must have influence, formal or otherwise, on peers, functional managers, and superiors. He or she must be able to gain the grass roots support required to move the organization structurally, functionally, and technically. Active communication of the company's intent to adopt CRM is also important. Communication can include discussing CRM intentions in the annual report, external company publications, Web sites, press releases, or speeches. Consider the following quote from C. Michael Armstrong, AT&T's chairman and CEO (from a speech to the Cable TV Association, June 1999), that communicates CRM direction and throws down a gauntlet to other companies in the industry:

> "When you look at the communications industry, it is almost immaterial whether you come at the challenge as a telephone company or a cable company, or for that matter an Internet company. As technology converges, success will go to the company that transforms itself out of the smoke stack mentality and into a broad-based consumer services company."

Third, the executive sponsor should take steps to ensure that the management team also gains a comprehensive understanding of CRM. Executive meetings and off-site strategy development sessions focused on CRM initiatives are one way to convey the concepts. CRM education should also be provided to the management team. Management participation in the identification, prioritization, and funding of CRM projects and initiatives is a third way to gain a buy-in. Without a buy-in and an active commitment from the management team, it will be difficult to achieve any of the technical, organizational, cultural, or strategic positions described in this chapter. With a buy-in, the organization can be well on the way to achieving the sort of customer focus that individuals like C. Michael Armstrong from AT&T espouse.

The Marketing, Service, and Sales CRM Roadmap

In the first part of this chapter, we described the five organization-wide critical success factors that are required to successfully transition your company to a customer focus. This section looks in more detail at the three primary CRM business areas: marketing, sales, and customer service. Here we provide specific best-practice examples of how to manage the CRM success factors previously described. The best practices include the following:

- Coordinating activity within marketing, sales, and service
- Adopting CRM plans and success measures
- Identifying and managing potential cultural issues as they relate to marketing, service, or sales
- Cooperating across marketing, service, and sales
- Integrating other business areas

Note that although these suggestions do not include every possible CRM best practice, they do provide examples of practices currently in place in CRM thought-leading companies throughout the world.

Roadmap for Marketing

The marketing organization is key to CRM success. Marketing typically drives CRM strategies, functioning as both an information consumer and an information disseminator. In the role as an information consumer, marketing is responsible for turning the available customer data into information that can be used to benefit the organization. As an example, through analysis and information modeling, marketing can transform customer transaction data into a profitability or customer value indicator. In the role as an information disseminator, marketing provides this transformed customer information, along with strategies to utilize it, to other functions with direct customer contact. In the case of the profitability or value indicator, marketing can combine this information with cross-sell suggestions and provide the results to the customer service areas. Given the link between marketing and CRM success, it is imperative that organizations manage the critical success factors that can have a negative impact on marketing efforts.

Marketing Activity Coordination

As we illustrate in the business strategy section of this chapter, it is common to have functions such as marketing performed in several locations or areas within an organization. Because of the possibility for duplication of activities, it is important to have mechanisms that coordinate the marketing activities across independent marketing areas. Several areas require coordination. First, the organization should have some mechanism to protect customers from over-solicitation when marketing is done simultaneously through independent channels. The following are two best-practice examples used to control over-solicitation:

- Any customer name included in a marketing campaign is listed in a central solicitation file. Prior to mailing, each campaign must match against the solicitation file to identify recently solicited customers. Customers that have received recent solicitations are eliminated from the campaign to prevent over-solicitation.

- A centralized marketing campaign calendar is used to document and coordinate campaigns across all business groups that can conduct a campaign.

A second area that should be coordinated concerns marketing and advertising space. Most organizations have a limited amount of room for mass-market messages to be displayed. Typically, competition exists among product managers or business units for the use of this limited advertising space. Thus, organizations that can coordinate across business area and product lines to control competition for limited shelf space in distribution channels are following another marketing "best-practice." The following are examples of display space that should be included in the coordination efforts:

Brick and mortar distribution channels: Sign space, banner space, brochure space, or display-stand space

Statements and invoices: Bill stuffer space in envelope, and message area available on actual statement or bill

Web: Icon space and prompt space available on the Web page

Call Center: Space available for recorded messages while on hold to call center

Kiosk: Icon, menu item, space available on ATM, and kiosk screens

Marketing CRM Plan

Another important factor to monitor is the focus of marketing activities. As described in a prior section in this chapter, it is not unusual for successful product companies to have developed efficient processes that revolve around the products themselves. When transitioning from a product focus to a customer focus, some of these product-oriented processes must change. Although it is desirable to have some product-based marketing, the organization should be performing customer-oriented marketing activities as well. It is key that marketing activities are planned and executed based on a marketing plan that is focused on customer concepts, rather than on product sales. Some examples of customer-focused marketing activities are as follows:

- Marketing actively defines and monitors customer segmentation.

- Marketing recognizes household relationships and influence value when calculating customer value and profitability.

- Marketing conducts customer satisfaction surveys and develops action plans based on the results.

- Marketing concentrates on retention activities, including the recognition of retention risks, proactive campaign activity on retention risks, and post-loss survey activity on customers that have left.

- Marketing focuses on share-of-wallet activities including the determination of the next best product to sell and the appropriate follow-up campaign activity.

Organization Culture and Marketing

As illustrated in the section on critical success factors, an organization's culture can play a key role in the success or failure of CRM activity. When considering the impact of your organization's culture, you should understand how the business areas relate to each other. In a customer-oriented environment, marketing should be viewed across the organization as a CRM-enabling business area, one upon which the other areas depend to "know their customers" and to achieve their performance objectives. The relationship between the distribution channels and marketing is of particular importance. The distribution channels should view marketing as an area key to their success. The following are two examples of positive interactions between marketing and customer contact areas:

- In a large insurance company, marketing provides the agents with customer profile information that enables the agents to know their customers.

- In the communications industry, marketing provides qualified leads and campaign advisory services to retail distribution store managers to help draw customers to the store.

Marketing Success Measures

Measures of success are key motivators of employee behavior. Organizations that are product-focused typically have success measures that are also product-focused. Changing activity and behavior to focus on the customer requires that the objectives and measures of success are also changed to focus on the customer. In the case of marketing activity, success measurements and incentives must include CRM-focused targets. The following lists some best-practice success measures for marketing that are focused on customers rather than on products:

- Marketing is measured by the contribution to increasing retention rates.

- Marketing is measured on how well it prompts the service channels for cross-sale activity. Measurements include the number of prompts delivered, customer reaction to the prompts, and the number of cross-sells or retention saves the prompts achieve.

- Marketing is measured on the rates of results, the response tracking it conducts, and on how these results and responses are incorporated into future campaigns. A response repository should be actively used to capture responses. In addition, if a customer rejects an offer, this information should be available and be actively used for the remainder of the current campaign or in future campaigns, so that customers do not receive the same solicitation every time they call in.

- Questions about marketing solicitations are included in customer satisfaction surveys and results are included in measurements.

- Cross-sell or share-of-wallet measurements are included in marketing performance evaluation.

- Increases in the value of targeted customers or the movement of customers into targeted segments should be included in measurements. Customer value should be measured across all the products they own or have influence over. The movement of a customer from a low value segment into a more profitable one also should be recognized and rewarded.

Marketing Integration with Other Business Areas

Earlier in this section we described the importance of understanding the culture of the organization and the marketing role in this culture. Creating an environment where marketing is fully integrated with the other business areas can facilitate a culture where a mutually beneficial relationship exists between marketing and the organization as a whole. One way to do this is to ensure that marketing information is actively disseminated throughout the organization, particularly to all points of customer contact. Marketing can take several steps to ensure this integration:

- Marketing works actively with all distribution channels to provide them with the information required to better understand the ultimate customers.

- Current marketing campaign information is clearly communicated to appropriate distribution channels.

- Customer segmentation information and action steps are communicated by marketing to the customer contact points throughout the organization.

- Customer satisfaction study results and the appropriate action plans are communicated to all points of customer contact.

- Marketing actively solicits feedback from service and sales representatives about customers' reactions to sales offers, competitive product features, competitor promotional offers, and so on.

- Marketing campaigns are actively modified based on feedback from both internal sources as well as feedback from customers.

Roadmap for Customer Service

The customer service functions are also integral to CRM success because they provide the primary means of contact with the customers. Customer service is a tremendous opportunity to positively influence the customer's feelings about the organization and to increase customer satisfaction and loyalty. It is an effective and non-intrusive way to collect information about the customer that can be used in all aspects of CRM analysis and strategy development. Lastly, it provides the contact mechanisms that can be leveraged to implement marketing and sales strategies and to apply the results of marketing analysis. The factors that influence CRM success in service are the same as those that influence marketing: activity coordination, CRM planning, CRM success measures, organization culture, and service integration across the organization. Equally important are the practical applications or best practices of CRM service activity.

Customer Service Activity Coordination

As with marketing, service activity can be performed in multiple places within an organization. As organizations develop new channels, coordinating the service activity across these independent channels becomes very important. In order to gain the benefits associated with top-quality customer service, the organization must have a mechanism to coordinate customer-oriented service processes across multiple service channels.

This coordination can be provided in several ways. First, if service centers are organized by product line (such as a cable service center and a cellular service center for same communications company), then all service centers should share a common customer information system and can route customer changes as required. Common customer information systems across service centers provide a strong benefit to a customer. A customer wanting to update his or her name and address information, for example, can call one location to facilitate the change. The called location takes the information and is able to make the change for all centers or can pass the information to the other centers.

Where possible, service centers should be equipped to deal with multiple lines of business or multiple products. However, if the organization does have multiple service centers or service channels, all customer-oriented service processes should be coordinated across all the disparate service centers. Some coordination practices for multiple channels are listed here:

- Organizations that have multiple service centers should provide the ability for one center to transfer the customer and his or her related information to another center, rather than requiring the customer to make another call.

- Call centers should facilitate the transfer of customers with telephony systems that can directly transfer customer and account information, rather than requiring the caller to reenter or repeat name and account numbers.

- A single customer-level identifier should be used across all product and service channels to provide seamless information transfers.

- Common training programs should exist across service centers for non-product-specific processes such as customer greeting and customer name change processes.

- Independent service centers should conduct regular meetings for cross-line-of-business service representatives to discuss issues and coordination mechanisms.

- Published guidelines should exist for common customer-oriented processes.

Customer Service CRM Plan

As with marketing, customer service should operate based on a CRM plan. The plan should ensure that all service policies, options, and training are developed and implemented according to an overall CRM plan. The CRM plan also should provide customers, both internal (distribution channels) and external (ultimate customer), with access to multiple convenience-based service options. The varied service options provided to Bob and his parents that are described in Chapter 1 are good examples of the types of options that should be facilitated by the CRM plan. Service options should be offered to sales representatives and customers alike. Such options should also include call centers, traditional retail standalone centers (such as branches, phone stores, or agencies), multipurpose retail stores (such as Radio Shack, which also carries cell phones), in-store kiosks (cell phone displays in a mall or grocery store), and Internet-based self-service mechanisms. The CRM plan should provide for the following types of best-practice policies at each channel:

- Valued customers are identified at all service points and are treated accordingly.

- Service representatives are empowered to conduct customer save activities and improve customer satisfaction where necessary.

- Service representatives are provided with training that enables them to become relationship managers, rather than product-level service providers.

- Service representatives are trained to recognize retention issues.

- Service representatives are provided with adequate sales training.

- Service representatives are trained to recognize the appropriate time to solicit additional information or attempt product cross-sell activities. This would include how to recognize customer signals.

Organization Culture and Customer Service

Organization culture can have a strong impact on the transformation of a service organization from a product focus to a customer orientation. In this case, the service representatives have most or all of the direct contact with the customers and must understand the impact these interactions can have. It is imperative that the organization has a stable and enthusiastic service representative force that can perform CRM-related activities. Several factors can be monitored to ensure that the culture will enable a customer focus:

- Service representatives understand the positive job effects that can result from satisfied customers.

- Service representatives are generally accepting and enthusiastic about the sales and customer satisfaction aspects of their position.

- The organization has a relatively stable service representative force, which would have low turnover rates.

- Service representative job skills have been assessed and are adequate for implementing a CRM strategy.

Customer Service Success Measures

It is important to ensure that the success measures and performance measures associated with customer service are customer focused. Many product-oriented service measures are geared around the volume of customers served rather than on customer satisfaction. In a CRM organization, traditional customer service performance measures must be adjusted to accommodate customer-oriented goals and objectives. The following are best-practice examples of CRM service measures that should be considered for incorporation into service policies:

- Some mechanism coordinates service measurements and incentives across multiple service centers.
- Customer satisfaction is included as a service objective and is actively measured.
- The ability of service representatives to handle all customer issues in one call is included in performance measures.
- Cross sales and retention saves are included in the performance measures.
- Traditional performance measures are adjusted to accommodate customer-oriented measures. For example, the acceptable call handle time could be increased, or the acceptable number of rings or hold time could be increased if required.

Customer Service Integration with Other Business Areas

As with marketing, the customer service functions should be fully integrated with all other business areas as required to implement CRM. This integration should include the relationship of customer service with both sales and marketing. Both of the following best-practice service integration points are dependent on the quality of this relationship across service, sales, and marketing:

- Customer service processes are evaluated utilizing feedback, both internal (organization-initiated) and external (customer-oriented).
- Service representatives are aware of recent marketing campaigns and sales solicitations and are trained to follow up as appropriate.

Roadmap for Sales

For obvious reasons, the sales area is also considered to be a high-impact CRM business area. As the primary distribution point for most organizations, sales relies on the customer information generated by marketing and on the customer satisfaction fostered by service. The sales organization typically generates and maintains the personal relationships that exist between the customers and the organization. In this capacity, the sales representatives are in a position to gather much useful information about the customers that can be passed onto the other business units as well. Thus, coordination, integration, CRM planning, success measures, and culture are all important factors to understand and manage in the sales area, as well as in marketing and service.

Sales Activity Coordination

Many organizations have multiple sales channels. This is particularly true in organizations that sell to other businesses, which is known as business-to-business (B2B) selling. Many corporate sales departments have sales representatives organized by product line and can have several individuals contacting the customer at the same time. Successful CRM requires that organizations have some mechanism for understanding, coordinating, and communicating multiple sales activities to the same customer. To better coordinate sales, corporate customer sales organizations should have overall account managers who direct all sales efforts to each client, and they should have sales teams with product specialists from different areas within the company. In addition, the contact management systems need to be available across business lines, and sales representatives from one product line need to know which offers are on the table to a customer through another business line.

Some best-practices for coordinating sales activity follow:

- Sales and deal teams are dynamic and flexible, pulling specialist resources as needed.
- Relationship managers understand the importance of recording sales contacts in the contact repository for use by all sales personnel.
- In the case of independent sales efforts across business lines, formal and informal communication mechanisms are mandated to ensure adequate communication on independent sales efforts to a single client.

Sales CRM Plan

Sales and distribution activities should be planned and executed based on a CRM business strategy that is focused on customer concepts, rather than on product sales. The following are the best practices for facilitating the customer-focused selling concepts:

- Sales planning focuses on customer needs and on the next best product to sell customers based on these needs.
- Sales management actively assists the sales force in understanding customer profiles and characteristics.
- Sales representatives have periodic account reviews with most customers.

- Sales training sessions address relationship management.
- Sales training techniques include solution-selling concepts such as active listening and problem confirmation before proposing products.

Organization Culture and Sales

As with customer service, the culture of an organization can have an impact on the CRM sales efforts. The key here is that the organization has a stable and enthusiastic sales force that can act as relationship managers. A successful CRM sales force typically has a lower than average turnover rate and has sales representatives that view themselves as customer representatives and can accurately describe the characteristics of their customer base.

Best-practices for improving the sales culture of an organization follow:

- Organizations with a high sales force turnover have transition plans to minimize the impact on clients.
- The sales force is relationship-oriented and has adequate knowledge of its customer base, including characteristics, buying motivators, and so on.
- Independent distribution channels place an organization's products high on their priority list. For example, independent insurance agents who can sell products from multiple companies understand the benefits of the organization's products and try to sell these first.

Sales Success Measures

Sales success measurements and incentives must be established to include CRM-focused targets. The following are examples of CRM-oriented sales measures:

- Sales incentives include measures for increasing the products held by existing customers.
- Customer satisfaction with the sales and distribution people and with the sales process is actively solicited and included in performance measures for sales and distribution channels.
- The compensation plan provides for the formation of sales teams to address customer needs across specialized products and services.

Sales Integration with Other Business Areas

The sales and distribution functions must also be fully integrated with all other business areas as required to implement CRM. The indicators of sales integration with marketing and service include the following:

- Sales and distribution channels receive leads from customer service areas and actively follow these leads to conclusion.

- Sales and distribution channels are involved in follow-up activities from direct marketing campaigns.

- Customer service and marketing are notified of the results of lead follow-ups.

- The organization conducts periodic coordination meetings with customer service, marketing, and sales and distribution.

Summary

Organizations embarking on a CRM initiative should establish critical success factors in the areas of business strategy, organization structure, organization culture, technology, and executive support. The enterprise must establish a set of cross-functional business strategies that focus on the customer. It must deploy an organizational structure that promotes the cross-functional coordination of customer-oriented processes. It must have an organizational culture that enables change and facilitates organizational cooperation and sharing. It must have an information technology environment that provides integrated customer information. Its executive management also must understand and actively support CRM.

Organizations must become aware of how to manage these critical success factors at both an enterprise level and at a business unit level. Detailed steps such as CRM planning, CRM-oriented success measures, activity coordination, cross-business unit information sharing, and spreading an understanding of and enthusiasm for CRM are good places to start when attempting any CRM initiatives.

Individual CRM initiatives may be successfully implemented without fully resolving all the issues detailed in this chapter. However, to implement a comprehensive, coordinated CRM program, all these issues must be identified and resolved. Chapter 5, "Getting Underway," introduces the concept of managing comprehensive, multi-project initiatives such as those required to move an organization towards CRM. It also discusses the teams that must be set up to accomplish the technology and business initiatives required to implement CRM strategies.

CHAPTER 5

Getting Underway

hapter 4, "Are You Ready? Tuning the Organization for CRM," gave us great insight into the critical success factors needed to implement a successful CRM strategy, such as the importance of formal and informal communication channels and the need for executive buy-in. Once the organization has set its priorities, defined an overall Customer Relationship Management (CRM) program, and assessed its structure, culture, and technology, the next step is to build the customer systems that will support CRM. Easy enough, right? Not necessarily.

Consider this situation: Another bank that Bob has dealings with decided that it too wanted to become a CRM-savvy organization. As its first step toward this goal, the bank chose to implement a customer segmentation and scoring analysis application. The VP of marketing described his requirements to the CIO over lunch. He wanted his department to be able to identify valuable customers and give them the "red carpet treatment." The CIO nodded his head and stated that he would get his best team right on it.

The CIO came back to his department, called in his manager of applications, told her to build a customer database, and went back to his office. The manager found three people that she could assign part-time to this project. She told them to spend a couple of months putting together a database with customer information in it, give the database to the marketing guys, and then go back to their normal maintenance programming assignments.

The team then went to work. They extracted a bunch of data from the billing system, bought an online analytical tool as an access mechanism, and proudly rolled out the new application to the Marketing Department after three months of effort. Needless to say, the marketers trying to use it were not involved in the design of the application and were not informed of what the Marketing VP had originally requested. These marketers deemed the new application unworkable, and unfortunately the enterprise ultimately declared their whole CRM effort a failure.

To avoid technology project failures like this one, you should define the leadership required in the technology area, determine the roles and responsibilities required to develop complex customer technology, and ensure that project teams are staffed accordingly. Building effective project teams requires that attention be given to the relationship between information technology and the business areas. The business areas interact with customers, define information requirements, and set the CRM strategy. The technology groups supply the systems that support customer interaction and enable the CRM strategy. For this relationship to work smoothly, the CRM strategy must be clearly defined and agreed on by both groups, and formal communications lines must be implemented. Without the bridge between the strategy setters (business) and the strategy supporters (technology), most complex technology projects are likely to fail.

In Chapter 2, "The Customer and the Corporate Information Factory (CIF)," we discussed the need for three sets of systems to support CRM: business operations, business intelligence, and business management. This chapter focuses on the roles and responsibilities of the teams that build the business intelligence and business management systems. The methodology and responsibilities for typical business operations projects are well defined in standard "software development lifecycle" books and will not be discussed further here.

It is important to note that all three sets of systems must ensure the integration of data. For example, customer service centers, call centers, and branch offices must have timely access to the customer profiles housed in a customer-centric operational data store (ODS). Without the integration of relationship and product ownership data found in the ODS, the bank would never recognize Bob's parents as both an economic unit and as individual customers. It would not recognize that the Bob who has a checking account and the Bob who uses investment services are the same person. Bank personnel also need the historical data and analytical results contained in the data warehouse and marts. Without this information, the bank would not know that Bob's parents enjoy luxury travel and are likely candidates for the bank's travel services. It would also not recognize Bob as a valuable financial investment customer. Only this tight integration can produce the desired end result, happy and profitable customers.

This chapter focuses on three important functions needed to implement and administer CRM systems within the Corporate Information Factory:

- The program management team
- The getting data in (GDI) team
- The getting information out (GIO) team

This chapter starts with a discussion of program management. This section emphasizes that implementing an integrated customer information environment is not a single project. Rather, it is a series of coordinated projects, all having the Corporate Information Factory as the roadmap for implementation and a CRM strategy as the ultimate goal.

Next we discuss what we have coined the GDI team and the GIO teams. Each team concentrates on a separate part of the CIF architecture, and therefore their team members have different roles and responsibilities. These specific roles and responsibilities are the topic of the last section, which details the skills required and challenges faced when implementing the CRM environment.

We recommend that both IT and business sponsors read this chapter to understand their level of involvement in building a CRM environment. Note that Chapter 4 contains additional non-people requirements for building this environment.

Program Management

Program management is one of the distinguishing characteristics of the Corporate Information Factory architecture. It should be readily apparent by now that building the CIF, especially in support of the move to CRM, is not a single project, but rather a series of projects. Why is this so? Because the technology required to provide seamless integration of customer information across business units is not a single system. Instead, it is the integration of the business operations, business management, and business intelligence that we described earlier. Further, for most companies, the question is not which single piece of CRM technology should be built, but rather which of the many required components should be built first, and how can the integration of the individual components be ensured when they're finally built.

How does a company achieve this integration? By making sure that the series of technology projects required to support CRM strategies is governed by a larger function: program management. Program management is the process of identifying, prioritizing, and selecting the appropriate projects for CRM support. For example, the enterprise may immediately request the following capabilities:

- Customer demographic profiling
- Customer segmentation and scoring
- Buying behavior analysis
- Sales channel analysis
- Customer contact information

We can't possibly build all of these simultaneously! Program management is responsible for setting the priorities of each of these projects and determining their implementation schedules. This function must also ensure that, at the end of the day, each project integrates with the others, (to ensure that your customer data can also be integrated). To help differentiate between a program and a project, the characteristics of each are shown in Table 5.1.

The enterprise embarking on a CRM strategy must assign members to the program management team before the start of the very first technology project. The goals of the program management team are as follows:

Business Strategy Alignment. The program management team's (this includes the business sponsor) top goal must be to ensure that the technological implementations of the CIF are fully aligned with the organization's business direction and vision. The team must be heavily involved in the decision-making and direction-setting processes for the organization as a whole. It must also ensure that all proposed projects are in keeping with the new vision. In Chapter 4, we state this critical success factor succinctly: The organization must have business strategies that promote CRM across functional boundaries. Simply stated—difficult to do! See Chapter 4 for more on this topic.

Repeatable and Reused Processes. The ideal of repeatable and reused processes can only be accomplished if a program management team is aware

Table 5.1 Characteristics of a Project versus a Program

PROJECT	PROGRAM
One-time	Ongoing and may consist of several projects
Specific perspective	Broad perspective
May not require architecture	Requires architecture
May ignore long-term goals	Focuses on long-term goals
May not realize benefits of standards or a reuse for new items	Realizes benefits of standards and reuse
Strategy is optional	Strategy is essential

of these processes and actively promotes their creation and use. Reused processes make the downstream projects less expensive and ensure the integration and coordination between projects that is needed to support CRM initiatives. One such process may be the creation of a reusable project plan for strategic applications (data marts). The construction of these applications is remarkably similar from project to project. The data changes, the requirements change, and the people involved change, but the actual implementation steps remain the same (or at least are very similar).

Project Prioritization and Funding. The program management team is the appropriate body to determine the sequence and priority of projects and their funding. Because this team knows the business strategy and vision, they are best suited to determine the priority and funding levels for the various CRM projects within and outside the CIF architecture. Chapter 4 contains the statement, "both business executives and technologists should pay careful attention to the presence or absence of customer-oriented business strategies and action plans when considering CRM initiatives." Read through the "CRM Strategy or CRM Systems, Which Comes First?" section in Chapter 4 carefully to get a strong understanding of what is needed to achieve this goal.

Business Community and IT Communication. Justifications, prioritization, funding, and resource allocations are all important decisions that should be communicated to the entire organization. It is critical to keep both the information technology (IT) and business communities informed of strategic decisions regarding CRM technology projects. This communication ensures ultimate organizational support for each project, which in turn facilitates project success. For example, we note in Chapter 4 that a technology plan is needed to coordinate activities. This plan is the basis for communications across the organization and it ensures the appropriate creation and integration of all the required CRM components.

"Getting Data In" versus "Getting Information Out"

For many large technology groups, specialization within the teams that build and maintain CRM technology is bipolar. One part of the team becomes very focussed on the operational systems, the integration and transformation layer, and the data warehouse—getting the data in. Another part of the team gravitates towards the building of cubes, marts, data sets, statistical subsets, and reports for the business community—getting the information out.

Even though both of these functions are necessary to build the seamless customer information environment provided by the Corporate Information Factory (refer to Figure 5.1), it can be difficult to manage the situation and to "synergize" the two groups. Without an understanding of this polarizing tendency, you may be asking yourself why once-happy team members are now feuding with each other over issues such as project priorities. Without a plan for maximizing team cohesion, you may be stuck with suboptimal results.

So, what's the plan? How do you set up a team structure that accommodates the widening gap between those who see the world of strategic and tactical decision-making as GDI and those who see it as GIO? First, you need to understand the goals of each group. Figure 5.2 shows these broad goals, which are discussed in detail in the next two sections.

Goals of the "Getting Data In" Team

Using the Corporate Information Factory architecture as a guide, Figure 5.3 illustrates that GDI focuses almost exclusively on the left side of the architecture: the operational systems, the data acquisition layer, the data warehouse and operational data store databases, and finally the enterprise data manage-

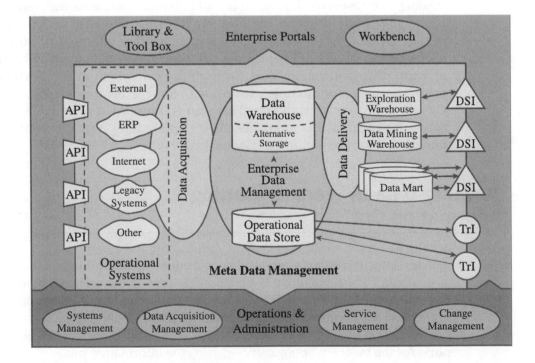

Figure 5.1 The Corporate Information Factory.

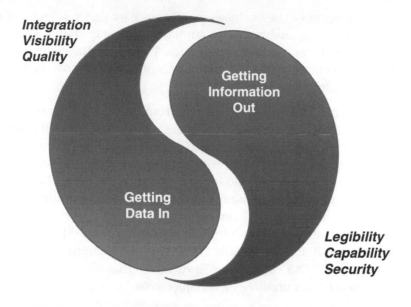

Integration
Visibility
Quality

Getting
Information
Out

Getting
Data In

Legibility
Capability
Security

Figure 5.2 The goals of GDI and GIO groups.

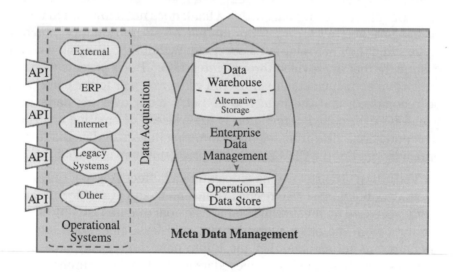

Figure 5.3 The focus of the GDI team.

ment processes, as defined in Chapter 2. Although the GDI focus is more technical in nature than its GIO counterpart, the business community still plays a large role. Business involvement is critical to the success of this part of the architecture because the business representatives verify sources of data, help develop algorithms, analyze information quality and currency, and validate the data models and associated business rules. These activities help make the information in the customer systems complete, correct, and broad enough to meet a variety of business unit needs.

The goals of this team are quite different from those of the GIO group discussed in the next section. First and foremost in the minds of the GDI team is the ability to capture, integrate, cleanse, and transform the fractured data from the myriad operational systems to the integrated, enterprise-oriented standard formats of the data warehouse and the operational data store. This effort can vary greatly depending on such factors as the age of the operational systems, the available documentation, the quality of the data and processes, and the complexity of the transformation rules and algorithms (this difficult process is discussed in detail in Chapter 8, "Quality Relationships Start with Quality Customer Data"). Our experiences have shown that 65 to 80 percent of the GDI team's efforts center on three broad objectives:

Integration. Many of the CRM determinations (such as customer value or the targeting of certain products to specific individuals) must have fully integrated customer data. Householding is a good example. Looking only at the operational product systems within a bank does not allow you to understand all the products owned by Bob's mother or by Bob's father, much less to understand their net value as a household. Without the integrated view of our customers that is provided through integration, Bob's parents would not be seen as an economic unit, their overall value as a pair to the bank would not be recognized, and the influence of Bob's mom over his dad's decisions would be overlooked. Integration is the process of creating a single, cohesive, enterprise view from the many differing flavors of data that exist in the organization. For the CRM-savvy enterprise, this step is crucial.

Data Visibility. To use the data efficiently and effectively, not only must it be integrated, but it must also reside in convenient and available formats and be easily accessed by those who need it. The goal of data visibility is to extract the data from the older, more difficult, and less understood technologies; document its format; and then put it into new, more easily accessible technologies. The GDI team has achieved its goal if the data warehouse contains a robust enterprise view of data that can be extracted and loaded into data marts to provide strategic decision-making capabilities to the organization. The team would also have achieved its goal if the ODS contains a robust enterprise view of data that can be used to feed other parts of the CIF and to make tactical decisions across the organization. This may mean a change in the technological platform for many organizations, usually from less robust networks or hierarchical databases (IDMS, VSAM, IMS and flat files) to a relational database (DB2, SQL server, Informix, Teradata, and Sybase) on a highly scalable platform (Unix, NT, MVS).

Quality. The last, but not least, concern of the GDI group is the quality of the data they are loading into the CIF. The first question from most users is "How good is this data?" Until the quality is known and measured, this question cannot be answered. Unfortunately, the quality of the data in most operational systems is relatively unknown. The first indication of a quality problem comes during the integration and extraction processes. The GDI group inherits these problems from the operational systems, and their goal is to correct them, so don't shoot the messenger! It takes a great deal of coordinated effort from both the business community and IT personnel to achieve major improvements in data quality. It may even require an overhaul of existing business processes and/or incentive plans to show these improvements. Quality expectations should be set for each CRM component. Chapter 8 covers this topic of quality in detail.

The activities of the GDI team generate a great deal of meta data, both technical and business. This meta data may include such information as where the data came from, which transformation and integration rules were used, which business and summarization rules were used, what is the target format, and which error detection and correction rules are in place.

Goals of the "Getting Information Out" Team

The people responsible for getting information out and into the hands of the business community have their own architectural concerns. Figure 5.4 shows that they are far more focussed on the right side of the architecture: the data delivery process, data marts, and the interfaces into both the data marts (the decision support interface [DSI]) and the ODS (transaction interface [TI]). It is important to note that meta data is also a part of the GIO's focus. In this case though, the meta data is more business-oriented, containing information such as the business definition of attributes and entities, applicable business rules, business aliases, data steward and owner names, and security specifications. However, the GIO team may also be responsible for delivering some of the technical meta data collected by the GSI team (such as the calculations used, the summarizations, and the aggregations created). It is mandatory that CRM personnel understand the definition of critical entities such as customer, product, and service, so that they understand the enterprise's view of these and act accordingly. Generally, the GIO team (or teams) is made up of both line-of-

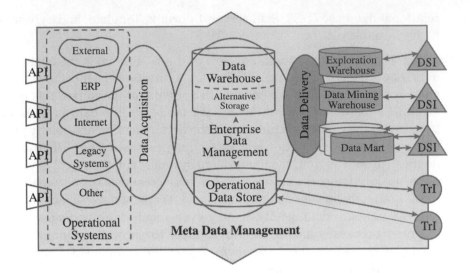

Figure 5.4 The focus of the GIO team.

business information technology people and personnel from the business community.

The GIO team also has its own set of goals, very different from those of the GDI team. These consist of the following:

Capability. The job of the GIO team is to understand the specific problems that the business community is trying to solve, to identify the information from the data warehouse (created by the GDI team) that is required to solve each problem, and to get that information out of the warehouse and into specialized data bases (data marts) for easy analysis by the business community. Each business problem typically equates to an analysis capability that can be provided through an individual data mart. What differentiates one business problem and its required analysis capability from another is the type of information required to solve the problem. In many cases, different business problems require different information. For example, if you create a data mart to analyze customer demographic profiling, it is unreasonable to assume that the information in this particular data mart can also support the analysis required to predict customer purchasing patterns. Those questions require yet another set of data formatted specifically for the business capability of predicting purchase patterns, another data mart. The GIO team turns the data warehouse into a pot of gold by providing the business community with the information they need to do CRM analysis. All it takes is time, dedication, resources, and, of course, an unwavering vision of the ultimate CIF environment.

Business Community Legibility. If the analysis capabilities provided by the data marts are to yield the pot of gold described earlier, the business community must know which data marts exist and understand which types of analysis these marts support. This thought highlights a key issue: the CRM technology is only as good as the meta data that supports this technology. Meta data (the data about the data, activities, reports, and usage) is the glue that holds the CIF architecture together. It is the information you turn to when you don't know what a calculation is, where a piece of data came from, who created which report, and other critical information. Without this type of solid understanding of the CIF, the business community could use information inappropriately or, worse, not use the information at all because they don't know how or because they didn't know it was there. The goal is to make the environment easy to use and easy to understand.

Security. The final goal of the GIO group is to ensure that this most valuable corporate asset—clean, accessible information—is not abused, stolen, or inappropriately accessed. Security can quickly become a highly political issue, especially if you make your CIF accessible through your intranet to the business community and to external entities. A carefully thought-out security plan will be invaluable to the well-being of your organization. Effective security requires that the business community specify the security (and privacy) requirements and that the IT staff implement these requirements. An important note: Data sharing is the counterpoint to effective security, but sharing critical data is mandatory for successful CRM. Therefore, a balance must be struck between data security and data sharing. Also, we recommend that a significant effort be made to educate the business community about the dire results of misusing data. Privacy issues are discussed in Chapter 14, "Preserving Customer Trust—The Role of Privacy," and should not be taken lightly.

Just as the GDI group cannot forget about the business community in its quest to get data in, the GIO group cannot forget about the architecture in its zeal to get information out. The GIO team must ensure that the required data exists in either the data warehouse or the ODS. To keep the architecture in sync, this team must also ensure that the GDI group is informed of new requirements, new calculations, new data marts, or any other new developments.

Ultimately, you may consider splitting these groups into two formal teams, a centralized GDI team and one or more GIO teams. Moving the GIO team(s) from the technology organization into the business community can provide these organizations an improved sense of control and can help ensure a buy-in to the CIF. Once split into two camps, you must ensure that the teams maintain a cohesive relationship.

The following cultural requirements all relate to the cooperation, communication, and coordination between business units and IT, as discussed in Chapter 4. Just as these coordination and cooperation issues are required on a larger scale to implement CRM strategies, so they are required at a more detailed level to implement CRM technology:

- Educating the teams on the nature and importance of each other's goals
- Ensuring that each team keeps the interests of the other in mind
  - The GDI team supplies the GIO team(s) with clear, well-documented meta data explaining the source of data, its quality, format, and content
  - The GIO team(s) constantly reports user feedback on data quality and communicates new data requirements to the GDI team
- Creating open communication channels
  - Critical e-mails are distributed appropriately
  - An intranet site for project/program notices, events, and implementations is developed
  - Formal and informal channels such as brown bag lunches, request-tracking systems, surveys, and user group meetings are created

Roles and Responsibilities of the Teams

This is perhaps the most important section of this chapter, the identification of the specific roles and responsibilities for each team. Filling each of these roles with qualified resources is a significant key to the overall success of your CRM initiative.

NOTE

It is important to remember that this section identifies roles and the associated responsibilities. One person may be able to perform more than one role; alternatively, you may need multiple people to correctly perform a single role.

Program Management Team

As we mentioned earlier, the implementation of a solid CRM environment cannot be done overnight. It takes a series of many smaller projects, created iteratively and perfected over several months, even years. The program management team must oversee these projects, ensuring that they all lead toward the goal of a fully integrated customer-focused enterprise. Program management consists of the following roles.

Business Sponsor

The Business Sponsor is the executive who is responsible for garnering business support and for obtaining business personnel and funding. Your organization may use more than one Business Sponsor. Chapter 4 highlights the need for the executive support provided by the Business Sponsor.

Important traits for this role are as follows:

CRM knowledge. The Business Sponsor must have an extensive knowledge of CRM and all that it entails. See Chapter 4 for more about the business sponsor's responsibilities.

Decisiveness. The Business Sponsor must be able to make or approve strategic decisions concerning the CRM program and related CIF projects.

Authority. The Business Sponsor must have the authority to enforce decisions and to acquire the needed funding and business resources.

Respect. The Business Sponsor must actively promote CRM initiatives and the CIF and should be respected within the enterprise management team.

Commitment. The Business Sponsor should be committed to the success of the CIF to facilitate CRM. The Business Sponsor must understand the value of the CIF to the company and must be willing to take appropriate actions to ensure success. Chapter 4 details ways to ensure this commitment.

The major challenges for this role are as follows:

Acquiring and retaining funding. The Business Sponsor must be able to obtain the needed funding. In a typical company, multiple projects and programs compete for limited funds and resources. The business sponsor must balance these competing projects to determine the best dispersal of funds and resources. Chapter 4 gives you suggestions on how you can use unsupported CRM initiatives to justify funding for the CIF implementation.

Maintaining interest. During the development of the CIF, there are periods of time when results are not visible to the business community. The Business Sponsor must communicate the importance of these activities across the organization so that interest in the program is maintained. These types of communications are discussed in Chapter 4 and include discussing CRM intentions in the annual report, external company publications, Web sites, press releases, or speeches.

Data Steward

The Data Steward is responsible for ensuring that the data provided by the Corporate Information Factory is based on an enterprise view. An individual, a committee, or both may perform data stewardship. It is advisable to have one Data Steward per data subject area, such as Customer, Order, and Product. Because a subject area cuts across the enterprise, this type of stewardship eliminates possible overlap and ensures an enterprise view.

Important traits for this role are as follows:

CRM knowledge. The Data Steward will be frequently called upon to settle integration issues, definitional disputes, and other significant clashes. Who "owns" the customer is a good example of a frequent and significant clash. To ensure appropriate resolutions to these issues, the steward must have a firm understanding of CRM principles and goals.

Enterprise perspective. The Data Steward must understand the often-conflicting viewpoints concerning the data. For example, the tellers may see customers as single individuals having individual checking and savings accounts. Marketers may want to view customers in relation to their households or as part of the larger consumer market (leads and prospects). Commercial account representatives are mostly concerned with businesses and not individuals. Each of these views is valid and must be accommodated in the definition of customer, as discussed in Chapter 1.

The commitment to managing data as an asset. To successfully support CRM, customer information must be recognized as a strategic asset and, as such, should be governed by the same level of enterprise planning and care that governs other corporate assets. The Data Steward's role for data is similar to the Chief Financial Officer's role for money. Neither owns the asset, but both are responsible for establishing practices concerning the acquisition, management, dissemination and disposal of the asset.

Negotiation. The Data Steward needs to help the interested parties arrive at solutions that reflect the enterprise view. This often requires effective negotiation and compromise. This process is similar to the one that takes place to facilitate cross-functional business strategies required by CRM.

The major challenges for this role are as follows:

Ensuring the enterprise perspective of data. Conflicting opinions, such as the customer definition mentioned earlier, happen frequently and the Data Steward must be prepared to facilitate the resolution of any significant differences.

Balancing individual and enterprise access needs. The success of CRM technology in support of customer-oriented business strategies depends on the appropriate sharing of information. The Data Steward must balance the desires to restrict access with the value of providing access for legitimate business needs.

Organization Change Agent

The Organization Change Agent helps the company understand the value and impact of the Corporate Information Factory and deals with the organizational issues. Chapter 4 discussed in detail the need for these types of agents in a CRM-savvy organization, for it is this role that is responsible for ensuring that the culture is appropriate to support CRM initiatives.

Important traits for this role were discussed in Chapter 4 and are summarized here:

CRM knowledge. The Organizational Change Agent has the important job of making certain that the organization is ready, willing, and able to conduct its CRM practices. This may entail reeducating personnel, finding and eliminating fear of the new changes, demonstrating benefits from CRM practices to the organization, and perhaps hiring new personnel with the proper CRM focus.

Visionary. The Organization Change Agent needs to understand and convey the value of the CRM program to both business and technology personnel.

Strong interpersonal skills. The Organization Change Agent must deal delicately with people whose responsibilities are changing.

The major challenges for this role are as follows:

Help people deal with change. Change can be traumatic, even if it is "for the good." The Organization Change Agent must help people whose responsibilities are changing. The help may include counseling and education.

Deal with displaced individuals. With the introduction of the Corporate Information Factory and the CRM program, some positions may be eliminated; others will certainly change significantly. The Organization Change Agent needs to work with the displaced individuals to help them deal with the change and potentially to help them find another suitable position.

Program Manager

The Program Manager is responsible for overseeing the entire CRM program and for managing day-to-day program activities within scope, budget, and schedule constraints. Generally, the Program Manager reports to the members of the Steering Committee.

Important traits for this role are as follows:

CRM knowledge. The Program Manager must have the respect of the program participants and must demonstrate a solid understanding of the CRM goals and objectives for each project.

Project management. The Program Manager should have experience in managing multiple simultaneous technology projects that involve multiple business areas.

Technical knowledge. The Program Manager must have a strong understanding of the CIF architecture, the role and positioning of the CRM-specific components within this architecture, and the associated implementation methodology. He or she is often called upon to explain the architecture and must be prepared to do so. Few, if any, projects apply the methodology exactly as written. The Program Manager needs to be well versed in the methodology and be capable of making rational decisions concerning the inclusion, exclusion, and modification of specific activities and tasks.

Commitment. The Program Manager should be committed to the success of the CIF and the CRM initiatives. The Program Manager must understand the value of the CIF and must be willing to take appropriate actions to ensure success. He or she must also continually review all projects to ensure that they are aligned with the CRM strategy and goals.

Communication. The Program Manager must have strong verbal and written communication skills.

The major challenges for this role are as follows:

Dealing with demands for quick delivery. The success of the CIF and the ensuing CRM program is dependent on building a strong foundation. The Program Manager may be continuously called upon to defend the need to build the procedural and technical infrastructure.

Prioritization. The CRM program and the CIF architecture do not directly provide business benefits; the use of the information in the associated customer systems provides the benefit. The Program Manager actively participates in setting priorities for the CIF projects within the CRM Program.

Project Leader

The Project Leader is responsible for managing day-to-day project activities and for delivering the products according to the scope, budget, and schedule. Responsibilities include keeping the Program Manager up to date with project details, ensuring that communication is open between the project team and the program management, and elevating difficult issues to the program members' attention for resolution.

The important traits for this role are as follows:

Project management. The Project Leader should have experience in managing major technology projects that involve multiple business areas.

Technical understanding. The Project Leader must have a strong understanding of CRM and the CIF, as well as the associated methodology. The Project Leader is often called upon to explain the architecture and how it supports the CRM initiative. Therefore, the Project Manager, just like the Program Manager, must be prepared to do so. Again, rarely will the projects use the methodology exactly as written. The Project Leader needs to be well versed in the methodology and be capable of making rational decisions concerning the inclusion, exclusion, and modification of specific activities and tasks.

Commitment. The Project Leader should be committed to the success of the project and to the overall CRM effort. The Project Leader must understand the value of the effort to the company and must be willing to take appropriate actions to ensure success.

Communication. The Project Leader must have strong verbal and written communication skills.

The major challenges for this role are as follows:

Expectation management. The business community and development team each have expectations with respect to the project. The Project Leader must understand the expectations and ensure that they are consistent with the approved scope and plan for the project.

Scope management. The scope of the project is defined at the outset. Throughout the life of the project, pressures will exist to modify the scope, either consciously or unconsciously. The Project Leader must employ an effective change management process for managing the project scope.

Architect

The Architect is responsible for developing the conceptual architecture for the Corporate Information Factory and for ensuring that the technical architecture is appropriate for the overall CRM effort. Specific exceptions may be necessary as the program advances, but it is the responsibility of the Architect to understand and communicate the trade-offs when exceptions are made.

The important traits for this role are as follows:

Technical understanding. The Architect is responsible for developing the architecture to be used for CRM. Therefore, the Architect must also have a firm understanding of the Corporate Information Factory and how the CIF supports the different aspects of CRM. In this capacity, the Architect also needs to be capable of discussing options with the technical experts and of ensuring that proper decisions are made.

Architectural decision-making. The Architect needs to be well-versed in the architecture and be capable of making rational decisions concerning the inclusion, exclusion, and/or modification of specific components.

The terrorist versus methodologist[1] mentality. The Architect must have a terrorist mentality. The Architect needs to make appropriate adjustments to the theoretical architecture so that it can be implemented within the enterprise's culture and physical environment. This is particularly important because the CIF must continually be realigned with the changes brought forth by the evolving CRM practices.

The major challenges for this role are as follows:

Balancing theory and practicality. The Architect needs to make appropriate adjustments to the theoretical architecture so that it can be implemented within the enterprise's culture and physical environment.

Dealing with demands for quick delivery. The success of the CRM program is dependent on building a strong foundation. The Architect may be continuously called upon to defend the need to build the procedural and technical infrastructure for the CIF.

Steering Committee

The Steering Committee is responsible for establishing priorities for the efforts pursued within the CRM program. It is often tasked with approving funding

---

[1]The difference is that you can negotiate with a terrorist.

requests and resolving difficult integration issues. Often these resolutions require significant changes in business processes or incentive programs to ensure alignment with the CRM objectives. Therefore, the Committee must support these changes and ensure their compliance within the enterprise. Members of the Steering Committee may include the business sponsor, the IT sponsor, and key executives in the CRM initiative.

A good example of a Steering Committee can be found in a large Canadian bank (one of the top five banks in Canada). The bank instituted a top-level Steering Committee that is responsible for all issues relating to CRM. It arbitrates all conflicts, approves all business plans, and obtains funding for all CRM technology. Another group, one level lower in the organization, assists the Steering Committee by doing all the legwork and initially viewing all proposals and issues.

The important traits for this role are as follows:

CRM knowledge. The Steering Committee is the most influential group in determining the CRM directions and goals. It must have a firm understanding and comprehension of CRM, its impact on the organization, and why the CIF architecture is so important to the overall success of the CRM effort.

Authority. The Steering Committee is responsible for approving priorities and funding, and it must have the authority to make difficult decisions.

High-level exposure. The Steering Committee must consist of executives that have good visibility in the organization. Business executives as well as IT executives should participate.

The major challenge of this role is determining relative priorities. Funds are typically not available for all worthwhile efforts. The Steering Committee must select the appropriate efforts to receive funding. They should consider the order of implementation of the CIF and how this order will affect the overall success of the CRM program.

Technical Sponsor

The Technical Sponsor is responsible for garnering business support and for obtaining the needed technical personnel and funding. Ideally, the Chief Information Officer or Chief Knowledge Officer should be the Technical Sponsor.

The important traits for this role are as follows:

CRM technical knowledge. The Technical Sponsor must understand the breadth of technology available to bring to bear on the organization's CRM initiative. He or she may not have a detailed understanding of each tool and technology but should have enough knowledge to determine the appropriateness and/or possible limitations for the enterprise. He or she should demonstrate substantial understanding of CRM and be conversant in how the CIF supports the overall CRM program.

Decisiveness. The Technical Sponsor will be called upon to make or approve decisions concerning the CRM program and related CIF projects.

Authority. The Technical Sponsor needs to have the authority to acquire the needed funding and technical resources.

Respect. The Technical Sponsor actively promotes the CIF and should be respected within the enterprise management and IT teams.

Commitment. The Technical Sponsor should be committed to the success of the CIF and the CRM program. The Technical Sponsor must understand the value that each component brings to the company and must be willing to take appropriate actions to ensure success.

The major challenges for this role are as follows:

Acquiring and retaining funding. The Technical Sponsor needs to obtain the needed funding. Within the corporate environment, other projects and programs are competing for limited funds. It is the Technical Sponsor's responsibility to understand the business strategies and support the alignment of CIF projects with those business strategies.

Maintaining interest. During the development of the CRM program and CIF projects, periods of time may occur when results are not visible to the business community. The Technical Sponsor needs to communicate the importance of these development activities so that interest in the program and the architecture is maintained.

Dealing with demands for quick delivery. The success of the CRM program is dependent on building a strong foundation. The Technical Sponsor should proactively promote the CIF architectural approach and resist shortcuts in the delivery process.

"Getting Data In" Team

The focus of the GDI is much more technical than that of its sister team, the GIO team. This does not mean that the GDI team works in a technological vacuum with little or no input from the business community. Their ability to garner the correct data with the highest possible quality is critical to the overall success of the CRM initiative.

The GDI team must, however, remain focused on the three goals stated earlier in this chapter. Their ultimate purpose is to create an environment in which the GIO team can easily and quickly extract information for strategic and tactical CRM analyses. The roles and responsibilities of the team are as follows.

Business Analyst

The Business Analyst is responsible for providing input concerning the CRM applicability, its content, quality, and delivery, as well as the human interface with the CIF. The Business Analyst must be able to communicate the business needs for specific functionalities and data to IT team members.

The important traits for this role are as follows:

CRM knowledge. The business sponsor is the direct representative of the business community to the IT professionals. They must impart to these professionals an understanding of the CRM principles and goals so that appropriate actions are taken.

A strong understanding of the CIF architecture. The Business Analyst must understand the role of the CIF and be able to effectively determine how it can best be applied to meet CRM goals.

Specific business knowledge. The Business Analyst must understand specific business needs and be able to effectively express these needs to the IT resources.

Analytic prowess. The Business Analyst is an analyst, and hence must possess the related skills.

The major challenges for this role are as follows:

A tendency to include everything. Business users often don't know exactly what they need, and sometimes follow a philosophy of "when in doubt, bring it in." The inclusion of extraneous data in the CIF is costly and increases development time. The Business Analyst must help the business community determine the scope of each CRM application and include only data most likely to be needed for that particular application.

Segregating CIF components. Each of the components of the CIF plays a specific role in supporting the overall CRM program. The Business Analyst must convey these roles to the business community to ensure understanding and a buy-in to the CIF.

Data Acquisition Developer

The Data Acquisition Developer is responsible for developing the applications to capture, cleanse, integrate, transform, and load data from the operational systems into the data warehouse and/or operational data store.

The important traits for this role are as follows:

A strong understanding of the Data Acquisition layer of the CIF. The Data Acquisition Developer must design and build the Data Acquisition layer with a sound understanding of the particular data integration issues that will be encountered in building the CRM components. A solid foundation in the CRM principles is necessary for this person to fully understand the relationship between the CIF and CRM.

Tool knowledge. The Data Acquisition Developer must be proficient with the data acquisition and data cleansing tools that are used to address data integration and quality.

Technical knowledge. The Data Acquisition Developer needs to be proficient with the target technological environment and must understand enough of the source environments to efficiently extract and integrate data from the operational systems.

The major challenges for this role are as follows:

Ensuring the enterprise CRM perspective. The operational systems are often focused on products and not customers. The Data Acquisition Developer must bring these together into a cohesive enterprise vision that supports the new CRM focus on the customer.

Dealing with disparate sources. The operational systems often exist on disparate platforms and employ a diversity of technologies. Additionally, information about these systems is not always readily available. The Data Acquisition Developer must understand these systems and technologies sufficiently enough to ensure that the data acquisition applications are properly designed and built.

Ensuring operating efficiency. The data acquisition programs may be very complex, and the process must operate within stringent time constraints. This acquisition process often needs to be executed daily, weekly, or monthly. The Data Acquisition Developer must design and tune the data acquisition applications to meet business objectives and data quality requirements.

Data Analyst

The Data Analyst is responsible for developing data models for specific CRM systems and for ensuring that these models are synchronized with the enterprise data model. The CRM program will not be successful without fully coordinated and integrated data models.

The important traits for this role are as follows:

An understanding of CRM concepts. The Data Analyst must fully comprehend the importance of CRM initiatives and how the various CIF component data models will support these initiatives.

An understanding of the CIF architecture. Each of the constructs (operational system, data warehouse, operational data store, and data mart) within the CIF has a different design philosophy, and the Data Analyst must ensure that the data model for each reflects its role.

Relational and dimensional modeling skills. The Data Analyst must develop the appropriate data models. Relational models are appropriate for not only operational systems, but also for the data warehouse and part of the ODS. Dimensional models may be appropriate for part of the ODS and the data marts. Other models may be needed for specialized data marts such as the exploration and data mining warehouses.

Repository and computer-aided software engineering (CASE) tool expertise. The primary tools used by the Data Analyst are the repository and CASE tools. The Data Analyst must be proficient with these tools. If a formal repository is used, a Repository Administrator may be responsible for day-to-day management of the repository.

The major challenges for this role are as follows:

Maintaining synchronization with the enterprise model. As with application development, the pressure exists to develop models that reflect the view of particular sponsors or business areas. The Data Analyst must ensure that the enterprise model view and the enterprise CRM strategy are preserved to provide a strong foundation for data integration.

Identifying data integration issues. The Data Analyst is often the first person to recognize and identify data integration issues. He or she must seek the appropriate resolution of these issues as he or she goes forward.

Database Architect

The Database Architect is responsible for designing and tuning the CIF databases and for implementing security constraints.

The important traits for this role are as follows:

An understanding of the CIF architecture. Each of the constructs (operational system, data warehouse, operational data store, and data mart) within the CIF has a different design philosophy, and the Database Architect must ensure that each is designed and tuned based on its role within the CRM program.

Strong DBMS technical knowledge. The Database Architect must be an expert with the database management system(s) being used for the CIF. Additionally, the Database Architect must be familiar with the database management system's optimization schemes for the CIF constructs and how each will be used in the CRM applications.

Relational and dimensional modeling skills. The Database Architect transforms the logical models into physical schemas. The Database Architect needs to understand the data modeling concepts and the business purposes of each component to be able to do this effectively.

The major challenges for this role are as follows:

Achieving performance goals. The Database Architect needs to understand the performance needs within each CRM initiative and take appropriate measures to meet them while minimizing costs for hardware.

Balancing acquisition with access needs. The CIF acquires and integrates data and then provides that data for data marts or for ODS interfaces. The Database Architect must balance these needs in meeting the service-level objectives for the CRM program.

Technical Meta Data Analyst

The Technical Meta Data Analyst on the GDI team is responsible for determining and satisfying the meta data acquisition, management, dissemination, and disposal requirements of the CIF architecture's technical components. These responsibilities include the design of the overall meta data structure that will house both technical and business meta data. They also include loading these structures with the meta data that is generated from the integration processes described earlier in the chapter.

The important traits for this role are as follows:

An understanding of technical meta data. The Technical Meta Data Analyst must provide the appropriate technical meta data for each of the CRM initiatives. The technical meta data provides the foundation for understanding source systems and building appropriate transformation and integration rules to get the data into the CIF.

An understanding of the CIF architecture. Meta data is integral to the CIF. The Technical Meta Data Analyst must understand the role of meta data in constructing, maintaining, and sustaining the CIF, as well as the interaction of meta data among the components.

Tool knowledge. The Technical Meta Data Analyst must be proficient with the meta data tools. In addition, the Technical Meta Data Analyst must be sufficiently proficient with other tools that create, manage, or disseminate meta data as an ancillary function of the CRM initiative.

The major challenge for this role is retaining interest in meta data. Like documentation, meta data is recognized as important but is sometimes ignored. The Technical Meta Data Analyst must ensure that appropriate resources are dedicated to meta data's creation and maintenance. Note that if a data acquisition tool is purchased, much of the technical meta data is automatically captured, making the maintenance of this information much simpler.

"Getting Information Out" Team

The GIO team must work closely with the business community. This team's ultimate responsibility is to build an environment that is easy to use and understand for both tactical and strategic decision-making. They must communicate freely and openly to the GDI team to ensure that the data warehouse and ODS remain the best sources of data for each of the analyses and interfaces they are responsible for building.

The architectural components that are within the domain of the GIO team are the variety of data marts and the transaction interface to the ODS. The roles and responsibilities of these team members are described in the following section.

End User Specialist

The End User Specialist is responsible for developing and configuring the end-user support environment. He or she also provides appropriate training on the access tools. The End User Specialist's focus is on the ease of use and appropriateness of the access for each data mart or ODS. He or she must understand the business community's requirements to determine the suitable tool (OLAP, mining, and exploration) for the particular capability.

The important traits for this role are as follows:

CRM knowledge. The End User Specialist must have a thorough understanding of the CRM principles and goals in order to create a supportive CRM environment.

An understanding of the CIF architecture. The End User Specialist must understand the role of the CIF and be able to effectively develop the end-user applications in the appropriate components. Understanding how the CIF components will be used in CRM activities is crucial to creating a proper atmosphere for successful CRM.

Tool knowledge. The End User Specialist must be proficient with the end-user access tools.

Technical knowledge. The End User Specialist needs to be proficient with the target technological environment.

The major challenge of this role is meeting expectations. The end users can be very demanding in terms of performance and flexibility. The End User Specialist needs to ensure that expectations are appropriately set and then needs to meet them.

Information Delivery Developer

The Information Delivery Developer is responsible for developing the processes for filtering, formatting, and delivering data from the data warehouse into the data marts and from the ODS into its transactional interface.

The important traits for this role are as follows:

A solid understanding of the CRM applications. The Information Delivery Developer must deliver the data or the interface with the appropriate understanding of how it will be used in the various CRM initiatives.

A strong understanding of the data delivery and the transactional interface layer of the CIF. The Information Delivery Developer is designing and building both of these layers.

Tool knowledge. The Information Delivery Developer must be proficient with the data delivery tools and the methods of accessing the ODS.

Technical knowledge. The Information Delivery Developer needs to be proficient with the target technological environment.

The major challenge of this role is ensuring operating efficiency. The information delivery applications may be complex, and the process, particularly if it is transaction-oriented or requires the daily delivery of historical data, must operate within stringent time constraints and performance requirements. The Information Delivery Developer must design and tune the data delivery applications to meet these service-level objectives.

Business Meta Data Analyst

The Meta Data Analyst on the GIO team is responsible for determining and satisfying the meta data requirements for efficient usage by the business community. Their primary job is to ensure that the people in the organization (both technical and business) who need meta data can access it. Understanding meta data requirements, ensuring that the meta data exists and is correct, and ensuring that people know where to go with questions and issues about meta data are all responsibilities of the meta data analyst.

The important traits for this role are as follows:

An understanding of the CRM program. The Business Meta Data Analyst must understand how the CIF will be used in the CRM program and how each set of users will access the business meta data.

An understanding of the CIF architecture. Meta data is integral to the CIF. The Business Meta Data Analyst must understand the role of meta data and the interaction of meta data among the components.

Tool knowledge. The Business Meta Data Analyst must be proficient with the meta data tools. In addition, the Business Meta Data Analyst must be sufficiently proficient with other tools that create, manage, or disseminate meta data as an ancillary function.

The major challenge for this role is retaining interest in meta data. Like documentation, meta data is recognized as important but is sometimes ignored. The Business Meta Data Analyst must ensure that appropriate resources are dedicated to meta data creation and maintenance.

Business Community End Users

The business community end users need to convey the information content and presentation requirements for the overall CRM program and work with each prototype to refine these requirements. These are also the individuals who will apply this information to obtain business value in the savvy CRM enterprise. Their ongoing communications on the validity of each component are critical to the overall success of the CRM initiative and for ensuring that the end users are satisfied and productive. Different types of business community end users exist, each with its own set of needs:

Tourists. These are executives and managers who typically look for exceptions or review summary trends. They need easy-to-use, intuitive tools that require minimal training. These executives are critical to the overall success of the CRM program. They determine whether or not the CRM initiative is a success. They continually look at key performance indicators to make these crucial decisions.

Farmers. Farmers consist of analysts who perform more in-depth analyses and often need to view the data through paths dictated by the information retrieved. The analyses generally are based on viewing the data using a set of predefined parameters, though the combination of parameters may vary.

Explorers. These are analysts who need to view data in unpredictable ways. These people occasionally need to access the data warehouse directly. They search for unusual or undetected data relationships and form hypotheses from these findings.

Data miners. These are analysts who apply statistical data mining techniques to analyze data. The types of analyses performed and the data-mining techniques or tools employed dictate their access. Miners use these techniques many times to prove or disprove that the hypothesis developed by the explorer is statistically significant.

Operators. Operators are business users who must act upon the intelligence given to them by farmers, explorers, and miners. These resources require instant access to current, fully integrated data to perform their functions and typically use the ODS.

The important traits for this role are as follows:

A broad understanding of CRM. It is for the business community end users that we are building this architecture. They are the resources that will interface with the customer implementing all the CRM functions to create the successful CRM enterprise. Therefore, they must fully appreciate and realize the value of the CRM program.

An understanding of the CIF architecture. The business community end user must understand the role of the CIF and determine how to effectively use it.

Front-line business knowledge. The business community end user directly interfaces with the CIF and must understand how to apply its various components to address business opportunities.

This role's major challenge is the tendency to designate a prototype as production-ready. In order to provide the business community end user with a view of the eventual deliverable, a prototype is often provided. The prototype may not contain the required functionality and quality, and it may also be built using processes that are not designed for regular execution. It is imperative to set the expectations of the business community end users so that they understand the limitations of the prototype as well as the possibility that it may take additional effort and time to develop the production-ready data mart and optimize the sourcing processes from the data warehouse.

Summary

To successfully implement a CRM program for business intelligence and business management, you must define appropriate roles and responsibilities and staff these accordingly. Generally, these roles and responsibilities fall into three groups: program management, getting data in, and getting information out.

As the CRM program advances, a natural evolution of the team structure goes from a single team sharing all roles and responsibilities to that of a central getting data in (GDI) team and one or more getting information out (GIO) teams. The GDI team is generally part of central IT with appropriate input from the business community. This team takes on the role of maintaining and sustaining the parts of the CIF relating to their specific area of interest (the left side of the CIF). These administrative functions were described in Chapter 2 and are briefly described here:

- *Systems management* guarantees that upgrades and new versions of hardware and software are installed with minimal impact on the CIF usage.

- *Data acquisition management* certifies that that data acquisition processes are working at peak efficiency and effectiveness.

- *Enterprise data management* consists of backup and recovery processes, and archival and retrieval procedures. Standard dimensions, calculations, and derivations are created (in the warehouse for use by data delivery), and data is partitioned according to usage.

The GIO teams fall into a combination of line-of-business IT and business community members. They too will evolve into a more administrative role that includes service management, which ensures that the business community requests and service-level agreements (SLAs) are handled properly.

Change management, the last of the administrative functions, must have the cooperation and contribution of both GDI and GIO teams. Without a controlled change environment, the CIF (and indeed CRM) will become chaotic and dysfunctional. Change management is defined in Chapter 2 as:

Confirming that changes made to any part of the CIF are reflected in all appropriate documentation (models, programs, meta data), structures (data warehouse, ODS, data marts) and interfaces (decision support and transaction).

Using the goals described in this chapter, you can determine who should be assigned to the GDI side of the house versus the GIO side. Each team focuses on different aspects of the Corporate Information Factory architecture, but each must rely on the other for optimal effectiveness and efficiency.

The program management team may evolve into a program management office (PMO), formalizing the team within the enterprise. The PMO, however, continues to report to the Steering Committee. Its role remains one that studies enhancements to the CIF components (new data attributes for existing capabilities, the creation of new reports, and the incorporation of new business community members), prioritizes them, and then determines the time frame for the enhancements' incorporation into the CIF.

The roles and responsibilities described in this chapter are necessary for the ultimate success of your CRM strategy. They are needed to implement the seamless integrated customer information environment that promotes the cross-functional business strategies developed for the CRM enterprise.

CHAPTER 6

Developing an Integrated CRM Technology Environment

hapter 2, "The Customer and the Corporate Information Factory (CIF)," introduced the CIF, which integrates the physical components of a complex information systems environment. It provides a clear migration path for moving information in the operational systems into the data warehouse, the operational data store (ODS), and the data marts. An integrated customer information environment is vital to Customer Relationship Management (CRM). But how do we get there?

To achieve a truly integrated customer information environment, we need an approach that is driven by clear business goals. In addition to driving specific objectives, these goals impact the information we need, the business processes, the technological infrastructure, the organizational structure, and the responsiveness that we provide to our customers. The objectives, required information, business processes, technical infrastructure, organization structure, and responsiveness make up six key dimensions that need to be addressed when designing our CRM environment.

This chapter introduces a framework, the Zachman Framework, which considers each of the six dimensions above and provides an approach that does just what we need—it links these six dimensions and helps us understand the information we need as we migrate from the planning activities to implementation. The Zachman Framework will help us build an integrated CRM environment that is driven by business goals and objectives. It will ensure that we consider more than just data and processes in the design of these systems, pushing us to look across all six dimensions during the creation of each CRM technology component. The Zachman Framework provides the glue that relates the development activities, and is described in the first section of this chapter.

After this review of the Zachman Framework, we explain critical business model development rules. The business model describes the environment from a business perspective, independent of system constraints. In the context of CRM technology, the business model incorporates a set of customer information standards that, if used in the construction of all customer-oriented systems, will help to ensure the consistency and integration so critical to CRM strategies. The model development rules discussed in this section apply the Zachman Framework to the creation of the CRM systems and databases. These rules help ensure the consistent view of customer information and help create an environment that will be resilient to change. This chapter concludes with information about developing the models required for each of the layers of the Zachman Framework. Sample contents for some of these models are also provided.

This chapter departs from the previous ones, as it is targeted for information technology (IT) managers and personnel who build the CRM environment. By skimming this chapter, a business manager can also gain an appreciation of the complex issues involved in building a truly integrated environment.

Overview of the Zachman Framework

The Zachman Framework, named for its creator, John A. Zachman, provides an architectured approach to viewing and communicating information about complex systems[1]. These systems are used to create products such as jets, buildings, and machines. Mr. Zachman reasoned that if this approach is useful for developing these items, which must function properly for decades, it should be applicable to application systems such as those used for CRM as well.

The Zachman Framework is represented by a matrix depicting a set of perspectives and a set of dimensions.[2] The perspectives, also called views, represent the information needed by different people involved in the development of a product (in this case, a CRM technology project): the planner, owner, designer, builder, and subcontractor. Table 6.1 relates these views to the roles

---

[1]For additional information, see *Data Stores, Data Warehousing, and the Zachman Framework: Managing Enterprise Knowledge* by W. H. Inmon, John A. Zachman, and Jonathan G. Geiger (McGraw-Hill, 1997).

[2]The term dimensions, as used in conjunction with the Zachman Framework, is not related to the use of the term in conjunction with a star schema.

Table 6.1 CRM Roles

FRAMEWORK DIMENSION	PROJECT ROLE
Planner	Business Sponsor, Technical Sponsor
Owner	Business Analyst, Data Steward, End User
Designer	Data Modeler, Systems Analyst, Architect
Builder	Developer, Database Administrator
Subcontractor	Developer, Database Administrator working on a module or database portion independent of the system into which it will be placed

typically involved in a CRM initiative (Chapter 5, "Getting Underway," provides detailed information about each of these roles).

The dimensions, which are also called abstractions, represent the six different aspects of the product's environment: the data, functions, locations, people, times, and motivations. In the chapter introduction, we provided examples for each of these:

- Required information is an example of data
- Business processes are addressed by functions
- The technical infrastructure is an instance of locations
- Organization structure represents people
- Responsiveness is an indication of times
- Objectives are within the motivations dimension

A matrix (see Figure 6.1) is often used to depict the Framework, with the perspectives appearing as rows and the dimensions appearing as columns. The cell at the intersection point of each row and column provides an isolated representation of the way someone views the product (that person's perspective) for a particular aspect (or dimension) of the product. This approach enables the business representative or developer to focus on a part in isolation while also being able to see how it fits into the whole. For example, the physical schema in the fourth row of the first column of Figure 6.1 represents the builder's view of the data dimension.

Each of the perspectives has a different view of the product and is subject to a different set of constraints (see Rule 4 in the following section, "Zachman Framework Rules"). Table 6.2 summarizes a CRM context by highlighting the way data is viewed for each perspective and identifying associated constraints.

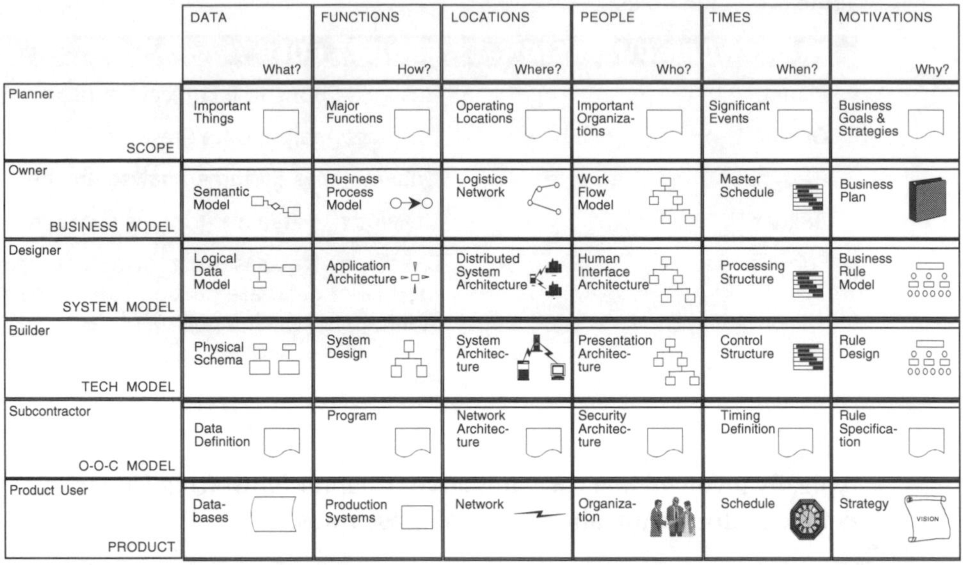

	DATA	FUNCTIONS	LOCATIONS	PEOPLE	TIMES	MOTIVATIONS
	What?	How?	Where?	Who?	When?	Why?
Planner SCOPE	Important Things	Major Functions	Operating Locations	Important Organiza- tions	Significant Events	Business Goals & Strategies
Owner BUSINESS MODEL	Semantic Model	Business Process Model	Logistics Network	Work Flow Model	Master Schedule	Business Plan
Designer SYSTEM MODEL	Logical Data Model	Application Architecture	Distributed System Architecture	Human Interface Architecture	Processing Structure	Business Rule Model
Builder TECH MODEL	Physical Schema	System Design	System Architec- ture	Presentation Architec- ture	Control Structure	Rule Design
Subcontractor O-O-C MODEL	Data Definition	Program	Network Architec- ture	Security Architec- ture	Timing Definition	Rule Specifica- tion
Product User PRODUCT	Data- bases	Production Systems	Network	Organiza- tion	Schedule	Strategy

Figure 6.1 Zachman Framework.

Table 6.2 Perspectives for CRM Data

PERSPECTIVE	VIEW OF DATA	CONSTRAINT
Planner	Subject areas impacting CRM	Financial and legal restrictions
Owner	Real entities (people, concepts, events, locations, and things) of interest to CRM	Company policies related to customers
Designer	Electronic representation (entities and attributes) of the real entities of interest to CRM	Business and technological environment
Builder	Customer database construction and assembly	Development facilities
Subcontractor	Reusable database or table components	Implementation and integration restrictions

Perspectives are described in Table 6.2 in terms of how they relate to your CRM data.

A good detective seeks answers to six basic questions, or interrogatories, and the Framework is organized into columns, each of which answers one of these questions. The data column addresses "what?"; the functions column addresses "how?"; the locations column addresses "where?"; the people column addresses "who?"; the times column addresses "when?"; and the motivations column addresses "why?". These six columns apply to each of the perspectives or rows. Table 6.3 expands the owner's perspective for CRM to delineate the contents for each of the columns. Expanding the designer's perspective ensures that when we design a system, we look beyond the process model (function) and address the data model (data), the network model (locations), the system users (people), the program schedule dependencies (times), and the business rules (motivations). A similar expansion can be made for each of the other perspectives, and in each case, the expansion ensures that we provide a complete perspective.

The Zachman Framework ensures that the approach to CRM considers all areas. It is governed by a set of rules that has remained constant since its inception over a decade ago and is compatible with any sound development methodology. If you choose to use another guiding framework, be sure that it encompasses all the needed perspectives and dimensions.

Zachman Framework Rules

The Zachman Framework helps to relate all of the CRM dimensions to each other in order to provide us with a synergistic view of our environment. The Framework is governed by a set of seven rules and derives much of its strength from its adherence to these rules.[3] The full set of rules is summarized in Table 6.4.

Table 6.3 Owner Perspective for CRM

ABSTRACTION	INTERROGATORY	CONTENT
Data	What?	Real entities (people, concepts, events, locations, and things) of interest to CRM
Functions	How?	CRM business processes
Locations	Where?	Places where CRM activities, including customer contacts, take place
People	Who?	Organizational units responsible for CRM activities
Times	When?	Schedule dependencies of CRM-related activities
Motivations	Why?	CRM business plan

[3]For additional information, see "Extending and Formalizing the Framework for Information Systems Architecture" by Sowa and Zachman (*IBM Systems Journal*, 31:3, 1992).

Table 6.4 Zachman Framework Rules

RULE NUMBER	RULE NAME	RULE
1	Column Importance	The order of the columns is not important.
2	Column Simplicity	Each column has a simple meta model.
3	Column Uniqueness	Each column's meta model is unique.
4	Perspective Uniqueness	Each perspective represents a unique view.
5	Cell Uniqueness	Each cell is unique.
6	Column Necessity	All columns are needed for a complete perspective.
7	Logic Recursiveness	The logic is recursive.

CRM is an enterprise-wide initiative. The Framework and its governing rules ensure that all of the relevant information is considered when building the database and supporting systems for CRM. Adherence to these rules will provide companies initiating a CRM initiative with a strong foundation for growth and expansion. The remainder of this section reviews each rule in detail and provides definitions and explanations for how to use each in the context of a CRM initiative.

Rule 1: The Order of the Columns Is Not Important

The order of the columns that appear in the matrix in Figure 6.1 does *not* imply anything about their importance or the sequence in which they should be addressed. The priority and sequence is dictated by the methodology that governs the development of the system or product. Figure 6.2 displays another way the Framework could have been represented. The alternative representation of the Framework presented in Figure 6.2 is also a valid way to approach a CRM initiative.

The implication of this rule to CRM systems is that we need to recognize that the sequence by which we address each of the six dimensions—data, functions, locations, people, times, and motivations—is dictated by our chosen methodology. For example, a data-driven approach dictates that we address the data first, while the process-driven approach dictates that we address the functions first. Both approaches are valid and both fit within the Framework. When we develop the methodology we use for our CRM initiative, we determine the sequence, and any sequence is consistent with the Framework.

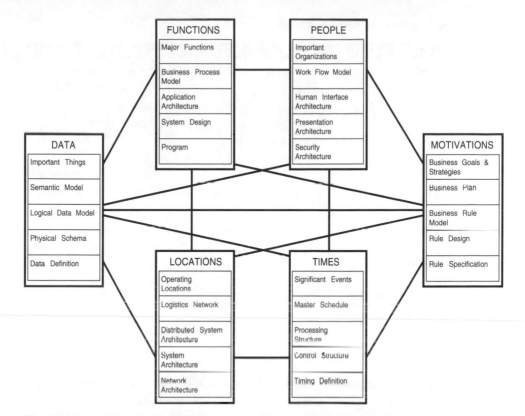

Figure 6.2 An alternative representation of the Zachman Framework.

Rule 2: Each Column Has a Simple Meta Model

As we explained earlier, each column answers one of the six interrogatives of what, how, where, who, when, and why. The basic structure, or meta model, of each set of answers is the same. Regardless of the perspective, all of the answers to what are represented by two entities that are linked by a relationship.

The items represented by entity and relationship change as we move from one row to another. In the owner's view, the entity is a business entity and the relationship is a business rule; in the designer's view, the entity is a data entity and the relationship is a data relationship; and in the builder's view (for a relational database), the entity is a row and the relationship is a key. Table 6.5 displays the meta model for each of the six columns. An example, using the owner's perspective, is provided for each meta model.

Table 6.5   Column Meta Models

INTERROGATORY	BASIC MODEL	EXAMPLE (OWNER'S VIEW)
What?	Entity, Relationship, Entity	Entity = Business Entity; Relationship = Business Rule
How?	Process, Input/Output, Process	Process = Business Process; Input/Output = Business Resources
Where?	Node, Line, Node	Node = Business Location; Line = Business Linkage
Who?	Agent, Work, Agent	Agent = Organizational Unit; Work = Work Product
When?	Time, Cycle, Time	Time = Business Event; Cycle = Business Cycle
Why?	End, Means, End	End = Business Objective; Means = Strategy

To picture this meta model, think about the entity relationship diagram that is commonly used for the data model. This diagram consists of entities joined together by relationships. Similarly, the data flow diagram used for the process model consists of business processes with an indication of the data flowing in and out of them.

The implication of this rule to the customer ODS (see Chapter 10, "Facilitating Customer Touches with the Customer ODS," for a detailed description of capabilities included in the customer ODS) or any other database we use for CRM is that we must use the same meta model during each of the stages of its development. For the data column (what?), at the owner's view, we relate the business entities to each other. For example, we may relate a customer to a product using a relationship of "acquires." As we design our database, the meta model stays the same. The entity transforms from being the real customer to being the electronic representation of that customer, and the relationship becomes the data relationship. The meta model is preserved as we move onto construction (the builder's perspective). For the builder, the electronic representation transforms into the physical schema, which, for a relational database, is the table and row, and the data relationship transforms to the referential integrity provided by the foreign key relationships. Using the same meta model as we progress through the development process ensures that the database we produce is consistent with the rules that are used to govern the business.

Rule 3: Each Column's Meta Model Is Unique

Rule 2 establishes a meta model for each column, and Rule 3 indicates that each of the column meta models is unique. This rule emphasizes the need to understand the bounds of each perspective and not to commingle aspects that should be independent.

Within CRM, we are concerned with marketing in two ways: as a business function and as a business unit. When these are used interchangeably, a common tendency is to build systems that are dependent on the organizational structure. We learned earlier (in Chapter 4, "Are You Ready? Tuning the Organization for CRM") that the organization structure may need to change as we implement CRM. By making sure that we look at the marketing function independent of the Marketing Department, we are more likely to build a system that will be able to evolve as your organizational responsibilities change.

Communicating the difference between the functions and the organizational units is difficult. Instead of naming both the function and the organizational unit "Marketing," consider naming the function "Marketing" and the organizational unit "Marketing Department." The distinction is small, but with this minor change, the Marketing Department will not be confused for the marketing function.

A matrix then can be developed to relate the organizational units to the functions or processes. (A similar matrix can be used to relate any single dimension to any other dimension.) Each set of relationships that is developed using this type of matrix has governing rules. A CRUD matrix is a common way of relating entities and processes. With such a matrix, we quickly identify the processes that create (C), read (R), update (U), or delete (D) each entity. For example, using a CRUD matrix, such as the one in Figure 6.3, that relates entities and processes, we know that:

- Each process should perform at least one activity on at least one entity. (Otherwise, why include it within our scope?) In Figure 6.3, Process 4 and Process 8 are either outside of our scope or perform activities on entities that have not yet been identified.

- Each entity should have at least one process (and ideally only one process) that creates it. When more than one process creates it, we are alerted to a potential redundancy. If no process creates it, it cannot exist. In Figure 6.3, Entity 3 is only read, and Entity 2 is only updated, deleted, or read. The processes that create these entities are clearly missing. Entity 1 is created by two processes. Care must be taken to avoid inconsistencies.

- Each entity should have at least one process (and ideally only one process) that updates it. When more than one process updates it, we are alerted to a potential redundancy. If no process updates it, it cannot change once created. In Figure 6.3, Entity 3 is only read. The process that updates it is clearly missing. Entity 1 is updated by two processes, and Entity 4 is updated by three processes. Care must be taken to avoid inconsistencies.

- Each entity should have at least one process (and ideally only one process) that deletes it. When more than one process deletes it, we are alerted to a potential redundancy. If no process deletes it, it can never be eradicated. In Figure 6.3, Entity 3 is only read. The process that deletes it is clearly missing. Entity 1 is deleted by two processes, and Entity 4 is deleted by three processes. Care must be taken to avoid inconsistencies.

- Each entity should have at least one process that reads it. (Otherwise, why include it within our scope?) In Figure 6.3, Entity 1 is never read. Either we are not concerned with this entity or we need to include the processes that read it.

A matrix can also be developed to relate the organizational units to the entities. That matrix would show which organizational units are responsible for which pieces of data. As we get into the data stewardship responsibilities that are explained later in this chapter, this would help determine the decision-makers for each set of data.

Entity / Process	Entity 1	Entity 2	Entity 3	Entity 4
Process 1	CUD	R	R	CRUD
Process 2		RUD	R	UD
Process 3	CUD	R	R	UD
Process 4				
Process 5		R	R	R
Process 6		R	R	R
Process 7		R	R	R
Process 8				
Process 9		R	R	R
Process 10		R	R	R

C = Create, R = Read, U = Update, D = Delete

Figure 6.3 A process-to-entity matrix.

Other matrices can also be developed. In each case, the matrix should relate one dimension of the Zachman Framework to another, being careful to remain within one perspective (or row). For example, although it would be appropriate to relate the business processes to the entities (the owner's perspective), and the systems to the tables (the builder's perspective), it would not be appropriate to relate the business processes to the tables directly.

Rule 4: Each Perspective Represents a Unique View

Each of the perspectives, represented by the rows in the matrix shown in Figure 6.1, provides a unique view and is governed by a unique set of constraints. Figure 6.4 shows these constraints.

- The business sponsor, in the role of the planner, addresses the scope and is governed by financial and regulatory constraints.
- The business analyst, in the role of the owner, describes the real-world product, and he or she is governed by the company's policies and constraints related to product usage.

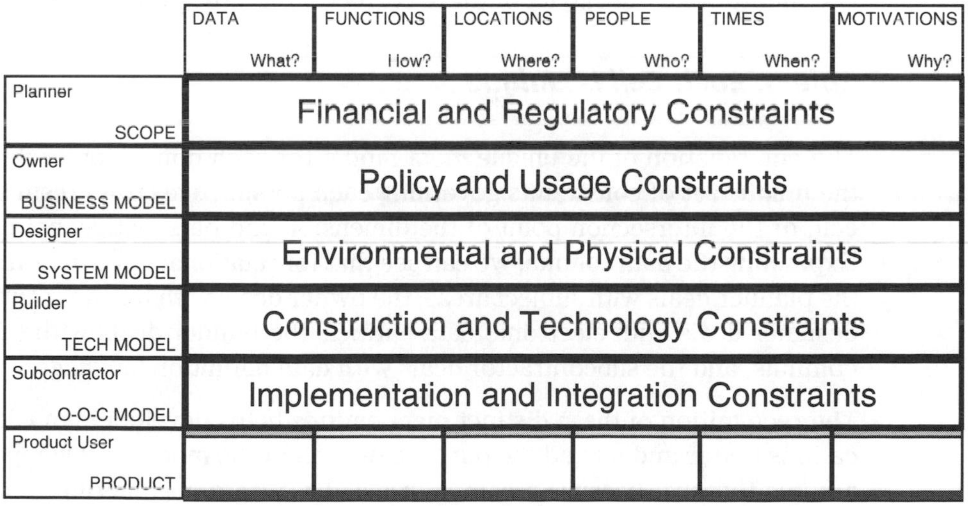

	DATA What?	FUNCTIONS How?	LOCATIONS Where?	PEOPLE Who?	TIMES When?	MOTIVATIONS Why?
Planner SCOPE	Financial and Regulatory Constraints					
Owner BUSINESS MODEL	Policy and Usage Constraints					
Designer SYSTEM MODEL	Environmental and Physical Constraints					
Builder TECH MODEL	Construction and Technology Constraints					
Subcontractor O-O-C MODEL	Implementation and Integration Constraints					
Product User PRODUCT						

Figure 6.4 Perspective constraints.

- The data modeler, in the role of the designer, describes an abstraction of the product for use in its development. The design constraints relate to the business and technological environment.

- The developer, in the role of the builder, describes the construction and assembly of the product, and he or she is governed by the state of the art of the available construction (or development) equipment.

- The developer, in the role of the subcontractor, describes the component construction. This perspective promotes the reuse of common components and is governed by the implementation and integration constraints.

Unlike the dimensions, the perspectives have an order. Each successive perspective depends on its predecessor, as demonstrated by the successive constraints. The scope definition, which is performed first, constrains the area being addressed, and all succeeding work must comply with that constraint.

The actual systems to support CRM are developed in the builder and subcontractor perspectives. For these to truly meet the enterprise's needs, the designer perspective, consisting of the set of system models, must exist. These system models should be based on the business models developed in the owner perspective, and these, in turn, should reflect the planner perspective as represented by the scope definition and the list of things that are important to the enterprise. The different types of models are defined later in this chapter, and the model relationships shown in Figure 6.5 demonstrate these dependencies.

The feedback loop in Figure 6.5 is also important. Sometimes errors are discovered in the physical database and people are tempted merely to correct the database. The return (upwards-facing) arrows emphasize the need to assess and incorporate the impact of these corrections on the preceding models.

Rule 5: Each Cell Is Unique

The combination of the unique meta model for each dimension (column) and the unique set of constraints governing each perspective (row) results in each cell, or the intersection point of the dimension and perspective, being unique. Expanding the data column, we can see that for relational information systems, the planner deals with subject areas, the owner deals with business entities, the designer deals with electronic data entities, the builder deals with tables and columns, and the subcontractor deals with data definition language.

The recognition of these distinct meta entities helps developers of CRM applications better understand the purpose of each of the models. Developers often assume that just because a computer-aided software engineering (CASE) tool provides a logical and physical view of a model, they truly have two different

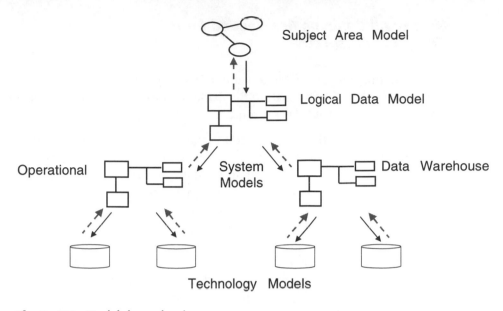

Subject Area Model

Logical Data Model

Operational

System
Models

Data Warehouse

Technology Models

Figure 6.5 Model dependencies.

models. The Zachman Framework tells us that we should have distinct models in row 3 (designer) and row 4 (builder). With some CASE tools, what we have is two representations of the same model and not two separate models. When the database administrator tunes the physical model to improve performance in a specific physical environment, the result becomes the technology model. When this happens, however, the system model is no longer technology-independent, and it becomes a view of the technology model. The system model is lost.

Ideally, each of the models should be maintained. In reality, companies need to deal with the available tools and evaluate the risk of losing the system model. If the CRM applications will be on a single platform and this platform is likely to be stable over time, the risk may be minimal. If multiple platforms will be used, or if the platform is expected to change, companies should consider using repositories or manually maintaining both the system and technology models so that they can gain leverage from the system model across multiple installations. Manual maintenance of these models is prone to error, and periodic model comparisons should be performed to ensure that the model differences are solely due to the technology differences.

Rule 6: All Columns Are Needed for a Complete Perspective

Each column is a part, or dimension, of a complete view. A complete perspective consists of a full row within the Zachman Framework matrix, and each column in that row must be represented.

The implication of this rule to CRM is that we need to consider all aspects of the relationship when dealing with our customers. It is not sufficient to just consolidate the customer information (data) to form a single view of the customer. From the customer's perspective, we also need to consolidate the way we view our processes so that our systems reflect this view and the customer is not hampered by our technically driven decisions concerning system design. The same applies to locations (customers should not be impacted by the physical location of the customer service facility, nor the location of the actual data), times (if a customer has several financial obligations to us, for example, we should be able to consolidate the payment due date information), people (customers should not be negatively impacted by our internal organizational structure), and motivations (the business rules need to support CRM). All six of these dimensions must be addressed in an effective CRM initiative.

The information engineering emphasis during the 1970s and 1980s influenced the development of numerous tools (CASE tools, for example) that dealt with the data and function columns. The major tools available for the remaining columns are traditional drawing, word processing, and scheduling tools. Although word processing software provides a means of documenting the information relating to motivations, for example, the documentation is not well integrated into the process or the data models that are developed using CASE tools. When we develop our meta data strategy, we need to address collecting meta data for each of the six abstractions. Figure 6.6 delineates the models that exist to represent each of the six dimensions for creating the complete designer view.

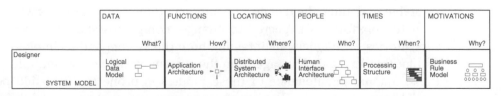

	DATA	FUNCTIONS	LOCATIONS	PEOPLE	TIMES	MOTIVATIONS
	What?	How?	Where?	Who?	When?	Why?
Designer SYSTEM MODEL	Logical Data Model	Application Architecture	Distributed System Architecture	Human Interface Architecture	Processing Structure	Business Rule Model

Figure 6.6 Six system models.

Rule 7: The Logic Is Recursive

The Framework logic establishes the different perspectives and the relationships among them. The aspect of the recursiveness that is most applicable to CRM is that the Framework can be used to describe an existing system as well as variants (an "as is" view and a "to be" view) of potential replacement systems. During the development of a CRM program, several alternatives might be considered. Often, these will be considered at a high level (a planner's perspective) to determine their viability. Some might be pursued in greater detail (an owner's perspective). At this level, procedures would be developed and a pilot without support of new information systems might be pursued. Once information systems enter the picture, the development of prototypes or final systems can be pursued by creating the appropriate models and products represented by the succeeding perspectives.

Business Model Development Rules

The Zachman Framework contains 30 cells in the top five rows, and a model can be used to describe each cell. These models are essential for any application that needs to provide an enterprise perspective and needs to be resilient to the changing business environment. CRM technology initiatives are such applications. Failure to consider each of the models entails a risk. Sometimes, the value of getting something implemented is worth the risk. The Framework helps us by ensuring that the acceptance of the risk is a conscious decision. For example, if we go straight to the physical database design (row four) without first developing the business data model (row two) and system data model (row three), it should not come as a surprise to us later if the implemented database does not match the business.

The business model represents the way the business operates and provides the focal point for the models that follow. It resides in the second row of the Framework and is subject only to financial, regulatory, policy, and business usage constraints. The physical and technology constraints are introduced in the subsequent models (refer to Figure 6.5.) The sixth rule governing the Zachman Framework tells us that each dimension must be represented in the business model to provide us with a complete view. Hence, the business model actually consists of six distinct models, each representing the data, processes, locations, people, times, or motivations, as shown in Figure 6.7. In this section, we will be referencing the business data model and business process model. Similar references could be made to the other four business model components.

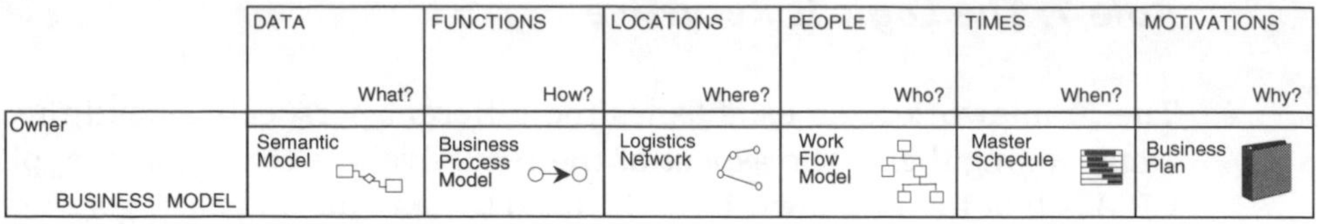

	DATA	FUNCTIONS	LOCATIONS	PEOPLE	TIMES	MOTIVATIONS
	What?	How?	Where?	Who?	When?	Why?
Owner BUSINESS MODEL	Semantic Model	Business Process Model	Logistics Network	Work Flow Model	Master Schedule	Business Plan

Figure 6.7 Business model components.

To help you with your development activities, we are introducing a few simple development rules pertaining to this model that take the concepts promoted by the Framework and bring them into practice. These rules are as follows:

- Only one business model exists.
- All business model components must be defined.
- An item may appear only once within the business model.

Many of the problems that exist with our legacy systems can be attributed to not following these simple rules. These problems often manifest themselves as we build the data warehouse. During that process, we must resolve anomalies in the physical databases that exist because each database is based on the developer's perception of the business model and not on the actual business model. In hindsight, we have learned that we must obey them. As we embark on our CRM journey, let's use foresight. This section expands on these rules with a particular emphasis on the business data model and business process model. The rules apply to the business models for the other four dimensions, locations, times, people, and motivations, and the concepts can be extrapolated to those models as well.

Rule 1: Only One Business Model Exists

The CIF architecture defines the databases of interest and the flow of data among them (refer to Chapter 5 for an explanation of the importance of approaching the CIF as a program). Because the business model is governed by the business and not by the physical systems and databases, it must be developed with a program perspective, and not with the perspective of each individual project.

If a company has several standards, it has no standard, because the sets of standards may conflict with each other. The same can be said for the business model. Because the business model is supposed to depict the enterprise, if an enterprise has more than one business model, it has no business model.

Business Data Model

The business data model, sometimes known as the logical data model, describes the major entities of interest to the company and the relationships between pairs of these entities. Table 6.6 delineates a few of the entities and relationships of interest to CRM which may be included in the business data model.

The key distinction between the business model and the models that are created subsequently in the development process is that the business model represents the enterprise perspective. Because it represents the view of the entire company, only one such model can exist.

We've encountered many systems development projects in which the project leader proudly declares that his or her team developed the "logical" data model for the system. In developing systems to support CRM, we need to be careful not to fall into that trap. Yes, we need a logical model to be part of our foundation, but no, we can't develop our own while ignoring any existing logical model. Otherwise, we end up with a logical model that is nothing more than a view of the physical model for our system. We must be sure that everything that is within the scope of CRM is included in the business data model. If one exists, then we need to review it and make appropriate adjustments. If no business data model exists, then we need to develop the portion of such a model to encompass the area of interest. We should not attempt to develop a full enterprise business model before getting started on our CRM initiative.

There is no such thing as a logical model for a system. The logical model exists for the enterprise. The model that is developed for a system is just that, a system model. In the Zachman Framework, this model falls into the third row, while the business, or logical, model falls into the second row. The major differences between these models are delineated in Table 6.7.

Table 6.6 CRM Entities and Relationships

SOURCE ENTITY	RELATIONSHIP	TARGET ENTITY
Customer	receives	Promotion Material
Customer	acquires	Product
Employee	responds to	Customer Inquiry
Agent	services	Product

Table 6.7   Differences between Logical and System Data Models

CHARACTERISTIC	LOGICAL MODEL	SYSTEM MODEL
Scope	A representation of the information used in an enterprise from a business perspective	A collection of the information used by a system
Quantity	One	One per system
Normalization	Fully (Third normal form) normalized	Denormalized based on system needs
Content	All enterprise entities, attributes, and relationships	Entities, attributes, and relationships within the scope of the system
Perspective	Enterprise	System
Organization	Business rules	Usage

The organizational structure impacts the development of the single view of the enterprise required in the business data model. A successful CRM initiative depends on the company being able to have a single, consistent view of its customers. If the marketing, sales and distribution, and customer service departments each develop its own business data model, then the view of the customer will not be consistent. The Marketing Department will create its view; the Sales and Distribution Department will create its view; and the Customer Service Department will create its view. Although each of these models will accurately represent a particular perspective, the models will differ from each other and will not provide an enterprise view of the customer. The implications of these differences are described subsequently within this chapter.

If the CRM initiative is the responsibility of a single organization, such as the Strategic Operations Organization described in Chapter 4, then the development of the model becomes simpler. If the organizational structure consists of distinct departments, the task becomes more difficult because of the cooperation and compromise that is required to arrive at the enterprise view.

Business Process Model

The business process model identifies and describes the major business functions and the processes within these functions. Table 6.8 delineates a few of the functions and processes of interest to CRM which may be included in the business process model.

Table 6.8 CRM Functions and Processes

FUNCTION	PROCESSES
Channel Management	Identify Emerging Channel, and Monitor Channel Performance
Customer Service	Process Customer Request, Open Customer Account, and Fulfill New Product
Marketing	Develop Direct Marketing Campaign, Execute Direct Marketing Campaign, and Monitor Direct Marketing Campaign
Sales	Conduct Customer Account Review, Establish Sales Team, Maintain Sales Team, and Conduct Sales Pitch

Like the business data model, the business process model is an enterprise-level model. Its existence enables the delineation of each process and function of interest within the company independent of the organizational unit that performs the function. For example, processes within the customer service function may deal with answering customer inquiries. The marketing function may also have such processes. In developing the business process model, the Customer Service Department and Marketing Department need to collaborate so that the process is described for the enterprise. This exercise does more than just build a model on paper. It forces the CRM management team to evaluate each of its processes. In addition to identifying and describing the processes for the model, the synergy could help identify an improved process.

The independent view of the process provides you with a number of benefits. In the Customer Life Cycle described in Chapter 3, "Understanding the Customer Life Cycle (CLC)," we emphasized the importance of the customer touch points. By defining each process once, the customer receives treatment based on the required interaction at each touch point and is not based on the person or department that is providing the service. From a systems perspective, it permits us to develop a series of reusable components to support the business needs. The reusability of these components enhances productivity as well as data quality.

Rule 2: All Business Model Components Must Be Defined

The usability of the model, both for development and for subsequent use by the business community, depends on each item within the model being defined and on the quality of these definitions.

Business Data Model

The business data model consists of entities, attributes, and relationships, represented in pictorial form as an entity-relationship diagram. The usability of the business data model, both for development and for subsequent use by the business community, depends on each entity, attribute, and relationship being defined and on the quality of these definitions.

You would be quite correct if you assumed that "Customer" is one of the entities needed in a CRM application. Customer data is one of the most important sets of data within any company. We suspect that if you asked 10 executives within your company to define "Customer," you would get at least 10 different definitions. (Our definition of customer is provided in Chapter 1, "The Customer Becomes the Center of the Business Universe.") Some of the definitions you may get from the executives include the following:

- The person who buys our product
- The company that leases our product
- The party that acquires our product
- The party that pays for the product
- The party that uses the product
- The party that is considering acquiring the product
- The household in which the product is used
- The agent who helps in the sale of a product

Some of these definitions appear to be the same, but each carries with it a nuance that has significant implications to the users and developers of customer-oriented applications. Some of the subtle distinctions and the problems they present are as follows:

- Four different types of entities are shown as person, company, party, and household. The distinction between person and company greatly impacts the data that is available (for example company name versus salutation, first name, middle name, last name, and name suffix), its representation, its relationships, and so on. The concept of party generalizes some of this information and provides for the entities "Person" and "Company" (or more accurately, the Organization) to be types of the entity "Party" for the purpose of capturing information and relationships that are unique at that level.

- The type of transaction is different. Some definitions assume that the product must be bought, others assume that it must be leased, and still others provide a more generalized form of being acquired. What is not known is whether these distinctions are intentional or just a poor choice of words.

- The concept of consumer (as opposed to the party that pays for the product) is introduced in one definition.

- The concept of people who help in the sale is introduced in one definition.

One way of visualizing the impact of the definition is to think in terms of counting the number of occurrences within an entity. For a typical company, if customers were counted using each of the previous definitions, the total number of customers would be different in each case. Without commonly accepted definitions, we should not be surprised if representatives from the Marketing Department, Sales Department, and Customer Service Department each come to a meeting with a different customer count. For a product such as Microsoft Windows, the Marketing Department and Sales Department have two distinct counts of interest: the number of entities (such as corporate accounts) that buy the product, and the number of people within those companies to whom the product is distributed. The Customer Service Department, on the other hand, is only interested in the customers that it needs to service. If Windows is delivered on a PC and service needs to be provided by the PC vendor, this may not represent a customer to the Customer Service Department.

"The more an organization knows and cares about a particular business entity, the less likely its members are to agree on a common term and meaning for it."[4] If we are to be successful in building CRM systems, we must ensure that common terms are created, that common definitions are adopted, and that these terms and definitions are conveyed to both the people developing your CRM systems and the system users. Only then can we count on the information being accurately portrayed both electronically and in the business setting.

Entity and Attribute Naming Definition Conventions

The rules for naming and defining entities and attributes should be established within each enterprise. Entities and attributes represent business-oriented views and the naming conventions are not limited by physical constraints. This section will describe some of the conventions to consider.

ENTITY NAMING CONVENTIONS

- Each entity should have a unique name.
- The entity name should be in title case (e.g., key words capitalized).

---

[4]Davenport, Thomas H. "Information Behavior: Why We Build Systems That Users Won't Use." *Computerworld*, September 15, 1997, Leadership Series Insert.

- Entity names should be composed of business-oriented terms:
  - Use full, unabbreviated words.
  - Use spaces between words.
  - Use singular nouns.
  - Avoid articles, prepositions and conjunctions.
- The length of the name is not limited. A good entity name would be Bill to Customer. A poor one would be BTC or Bill-to-Cust.

ATTRIBUTE NAMING CONVENTIONS

- Attribute names should contain one or more prime words, zero or more modifiers, and one class word.
  - The prime word describes the item. It is often the same as the name of the entity within which the attribute belongs.
  - The qualifier is a further description of the item.
  - The class word is a description of the type of item.
- Each attribute should have a unique name within an entity. If the same attribute name is used in several entities, it should always have the same definition.
- The attribute name should be in title case.
- Each attribute name should be composed of business-oriented terms:

  - Use full, unabbreviated words.
  - Use spaces between words.
  - Use singular nouns and adjectives.
  - Avoid articles, prepositions, and conjunctions.
  - The length of the name is not limited.

ENTITY AND ATTRIBUTE DEFINITION CONVENTIONS

- Definitions should use consistent formats.
- Definitions should be self-sufficient.
- Definitions should be clear and concise.
- Definitions should not be recursive. A word should not be used to define itself.
- Definitions should be business-oriented.

- Definitions should be mutually exclusive.
- Definitions should be independent of physical system constraints.

Business Process Model

The business process model consists of functions and their dependent processes represented in pictorial form as a function decomposition diagram. (The processes are subsequently decomposed further.) The usability of the business process model, both for development and for subsequent use by the business community, depends on each function and process being defined within the model and on the quality of these definitions.

The rationale for using common terms and definitions is the same as that for the business data model. Only with a common set of terms and definitions can we expect our systems development staff to build the systems that are needed and our business community to effectively use them.

Business Process Model Conventions

The rules of the business process model should be established within each enterprise. Some of the conventions to consider are as follows.

FUNCTION AND PROCESS NAMING CONVENTIONS

- Function names should be gerund verbs.
- Function names should be in upper case.
- Process names should consist of a verb and an object.
- Process names should be in title case.
- Function and process names should be unique.
- Function and process names should be composed of business-oriented terms.
- Use full, unabbreviated words.
- Use spaces between words.
- Avoid articles, prepositions, and conjunctions.
- The length of the name is not limited.

DIAGRAM CONVENTIONS

- Each level should have three to eight functions or processes. This accomplishes two important objectives. It reduces the complexity of the model by limiting the scope of each decomposition layer, and it facilitates printing the function model so that three levels can appear legibly on a page.

- The sequence in which functions and processes appear is inconsequential.

The definition conventions are as follows:

- Definitions should use consistent formats.
- Definitions should be self-sufficient.
- Definitions should be clear and concise.
- Definitions should not be recursive. A word should not be used to define itself.
- Definitions should be business-oriented.
- Definitions should be mutually exclusive.
- Definitions should be independent of physical system constraints.

Rule 3: An Item May Appear Only Once within the Business Model

Within the business model, each item can appear only once. The ramification of breaking this rule is that we will lose our single view of the enterprise.

Business Data Model

Within the business data model, each entity and attribute can appear only once. This rule does more than just avoid something with the same name (such as customer) from being included multiple times. It also precludes two entities that mean the same thing being included in the model. For example, if the definitions for the entities "Customer" and "Account" are the same (and frequently they differ), then both cannot appear in the model. The following are two consequences of an item appearing in the business data model more than once.

If "Customer," for example, is included in the model more than once, for each of its occurrences, a definition will be created, a set of attributes will be defined, and relationships will be established. It is highly unlikely that these will all be identical, and if they are not the same, then we have not actually defined customer for the enterprise.

The second consequence affects our supporting systems. An effective CRM program requires that we have a single view of our customers. If customer information is duplicated in the model, we can fully expect that it will be duplicated in the systems, because the system data models are based on the business data model. When customer information is duplicated within the systems, it is not consolidated, and our ability to get the single view of the customer is significantly hampered.

Business Process Model

This rule applies to the business process model as well. Within the business process model, a function or process may appear only once. A common CRM function is Sales Follow-up. Does this function belong within the higher level function of Sales or Customer Service? The answer is that it doesn't matter as long as it is not placed under both of these higher level functions. It should be placed within the function that makes the most sense to your company. If you place it under both functions, then you will probably define two distinct functions even though only one really exists.

The business process model is not an organization chart, and hence the location within this model does not imply that a particular department is performing the function. Both the Sales Department and the Customer Service Department may perform this function, but the function remains the same (nuances can be addressed within the description of the function). For the business process model to provide a foundation for creating a consistent face to the customer, we need to define and describe the function only once within this model. That definition and description will eventually translate into business procedures and supporting systems.

Another consequence of the distinction between the business process model and the organization model is that the business process model accommodates functions and processes for which multiple organizations are responsible. Examples of these cross-functional activities are described in Chapter 4, "Are You Ready? Tuning the Organization for CRM."

Corollary to Rule 3

A corollary to having each item appear only once in the business models is that every item must appear in the business models. The business data model is the consolidation point for all the data that exists in the application systems, and it provides an enterprise perspective for these items. An element that appears in a system without being present in the business data model is not defined from an enterprise perspective. Without the enterprise perspective, each system establishes the definition for the element, and consistency among systems is not assured.

Similarly, if a system is developed for a process that is not defined in the business process model, we have a technical solution to an unrecognized business process. Without the enterprise perspective, each system's development project implicitly defines business processes, and these processes are unlikely to share common names, definitions, and descriptions. The net result, as John Zachman would say, is that we have "disintegrated" our enterprise.

Models

Ultimately, CRM will be supported by application systems and a customer database. The Zachman Framework delineates a series of models that provides the foundation for the systems and the database. This section explains how to build the models for the processes and data, beginning with the models that support the first row of the Framework. Information about their content is provided to help you get started.

Function Model

The function model depicts the major functions, or groupings of business processes, of interest to the enterprise. In the Zachman Framework, it belongs in the second column of the first row. At the highest level, a function model could consist of the following major functions:

- Customer Relationship Management
- Distribution
- Production
- Resource Management
- Administration

The function model can be decomposed into subfunctions or directly into processes. If the function model begins at a high level with functions such as those previously listed, it should be decomposed into subfunctions first. The decompositions for two of the major functions are as follows:

- Customer Relationship Management
  - Channel Management
  - Customer Service
  - Marketing
  - Sales
- Resource Management
  - Facilities Management
  - Financial Management
  - Human Resource Management
  - Information Management
  - Materials Management

The function model consists of two major components: a pictorial representation and a set of definitions.

Pictorial Representation

The pictorial representation consists of the functions displayed in a hierarchical fashion. The pictorial representation of the function model just described is depicted in Figure 6.8. The figure is structured so that the function of interest is at the second level. In this manner, it is put into perspective with its parallel functions, and its subfunctions can also be presented.

Definitions

A definition for each of the functions is critical so that the developers and business users have a common set of assumptions concerning the meaning, scope,

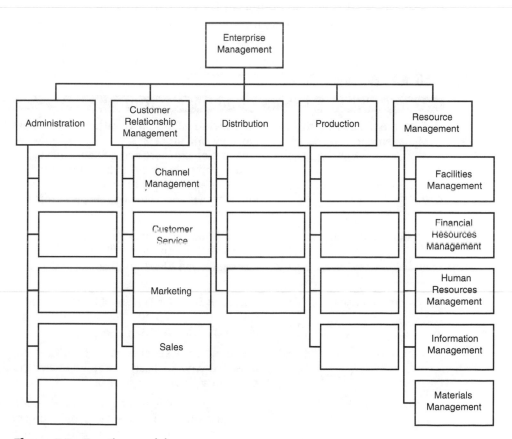

Figure 6.8 Function model.

and implications of each. Because this book is limited to CRM, only the subfunctions for Customer Relationship Management are defined in Table 6.9.

Subject Area Model

The subject area model groups the major categories of data for the enterprise. It provides a valuable communication tool and also helps in organizing the business data model. In the Zachman Framework, it belongs in the first column of the first row. A typical company has 12 to 15 subject areas, some of which are of interest for CRM. As the foundation for the business data model, it provides a map for grouping the data. The subject area model consists of two major components: a pictorial representation and a set of definitions.

Typical Subject Areas

Table 6.10 contains a list of some of the subject areas that are common to many enterprises and a sample definition for each. This list is not intended to be a complete list of subject areas for an enterprise. The inclusion or exclusion of a

Table 6.9 Function Definitions

FUNCTION NAME	FUNCTION DEFINITION
Customer Relationship Management	Customer Relationship Management is the set of functions and processes that align business strategy, organization structure and culture, and customer information and technology so that all customer interactions can be conducted to the long-term satisfaction of the customer and to the benefit and profit of the organization.
Channel Management	Channel Management is the set of functions and processes that coordinate all the activities involved in moving the product from the company to the customer.
Customer Service	Customer Service is the set of functions and processes for interacting in a non-sales capacity with existing or prospective customers.
Marketing	Marketing is the set of activities for identifying prospects who are likely to acquire one or more of the company's products or services.
Sales	Sales is the set of functions and processes for obtaining a customer commitment to acquire one or more of the company's products or services.

Table 6.10   Common Subject Areas

SUBJECT AREA	DEFINITION
Campaigns	Campaigns are organized sets of activities designed to improve customer relationships, the company's community position, or sales.
Channels	Channels are the means by which the enterprise provides offerings to customers.
Customers	Customers are parties that acquire or use products.
Facilities	Facilities are physical places where activities by or on behalf of the enterprise are performed.
Financials	Financials consist of money that is received, retained, or expended by the enterprise.
Human Resources	Human Resources are the people who perform services for the enterprise.
Locations	Locations are the physical and electronic places of interest to the enterprise.
Materials	Materials are the goods and services that are consumed or used by the enterprise in its operation.
Offerings	Offerings are the products and services that the enterprise provides to customers.
Suppliers	Suppliers are organizations, external to the company, that provide materials to the enterprise.

subject area in this list depends on a number for factors. First and foremost, the subject area needs to be commonly viewed as a major grouping of information of interest to the enterprise. Additional factors to consider are that the subject areas should be at approximately the same level of abstraction, that each could include between five and 15 entities, and that the number of subject areas is less than 15.

Subject area names are plural nouns. The rules for defining the subject areas are similar to those for entities. In examining the previous definitions, you may conclude that we violated one of the rules. The definitions for customers, human resources, and suppliers do not appear to be mutually exclusive because the same person may, in fact, be an employee who provides materials to the enterprise and who acquires products from the enterprise.

These definitions are indicative of the relationships that parties such as people and organizations may have with the company. From a purely theoretical point of view, we should define a subject area called Parties, which would consist of organizations and people of interest to the enterprise. Although this solves the theoretical problem, it is difficult to communicate the concept to business people. If we presented a list of potential subject areas to executives and used the generic Parties subject area, we are likely to lose credibility. The business people will quickly notice the absence of customers, and we will be faced with an uphill battle to explain the technical reasons that we decided to portray things in a way that is confusing to business people. This is not the route to success!

Ignoring the fact that customers, human resources, and suppliers are each of the roles of generic Parties, however, creates downstream problems. We could end up with multiple points at which we maintain information about someone who has several relationships with your company. A compromise is to combine the two concepts by using Parties as a subject area and establishing Customers, Human Resources, and Suppliers within that subject area. With this approach, we can selectively present the information in the way that is best received by the audience we are addressing. The diagram presented in Figure 6.9 uses the compromise approach. The use of Parties is further described subsequently in this chapter.

Subject Area Diagram

The subject area diagram is the pictorial representation of the subject areas. It consists of the subject areas themselves and the major relationships between pairs of subject areas. A subject area model for the subjects previously delineated is provided in Figure 6.9.

The Relationship between Major Functions and Subject Areas

Information engineering concepts teach us that a relationship exists between the data and the processes. To assist with application development, that relationship is often represented in the form of a CRUD matrix that shows the relationship between the lowest level of business processes defined in the function/process diagram and the data entities.

The CRUD matrix is valuable for application development, and a similar matrix can be developed at the major function and subject area level to assist with scope definition. In this matrix, the major functions are presented along one axis, and the major subject areas along the other. At the intersection points, notations can be made concerning the type of interaction. Figure 6.10 is an example of such a matrix for just the four subfunctions of Customer Relationship Management, with the intersection points indicating the level of interaction.

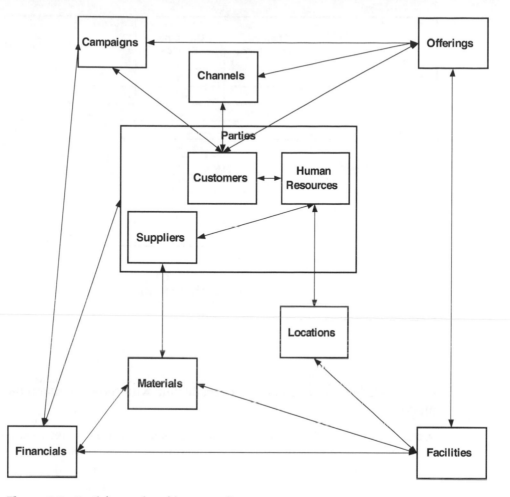

Figure 6.9 Partial generic subject area diagram.

Business Data Model

The subject area model provides a framework for organizing the data of interest. The business data model provides a similar function, but it does so from a different perspective. It describes the major concepts, people, places, events, and things of interest to the enterprise and their interactions, independent of any technological constraints. In the Zachman Framework, the business data model belongs in the first column of the second row. The perspective of the business data model entails entities and attributes, as well as the relationships between pairs of entities. These entities and attributes eventually get represented as tables and columns in the physical databases. The relationship among

Function Subject Area	Channel Management	Customer Service	Marketing	Sales
Campaigns		N	J	J
Channels	J	N	J	J
Customers	J	J	J	J
Facilities				
Financials		N	N	N
Human Resources		J	J	J
Locations	J	J	J	J
Materials				
Offerings	N	N	N	N
Suppliers	N	N	N	N

J = Major; N = Minor

Figure 6.10 Function to subject area matrix.

the models is described in the section dealing with the system and technology models.

A starter business data model that includes some of the entities needed to support CRM is provided in this section. Within some industries, more complete models are also available. Generic models can be used to speed up your model's creation. Each company using a starter model should expect to modify it to suit its particular environment. Before developing the full model, a few areas deserve special attention.

Parties

The business view of parties,[5] at the subject area level, is best provided by segregating the customers, human resources, and suppliers and treating them as separate subject areas. Due to the downstream implications, combining these as parties for purposes of model development has many advantages. As previously stated, parties are organizations and people of interest to the enterprise.

[5]For additional information on parties, see *Data Model Resource Book*, by Len Silverston (John Wiley & Sons, 2001).

Parties encompasses all persons and organizations, regardless of their relationship with the enterprise. Using this subject area facilitates capturing generic information about an organization once and applying it wherever it is needed. For example, if a company can be a supplier and a customer, the name and address information of the company is captured within Organization, and only the information specific to each role (such as supplier and customer) is captured at the role level.

One of the complexities organizations face is finding a way to capture the information about a customer in one place. This task is daunting enough, but what if the customer is also an employee? What if it is also a supplier? Most enterprises have distinct systems for managing customers, employees, and suppliers. If one person were simultaneously a customer, employee, and supplier, that person would likely be represented in three distinct databases. Further, because of the typical myopic approach of systems development, these systems would be unlikely to share data about the individual.

From a modeling perspective, using a generic parties concept helps resolve the situation. A party is any person or organization of interest to the enterprise. Its two subentities (see Figure 6.11), as implied by the definition, are Person and Organization. Table 6.11 provides definitions for the two subentities.

The party concept enables enterprises to view the individual as a person first and as a customer, employee, or supplier second. By first viewing the individual as a person, information about the person that is not dependent on that person's role as a company representative (employee or agent), customer, or supplier can be consolidated. Information specific to the person as a customer

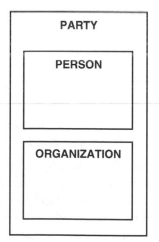

Figure 6.11 Party, Organization, and Person.

Table 6.11 Party Subentities

ENTITY	DEFINITION	EXAMPLE
Person	A Person is an individual of interest to the enterprise.	
Organization	An Organization is a group of people or a legal entity of interest to the enterprise.	

would be contained within the customer entity, information specific to the person as an employee would be captured within the employee entity, and information specific to the person as a supplier would exist within the supplier entity. Table 6.12 identifies information that pertains to the party, independent of its being a person or organization, and to the person and organization, independent of its role.

Figure 6.12 relates Party to Party Role. Using the subentity concept, Customer can be reclassified into Buying Customer and Using Customer, for example, if these are the significant distinctions.

Having refined the party relationships, we now focus on the customer, and in this capacity, we need to refer back to the definition of customer from Chapter 1. In that chapter, we define customer as "A party who is involved in the acquisition and use of the company's goods and services." Several different types of customers exist. One of the distinctions deals with the culmination of the acquisition. Here we distinguish between a customer as one who has already acquired the product and a prospect as one who has not. Although it's very common for a customer and prospect to be one and the same (as in a cross-selling opportunity), through the use of the party and customer roles, we provide a structure for capturing the common data only once.

Locations

Locations provide another useful means of coordinating common information. Many systems have been built with address information being included within the customer record. This inclusion presents a number of problems:

Customers often have more than one address. For example, the customer may have a billing address, a service address, a delivery address, an emergency contact address, and so on. If the address is included in the customer record, then the record needs to be expanded to account for the worst-case scenario in terms of the number of addresses. Further, a service address may be a postal address for some customers and a geographically based address

Table 6.12 Role-Independent Attributes

ENTITY	ATTRIBUTE
Party	Identifier
	Tax Identifier Number
	Annual Income
Organization	Name
	D and B Number
	Industry Code (derived through a foreign key relationship)
	Establishment Date
Person	Last Name
	First Name
	Gender
	Birth Date

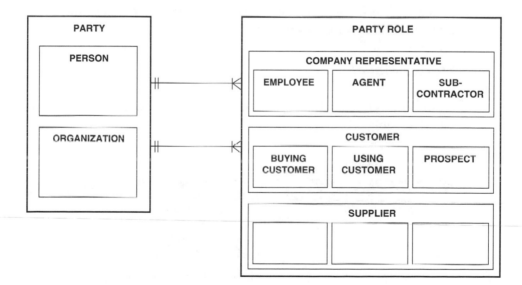

Figure 6.12 Parties and roles.

for others. This approach adds unnecessary complexity to the model and wastes a significant amount of storage space.

Customers have more than one type of location. In today's business environment, customers have both physical (geographically based) addresses and electronic addresses. Just as the customer may have multiple physical addresses, the customer may have multiple types of electronic addresses and multiple instances of each of these. Examples include e-mail, telephone, facsimile, and pager.

Within the context of CRM, it is often important to know where a contact with the customer transpires. If the location is embedded within the customer record, then the location of the contact is much more difficult to capture. Further, the contact may be made at a location that is not typically associated with the customer.

The location information therefore should be segregated, and this is done through the Locations subject area. The major fundamental entities are Electronic Location, Geographic Location, and Geographic Area. The definitions for these entities are provided in Table 6.13.

The foregoing discussion described the relationship between the customer and the location. In reality, the relationship is independent of the party role, and hence it is between Party and Location. Figure 6.13 portrays the Location entities and their relationship to Party.

Starter Model

A starter model for CRM is presented in Figure 6.14. Entity definitions are provided in Table 6.14.

Table 6.13 Location Entities

ENTITY	DEFINITION
Electronic Location	An Electronic Location is the address at which an electronic message may be sent or received. Examples include e-mail addresses, telephone addresses, and network IP addresses.
Geographic Location	A Geographic Location is a physical point of interest on the earth. Examples include mailing addresses, service addresses, and latitude and longitude locations.
Geographic Area	A Geographic Area is a region of interest on the earth. Examples include geopolitical areas (such as city or country), the area encompassed by a lake, and the area encompassed by a piece of property of interest.

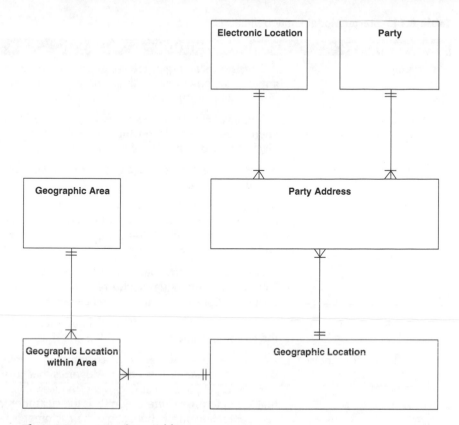

Figure 6.13 Location entities.

System and Technology Data Model

The system data model is the technology-independent model of the data needed to support a particular system. In the Zachman Framework, it belongs in the first column of the third row. The system data model must be consistent with the business data model. It typically consists of a subset of the business data model that is based on the data required to support a particular system. For example, if we were developing a system to handle wholesale customers, we would create a system data model that would deal only with these customers and not with the retail customers. Due to the relationship between the system data model and the business data model, we are assured that the business rules of the enterprise will be preserved.

The technology data model is the technology-dependent model of the data needed to support a particular system. In the Zachman Framework, it belongs

Table 6.14 Starter Model Entity Definitions

ENTITY NAME	ENTITY DEFINITION
Campaign	A Campaign is an organized set of activities designed to improve customer relationships, the enterprise's community position, or the sales of its offerings.
Campaign Event	A Campaign Event is a specific activity designed to improve customer relationships, the enterprise's community position, or the sales of its offerings.
Channel	A Channel is a means by which the enterprise contacts or provides offerings to customers.
Company Representative	A Company Representative is a person or organization that is acting on behalf of the enterprise when dealing with a customer. Subentities include Agent, Employee, and Subcontractor.
Customer	A Customer is a party that acquires or uses an offering. This includes subentities such as Prospect, Using Customer/Consumer, and Buying Customer.
Customer Account	A Customer Account is the financial information about the customer's interactions with the enterprise.
Customer in Household	A Customer in household is the customer in its role as part of a household. This entity recognizes that customers may participate in several (extended) households, and that the enterprise's interaction with the customer may vary depending on the household the customer is representing.
Customer Segment	A Customer Segment is a grouping of customers of interest to the enterprise.
Customer Touch	A Customer Touch is an interaction between the customer and the enterprise. Subentities include the Sales Transaction, Service Request, Customer Complaint, and e-Mail Marketing Message.
Customer Touch Location	A Customer Touch location is the electronic and/or geographic location at which the customer touch takes place.
Demographic	A Demographic is a characteristic about a customer that is of interest to the enterprise.
Demographic Set	A Demographic Set is a grouping of customer characteristics that is of interest to the enterprise.
Electronic Location	An Electronic Location is an electronic address. Its subentities include an e-Mail Address, Phone Number, and Fax Number.

continues

Table 6.14 Starter Model Entity Definitions (continued)

ENTITY NAME	ENTITY DEFINITION
Geographic Area	A Geographic Area is a bounded set of geographic locations. Subentities include a Geopolitical Area (city or country), Sales Area, and Demographic Area.
Geographic Location	A Geographic Location is a physical place.
Household	A Household is a grouping of one or more customers.
Incentive	An Incentive is an inducement provided to a customer to influence a particular action.
Location	A Location is a physical or electronic place of interest to the enterprise.
Medium	A Medium is a method for communicating a message. Medium types include newspaper advertisements, e-mail messages, and messages sent by regular mail.
Message	A Message is the content of the communication the enterprise is transmitting to the customer.
Offering	An Offering is a product or service that the enterprise provides to customers.

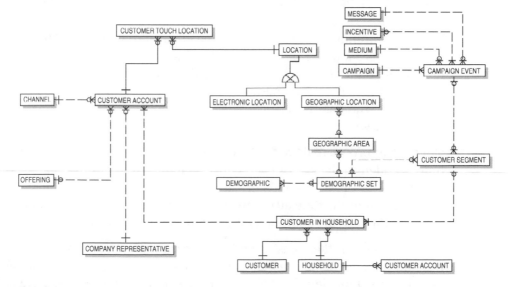

Figure 6.14 Starter data model.

in the first column of the fourth row. Occasionally, the same system resides on multiple platforms. The technology data model begins with the system data model and then applies changes needed to help the system perform on the selected platform. We could, for example, have a data warehouse that resides concurrently at headquarters on a mainframe computer using DB2, at a regional office (possibly with only that region's data) on a Unix server using Oracle, and at a district office (possibly with only that district's data) on a Windows 2000 server using SQL Server as the database management system. The three instances would require three technology data models, but only one system data model. The relationships among the different types of models are presented in Figure 6.5.

Three sets of system data models are of interest for CRM.

Operational System Models

The first is the set of data models for the operational systems that contribute to CRM processes. In the context of the Corporate Information Factory, these were described as the systems supporting business operations. The model is created by determining the data needed to support that system's scope. Subsequently, it is transformed to a technology data model that considers the performance implications.

Data Warehouse Model

The data warehouse is also based on the business data model. The first step in creating this model is the same as the first step for the operational system model; the data of interest is selected. For the operational systems, the data selected is based on the operational activities being performed. For the data warehouse, the data is selected based on its need to meet strategic decision support activities.

Once the appropriate data is selected, the systems data model is reviewed, and time is added to the key of each entity. The inclusion of time enables the data warehouse to provide the historical perspective needed for strategic analysis. The addition of the time attribute creates some data model anomalies that get resolved through the addition of associative entities and attributive entities.

The third step in the transformation process is the addition of derived data. Derived data elements are calculated fields that are defined so that all users have a consistent view. In step four, we ensure that the level of granularity, or detail, can support the analysis that needs to be performed.

The next four steps entail adding summary data to enhance the access to information, merging tables together (if usage dictates and if they share common keys), adding arrays if appropriate, and segregating data based on its stability.

Once the system data model for the data warehouse is completed, additional measures are taken to optimize performance. These measures include replicating fields, partitioning the data, adjusting indices, and so on. Figure 6.15 shows the transformations leading to the data warehouse model.

Data Mart Models

The data mart model is designed to help the end users get to the data, and the dimensional model is the most popular approach. Other approaches also need to be considered to reduce the overall cost of ownership of the data warehouse or to support specific needs.

The dimensional model supports many of the CRM requirements. The first step in the dimensional modeling process is to distill the business questions and to identify the data elements, including the metrics, or facts, that will be needed. The dimensions are then refined by adding attributes, incorporating hierarchies, and

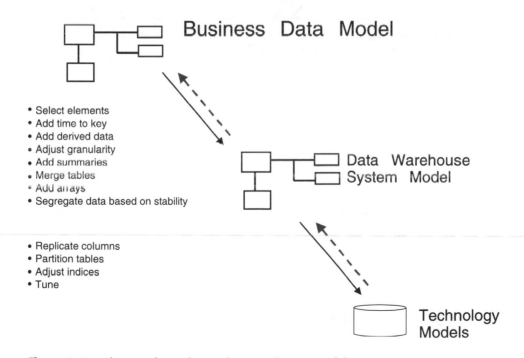

Figure 6.15 The transformation to data warehouse model.

ensuring that the keys are appropriate. If multiple data marts are needed, opportunities to reuse dimensions are pursued to promote consistency and improve the efficiency of the data delivery process. Additional steps address the history requirements of the dimensions as well as opportunities to improve performance by normalizing the dimensions. Figure 6.16 shows the steps leading to the data mart model.

For many statistical, data mining, or exploratory applications, the dimensional model has a fundamental flaw. These applications require that the data be completely without bias, and that no predefined relationships exist. The process of creating the dimensional model often involves filters that introduce a bias, and the star schema is created by predefining relationships. Special technologies are specifically aimed at meeting these needs, and the design of the data mart needs to consider both the business requirements and the technology being deployed.[6]

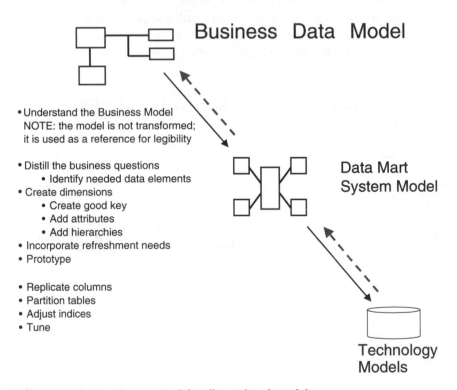

Figure 6.16 Development of the dimensional model.

[6]For additional information, see *Exploration Warehousing* by W. H. Inmon, Claudia Imhoff, and R. Terdeman (John Wiley & Sons, 2000).

Managed query environments and certain ad hoc requirements, while they can be supported by the dimensional model, may not require such a model. The needs in this environment can often be met with a denormalized or normalized structure aimed at the stated business requirements. Figure 6.17 depicts some of the criteria for selecting the data mart model structure.[7]

Summary

The Corporate Information Factory provides the framework for a consolidated set of information to support CRM. The information that flows through the CIF includes data about customers and their interaction with the organization. The use of business process and data models provides a common set of definitions for the activities and information groupings. It also provides an enterprise perspective of these groupings. With that perspective, individual systems can be developed to focus on individual CRM components, with the assurance that the data represented by these systems can be shared by other systems.

Development efforts are often limited in scope based on financial, political, or scheduling constraints. The Zachman Framework provides us with a background for approaching our CRM initiative from an enterprise perspective.

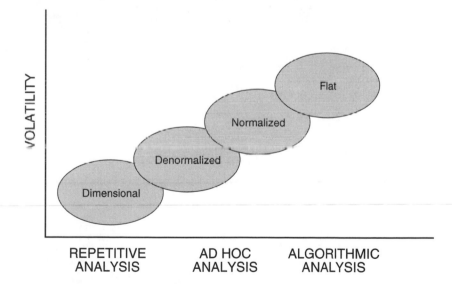

Figure 6.17 Data mart structure options.

[7]From "If the Star Fits—Part 1 and 2" by Claudia Imhoff and John Ladley, *DMReview*, April–May 2000.

Using the Framework, we can gain a better understanding of the impact of the limited scope and the associated risks. As we develop our related systems and databases, we need to observe a few fundamental business model development rules, such as the ones delineated in this chapter. Make sure that you maintain a set of semantically consistent models that encompass all of the perspectives, from planner to builder and subcontractor.

The systems and databases are developed through an evolution of the governing models. For the customer database, for example, we must start with the subject area model and transform it into the business data model. The system model is developed for the specific CRM application using the business data model as the foundation. A technology model is then developed to ensure that the database performs properly on the selected platform and database management system.

By ensuring that conscious decisions are made concerning the extent to which each model is developed and the extent to which each abstraction is considered, we stand a better chance of building a strong foundation for our CRM initiative.

CHAPTER 7

Capturing Customer Information

We began our book with a story about Bob and his parents and their relationship with their local bank. It is important at this point to review how the bank was able to treat these customers in such different but beneficial ways. The bank, like all organizations, has a wealth of information about its customers. Some examples of the information captured within the banking systems are as follows:

- Credit card transactions that indicate where customers spend their money and how they spend it

- Offers from the bank that customers have accepted or responded to

- Loan applications that provide a full financial picture of the applicant

- Channel activities, such as ATM transactions, that show customer interaction preferences

- Investment activities that demonstrate patterns of risk, speculation, and retirement savings

- All forms of customer contact information (name, address, and phone numbers)

- Product usage statistics that show customer behavior and indicate retention risks

Bob and his parents receive great service from their bank because the bank is able to identify and use these informational assets. From the credit card transactions, the bank can offer travel packages that fit their lifestyles. From the channel usage information, the bank can offer specific product packages with prices tailored to each person's preferences. (Bob uses the ATM machine for free but must pay a fee if he uses a teller; his parents use the teller for free but pay a per-transaction fee for the ATM machine.) The different investment activities of Bob and his parents give the bank great insight into the financial needs of each, enabling the bank to identify specific investment opportunities.

We can capture customer information in various ways. The traditional way is for an employee to type new customer information into the account setup system (such as the checking application system in a bank). New account setup systems like the checking application form the business operations category within the Corporate Information Factory (CIF). These systems are the ultimate source for most of the information that makes its way into the rest of the CIF, the business management and business intelligence systems. Although you have some control over how the information in business operations is entered and processed, many of these systems are old, undocumented, and difficult to change. This leaves a difficult cleanup and integration job to be completed prior to moving this operational information into the data warehouse and the operational data store (ODS). This data cleanup and integration is called the data acquisition process, and it is key to ensuring that the customer information assets within your organization can be leveraged to the extent described earlier. This chapter focuses on the data acquisition process, defined as the process of extracting and integrating data from the operational systems and moving it into the remainder of the Corporate Information Factory.

Data acquisition, as described in this chapter, can move data from the operational systems into the data warehouse or into the ODS. This process, when used for the ODS, has some similarities and some differences to the same process used in acquiring data for the data warehouse. Certainly, the activities involved in mapping the sources to the targets, integrating and transforming the data, all involve similar tasks and functions for both databases. Differences occur mostly in the timing of the capture of data (the scheduled capture for the data warehouse versus the mostly unscheduled capture for the ODS) and in the way that the data is ultimately loaded into these two environments (record appends for the data warehouse versus true updates to records for the ODS). These differences are explained in more detail in the appropriate sections of this chapter.

NOTE Your organization can take certain measures to clean up customer data directly in the operational systems. In addition, data hygiene tools that focus on customer names and addresses can be applied to the ODS data during the data acquisition process as described in this chapter (see Chapter 10, "Facilitating Customer Touches with the Customer ODS," for more on this real-time process). Chapter 10 also describes how customer information can be entered directly into the ODS, bypassing the data acquisition process. Using data quality tools in this approach can help ensure the quality of customer information. Chapter 8, "Quality Relationships Start with Quality Customer Data," provides a detailed discussion of the role of quality in Customer Relationship Management (CRM) and shows how and where to apply these tools. This chapter focuses exclusively on the discreet data acquisition process that will feed most of your operational information into the Corporate Information Factory.

The first step in data acquisition is to understand the information assets already available in your operational systems and the assets that come from external sources. To identify these assets, a process is developed in which each piece of data required by the Corporate Information Factory is mapped to its ultimate source. Mapping these data sources to the target database schemas described in Chapter 6, "Developing an Integrated CRM Technology Environment," creates an inventory of available data, facilitates a gap analysis, and highlights data deficiencies.

This chapter starts with a definition of data acquisition as we have indicated and lays out the various processes that comprise it. We then discuss these processes, one by one. First is the mapping process in which the sources of data are mapped to the ultimate targets. We cover the ways to select the best data from the operational systems. We discuss the programs responsible for extraction, cleansing, and transformation. And, we deal with the guidelines for capturing data, the processes for filtering data, data cleansing routines, integration tips and techniques, and the transformation procedure. The load process is our next topic, where we discuss the differences between loading a data warehouse versus an operational data store.

The chapter concludes with a discussion of the audit and control processes that ensure the quality of data entering the data warehouse and ODS, as well as the meta data that is generated from the data acquisition process. Although it is impossible to discuss all of the possible nuances of the data acquisition process, this chapter covers the most important aspects and gives you a solid understanding of the process as well as a set of guidelines to use as you go through your data acquisition steps.

This chapter contains various technical strategies and practical advice gleaned from our own experiences in constructing this environment. Your situation will dictate which of these strategies will be most effective in your environment.

What Is Data Acquisition?

Data acquisition is a complex set of processes and its sole purpose is to attain the most accurate data possible and make it accessible to the enterprise through the Corporate Information Factory. Figure 7.1 shows that data acquisition brings data from the operational systems into the data warehouse and ODS. The entire process began as a manually intensive set of activities. Hand-coded "data suckers" were the only means of getting data out of the operational systems for access by business analysts. This is similar to the early days of telephony when operators on skates had to connect your phone with the one you were calling by racing back and forth and manually plugging in the appropriate cords.

Fortunately, we have come a long way from those days and the data warehouse industry has developed a plethora of tools and technologies to support the data acquisition process. Now most of the process can be automated, much like the

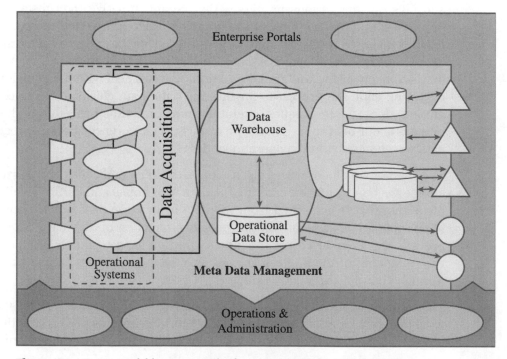

Figure 7.1   Data acquisition process in the Corporate Information Factory.

progress in today's telephony world. Also, similar to telephony advances, this process remains a difficult, if not temperamental and complicated, one. No two companies will ever have the same data acquisition activities, or even the same set of problems! However, the overall process is similar for all enterprises and we will discuss the guidelines for creating an efficient and effective data acquisition process.

Data acquisition is far more than just extraction, transformation, and loading (ETL) of the data. It also consists of the following activities:

Mapping. This is the process of linking the data in the database schemas of the ODS and the data warehouse to the ultimate sources (internal operational systems and external or purchased data, such as credit data, demographic data, competitor data). This includes the logic for choosing the appropriate source systems and analyzing the quality of the data in those systems.

Extraction, Cleansing, and Transformation. These are the programs for capturing the data from its sources, determining the necessary transformation rules for data integration, creating the code to enforce transformation rules, and then cleaning the data as much as possible. Transformation rules include logic for matching disparate sources of similar data, algorithms for integrating customer data into an enterprise view, and householding rules for properly aggregating consumer data. The cleansing process includes data hygiene algorithms for customer matching as well as the identification, and potential correction, of errors in the data.

Loading. This is the process of delivering data to the appropriate target, either the data warehouse or the ODS. For the data warehouse, this includes the processes to append or insert historical snapshots into the database. For the ODS, this includes the appropriate commit and rollback processes required to update records.

Audit and Controls. These are the processes that are necessary to permit comprehensive reconciliation and rationalization of the data entering the data warehouse or the ODS.

Each of these processes creates a significant amount of invaluable meta data that must be stored in some form of repository. This predominantly "technical" meta data is the heart and soul of understanding and maintaining the technical expertise in your Corporate Information Factory. It is the source of information for monitoring data problems, tracking improvements in data quality, assuring the business community of the proper sources of data, and for documenting the audit trail from start to finish for the data entering the CIF. If you use programmers rather than ETL tools to create your data acquisition process, you must ensure that the programmers create and maintain the meta data that accompanies their code. Figure 7.2 contains a minimum list of technical meta data that should be maintained either by the programmers or within the repository in your ETL tool suite. Our recommendation is that the entire data acquisition process be meta data-driven from the ETL tool, rather than code-driven with meta data as an afterthought.

Data acquisition must satisfactorily perform the following actions:

■ It must efficiently and effectively extract data from the source systems.

■ It must successfully move data from one location to another.

■ It must enable easy updates and changes to its processes.

■ It must supply sufficient audit information to permit successful reconciliation back to the operational sources.

- Error detection and correction routines

- Archiving criteria

- Data owner/steward names

- Entity and attribute definitions

- Access patterns

- Data quality indicator

- Reference tables/encoded data

- Defaults used and their reason(s)

- Security

- Source system map

- Transformation rules

Figure 7.2 Technical meta data examples.

The following sections give you time-proven guidelines for a sound data acquisition process, leading to a successful Corporate Information Factory to support your CRM initiative.

Mapping the Sources to the Targets

Once the data models for the warehouse and ODS have been created and validated with the business community, the difficult process of choosing the best operational source(s) for each data attribute begins. Mapping consists of these four activities:

- Creating a sustainable set of identifiers for critical data elements such as a Customer ID
- Choosing the appropriate sources for all needed data elements
- Determining the refreshment frequency of the data
- Determining summarized, derived, and aggregated fields

Creating Sustainable Identifiers

Let's start with a look at a key identifier for any CRM environment, the customer ID. Unfortunately, customer information can be found in many operational systems (Bob's information can be found in the demand deposit system, in the mortgage tracking system, in the credit card transaction system, and even in the GL systems) and each system has its own set of customer identifiers. To make matters worse, this customer information often conflicts across systems.

Regardless of the complexities involved, an effective CRM program requires a consistent customer view across all systems, so the first question you need to answer is, which of the possible sources should you use for the customer identifier for your data warehouse and ODS? Or should you create your own identifier, a surrogate key? In either case, you have to set up the algorithms and cross-reference tables to match the IDs from these systems with the chosen identifier. An example of a customer ID cross-reference table is shown in Table 7.1.

Whether we use an existing identifier from an operational source or we create surrogate keys, these identifiers must satisfy several criteria before they can be safely used in the CIF. The identifiers for your customers are as follows:

Not null over the scope of integration. This means that customer data can never enter the system without being identified by or attached to a customer ID.

Table 7.1 Customer ID Cross-Reference Table

CUSTOMER NAME	OPERATIONAL SYSTEM KEY	OPERATIONAL SYSTEM NAME	CIF SURROGATE KEY
Bob Jones	089824-190	Checking	10000234-01
Bob Jones	089835-101	Checking	10000234-01
Bob Jones	Bob15395	Mortgage Tracking	10000234-01
Bob Jones	1999-12953	Credit Card	10000234-01
Don Smith	Don12952	Mortgage Tracking	10000235-01
Mary Jones	783716-300	Checking	10000236-01
Mary Jones	Mary9383	Mortgage Tracking	10000236-01
Mary Jones	1999-39022	Credit Card	10000236-01
Robert Jones	1998-43829	Credit Card	10000237-01
Robert Jones	492833-289	Checking	10000237-01

Unique over the scope of integration. Two customers cannot have the same identifier or a customer identifier cannot be reused for another customer.

Unique by design not by circumstance. The designers of the system must put thought into the creation and design of these identifiers to make them unique. For example, they could create a serially generated key for each new customer.

Singular over the scope of integration. This means that the customer will have one and only one identifier throughout his or her existence in our CIF.

Persistent over time. Because customers will exist in our data warehouse for a long time, perhaps many years, the identifier must remain constant. We do not want to have to create new keys for all our customers because we did not design a persistent identifier for them. For example, if we created a key that contained only five numeric places, we would need a new set of IDs when we reached our 100,000th customer.

In a manageable format. Generally, we will use a format such as a numeric or alphanumeric field that our database management system can handle easily.

Not intelligent. There is a natural impulse to build "intelligence" into customer identifiers, such as using the state two-letter code at the beginning of the customer ID. This makes it easy to determine which state a customer lives in just by looking at his or her ID. For example, we could identify Bob as CO1234897, giving Bob's identifier an intelligence that indicates that he currently resides in Colorado. It certainly makes it easy to sort all the customers into their various states, but you can also immediately see the problem. What happens if Bob moves to Pennsylvania? He either gets a new ID (unacceptable if we are to see an integrated, single view of Bob) or he continues to be included with the Colorado customers (also unacceptable because it is wrong).

Once these criteria are met, you can then build the cross-reference table shown in Table 7.1 to match your standard customer identifier with the other forms of customer identifiers used in the operational sources. This table has two major functions. For data acquisition, it translates the key from the source system to the key that is used in the ODS or data warehouse. For a direct update of the ODS (introduced in the note earlier in this chapter and detailed in Chapter 10), this table is used to generate transactions for updating the appropriate operational systems with the new data, which is entered into the ODS first and pushed out to the operational systems as appropriate.

Choosing Appropriate Sources

The next step in the mapping process for data acquisition is to decide which of your source systems you will use to populate the rest of your customer data. Again, this is not an easy process, but a number of criteria are available to help you choose the appropriate source of operational data. A good source is one that contains the following characteristics:

It is the point of origin of the data item. Often the best source of data is the system in which the data is originally entered. For example, a new customer may first be entered into the order entry system. The customer service representative (CSR) may be very careful in entering that data because the shipment of the order is dependent on accurate data. That data may then be sent for further processing into the billing system and into the GL system through various manual or automated interfaces. Many things can happen to the data as it flows from system to system, causing it to lose some of its quality. For example, the street address contained in the checking system accommodates international addresses. The GL system does not; it is set up only for U.S. addresses. As the data moves from the checking system to the GL system, the address data loses some of its meaning (postal codes are different from zip codes, shires are different from states, and a country code may not even be in the GL system).

It is the most complete record of the data item. You may reach a point in your operational processing when much of the needed customer data comes together in a single record. For example, Bob's most complete product usage information may converge on the GL system. In this case, you may choose to use that source, thus negating the need to piece the same data together from the other systems.

It is the most reliable source of the data item. Some systems may have tighter edit checks or better business processes that make their data more accurate or complete and therefore, a better source of your CIF data.

It is the most current source of the data item. Again, as the data flows between systems, the currency (and therefore the accuracy) of this data may vary. Perhaps the billing system is a better source of the customer's contact information than the order entry system because it is used for sending bills and for supporting collection processes. You may decide that the billing system is the best source for this specific data item.

It is the most thoroughly documented. Obviously, the more you can understand about an operational source of data, the better chance you have of getting it right. Therefore, you may choose a newer operational source that has thorough documentation (data models, data dictionaries, and documented processes) over an older one in which the documentation is non-existent.

It is the most accessible. Often, an enterprise has old or fragile operational systems or their processing may be outsourced and managed by a third party. The data contained in these systems may be in inaccessible technologies (such as proprietary databases) or may simply not be accessible due to other reasons. If so, you may have to get the data from a downstream system that permits access.

It is best in terms of the timing of the updates. If the Corporate Information Factory is updated nightly and the GL system is updated with new customer data only once a month, it would be inappropriate to use the GL system as the source for customer information.

One final consideration is the politics behind the selection. There may be non-technical reasons for choosing a system. Will the business community use the Corporate Information Factory if its data comes from a system they don't trust (even if there is no obvious reason for the distrust)?

Once you have determined the logic behind the best source of data, this logic must be formally documented and stored for future reference in the meta data repository.

Determining Refreshment Frequency

Another step involved in mapping is to determine the frequency with which data is updated or refreshed. This is as important to the data warehouse as it is for the ODS. How often we capture data for use in strategic and tactical decision-making depends on these considerations:

Business needs. For very stable data, we may not need to update the ODS or data warehouse as often as we do for the most volatile data. For example, in the ODS, we may have ATM location data that we update once a day or maybe even once a week. We may also have customer contact information that we update almost immediately.

Referential integrity requirements. Even though the business may dictate that it does not need to see the ATM location changes above more than once a week, we may need to update the data more frequently to enforce referential integrity. If the transactions associated with an ATM are updated once a day, then the locations of these ATMs will also need to be updated daily. This eliminates the problem of what to do with daily transactions for an ATM whose physical location has already changed, but the warehouse information is not due to change for another week.

Production cycle dependency. If the volume of data being extracted is large or we cannot preprocess the data throughout the day, we may run into problems with the operational window of the source system. We may not be able to stop operations of that system long enough to do frequent extractions of information to push it into the warehouse and ODS.

Transformation time and complexity. The shorter the refresh window, generally the simpler the transformations that can occur. This is particularly important for the ODS. If the transformation is quite complex, we may not be able to update the ODS immediately; it may take several minutes to an hour or more to ensure that the update is properly transformed.

Differences in refresh cycles for different pieces of data. Not all data is on the same refresh cycle, especially for the data warehouse. However, if different refresh cycles are used, you must make sure that these different cycles do not affect referential integrity as described in the ATM location example earlier.

Determining Summarized, Derived, and Aggregated Fields

The last step in the mapping process is to ensure that the necessary detailed data exists to create all summarized, aggregated, and derived fields. The data models contain the meta data about these fields (such as how they are calculated and what fields go into their calculation) and are used to make this final determination. For example, we may decide to calculate Bob's total utilization by product (credit card, ATM, or Internet transfers) for each week and store that history in the data warehouse. The people creating the mapping process must understand which detailed fields go into these calculations and ensure that the details are mapped to the appropriate systems for capture and ultimate inclusion in the calculations. It is often advisable to capture both the details as well as the calculated fields, so that the derived data can be recalculated if the formula changes down the road.

Creating the Extraction, Integration, Cleansing, and Transformation Processes

Now we are ready to begin the process of creating the processes that will capture, integrate, cleanse, and transform our operational source data into the CIF data to be used by our customer-centric enterprise. Figure 7.3 is a pictorial view of this complicated set of processes.

These processes consist of the following activities:

Capture. The first step is to extract the appropriate data elements from each operational source at the right time without impacting the performance of the system being extracted.

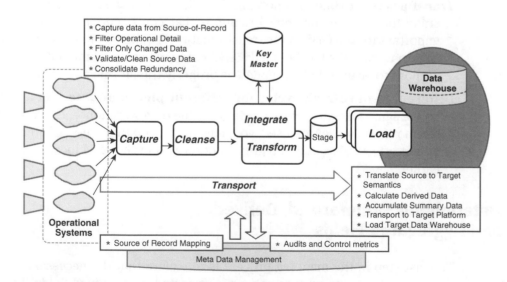

Figure 7.3 Data acquisition processes.

Cleanse. The extracted data is authenticated and its appropriateness is confirmed. This process includes data hygiene processes as well as error-detection and correction processing.

Integrate. The bits and pieces of customer data are matched up and consolidated into a single version of the truth.

Transform. The integrated data is transformed into the enterprise standard (data format) for ultimate delivery into the data warehouse or ODS.

The final process, load, will be discussed in the next section of this chapter.

Capturing Data

The first decision facing the creators of the CIF environment is the logic to use in capturing data from the operational systems, and the filters to apply to each system's data. Because customer data flows throughout our systems, the timing of its capture and the completeness of the record must be planned and charted. For the ODS, the capture process must be performed multiple times per day and at unscheduled times, every time that a new transaction occurs. For the data warehouse, a capture occurs on a regularly scheduled interval: every day, week, or perhaps month.

This section begins with a discussion of a common source system issue that immediately surfaces in the capture process: logic problems. You'll be given guidelines for building your capture processes to mitigate this issue. Next, the different formats and forms that operational data can take within a system and the characteristics of each are discussed. The section ends with a discussion of the filters you will need for your capture activities.

Logic Problems in the Capture Process

Problems always occur when different parts of the integrated customer record come from different systems. This section focuses on two specific problems and suggests solutions to these.

Sometimes we get only a partial customer record. This may occur because the source system has not been fully updated, or because it is not designed to contain certain information. For example, the customer complaint system may not contain information about the customer's purchases, so we need to develop logic to handle the incomplete record. One solution is to store the record in a staging area until the rest of the operational systems are updated and the data is available to complete the record. A second method is to use defaults or not available (NA) to fill in the blank or missing fields (marking the record as an incomplete one) and let it continue on into the data warehouse or ODS. When the data becomes available in this second case, the record must be updated and returned to its target.

Neither solution is ideal. In the first one, holding up the customer record until it is complete may cause us to have under-recognized sales and finance information. Also, we have no information on that customer at all in the CIF. On the other hand, loading an incomplete record and filling in the fields at a later time increases the processing complexity (especially for the data warehouse). The solution in your environment depends on the criticality of having this data available and on the amount of time it takes to get the complete picture. If the incomplete record will be completed within two or three hours, then holding the incomplete record in a staging area may be reasonable. If it takes significant time, more than 12 hours or even days, to update the downstream systems, then the use of defaults is preferable.

A second problem, common to most CIF implementations, is that fields in the operational systems are used for multiple purposes depending on various scenarios in the business environment. For example, in an order entry system, we may use the Customer Type field to contain a standard industry code for commercial customers. For a residential customer, we may use the Customer Type field to indicate the income level of the household. Obviously, the capture process must use a fair amount of if-then-else logic to direct these different records to the proper integration processes.

Guidelines for Handling Logic Problems

Both of the previous examples demonstrate how quickly this activity becomes quite complicated and complex. As your CIF grows in both data and complexity, you will find that literally thousands of algorithms are needed to capture the right data and then direct it to the appropriate integration activities. Here are some guidelines to help you with this process.

- Consider preprocessing the data throughout the day, rather than waiting for the batch window to process all your data. For example, as soon as a customer record is added to an operational system, your capture process may begin by obtaining that data and storing it in the beginnings of a customer record for the CIF. If the record is for a new customer, a customer ID may be generated using the serially generated process. Other pieces of customer data can be brought into the record as that data becomes available from other systems. At the end of the day, all the new customers have been pre-processed to have their new IDs and bits of their record have been built. You should consider these characteristics when thinking about processing data during the operational day:

- Network speed or reliability: Will your network support the transfer of massive amounts of customer data all day long?

- Impact on production systems: Will you cause performance problems for critical operational systems by permitting access to them during their up time in order to pre-process data?

- Extract schedule: Does the schedule of extractions from other operational systems match up with the pre-processing schedule or is processing dependent on the coordination with other systems?

- Extract frequency: Will the pre-processing match up with the extraction frequency of the other operational systems (for example, all systems are on daily extract cycles)?

- Requirements for a staging area: Will the pre-processed data have to wait in the staging area for other systems to catch up?

- Determine your method of capture. This depends on the technology used in the various operational systems. You may be able to use bulk unloads of source systems or programmatic unloads based on activity dates to capture the data. If the technology of the operational system supports a DBMS log, you may be able to capture only changed data. This will be discussed in more detail in the next section.

- Consider purchasing an ETL tool. Part of the selection process for the tool should include a thorough understanding of how the ETL tool works so that you can design your ETL processes accordingly.

Formats and Data Storage Forms

The next decision for the data acquisition process concerns the different ways that operational data can be stored. Operational data comes in three varieties: archived, in-use, and changed data. Each storage mechanism has its own characteristics and reasons for usage in the Corporate Information Factory. If a great deal of customer history is needed (data that is more than two years old), then we may have to retrieve these records from a tape or optical disk. If we are using only the current history of our customer (within the last six months or so), the data may still reside on the disks for each system and archived data may not be needed. For future additions to the Corporate Information Factory databases, we may choose to capture only appropriate data that has changed from the last capture process. Let's examine each of these types of stored data to understand the best approach to capturing data from them.

Archived Data

Archived data is operational data that is no longer needed online in the operational system. Historical data is not as critical for the ODS and may not be needed at all. It is an invaluable source of data for historical purposes though, and therefore, it is critical that it be included in the data acquisition processing for the data warehouse. For example, credit card transactions from two years ago are invaluable in determining product utilization trends. Fraudulent cases can be retrieved and analyzed to determine patterns of fraudulent behavior.

Archived data is usually used for the initial load of that source system's data into the data warehouse. Once loaded, we rarely have to go back to the archive to retrieve more data. This form of data has a number of characteristics that make it difficult to work with:

- It is usually stored on tape, which may be difficult to read. Often the device reader is no longer available or is in limited supply. Older tapes can be damaged and no longer readable.

- The format of the records may have changed over time, making the archive difficult to interpret.

- The meaning of the data fields may have changed over time, contributing to the difficulty of interpreting the data.

- The content or codes of fields may have changed requiring significant effort to bring the codes up to the current set.

- Many archived sets of data have little or no documentation describing their content, format, or even what data is contained within them.

- Finally, the volume of data stored in archived media is usually enormous, making the effort to recover it even harder.

Archived data is a difficult type of data to deal with, but does give our strategic CRM applications a tremendous wealth of knowledge and intelligence about customers, the products they prefer, the usage of the products, and other important pieces of information. If significant history is required by your enterprise for its CRM initiative, we suggest that you deal with archived data in a separate project, focused on just that media. Much can be gained from getting the more easily accessible data (in-use and changed data) in the hands of the business community quickly and then bringing in the archived data at a later date. Furthermore, you may find that the archived detail data is not as useful as the aggregated information from the archives.

In-Use Data

In-use data consists of the operational source data that is still being actively used and is stored online on disks within the application. Examples of this type of data are abundant, including the current transactions from Bob's credit card, recent investment activities, or the checking account activity by Bob's parents. In-use data too is generally used only once for the initial load of the project and then it is not necessary to gather it again (unless we missed a piece of data the first time around). It is the most valuable data we can bring into both the data warehouse and ODS.

Certain characteristics of in-use data should be taken into account when building the capture processes for it. Some of these considerations include ensuring access to the operational system's maintenance resources and the use of any documentation for the systems. Some of the operational programmers and database administrators may have limited time to work with your team and should be given a heads-up when their knowledge will be needed. Some of the documentation may be lost or stored in unusual places and may take time to find. Here are some of the other considerations to keep in mind when using in-use data:

- In-use data shares a common format and content within each specific source, but rarely across sources. The format and content must be studied to ensure that undocumented features such as fields used for different purposes have not occurred.

- Generally, we have documentation available for in-use data. Unfortunately, this may be limited to the knowledge inside the heads of the maintenance programmers within the enterprise or to a simple data model that came with the original package.

- Usually, we are dealing with a large volume of data when we capture in-use data. Fortunately, once the operational system is understood, it becomes relatively routine and predictable to capture the data from it.

- The capture process competes with the production application for resources, such as the central processing unit (CPU) or input/output (I/O). We may find that the capture process must be postponed until the nightly batch window to prevent any degradation of performance in this system.

Changed Data

Once the initial load of the data has been completed in the ODS and data warehouse, you may now choose to use delta or change data mechanisms to capture only the data that has changed since the last extract process. A changed data capture process deals with data volumes that are significantly smaller than the entire set of data in the operational database. Here we are gathering only the transactions from Bob's credit card usage or the checking account transactions for his parents that have occurred since the last capture. This mechanism of capture is useful for the ODS where data currency is critical and for the data warehouse where data volumes are enormous.

Six methods for capturing data changes are available:

1. Use source timestamps. Modern operational systems have database management systems that place a timestamp on the record indicating when it was created or last updated. Unfortunately, this mechanism may not be available for older operational systems, but for those that do perform this time stamping, we can capture the updated and new records with minimal effort. Note that this method of capture cannot be used to determine deleted records if physical deletes are performed (no record will show this deletion).

2. Read the DBMS log. Tools are available today that can capture the history of all the changes occurring within a DBMS. These can be very useful in a persistent staging area, as discussed earlier in this chapter. The changes are brought into the staging area and are matched up with the partially constructed records for a completed one, ready for the next process, integration.

3. Modify the operational source system application. For example, you may have the opportunity to incorporate new code into your credit card transaction system so that it creates a transaction file of all the activities your customers make with their credit cards. If updates and inserts were performed in a batch fashion using a batch file, these same files can be used instead as input into the capture process, thus eliminating the need to capture data from the operational system.

4. Compare before and after images of the database. To make this process easier, we recommend that you use the backup files (image copies) and a compare utility like Comparex, Superc, or Syncsort. Comparison may be your only choice for older batch systems. It can be a slow process to identify those records that have changed since the last compare. Once identified, the records or the fields are extracted and put into a file for further integration.

5. Create snapshots of the operational systems and use these in the capture process. This usually requires a complete reload of the tables and works best in the ODS. If used for the data warehouse, then all history must be rebuilt.

6. Use database triggers from the operational system. This mechanism requires that the operational source has a relational DBMS and that it saves inserted, updated, or deleted records of interest. Unfortunately, this also creates twice the workload on the operational system. For example, upon the insertion of a new record, the database fires a trigger not only to insert the record into its own database, but also to update another table for our use in data capture.

Capturing changed data makes for a very efficient process but may not always work in your environment with your particular set of technologies. A chat with your operations people, application maintenance staff, database administrators, and technology vendor may help you determine if this will work for you and which mechanism is best suited.

Filtering Guidelines

Filtering is defined as the process of selecting data elements that will be extracted from the operational systems. An example would be the credit card transaction records created in the operational credit card system. The transaction record contains many fields that are only needed by the credit card system to process the transaction. These include fields for the audit time and date stamps for the transaction's posting and its creation, system IDs for sending this transaction on to other systems (such as the GL system), and fields used to identify price codes. Many of these fields are not needed for either the data warehouse or the ODS. Therefore, a filtering mechanism is needed to eliminate these fields during the capture process.

This process has two schools of thought. The first recommends that you replicate all of the data from any operational system you use in your CIF, capture what you need from that copy for your immediate needs, and remove any elements that are purely operational in nature, redundant, or no longer being used. Then store the rest in an archive file for future usage. The rationale for this is as follows:

- You have a complete set of data from that time period.
- You are not dependent on the operational system for future enhancements or additions to the CIF.
- This process eases the "analysis paralysis" that may occur when designers agonize over which elements to include in their CIF.

The other school of thought is to eliminate elements, tables, or files that are not within the scope of the project. The capture process would gather only data requested for the first project or data that has a high likelihood of use in the first iteration. The rationale behind this process is as follows:

- Each captured element takes time, money, effort, and resources that may be in limited supply.

- The operational data may change over time due to prior period adjustments or corrections made at a later date that would not be captured in the static one-shot capture mechanism.

- Each element needs to be loaded into the data warehouse.

- A storage and performance impact occurs as well. Each element you capture, and its history, must be stored from now on.

As with all guidelines, you must determine which of these two mechanisms works best in your environment. Use the guidelines provided for choosing the best method for your situation.

Data Cleansing

One area in which a large gap occurs between the business community's expectations and the implementers' ability to deliver is the area of data quality. This is typically due to a number of factors:

- A lack of knowledge of the quality of data in the operational systems

- A lack of knowledge of what the values should be

- An unwillingness to take ownership of poor business processes that cause poor data quality

- A lack of interest by critical parties

For an enterprise to truly improve the quality of data used in its CRM initiatives, these factors must be overcome, usually through a company-wide education program or effort. Chapter 6 discusses the various quality issues and provides guidelines to help you attain quality data in your enterprise.

Data cleansing is a process that cleans and validates (to the extent possible) the data coming from operational sources. This may be as simple as a format validation (for example, numerics contain only numerics and date fields contain valid dates), range checks (for example, a zero or a negative number is a valid value and future dates are valid), or the standard representation of unknown or not applicable.

Data cleansing for a CRM initiative, however, is usually much more complex and complicated, as these simple examples illustrate. Processes like name and address hygiene are generally difficult and require the use of a cleansing tool from vendors such as Innovative Systems, i.d.centric, or Trillium. Each operational source's data must be run through the data hygiene programs, where it is corrected, standardized, and deduped (duplicates are removed). The data cleansing routines are run against each source of data until each source's data is as good as can be. Only then is the operational source ready for the integration process. Chapter 6 discusses this topic in great detail.

WARNING

The data in the Corporate Information Factory, especially the data warehouse, may never be perfect. This does not mean it is unusable. We can make correct and significant decisions with imperfect data, *as long as it is consistently bad*. If the data is always 10 percent off in the warehouse, you can adjust your thinking and decision-making to account for that. But if you don't know how bad it is, or if it is inconsistently off, adjustments cannot be made and you can't trust what you have received. The goal is to analyze where and how the poor quality is occurring and fix the problem. Please don't shoot the messenger!

Integrating Data

The integration process brings together all the bits and pieces of cleansed data we have gathered from the various operational systems and stitches them together into a cohesive view of our customers, products, and services. This process consists of an involved set of algorithms and equations that ensures an organized and functional grouping of information.

The process begins after the data-cleansing routines have been run. For the initial delivery of customer information into the data warehouse or ODS, the captured and cleansed data from the separate operational systems is copied into a staging area. Once there, the same data hygiene tools can match the data from one system with the data captured from the other systems. The same routines used to match the names and addresses within one system can now be used to match data between systems until we have a single version of the customer.

For other data not based on names and addresses, we can set up programs that contain sets of algorithms such as processes and rules for use in matching. Typical matching programs first parse the customer name and address record into a set of data elements for use in the matching process. The algorithms then compare the elements from several records to look for possible matches. Robust programs enable your organization to look at various combinations and choose those that are likely matches based on the conditions that occur in your data. You should be able to designate some combinations as definitive matches (automatically marked as a match by the software), some combinations as possible matches (marked by the software for manual review), and some combinations as non-matches (not combined or marked). In addition to these processes, you may have to send some of the data out to an examination process where a person has to manually perform the matching.

The integration process must include maintaining a key master table (refer to Table 7.1) that contains the keys from operational systems and the key for the data warehouse and ODS. This key master is mandatory when we have two or more operational sources that are merged together because we usually need to communicate back to old systems. In Chapter 10, we will see how the ODS communicates back to the operational systems in an immediate fashion, that is, real time integration to/from ODS and operational systems.

The integration process must have algorithms or business rules built into its programs to handle complex and confusing situations such as the following:

- Data from different systems that is the same data, but has a different name. For example, customers may be called accounts in one system, but customers in another. The integration process must recognize that these two are really the same.

- Data from different systems that has the same name, but is really different data. For example, two systems may have a record called account, but in one case it is the customer and in the other it is the financial account for the enterprise. Certainly, these are not the same and our process must recognize that difference.

- Data from different systems that is the same but encoded differently. For example, the product fields from two systems may be based on a completely different set of codes. The integration process must match these together and come up with the single integrated view of this data.

- Finally, the field name and meaning in different systems may be the same, but the field is calculated or measured differently. For an international company, product revenues may be calculated in the native monetary unit of the country that creates them. In England, revenue is measured in pounds; in the U.S., it is in U.S. dollars; and in Canada, it is in Canadian dollars. The integration process must be able to interpret each currency and calculate each number to the enterprise standard currency.

Transforming the Integrated Data

The transformation process is the final step before we deliver the data into the data warehouse or ODS. Transformation involves a conversion of the cleansed and integrated data into the standard format for the CIF. These transformations include the following examples:

- Reference data is converted to the enterprise standard. For example, state, gender, product, and other codes are converted to the corporate standard.

- Date fields are converted to the standard date format.

- Measurements are converted to the enterprise standard.

The transformation process is also responsible for creating record-level summaries or derived fields. These include rolling summaries; monthly, weekly, and daily sales totals; customer account balances; revenue numbers; and aggregations of information, such as a customer's total product usage statistics. We have ensured that the details for these calculations are present in the mapping process, so this step should simply be the process of creating the summaries, aggregations, or derivations.

Loading the Data Warehouse or Operational Data Store

The load process for the data warehouse and ODS is completely separate from the integration and transformation steps because it is usually performed by load utilities found within the DBMS technology. Therefore, this process is greatly influenced by the choice of technology for the DBMS and its platform. If your data warehouse or ODS is implemented on different technologies, the load process is more complicated by virtue of the multiple technologies. Also, a significant difference exists between the load process for the data warehouse and the ODS. This section will look first at the load process for the data warehouse, and then examine it for the ODS.

Loading the Data Warehouse

The data warehouse is a series of static (non-changing) snapshots of historical data (see Chapter 9, "Business Intelligence: Technologies for Understanding Your Customers," for a complete description of the data warehouse). Its load process, while not simple, is certainly easier to accomplish than the one for an ODS. For example, generally, the load process for the data warehouse runs after hours (during the batch window) and involves appending or inserting whole records into the existing files. These actions are easier to perform than the cascading updates and deletes that occur in the ODS.

Rarely do we need to change an existing record in the data warehouse. This would destroy the historical integrity for that customer. Rather than updating an existing record, we would insert a new snapshot with any corrections or updates to the historical record while still preserving the original record. After all, decisions were made based on the data that was available at that time. It would be misleading at best, and incorrect at worst, to recreate history and then examine the decisions made at the time using the newly recreated history.

The following are some guidelines to follow when loading data into the data warehouse:

Collect the data in a staging area to prepare it for the load process. You may choose to also use this area to do preliminary quality checks. If the data does not pass these preliminary checks, it does not get loaded. Also, you may need to sort the data for load sequencing before presenting it to your load utility. This can speed up the process by putting the data into the proper order before it is loaded, rather than depending on the load utility to do this.

Make a backup copy of the incoming new data. The time to create your backup file is right before you load the data into the data warehouse. The backup may be needed in the event of data corruption or a hardware failure.

Determine source precedence. Certain sources of data must be loaded before others to ensure proper referential integrity. For example, we must load the data sourced from the product system before loading a customer's product usage. Fortunately, this step has been made easier by the advances in your ETL tools. Some of these can schedule the sequences of input files through their meta data layer.

Determine the data precedence. The loading of the data has an order to be followed as well. The customer data (customer ID and customer type code) must be loaded, either into memory or into the actual database, before loading the customer's product information (product ID, start date, or campaign ID). Again, the ETL tools are of great benefit in scheduling the data precedence.

Utilize the bulk load capabilities of your DBMS. These utilities are very useful for loading (and unloading) entire files or sets of data. For example, you may want to reload a product code table or other reference table. The bulk load utility can easily load the product code table with the new codes. Each DBMS is different in terms of the tricks and techniques you use to optimize the bulk load utility performance. You must learn from your DBMS vendor what works best in terms of tuning their load performance.

Drop the data warehouse indexes before loading. This may be for initial loads only and thereafter you should benchmark the load performance to determine the efficiency and necessity of index creation.

Determine appropriate storage parameters. Figure 7.4 is a comparison of the different storage requirements for the operational systems, data ware-

Type of Data	Operational System	Data Warehouse	ODS
Static Data	95-100%	95-100%	95-100%
Static Index	95-100%	95-100%	95-100%
Dynamic Data	60-80%	N/A or 90-100%	60-80%
Dynamic Index	60-80%	N/A or 90-100%	60-80%
Clustered Index	65%	65%	65%

Figure 7.4 Storage requirements for the Corporate Information Factory.

house, and ODS. Because of the static nature of much of the data warehouse, there is little need to leave unused free space.

A number of other tasks should be completed to ensure good performance of your data warehouse. Some are after every load and others are part of the routine maintenance of the database:

Partition the data for performance. This activity can enhance the data delivery process: the process for delivering data into the data marts. Partitioning can be done in two fashions: vertical and horizontal partitioning. Figure 7.5 demonstrates the difference between these two types of partitioning. Horizontal partitioning separates whole records into two or more files based on specific record criteria. It creates horizontal slices of the data. For example, you may choose to separate your retail customer records from your commercial customer records. By dividing the data into different partitions, such as by geography, customer type, or market segment, we can easily create data marts with just commercial customers or with just customers from a specific geographic area or market segment. Vertical partitioning separates a table into two smaller tables. It creates vertical slices of the data. For example, you might separate the customer's geographic information from his or

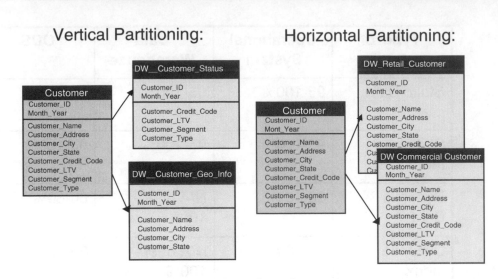

Figure 7.5 Partitioning in the Corporate Information Factory.

her credit information in the data warehouse because you may choose to capture the geographic data at a different refresh cycle than the credit information (more volatile information is captured more frequently than the more stable data). This can reduce the need for storage because you are not bringing in stable data at the same refresh rate as volatile data.

Rebuild the indexes after the successful load. Each enterprise should determine its indexing strategy for its data warehouse. The levels of granularity (aggregations), the volume of load data, the data delivery process, and the amount of direct access to the data warehouse by the business community all have an impact on your indexing strategy. Indexes can greatly speed up these activities but must be built based upon the appropriate sets of data.

Perform quality metrics and checks. Once the load is successfully completed, the process of examining and reconciling the data begins. Critical data elements should be studied for data quality problems such as null or incorrect values. Metrics for quality are used to monitor and measure the level of data quality reached. The publication of these metrics is essential to garner the business community's confidence in the data.

Loading the ODS

The ODS is a very different animal from the data warehouse. It is a "live" database in the sense that it is constantly being updated with information from the operational systems. Chapter 10 describes the ODS in detail, but suffice it to say that the ODS load process is more similar to the online transaction processing that occurs in the operational systems than it is to the load process for the data warehouse. Data is moved into the ODS through one of four different mechanisms:

Record insertion. This is the simplest way of getting data into the ODS. The source data record in transferred to the ODS and simply put in. For example, a new customer record would simply be inserted into the customer file.

Record insertion/replacement. This is a variation on the simple insertion mechanism. In this case, if data with the same key is found in the ODS, the entire record is replaced with the new one. For example, Bob's record already exists, but we replace it with a record having the new information contained within it. If an existing record is not found, the new record is inserted.

Field replacement. In this case, only the new field data is replaced, rather than the entire record. For example, if the customer's phone number has changed, we would update only the Phone Number field, rather than replacing the entire record.

Field accumulate. In this case, the data from the operational sources is accumulated and then stored into the ODS. We may choose to populate the accumulated fields less frequently than the other fields. For example, Bob's account balance can be kept in the ODS, but we do not want to store every single transaction Bob makes against that account, only the balance. Therefore, we may accumulate the transaction amounts and update the ODS account balance for Bob every 30 minutes.

Like the data warehouse load process, the ODS load process has certain guidelines. These include the following:

- Referential integrity is quite similar to that found in operational systems. Cascading updates and deletes are necessary, as are edit checks for certain fields (such as dates and range validations). Other concerns here are the primary key/foreign key matches, triggers and stored procedures used to enforce business rules or update another table, and "not null" constraints.

- The more current (or synchronous with the operational systems) the ODS is, the harder it is to maintain. You may need to build reinitialization and restart programs to maintain currency. You will need monitoring programs to ensure that synchrony is maintained.

- Determine the appropriate storage parameters. Refer to Figure 7.4 for a comparison of the different storage requirements for the operational systems, the data warehouse, and the ODS. The ODS has a profile very similar to the operational systems in terms of free space.

- Messaging software can be very useful in an ODS with a high frequency of updates occurring. Message brokers act as traffic cops, delivering messages or transactions to and from the ODS. These brokers form a key component in the load process technology.

Creating the Audit and Control Processes

Enormous amounts of time, effort, and anguish are spent trying to reconcile the data warehouse and ODS data back to the operational sources. Most companies use laborious manual processes to perform this reconciliation. It is still only adequate at best and does not really give the business community a good understanding of what is happening in their CIF environment.

The primary difficulty in measuring the data is that because it's intangible, many aspects must be measured. For example, how many records were read? How many were integrated and transformed? How many had errors in them and so were rejected? What types of errors were encountered? How many errors were corrected and then integrated? The list goes on. What's more, the integration/transformation layer can complicate measurement by distorting these dimensions. For example, we may have read 1,000 records, but only loaded 698 into the data warehouse. The numbers themselves do not tell us if the process worked, since we may have combined some records and rejected others.

The solution to the problem is to implement strategies that audit the processes that gather the content before it gets loaded and then to continue monitoring it after it is loaded. This overall process is the audit and quality control program.

NOTE Reconciliation does not mean that the data in the data warehouse is equal to the operational systems. Rather, it means having confidence that everything worked correctly and we have a track record to explain any differences that occur.

The data warehouse must be sufficiently accurate for performing strategic analyses. The ODS must have additional edit checks and referential integrity checks to ensure its accuracy for tactical decision-making and for the operational processing needed to support CRM. This means that the data in the data warehouse and ODS must have a proven and dependable level of data accuracy, consistency, and integrity for their respective intended business usage. Therefore, the minimal objectives of an audit and quality controls program are to:

- Validate the accuracy and completeness of the source data loaded into the data warehouse and ODS.

- Maintain a proactive approach for identifying audit and quality control problems as early as possible. This means that we should stop problems at the source (probably the operational source) rather than trying to fix them after they have entered into the data warehouse or ODS.

- Establish the meta data repository as an active system component to aid in measuring and reconciling the load processes.

- Provide the infrastructure to record and monitor the load processes as well as the quality of data over time. You may need to expand your meta data repository to accommodate these new fields.

A comprehensive audit and quality controls program consists of four major components:

Data acquisition architecture. This identifies where the processes of audit and control should be applied so the appropriate processes can be implemented. This chapter describes this architecture in detail (refer to Figure 7.3). An audit and control process should be in place for each activity: capture, cleanse, integrate, transform, and load.

Meta data repository. This defines, captures, and tracks the audit and control measurements. The audit and control programs should read and write to this repository. The book, *Building and Managing the Meta Data Repository* by David Marco (John Wiley & Sons), is an excellent resource describing this important component.

Human resources. A successful program requires resources from the business units as well as the technology organization in order to create and monitor the audit and control processes. Chapter 5, "Getting Underway," describes the roles and responsibilities of the technical and business meta data analysts. It is critical that the enterprise must commit these resources to this important function of capturing, maintaining, and making accessible meta data.

Methodology. This identifies the analysis, design, construction, test, and ongoing operational activities involved in the audit and control program. The methodology for a solid audit and control procedure will be discussed in the next section. This methodology is used to audit both the processes that capture, integrate, transform, and load data into the data warehouse or ODS as well as to monitor the actual data or content itself.

Audit and Control Methodology

The audit and control processes are more extensive than traditional data processing program-to-program audits. The objective is to measure and validate the assumption that all the appropriate data was extracted from the operational systems and then transferred, integrated, cleansed, transformed, loaded, and distributed without any losses. Essentially, these measures should be used to proactively account for the data, as well as the processes for extracting and integrating that data, prior to anyone using it for decision-making functions.

Many organizations perform some measurements in their data acquisition program code today. However, the results of these measurements are produced on hard copy reports that are viewed by only the CIF administrators. Business users rarely see these reports and may not be aware of a problem occurring within the data acquisition process.

Business users require a level of confidence in the completeness and accuracy of the data warehouse and ODS before they will use them. They will often query the ODS or data mart, and then look at reports from the operational systems to compare the numbers from each. It is a rare event that all the numbers will be identical because of the time of extractions, the filters on the extractions, or the marked error records encountered.

If the numbers don't match, the users must have an explanation that enables them to have confidence in their analyses. Unfortunately, most administrators today cannot provide the needed supporting intelligence to the business users to reconcile any discrepancies, thus calling into question the validity of the data itself. This is where the implementation of the audit and control program is needed to explain and justify the differences.

Four high-level activities are used to develop and operate the audit and control program. The methodology applies to the data acquisition processes as well as to the data in the data warehouse or ODS. The detailed tasks and scope vary for the data acquisition processes versus the data in the data warehouse and ODS and will be discussed in the next section. The four high-level activities are as follows:

- Define the process steps and data attributes that must be audited and measured.
- Assess the existing capability to measure both the processes and the quality of the attributes.
- Measure the processes and quality, record the results in the meta data repository, and report on each load cycle.
- Correct the processes or the data and then reprocess.

Figure 7.6 further defines these four activities and shows the relationship between activities.

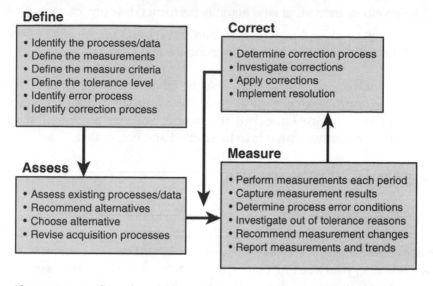

Figure 7.6 Audit and control processes.

Define Processes and Data Attributes

The purpose of the define activity is to identify strategically important processes and data attributes. In this activity, we define and begin to understand the quality expectations of the business community. We must identify all known actual values and the quality issues in the operational sources.

Second, we must identify the percentage of errors that the business can tolerate and specify the actions to be taken when the tolerance percentages are exceeded. These actions range from stopping the entire data acquisition process to correcting the error and to continuing the process with warnings about the errors found.

Finally, the define step must include the determination of the error-detection responsibilities within each organization's business unit and information technologies (IT) unit. This includes the following groups:

■ The group or individual who determines when an error has occurred and its severity

■ The group or individual who determines where the error can be corrected (at the operational source or before the entry into the data warehouse or ODS)

- The group or individual who actually performs the correction
- The group or individual who monitors and reports on the level of errors and the data quality in both the warehouse and ODS

The define activity should be started at the commencement of the CRM initiative. The error-processing steps and the organizations that will be responsible for this procedure are critical to the overall success of the CRM initiative because they determine what is to be audited and controlled.

Assess Process and Data Quality

The purpose of the assess activity is to document the existing data quality in the data warehouse and ODS. This baseline assessment is used to negotiate data quality expectations and communicate these negotiated tolerances to the enterprise. It is also your starting point for determining the improvement (or lack of improvement) in specific data attributes and/or processes.

This activity recommends and documents the error-correction processes. When an error is detected, it must be studied and the appropriate action taken. This may mean correcting the error at the source if possible, correcting it before its entry into the data warehouse or ODS if not fixed at the source, or analyzing it for the impact on the usefulness of the data warehouse or ODS if completely unfixable. The assess activity may develop revised error tolerances or error-detection processes if the proposed tolerances or processes are impossible to attain or perform.

Measure Process and Data Quality

The measure activity is used to calculate, record, and monitor the quality of the data and the processes found in your CIF. These measurements are documented in the meta data repository and are reported back to the business units and IT for monitoring purposes.

The CIF administrator is notified of any out-of-tolerance levels detected in the processes or data content. He or she also studies those attributes and processes that are nearing the tolerance levels. A proactive action may be taken to deter a possible out-of-tolerance situation.

The following list is a starter set of measurements for you to use in implementing your audit and control procedures. These can be used to define the actual steps in the methodology. Each measurement should have a step defined to conduct the actual measurement and to deal with results out of the accepted tolerance level. These measurement activities should be embedded within the data acquisition processes and the results should be recorded in your meta data repository for each load period:

- Count and cross-foot checks of record numbers read, dropped, and output by each process
- Sum and cross-foot checks of dollar amounts read, dropped, and output by each process
- Comparisons of the record count and dollars output from the previous process to those input into the next process
- Comparisons of the record counts and dollar amounts received from an extract file
- Comparisons of the count and dollars loaded into the ODS, data warehouse, and the data marts
- Counts of the results from special integration processes, such as merging customer accounts, householding, and data cleansing routines
- Measurements of the completeness and accuracy of attribute values
- Computed percentages of data errors and tolerance levels
- Counts of occurrences of specific attribute values (blanks, defaults, and in-range values)

The measures are uniquely identified by an audit and control process ID and a run date. This supports the automated balancing of the processing for each data acquisition cycle (as opposed to the manual processing described earlier).

Correct Errors

Once you begin to capture the audit and control measures in your meta data, you open up a plethora of opportunities. Business users can query the meta data to determine:

- When new data has been loaded
- How much new data has been loaded
- Which data has been integrated
- Which transformations were completed
- How many errors and their types were encountered

CIF administrators can query the meta data to:

- Resolve questions concerning the growth trend for the data warehouse
- Determine the impact on processing time by the growth of the databases

- Reconcile the differences between the various databases that exist in the CIF with the sources of operational data

The purpose of the correct activity is to ensure that the negotiated quality levels for data and processes have been met and maintained. Once the appropriate correction process has been identified (in the assess activity), it must now be applied to records with errors. The correction process consists of one of the following actions:

- It enables the error to enter unchanged into the data warehouse or ODS. The error is not severe enough to warrant exclusion and is necessary for the completeness of the data. A study of the operational system generating the error should be undertaken to eliminate the continuation of the error. Perhaps the error occurred in the customer's middle initial or some other non-critical piece of information. Though flawed, the record is still useful.

- It corrects the error before the data enters the data warehouse or ODS. A solution to the error condition is possible and feasible in the time frame of the data acquisition process. The operational source of the error should be analyzed to determine if the error could be fixed at the source. An example of this type of error and its correction is an instance of a bad address abbreviation (Sr instead of St for Street).

- It uses a default value. If a correction is not possible and the inclusion of the data is mandatory for analysis, a default may be used. The record should be marked as containing a default, and a correction to the original source should be performed if possible. An example of this would be a record that had a bad date, such as February 29, 1999. That year was not a leap year, so a decision must be made as to whether a default of February 28, 1999 or of March 1, 1999 should be used.

- It rejects the errored record. If the error is too severe and a correction is not feasible, you may have to reject the record outright. The operational source should be corrected and the corrected record reprocessed. An example of this would be an incorrect transaction code. You have no way of determining what the code should have been without studying the original entry or contacting the customer.

The Role of Audit and Control Meta Data

The meta data captured during the audit and control process is used to prove that you have indeed met (or exceeded) the business community's expectations on data quality. It is also used to alert these users to possible data quality problems and to track the performance of your quality improvement programs.

Finally, the audit and control meta data is used to ensure that the Corporate Information Factory has processed all the inputs correctly.

You may want to produce many types of reports, such as the following:

- Attribute errors by source
- Overall accuracy summary by attribute
- Process start and end times
- Process total counts and sums
- Process cross-foot errors (such as out-of-balance situations)
- Process failures
- Process integration activities (such as records merged or householded)
- Tolerance levels exceeded and tolerance level early warnings
- Total defaults applied

These reports are generated from the meta data captured during the audit and control process. A list of the meta data fields that you will need to incorporate into your meta data repository is shown in Figure 7.7.

- Process definition

- Process audit reference

- Process measurements

- Attribute definition

- Attribute control reference

- Attribute measurements

- Attribute valid values

- Process error conditions

- Attribute error results

- Attribute content summaries

Figure 7.7 Audit and control meta data attributes.

Meta Data Capture and Maintenance

The meta data involved in the overall data acquisition process has been discussed throughout this chapter. The majority of the meta data captured is very technical in nature (sources of data, targets of data, transformation rules, error conditions, audit, and control measurements) and is predominantly used by the implementers and administrators of the Corporate Information Factory. However, a fair amount of business meta data also will be captured during this process and will be of interest to the business community using this environment. For example, the business rules for data integration (such as a transaction must be connected to both a customer and a product) are useful to both the implementers as well as the users of the data. Definitions of entities, attributes, and calculations are of great help in understanding and using the environment. Once published, these pieces of meta data assure the business community that they are using the correct data or that the information was calculated in the same fashion in which they would have calculated it.

The job control process also captures useful meta data about the completion of job runs and the statistics associated with those runs (such as start and stop times and the completion statuses of programs). Other meta data is used to kick off the data acquisition programs in the proper order. Job scheduling can be complex, especially when many operational sources are involved in the process.

Our recommendation is that you seriously look into the purchase of a mature data acquisition tool suite. The suite should have a robust set of integration algorithms, be able to interface with data cleansing/quality tools, and have a meta data architecture that is open and can be interfaced with your meta data repository.

Summary

Data acquisition is critical to the success of your CIF and CRM initiative. You will encounter any number of data integration difficulties, political and cultural issues, and technological hurdles when you embark on this activity. Our experience has shown this to be the single most difficult step in the overall construction of this environment. If it is not done properly, the success of your entire CRM effort may be in jeopardy.

Once available customer data is identified and mapped to the components of the Corporate Information Factory, the data must be captured and integrated.

Customer information is usually scattered in many operational systems. These systems often have different versions of the truth. External sources of data must be integrated with information from within the enterprise. These key data integration decisions will ultimately define how the enterprise will interact with customers.

The programs must then be written to capture, integrate, cleanse, and transform the data from operational systems and external sources. Next, the data is loaded into the ODS or data warehouse. Proper audit and control procedures must be embedded in these processes to ensure that the data is the best it can be and that it can be reconciled back to the original sources. Finally, the all-important meta data created during this process must be captured in a maintainable fashion and be presented to both the implementers and the business community.

Quality Relationships Start with Quality Customer Data

In Chapter 1, "The Customer Becomes the Center of the Business Universe," we introduced Bob and his parents, who were used to illustrate the traditional and extended households. Bob's parents constitute a traditional household. These are two individuals who act as a single economic unit. However, Bob and his parents together constitute an extended household. These are two sets of people who act as two independent economic units, but who also have a relationship that, if recognized, can be nurtured to the benefit of the customers and the profitability of the bank. Simply having correct and complete information about Bob and about his parents is not enough; the relationship between them must also be recognized. To serve customers like these well, the bank needs quality customer data.

The quality of customer data cannot begin with the data itself. Instead, it must begin with the business processes that determine which data is to be collected and how that data is to be used to benefit both the enterprise and the customer. This chapter starts by defining what quality is and isn't. We then examine the basic foundations of any quality program, as espoused by one of this century's leading quality experts, W. Edwards Deming. Armed with an understanding of these foundational principles, we'll look at how they can be applied to Customer Relationship Management. In particular, we will examine the steps for capturing, cleaning, and transforming data to ensure the quality of customer information. Thankfully, automated tools can be used to help in this process, and this chapter reviews how they can be used. This chapter also explains the important role of the data steward in championing the cause of data quality.

Quality Defined

If you ask 10 people to define quality, you should expect many to indicate that it is synonymous with perfection. If you ask which type of car, luxury or economy, has a higher level of quality, most people would pick the luxury car. Further, if you ask if quality is expensive, many people would say yes. If you ask how to measure quality, some would even tell you that quality is subjective and cannot be measured.

If you address these same questions to the leading authorities on quality, you will get very different answers. The four myths that follow provide a definition of quality and explain how it differs from common perceptions.

Myth 1: Quality Means Perfection

Quality does not mean perfection. It means "conformance to requirements."[1] The key to determining quality, therefore, resides in determining the requirements.

The people responsible for a business function must set requirements or standards. In the case of customer data quality requirements, these need to be set by representatives of Sales, Marketing, Customer Service, and Fulfillment. If the enterprise has adopted the organizational structure recommended in Chapter 4, "Are You Ready? Tuning the Organization for CRM," the Strategic Operations group can ensure that the requirements are set and coordinated. The key factors to consider are completeness, accuracy, timeliness, delivery, and cost:

Completeness is a measure of the extent to which we include all germane data. For the net sales revenue generated by a customer, completeness would be an indication of the degree to which we include all appropriate sales transactions and all data about each sales transaction. Completeness also encompasses recognition of the relationships for a household.

Accuracy is a measure of the correctness of the data. Although completeness is a measure of the inclusion of all appropriate transactions, accuracy is an indication of the correctness of the information provided. In a formula for calculating net sales that accommodates internal costs, taxes, and commissions, accuracy reflects the extent to which the formula is properly applied. It also addresses the validity of all information maintained about each customer.

[1]Philip B. Crosby, *Quality Is Free.* (Penguin Books, 1979).

Timeliness is a measure of the availability of the data when it is needed. Financial institutions are a good example of timeliness requirements. Updating account balance information on a daily basis may be acceptable for some purposes, but up-to-the-minute information may be required for other purposes. Setting a timeliness measure requires that the organization agree upon an acceptable delay factor for the availability of data. In the Customer Relationship Management (CRM) world, timeliness also addresses the speed with which changes to a customer's information (such as a new address or phone number) are available to systems and to customer service personnel.

Delivery is a measure of the extent to which the data is delivered in a way that the business user finds acceptable. If the user is expecting graphical displays and we provide only tabular displays, we have not provided quality in the area of delivery. If our customers have access to information through our Web site, delivery is also a measure of the extent to which the navigation path through our Web site meets their expectations.

Cost is also a measure of quality. If cost were not a factor, then the demands for completeness, accuracy, timeliness, and delivery would be set substantially higher than what is actually needed. Cost, as a factor of quality, ensures that the business value of the requirement is considered. The definition of CRM indicates that customer interactions should be conducted to the long-term satisfaction of the customer and to the benefit and profit of the organization. The cost of the CRM environment must be considered because it is a factor in determining profit.

As you may have deduced, conflicts can occur between the quality components. For example, if we want complete data, we may have to sacrifice timeliness. If we want perfect data, we may have to pay more. The requirements must be set through a negotiation process involving all key parties that provide, manage, and use the data. Figure 8.1 displays metrics for the five components of quality. Within the figure, the circular point on each axis represents the quality expectation. For the set of data portrayed, quality is achieved for cost and accuracy, but not for completeness, timeliness, and delivery. In other words, the effort costs less than expected and provides better accuracy than expected. However, it does not provide as much data as expected, and the data is provided late and not in the agreed form.

Quality either exists or does not. Data may have a high level of completeness, but it is either quality data or non-quality data, depending on whether or not the level of completeness is above or below the established requirements. Figure 8.2 demonstrates the road to quality. An initial target defect standard is set through the negotiations described earlier. At first, the actual defect rate is above this standard, and until the defects fall consistently at or below the agreed threshold, we do not have quality data. Time has an interesting impact

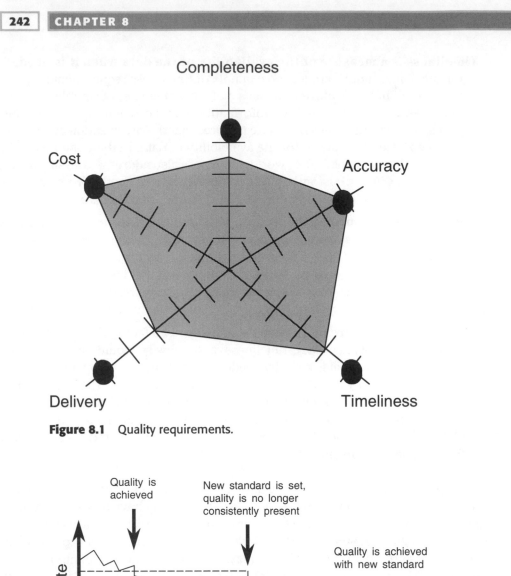

Figure 8.1   Quality requirements.

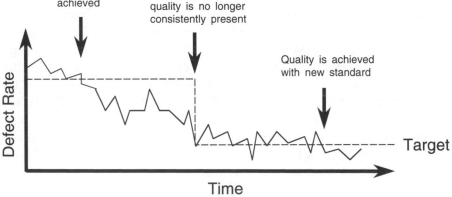

Figure 8.2   The road to quality.

on quality in this example. Although the initial defect rate is realistic given the state of the data, it changes considerably from the beginning of the process to the end. As the data quality level improves to meet the initial standards, the standards are reevaluated and made more stringent. Over time, the organization progresses in a stair-step method: setting a realistic quality standard, improving the defect rate to meet this standard, and then lowering the acceptable standards again. The road to quality reflects the continuous cycle in which we evaluate our current state, establish a standard, measure results, and, if needed, take actions to implement improvements.

Myth 2: Quality Means Luxury

Quality does not mean luxury. If we adopt the definition of "conformance to requirements," then we will see that the quality of the luxury car versus that of the economy model depends on the expectations of each car's owner. Customers looking for a luxury car have expectations with respect to size, luxury appointments, defects, gas mileage, ride smoothness, and price. Economy car purchasers also have expectations with respect to these factors. However, the expectations of the two sets of customers are quite different. In each case, if the delivered automobile meets expectations, then the customer has received a quality automobile; if it does not, then the customer has not received one.

The analogy extends to our CRM data and systems. Some companies implement elaborate CRM systems, while others implement simple ones. In each case, if the system meets the standards set by the business community, then quality exists.

Myth 3: Quality Is Expensive

The quality experts are consistent in one message: quality is not expensive—the lack of quality is. If all costs are considered, including the cost of errors, it is less expensive to build a quality product than a non-quality product. In other words, building a product that conforms to requirements is less expensive than building one that does not.

When we build a data warehouse or operational data store (ODS), the main cost we incur is the cost of "unquality," or the cost of not having quality. Data cleansing and data integration are two major activities that must be performed when moving data from the operational systems to the data warehouse or ODS. Virtually all of the related data cleansing work is a cost of unquality, which is the cost of detecting and addressing errors that exist in the operational environment. Similarly, much of the data integration work compensates for our previous failure to build systems with a single view of the customer. When we develop data collection processes and systems, it is important to build them with quality in mind. The absence of quality in our source systems is a major contributor to the development cost and time for data warehouses and ODSs.

Let's examine data cleansing. Some people will assert that the costs associated with data cleansing are the costs of quality. However, these are not the costs of quality—these are the costs of the lack of quality! The data cleansing costs are incurred primarily because the data that is acquired does not conform to the established quality standards. Measures are finally being implemented to help cope with the errors, but most of the activities are merely to correct situations that should not have existed in the first place. Had the source systems and the related business processes been created such that they produced quality data, the data cleansing task would be substantially reduced.

Now let's examine data integration. Data integration costs could be incurred for a number of reasons. Sometimes these are truly costs of quality, and sometimes they are costs of unquality. When we attempt to enter a new customer into our customer database, our process should include an analysis to determine if this customer already exists. This analysis may be performed through a combination of manual and automated methods, and if performed properly, it does add cost to the initial data collection. However, it also saves a tremendous amount of money in the data integration effort subsequently needed to ensure that we have a single view of the customer. The costs of the integration needed to bring data together from individual systems typically reflect myopic development efforts that consider only the project sponsor's view and not the enterprise view. These are the costs of unquality and they are needed to overcome quality deficiencies that we are inheriting from source systems. Note that, if this type of integration is needed to bring data together from systems that originated in different companies that have since merged, then the costs could be considered to be costs of quality.

The distinction between the cost of quality and the cost of unquality may seem overstated, but it really isn't. When we embark on a CRM initiative, we will need to obtain funding. Quantifying the costs incurred due to the lack of quality, and distinguishing between these costs and the costs of ensuring quality can help us to demonstrate the value of providing an enterprise view of customer data.

Myth 4: Quality Cannot Be Measured

The definition of quality, conformance to requirements, holds the secret to its measurement. "Conformance to requirements" implies that a set of requirements is defined. These requirements may pertain to tolerance levels, production costs, defect rates, or anything else that the people setting the requirements feel is appropriate. Measuring quality entails the establishment of a standard and of a metric that can be used to determine whether or not the standard is satisfied. Quality is binary. If we meet or exceed the standard, we have quality. If we fall below the standard, we have unquality.

Table 8.1   Quality Measures

QUALITY COMPONENT	POTENTIAL MEASURES
Completeness	Percent of data available
Accuracy	Percent of records with errors (may be for data or relationships)
Timeliness	Percent of time data is available at prescribed time
Delivery	Percent of users satisfied with delivery method (may be obtained through customer survey)
Cost	Actual versus budget

Previously, five types of quality requirements were identified. Table 8.1 lists potential measures for each requirement. Service level agreements (SLAs) provide a useful method for documenting the agreed-upon quality expectations.

Reality Check

The reality is that quality does not mean perfection or luxury; it means conformance to requirements. Quality itself is not expensive. Enterprises often incur significant expenses when they initiate a quality program, but these costs are costs of not having quality. They are the costs for ridding the enterprise of practices that have led to its current (often unacceptable) state of unquality. Quality can be measured. A standard can be established for each of the significant requirements, and a process for measuring conformance can be implemented. Now that we have a definition for quality, let's examine what we should do to instill a quality-oriented culture for our CRM initiative.

The Foundations of a Quality Program: Deming's 14 Points

W. Edwards Deming is responsible for helping major companies, primarily in Japan and the U.S., migrate to a quality environment. Following World War II, business was booming in the U.S., but Japan was recovering from a devastating war. Dr. Deming, who could be called "the man who discovered quality,"[2] attempted to help improve quality within companies in the U.S., but his

---

[2]This is the title of a book by Andrea Gabor about Dr. Deming's efforts.

attempts were not well received. The general attitude was, "business is good—why improve quality?" The situation in Japan was very different; they readily accepted Dr. Deming's advice, and during the ensuing decades, Dr. Deming was instrumental in helping quality infiltrate the Japanese business culture. To this day, the most coveted award for quality issued by the Union of Japanese Scientists and Engineers (JUSE) is the Deming Prize for quality.

During the 1970s and 1980s, the actual and perceived quality of Japanese products improved, while the actual and perceived quality of American products declined. When this began to hit the bottom line (when U.S. consumers began buying more and more Japanese cars), U.S. corporations joined the quality bandwagon and solicited help from Dr. Deming and others. In 1989, one U.S. company, Florida Power & Light, successfully vied for the Deming Prize. Its executives were instrumental in influencing Congress to establish a similar prize in the United States, and as a result, the Malcolm Baldrige National Quality Award[3] was created in 1987 to recognize companies that exhibit excellence in the areas of leadership, strategic planning, customer and market focus, information and analysis, human resource focus, process management, and business results. In line with the criteria for the Deming Prize, the criteria[4] for the Malcolm Baldrige National Quality Award are designed to help organizations enhance their performance through a focus on

■ The delivery of ever-improving value to customers, resulting in market-place success

■ The improvement of overall organizational effectiveness and capabilities

Dr. Deming delineated 14 points that he felt were required to establish a firm foundation for any ongoing enterprise. On the surface, these points appear to be simple, and when looked at individually, most people would agree that they provide a logical way to manage an enterprise. Most enterprises, however, do not fully adopt (or adapt) the 14 points. As we embark on a CRM initiative, we need to examine the extent to which our enterprise follows the concepts proposed by these points. The further along we are, the stronger our foundation. If the organization does not observe these points, it must recognize the resulting deficiencies and address them to the extent needed within its CRM initiative.

---

[3]The award is named after Malcolm Baldrige, Secretary of Commerce from 1981 until his death in 1987. Mr. Baldrige's managerial excellence contributed to long-term improvement in efficiency and effectiveness of government.

[4]Baldrige National Quality Program 2000—Criteria for Performance Excellence.

Point 1: Create Constancy of Purpose for the Improvement of Products and Services

Constancy of purpose is at the heart of an organization intent on ensuring quality. It entails an emphasis on a long-term perspective, with particular focus on the customer. An organization focused on constancy of purpose considers all actions in light of the downstream impact on its ability to continue meeting customer needs. An organization with this focus is willing to relinquish the emphasis on short-term objectives, such as measuring monthly profitability, in the interest of building a foundation that will enable the company to survive, and even thrive. These companies are willing to invest in research and in helping to grow their workforce.

Within the context of CRM, the long-term focus is critical. Successful CRM programs don't just happen; they require careful planning and an infrastructure that can stand the test of time. The data model, described in Chapter 6, "Developing an Integrated CRM Technology Environment," is a critical component. Creating an enterprise view in the data model takes time, and it takes commitment. Building this model will typically add to the development time for the first project, but it also has an immediate data quality payback, even for the first project. The data modeling process examines both the data needed about the customers and the governing business rules. Part of this process, for example, includes the delineation of different customer types and the definition of each element maintained about the customer. The discussions that lead to the conclusions reflected in the model often uncover data quality problems that can be addressed in the data acquisition process.

Additional payback comes in subsequent projects. Each succeeding project can piggyback on the work previously performed. If "customer" is defined for the first project, it does not need to be redefined in a later one. If the business rules between "customer" and "product" are resolved for the first project, subsequent projects can use and possibly refine them based on additional information.

The architecture embodied by the Corporate Information Factory (CIF), introduced in Chapter 2, "The Customer and the Corporate Information Factory (CIF)," is part of this foundation. At the start of a move to CRM, the business strategy should define the guiding conceptual architecture. The technical architecture can be built incrementally over time, but without some forethought as to how everything will fit together, there is a greater chance that some of the components will not be as scalable or flexible as needed.

Deming's 14 Points[5]

1. Create constancy of purpose for the improvement of products and services.
2. Adopt the new philosophy.
3. Cease dependence on mass inspection.
4. End the practice of awarding business on price tag alone.
5. Improve constantly and forever the system of production and service.
6. Institute training.
7. Institute *leadership*.
8. Drive out fear.
9. Break down barriers between staff areas.
10. Eliminate slogans, exhortations, and targets for the workforce.
11. Eliminate numerical quotas.
12. Remove barriers to pride of workmanship.
13. Institute a vigorous program of education and retraining.
14. Take action to accomplish the transformation.

Point 2: Adopt the New Philosophy

The second point, adopt the new philosophy, is perhaps one of the most difficult to implement in successful companies. The new philosophy refers to becoming intolerant of poor workmanship and service. Within successful companies, the executives may look around and ask themselves, "Why should we change? We're successful!" This is exactly what happened when Dr. Deming first tried to introduce his concepts in the U.S. Unsuccessful companies have a much easier time understanding the importance of adopting the new philosophy.

Even if your organization is successful, try to look into the future and consider whether or not your current practices will enable you to continue being successful. CRM demands that we consistently provide our customers with the workmanship and service they expect. This can only be accomplished if we accept this point and if we adjust our culture so that everyone in the organization knows that we value quality in everything we do. Adopting a new culture does not happen overnight. It takes executive commitment, and it takes time. In keeping with the first point, you must be willing to spend the time to build this philosophical change into your foundation.

[5] Mary Walton. *The Deming Management Method.* (Dodd, Mead & Company, 1986.)

The organizational structure promoted in Chapter 4 is a critical component of adopting the new philosophy (see Figure 8.3). This organizational structure recognizes the importance of properly serving the customer and of providing a unified approach at all customer touch points.

The data stewardship function (described subsequently in this chapter) can flourish in an organization that adopts the new philosophy. One of the roles of the data steward is to establish and then enforce practices designed to meet quality expectations. The scope of the steward's involvement includes the business processes that collect the data from the customer, the processes that transfer that data into electronic form, the systems that maintain the electronic data, and the application of the data by the business community. An effective stewardship program can go a long way towards ensuring data quality.

Point 3: Cease Dependence on Mass Inspection

Quality cannot be inspected into a product; it must be built into it. Deming's third point emphasizes the need to establish processes that create quality products. The typical systems development life cycle includes a significant testing cycle just prior to implementation. The third point does not preclude providing an inspection to verify that quality has been attained, but it does preclude establishing the inspection with the intent of improving quality. Data quality inspections

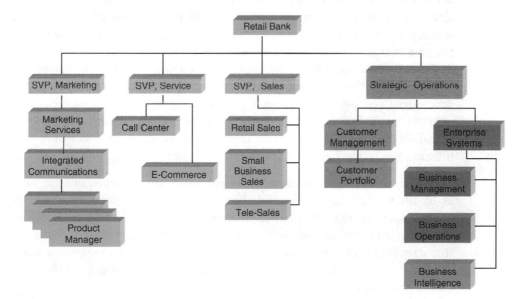

Figure 8.3 The organizational structure that promotes the new philosophy.

are commonly performed to support CRM initiatives. A variety of data quality analysis and data scrubbing tools that are specifically oriented towards customer data can be used in such inspections. In keeping with this point, these tools include features for improving quality based on the inspections, thereby building quality into the product. (These tools are described later in this chapter.)

The methodology for traditional systems development includes a clear definition of the requirements and specifications, as well as a verification that these are appropriate. The methodology for decision support systems includes steps for defining the needed information from a business perspective and for modeling the relationships among business entities. Once development begins, the process includes various peer reviews, the involvement of key people throughout the cycle, and the verification of each component as it is developed. If everything is developed properly, then the final testing cycle should merely confirm that quality has been achieved. Problems found during this final test are several times more costly to correct than they would be if detected and corrected during development. This is another example of a cost of unquality.

To illustrate the importance of verifying quality, consider its impact on one key CRM function, the fulfillment of customer orders. We cannot wait for the customer's inspectors at the receiving dock to tell we that we have shipped the wrong product, the wrong product quantity, or a defective product. We need to build a process, beginning with our first customer contact, which ensures that we understand the customer's needs and that we ship exactly what the customer requests. In Chapter 6, both the process model and the data model are presented. The fulfillment function is defined near the top of the decomposition diagram. It is then decomposed into its contributing processes, and eventually these processes are described. Data flow diagrams are used to describe the processes that need to be implemented in computer systems. The creation and maintenance of the process model enables us to understand business processes so that appropriate systems and procedures can be developed to support these processes. The better we understand the process, the more equipped we are to ensure that we build quality into it. By understanding the business processes and transforming them into the data flow diagrams, we have a continuous flow of information to the people responsible for building the supporting systems.

The process model is not used for decision support systems, but the data model is. In developing the data model, the data analyst and business representatives spend much needed time to ensure a common understanding of each element and group of elements (such as an entity) that are to be included. Going through this exercise eliminates surprises such as when end users use or inspect the data only to discover that their definitions and the meaning of the data in the databases differ.

Establishing a test database of customer data is one way of ensuring that quality is built into the process. This applies to the development of operational systems as well as to the development of the data acquisition and delivery processes associated with the data warehouse and operational data store. If the databases are built on statistically valid segments of the population, they are invaluable both in testing new routines during development and in performing sanity checks on the demographics of the customer data itself.

Point 4: End the Practice of Awarding Business on Price Tag Alone

Most enterprises depend on goods and services from other enterprises. These goods and services may be used internally or they may be used within the products provided by the company to its customers. In a competitive environment, companies tend to provide products at competitive prices. Enterprises with a quality culture look at more than just the price; they examine value. Value considers the price along with other factors such as quality, ease of use, maintenance requirements, available features, and extensibility. These other factors are included in what is sometimes known as life cycle cost.

Within the typical systems organization, the development teams are under constant pressure to complete projects as quickly as possible. This is another manifestation of awarding business on the basis of price tag alone. The team that gets done first gets the accolades. Additionally, the development manager can be under pressure to reduce costs and can therefore avoid investing in tools that could ensure data quality. It should come as no surprise that when we promote this type of behavior, project teams often take short cuts that do not consider the enterprise perspective or the downstream implications. Many systems built like this encounter a rough break-in period. The net result is that the data produced by these systems does not meet the quality expectations. Ending the practice of awarding business on price tag alone means that the development project timeframe and cost reflect all of the activities needed to ensure that a quality system is produced. When we consider the cost of having inaccurate data, the additional cost incurred to provide quality data is easily justified.

Consider the case of a direct marketing firm that is sending brochures to customers with selected profiles. If the data in the database is inaccurate, brochures are sent to many customers that don't really match the intended profile, which wastes the money associated with printing and distributing these brochures. More significantly, many customers that should receive the brochure do not get it, generating a tremendous opportunity loss.

In Chapter 1, the supplier is included in the broad definition of customer. For us to succeed, our suppliers must also succeed. We definitely need to consider price in our decisions, but the price has to be balanced with other factors. Remember, to our customers, we are the supplier. We should treat our suppliers in the same manner that we would like our customers to treat us. The CRM philosophy indicates that we should conduct all customer (and hence supplier) interactions to the long-term satisfaction and benefit of both parties.

Point 5: Improve Constantly and Forever the System of Production and Service

Point 5 teaches us not to be satisfied with the status quo. Organizations that adopt the quality philosophy spend a significant amount of time documenting their critical processes. Within the process documentation, various checkpoints are included so that both process quality and process results can be measured. Documentation of the process is the first step of the continuous improvement cycle. This cycle consists of four steps—plan, do, check, and act (PDCA)—and is represented diagrammatically in Figure 8.4 as a revolving wheel.

Plan: Planning consists of determining how something will be done and documenting that process. The documentation should include mechanisms to ensure quality (as promoted by the third point), and mechanisms to verify compliance with the quality standards. As an example, CRM applications

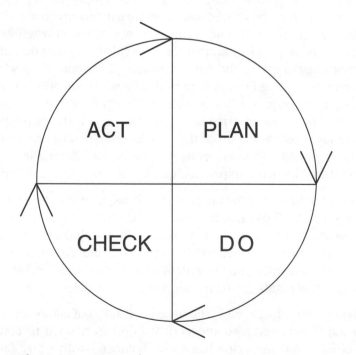

Figure 8.4 PDCA cycle.

often require accurate customer contact information. During planning, we define the business processes and the associated systems and tools to acquire and maintain quality customer contact information.

Do: Doing consists of actually performing the prescribed process. In our customer contact example, Do includes acquiring and maintaining the customer contact information in accordance with the prescribed processes.

Check: Checking consists of verifying that the results meet quality expectations. As part of the planning effort, measurement points should be inserted into the process. For example, we may want to measure the accuracy of the customer contact information on a weekly basis. If our quality standard is for 98 percent of the information to be accurate, then we regularly check the actual accuracy against the quality standard. Control charts provide a useful technique for monitoring the results of the processes like this one.[6] The control chart in Figure 8.5 sets the quality standard for the acquisition and maintenance of customer contact information to an inaccuracy level of two percent.

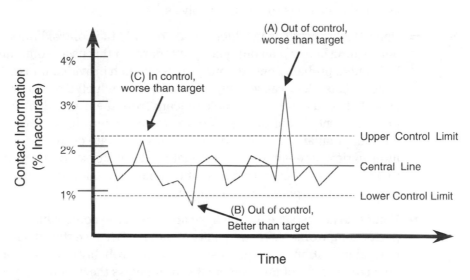

Figure 8.5   Control chart.

[6]Control charts were first introduced by W.A. Shewhart in 1927 to eliminate abnormal variations by distinguishing between variations due to assignable causes and due to chance causes. For additional information, see *Statistical Methods for Quality Improvement* by Hitoshi Kume (The Association for Oversees Technical Scholarship, Japan, 1985).

In a control chart, measurements are plotted over time. In the example, we would plot the percent of customers with invalid contact information each week. Statistically speaking, if a process is in control, 99.7 percent of the values should be within three standard deviations of the center value. In Figure 8.5, the Upper and Lower Control Limits mark these three standard deviations from our acceptable inaccuracy standard of two percent. Anything falling between these outer limits is considered to be "in control" and thus close to acceptable quality standards.

Three points within Figure 8.5 require special attention:

- Point A is an instance in which we are both outside the control limits and are performing worse than our quality standard. A point that lies outside of the control limits is an indication that something unusual is occurring, and every point that lies outside the control limits should be investigated to identify the assignable cause. In this case, we are looking for something that is probably outside our process that contributed to the unfavorable result. For example, we may have just acquired another company (one with inaccurate customer contact information) and entered its information. A common technique for investigating the assignable cause is root cause analysis.[7]

- Point B is an instance in which we are outside the control limits and are performing better than our quality standard. In this case, something happened, probably outside our process, which provided unusually good results. Root cause analysis should be conducted on these points as well, because we may be able to learn from them and identify improvements in our process. For example, we may have just acquired another company (one with exceptionally accurate customer contact information) and entered its information. In this case, we may choose to analyze the process used by that company and modify our own process to incorporate improvements.

- Point C is an instance in which we are within the control limits and are performing worse than our quality standard. Because this is within the normal operation of the process, we would probably take note of this occurrence but not take remedial action unless the accuracy rates continue to fall short of our quality standard.

Act: Acting consists of taking the steps needed to eliminate assignable causes and improving the process itself. Once we identify the root cause of a prob-

---

[7]Root cause analysis is outside the scope of this book. For additional information, see *Statistical Methods for Quality Improvement* by Hitoshi Kume (The Association for Oversees Technical Scholarship, Japan, 1985).

lem, we can initiate appropriate actions to prevent the same situation from occurring again (or to prevent it from impacting our process should it occur again). In the previous example, two actions would be appropriate; the first is to review the processes used within the company being acquired, and the second is to verify data accuracy prior to absorbing its data. When the process is in control, we need to examine whether or not opportunities exist to improve the overall performance. This would be the case if we continue to have measurements similar to Point C. In so doing, we may, in fact, be redefining the quality because we would be establishing a new standard.

Our customers demand quality. The fifth point teaches us not to be satisfied just because we meet the customer demands today. We need to constantly examine our processes and look for improvements. This can be accomplished by defining the processes (plan), performing them properly (do), verifying the results (check), and taking actions to eliminate deviations due to assignable causes, as well as taking actions to improve the overall performance of the process (act).

Point 6: Institute Training

Our workforce must understand what it needs to do, how it needs to do it, and why it needs to do it. We can do a fantastic job documenting our processes, but if we don't train the staff, then all we have are sheets of paper in a notebook. When problems occur within the quality-oriented company, the underlying assumption is that it is a process problem and not a people problem. When a process is out of control (see point 5), the root cause may be inadequate training.

People will generally do a better job if they understand the task and the reasons for it. Therefore, the place to start is to ensure that everyone in the company understands the new philosophy. When Florida Power & Light implemented its Quality Improvement Program, it conducted an extensive training program for its entire workforce. This training provided information on the program and on the reasons why the company deemed quality to be so important.

Inaccurate customer data can often be attributed to data entry problems. When the customer service representative (CSR) is speaking with a customer, useful information is collected. Sometimes the CSR will pay particular attention to the data he or she needs to perform his or her job and ignore other important data. During the conversation, the representative may be in a position to collect data relating to the customer's age and income level, for example, but because the CSR won't be using that information, he or she may either not seek it or just enter any value (such as ZZZZ if it is a required field). Given the typical compensation practices in a company, it is not unusual to have people focus only on what they need to perform a task so that they can complete their work faster.

Training will help the employee understand how information can help the company meet its business goals, thus highlighting its value.

The training curriculum should address CRM principles as well as the company's goals and philosophy with respect to CRM. It should also address the specific processes with which the individual will be involved. Once the workforce understands the philosophy, each member of the workforce must be trained on his or her specific job, on how that job impacts others, and on the importance of teamwork. Within the context of CRM, this education helps ensure that all people who provide service to the customer do so using a common set of procedures. It also helps ensure that these people understand the downstream implications of their work so they will work together to provide the required level of service.

Point 7: Institute Leadership

Leadership is the management process that causes each person to perform his or her assigned work in a quality manner. For sustained results, the leader must establish understandable goals and objectives, ensure that individuals are committed to these goals and objectives, define the measurement methods, and then provide the environment within which people can perform their work. Point 6 addresses the first responsibility of the leaders by ensuring that people understand their jobs. The biggest challenge is often in providing the proper environment. This starts with points 1 and 2, creating the constancy of purpose and adopting the new philosophy. The leader needs to serve as a coach, not as an enforcer. The leader's responsibility is to help all employees achieve the quality objectives.

Leadership must start at the top, and it must filter through each successive level of management. For a CRM initiative to be successful, the executives of the organization must understand its implications, and they must institute a supportive culture. The executives must also create an environment in which people who interact with the customers understand what to do and how to do it without fear of repercussions for making mistakes. Part of creating that environment is ensuring that the successive levels of management buy into these concepts and promote them.

Nordstrom's embodies this philosophy with respect to customer service because members of the Nordstrom family provide leadership within the company. Their confidence in the employees is embodied by the company's only rule: "Use your good judgment in all situations. There will be no additional rules. Please feel free to ask your department manager, store manager, or division general manager any question at any time."[8] Nordstrom employees understand the importance of serving the customers. They further understand that they each have great discretion in how to carry out that mission.

The data steward (or stewardship committee) provides leadership with respect to data quality. This person (or group) sets the expectations and establishes the processes to ensure that people understand and can meet these expectations. A common focus for the steward is to resolve differences in opinion with respect to the meaning of terms such as customer. Part of the issue resolution process for customer includes obtaining agreement on the definition and spreading the word about this definition and the associated information so that the organization understands what is available.

Point 8: Drive Out Fear

Fear must be driven out so that everyone can work effectively for the company. When people are afraid, they cannot be fully productive. A new employee should not be expected to fully understand the job on the first day. In addition to providing training (point 6), it is important to create an environment in which the employee is comfortable asking questions. We must recognize that people will make mistakes and fear of consequences can cause them to try to hide these mistakes. This situation creates two problems. First, if nothing is done to help the person understand how to avoid the mistake when it happens the first time, it is likely to occur again. Second, when the mistake is ultimately discovered, and it will be discovered, the cost of taking the corrective action (the cost of unquality) will be higher.

The good judgment rule for Nordstrom employees is designed to drive out fear. Nordstrom employees know that they will never be criticized for actions they take to service a customer. Stories abound about heroic actions by these employees. Although these actions often cost the company money in the short term, Nordstrom recognizes that profitability will come through long-term relationships, and that its employees are critical in establishing and nurturing these relationships. Nordstrom employs measures to ensure that employees feel comfortable with making decisions on their own. The company has enjoyed a reputation for customer service for over a century, and its non-threatening environment is one of the factors responsible for its success in this area.

[8]Robert Spector and Patrick D. McCarthy. *The Nordstrom Way, 2nd Edition.* (John Wiley & Sons, 2000.)

The way in which the data steward approaches his or her responsibilities can discourage or encourage people to identify problems. If an employee finds a definition discrepancy, he or she should feel free to discuss it with the data steward. If the steward gives any indication that the person is a troublemaker who should just stick to the basic job at hand, the employee may be afraid to point out problems in the future. If, on the other hand, the steward welcomes these constructive comments and enlists help in resolving the problem, the employee is likely to feel good about helping the company improve quality and will be more inclined to assist in identifying or resolving problems in the future.

Point 9: Break Down Barriers between Staff Areas

Organizational structures often create barriers to teamwork. These structures may create incentives for individuals or groups to hoard information. We've been involved in numerous sales-oriented data warehousing efforts in which the team is instructed to build the data warehouse, but to restrict one region's access to another region's information, even though the same customer may purchase goods from both regions. We've also been involved in efforts in which the inventory management department requested that information about material deliveries and turnover not be provided to the procurement department. These situations are often the result of incentive programs that discourage information sharing.

Teamwork is a requirement for a quality-oriented organization. If we are to properly serve our customers, we need to have as complete a picture of the customer's business with our organization as possible. Without a cross-regional enterprise view of customers, an effective service cannot be accomplished. Chapter 4 describes the problems with the traditional organization that consists of distinct Sales, Service, Marketing, and Fulfillment. As shown in Figure 8.3, we must create an organizational structure and philosophy that promotes the sharing of information among these areas.

When it comes to data quality, part of the steward's job is to look at data horizontally (cross-functionally) and not vertically (for a single functional area). Often, a committee performs the stewardship function to ensure that the various staff areas do indeed work together. As a team, this committee can understand all viewpoints and arrive at a solution that is best for the enterprise as a whole.

Point 10: Eliminate Slogans, Exhortations, and Targets for the Workforce

Slogans, exhortations, and targets for the workforce in themselves don't help people do a good job. Just saying that "quality is our most important job" or "we're here to serve the customer" isn't enough. These slogans generally imply that attainment of the goal is dependent on extra effort by the employees. It is management, not the employees, that must set the stage for quality improvement. Management must create a nurturing environment and provide the necessary tools and systems to ensure quality improvement.

Slogans may provide a focus, but if these are empty slogans, they quickly get discarded as the fad of the day. We don't need to establish a slogan that emphasizes CRM. We need to ensure that all our employees understand what we mean by CRM and that the processes we have in place facilitate customer interactions, which are conducted to the long-term satisfaction of the customer and to the benefit and profitability of the organization.

Data quality is no different. A slogan such as "we won't tolerate data errors" is actually counterproductive. For one thing, the implied goal is not attainable. Further, it implies that the data errors are caused by the workers, not by process defects or by a lack of quality-related tools. It's fine to have a goal of eliminating (or reducing) data errors, but this goal becomes meaningful only if it is supported by management actions that develop sound practices and by a methodology that includes all required steps, such as development of the data model.

Point 11: Eliminate Numerical Quotas

Numerical quotas are effective for influencing short-term behavior, but they are not effective for influencing long-term quality results. Think about the following situations:

- A company has a profitability objective for the quarter. In an effort to reach that objective, the most profitable division is sold. Result: The profitability objective for the quarter is met, but the company's long-term viability is jeopardized.

■ A police officer is expected to issue five speeding tickets a day. Result: If by the mid-afternoon the officer issued less than five speeding tickets, he or she may be more critical than usual and may actually issue a ticket to someone who isn't speeding. Alternatively, if by the mid-afternoon the officer already issued five speeding tickets, he or she may ignore drivers who are speeding.

These are two examples of incentives that influence behavior to meet the quota, while losing sight of the true objective. The other problem with numerical quotas is that these quotas generally presume that the person performing the work, not the underlying process and supporting systems, is responsible for the end result.

A CSR may be expected to field 10 calls per hour. The representative's ability to meet this quota may depend on a number of factors, including the nature of the call, the availability and performance of the supporting computer system, the availability of information from others who may need to support him or her, and the customer's demeanor and level of concern. A quality service organization will indeed measure the time for each call, but it should not, however, use this as a quota. If the CSR views this as a quota, then as a call approaches five or six minutes, he or she might be inclined to stop asking questions that are needed to provide data for downstream processes. Even worse, he or she may start being rude to the customer in an effort to close the call. Not only will the data quality suffer, the relationship with that customer may suffer as well.

This is the third step in the PDCA cycle, check (see point 5), and it is a very important part of the quality improvement cycle. When a call takes an abnormal amount of time, it may fall outside the control limits, and it should be analyzed to determine the assignable cause. Appropriate corrective actions, if any, (which may include additional employee training) can then be taken.

Point 12: Remove Barriers to Pride of Workmanship

People naturally like to do a good job. Part of the leader's job (see point 7) is to ensure that the people can do so. Too often procedures encumber good performance. Think about systems development and maintenance activities. In the typical company, the people who are most respected are those who complete their systems development work quickly and those who quickly fix problems when the program doesn't function properly. What about the person who takes a little longer to build a system but whose system never fails? We must be sure to develop an environment that promotes the latter behavior. We should not penalize someone for taking a little longer to develop a system if the result is that the system is more likely to perform properly and reliably.

As previously cited, Nordstrom took great strides in removing barriers to its sales representatives' pride of workmanship. These people were empowered to do what it took to serve the customers, their job satisfaction was high, and customer needs were met.

The data steward's role in driving out fear (point 8) also helps to remove barriers to pride of workmanship. Part of the steward's job is to ensure that all people involved with data—the data modelers, data analysts, business analysts, database administrators, and those who enter and use data—are concerned with the quality of that data. Each should take pride when the data meets or exceeds quality expectations. Given the compensation systems that often exist in companies, the steward, with management support, must often find innovative ways to recognize people who exert the extra effort to ensure data quality. This recognition need not include financial rewards. It could be as simple as visiting the person in his or her office or announcing the person's accomplishment. Above all, the steward must maintain an environment that encourages people to take the actions necessary to ensure data quality.

Point 13: Institute a Vigorous Program of Education and Retraining

The initial training described in point 6 prepares people to work in a quality-oriented environment, but we can't stop there. Employees can rightfully be expected to perform their jobs to the best of their abilities. Similarly, management can rightfully be expected to provide the appropriate environment and to ensure that the people understand how to perform the work. Continuing education programs are needed for two major reasons. First, the environment changes over time and, as a result, the processes evolve, new tools and techniques are introduced, and the manner in which work is performed must change. If we expect our employees to do the job properly, we must equip them to do so, and that includes education and retraining. Secondly, people often want to advance or change jobs. Before we place someone in a new job, we must ensure that they are properly trained.

CRM programs also evolve. To ensure the responsiveness to change and personal growth, training must not stop after the initial programs. When processes change, we need to inform our employees. When we learn of better ways to perform a process (from our competition, for example), we should educate our workforce so we can improve our own activities. When we bring in new people, we should ensure that they receive the necessary training. One way to accomplish this continuing education is to send employees to off-site training and conferences. These forums provide an opportunity to learn from others and then share what they have learned within the company.

Point 14: Take Action to Accomplish the Transformation

A quality-oriented CRM program does not just appear; it must be created. Creating this program requires a core group of executives that adopt the new philosophy, educate the organization in this philosophy, and provide the environment (including the tools, systems, organizational structure, and incentive programs) to successfully deploy and nurture CRM.

The actions needed to establish a quality-oriented CRM program are embedded throughout this book. They include the adoption of the appropriate organizational structure and culture, as defined in Chapter 4, and the establishment of a sound architecture, as defined in Chapter 2.

Establishing Quality Customer Data

Quality customer data must conform to CRM requirements. A new company has the opportunity to establish a CRM environment that from day one supports Deming's 14 points. Most of us, however, work for established companies and need to deal with existing business processes and data. Data acquisition, described in detail in Chapter 5, "Getting Underway," and Chapter 7, "Capturing Customer Information," is key to providing quality customer data. Two data acquisition processes need to be examined. The first deals with the initial data capture into the operational systems, and the second deals with the acquisition of data from the operational environment into the data warehouse and ODS. A new company, or a company building a new customer system, should ensure that the initial data capture provides quality data. Established companies often inherit data problems endemic in their source systems, and they must address the data quality when they capture, integrate, transform, cleanse, reengineer, and load source data into the data warehouse and ODS. Most of the remainder of this chapter deals with the latter data acquisition process, which is shown in Figure 8.6.

The data acquisition process requires that we view data from an enterprise perspective. This process includes activities such as determining the proper source for the data, establishing quality expectations with respect to the data, ensuring that the data meets these expectations, integrating data from multiple sources, and loading the data into the data warehouse and ODS. Each of the five major processes—data capture, data cleansing, data integration, data transformation, and data loading—are described within this section, and then the tools to support these processes are presented.

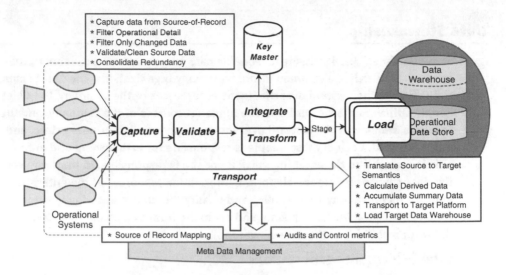

Figure 8.6 The data acquisition process.

Data stewardship is the function that is largely responsible for managing data as an enterprise asset. This function supports each of the data acquisition processes and the related business processes.

Capturing Data

For the data warehouse and ODS, capturing data consists of the steps needed to physically acquire data from each of the relevant sources. In its simplest form, this entails extracting information from each of the sources. This process has three major challenges. The first deals with establishing the proper source(s) for each data element, the second deals with the myriad technologies on which the data may reside, and the third deals with minimizing the extraneous data that is captured. Some tips for capturing data follow.

Preprocess the data at the source to the greatest practical extent. This enables each extract to be performed at the time that best suits the source system without requiring all the extracts to be performed simultaneously. Further, this approach takes advantage of processing cycles that may be available on the source platform. Consideration should be given to processing data throughout the day.

Data Stewardship

Stewardship entails exercising reasonable care over resources entrusted to the steward. Stewards are common throughout many organizations. The Chief Financial Officer is the steward over the financial resources of the company, the Chief People Officer is the steward over the human resources of the company, and the Facilities Manager is the steward over the company's buildings, real estate, and other facilities. Each of these people is responsible for establishing and enforcing policies relative to the asset for which he or she is responsible. In the same vein, the data steward is responsible for the information resources of the enterprise to improve its reusability, accessibility, and quality. The data steward may actually consist of several business people and act in the form of a committee. Some of the responsibilities of the data steward follow.

Establish Quality Expectations

The data steward is responsible for establishing the valid requirements concerning the accuracy, completeness, timeliness, delivery, and cost of the data. The data steward must carefully evaluate the existing data quality, because this will often limit the quality that can be provided through the data warehouse or ODS. Once the quality of the source data is understood, the data steward can establish the quality requirement for the data that will be available to the CSRs, and this requirement in turn dictates the types of activities required in the cleansing process.

In carrying out this responsibility, the steward might establish the following data quality expectations:

- Customer contact information shall be at least 98 percent accurate.
- The customer integration process shall be at least 95 percent effective.
- Information about the customer's age and income level shall be available and accurate at least 80 percent of the time.
- Information provided by a customer shall be available to all service representatives (through the ODS) within 15 minutes of receiving the information.

Establish Data Definitions

The data steward is responsible for defining the data elements. These definitions reflect the business meaning of the terms, and this activity is often performed during the development of the data models. Often, the same term (such as customer) means different things to different people. The key challenge faced by the data steward is to arrive at a set of definitions that everyone supports.

Imagine a world in which the person entering customer information, the person designing the system for handling, and the person using that system each have a different definition for customer. What are the chances that anything we report about the customer will be accurate?

Document the Business Rules

The business rules that govern the data relationships are often documented in the data model. The data steward should be an active participant during the modeling process to ensure that data relationships are reflective of the governing business rules. Within conventional modeling methods, the relationship may not be fully descriptive. For example, if a department may have no more than five employees, the typical data model merely indicates that a one-to-many relationship exists between department and employee. The steward must be sure to convey the limitation of five employees per department, and the data modeler must find a way to capture that information.

When we deal with customer data, the key areas that business rules need to be defined for are customer, household, and extended household. Understanding the relationships among these three entities will significantly impact the company's ability to use any information it collects.

Resolve Data Integration Issues

Arriving at a common set of data definitions is not enough. Often, the same data element exists in multiple source systems. The data steward needs to understand each of the source systems, to make decisions concerning the source systems to be used for each data element, and to determine how to resolve conflicts among source systems.

A customer may exist in multiple systems. We may choose to ignore this, but then we would not have a single view of the customer. We can't merely combine the information from these systems because conflicts may arise between systems. The steward needs to establish the rules first for detecting that the same customer exists in each of these systems and then for resolving the differences.

Establish Data Security Requirements

Although data needs to be shared among all who have a legitimate business need for this information, it also needs to be protected from access by others. This is not always a straightforward process. Information is power, and people often establish security barriers for the wrong reasons. The data steward needs to understand the reasons why people are reluctant to share information and must then work to define the data that will be available for each set of business users.

Enforce Adherence to Standards

The responsibility of the data steward goes beyond merely defining quality and security rules. The steward should also be empowered to enforce these standards and rules. This authority means that the data steward has the power to examine and initiate improvement actions related to any business or electronic process that can impact data quality. Along with this power comes the responsibility to ensure that people receive the proper training so that they understand standards, security restrictions, and the reasons for implementing security.

Extract only changed data to the greatest practical extent. The source system contains information that may have been extracted before. Extracting that information again entails extra work throughout the data acquisition process. If possible, the extract criteria should be established so that only data that changed since the last extract is processed. (This is often not possible without changing the source system.)

Capture also applies to the operational systems. After all, this is where the electronic data for the data warehouse and ODS originates. The methodology for building the operational systems needs to include all the necessary steps to ensure that these systems are capable of producing quality data. As we will see in the next section, some of the tools that are applied to cleanse data as it migrates to the data warehouse and ODS can also be used within the operational processes.

Data Cleansing

Data cleansing is needed within the operational systems as well as within the data acquisition process. If stringent data-cleansing processes and algorithms are included within the operational systems, we will have two very positive outcomes. First, the users of those systems will have better data, and second, the data acquisition process will not need to handle as many error conditions. Name and address cleansing and household creation are examples of data-cleansing activities that may occur at either juncture.

Operational System Data Cleansing

Part of the design of any operational system includes the anticipation of error conditions and the development of processes to handle them. The CRM program is heavily dependent on valid name and address information and on valid household definitions. We are fortunate in that several tools are available to help us in this area. Some of the features of these tools include the matching of addresses to valid postal addresses, and comparing customer name and address information to discern relationships that may result in identifying households. The tools are described in greater detail subsequently in this chapter.

A real-world problem that we'll need to handle is that we won't always have complete or accurate information. When a CSR enters information about a customer and lacks some critical information, we're faced with a dilemma. Do we reject the customer information, or do we accept it knowing that it is incomplete or inaccurate? Often, we'll decide that recognizing the customer is sufficiently important that we'll take the best information we have available. We may even build logic into the operational system to trigger a subsequent analysis to obtain the missing data or to correct known errors.

Data Acquisition Data Cleansing

Data cleansing within the data acquisition process consists of the steps needed to ensure that data in the data warehouse or ODS conforms to quality specifications. This may require a combination of manual and electronic processes. As each record is processed, certain quality checks are performed, and one of four actions must be taken. The data may be rejected, the error may be ignored, the data may be corrected, or a default value may be substituted for the incorrect value.[9]

Sometimes the record received from the source system contains an error that prevents it from being processed further. When this occurs, the data acquisition process has no choice but to reject the record. For example, a customer order may be received from the source system with no order date or order quantity. This condition could be one of those defined by the data steward as a condition that would cause a record to be rejected.

Sometimes data from the source system is incorrect, but it is accepted anyway. This happens when the data still conforms to the quality requirements. For example, we may have a customer record that contains a birth date of February 15, 1833 for an active customer. Our quality expectations may be such that we consider this information to be inconsequential, and if that is the case, we may choose to accept this record even though it contains an error.

The last two conditions are similar. In the first case, we encounter an error, but the error is of the type that we can correct. For example, we may detect an invalid state within a customer address. If we also have the postal code available, we can derive the state and correct the data. In the second case, we may encounter an invalid code for the type of customer (assuming we have a set of valid codes). In this case, we may establish a rule that changes that code to Unknown.

Taking one of these four actions will improve the data available within the data warehouse or ODS. It will not, however, prevent the recurrence of these errors. A quality-oriented CRM program would also include measurements for the error conditions (check) and the initiation of corrective actions that address the root causes of the error conditions (act). These corrective actions may

[9]Imhoff, Claudia and Jonathan G. Geiger. "Data Quality in the Data Warehouse." *DM Review*, April 1996.

include changes to the source systems, to the processes used to build and maintain these systems, or to the business processes that create the data in the first place. Once we identify the root cause, completing the feedback loop through actions like those listed previously helps ensure that errors will not reoccur.

Integrating Data

Data integration consists of the actions needed to determine how to merge data from different sources and to actually perform the merging. Often, customer data exists in multiple systems, and each of these systems may have data about the same customer. During data integration, we'll need to analyze the data to identify that we are dealing with the same customer, and this is often a daunting task because the systems are unlikely to share common keys. Once we know that we are dealing with the same customer, we then need to establish the single correct view of that customer.

The name and address matching and cleansing tools previously mentioned also help with merging customer data from multiple systems. If the two systems share a common set of keys, identifying the common customers is not a problem. This is, however, very unusual. Generally, each customer system has its own key, and we can't use the key to identify the common customer. We need to look at information about the customer, such as the name and address, to detect commonality. When these match exactly, we'll know how to proceed. But what about near matches, as shown in Figure 8.7?

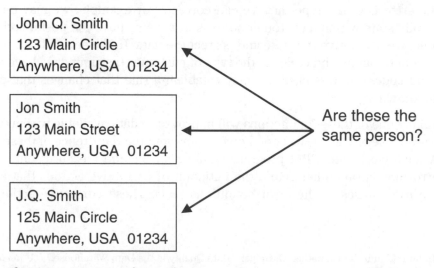

Figure 8.7 Customer integration.

The name and address cleansing tools provide algorithms for identifying potential matches and a means for helping the tools make decisions based on business rules. For example, the tool could score each pair of customers, and based on thresholds set by the people responsible for data cleansing, the tool could either assume that the three records belong to the same customer and perform the merger, determine that the three records probably belong to the same customer and provide for a manual verification prior to performing the merger, or determine that the three records probably don't belong to the same customer and treat them as different customers. The same process can also be used to identify households, as shown in Figure 8.8.

Transforming Data

Data transformation consists of the actions needed to create a homogenous view of the data. Even when systems don't have conflicting data, they may represent data in different ways. For example, gender may be represented in one system as MALE and FEMALE, in another system as M and F, in another system as 0 and 1, and so on. When the data is brought into the enterprise view, that data must be transformed to a single representation. In the case of gender, once the enterprise coding structure is determined, a simple algorithm can be created to convert each of the individual representations to the enterprise representation. Data transformation is not always that simple, and sometimes manual intervention is needed if electronic rules cannot be established.

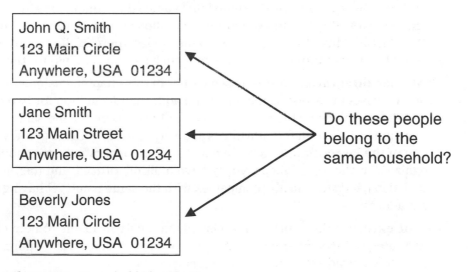

Figure 8.8 Household identification.

Loading Data

Loading consists of the actions needed to physically place the data into the data warehouse and ODS. This action takes the resultant data that has been cleansed, integrated, and transformed and moves it into the data warehouse and ODS. In some cases, this data may replace data already there; in other cases, it creates another historical instance of information.

Tools

Commercially available tools, such as data scrubbing, data matching, and data householding tools, can be used to improve the quality of customer information. In this section, we provide an overview of the major functions these tools perform, individually and in combination with one another.

Name and address cleansing and standardization. This function dissects the name and address information and ensures that each component obeys the governing rules. The name, for example, is divided into the salutation, first name, middle name, surname, and suffix. The address is similarly decomposed into the house number, the street name, and the street type. Each of these is validated, sometimes using external tables that are known to contain valid information. A customer record that conforms to a set of specifications concerning the name, street address, and so on is then created.

Name propagation. Often, customer information is provided for a couple (such as Mr. and Mrs. Jim Jenkins). Name propagation consists of segregating the reported name into the individual names that comprise it. In this case, Mr. and Mrs. Jim Jenkins would be decomposed into Mr. Jim Jenkins and Mrs. Jim Jenkins. If the wife's first name is elsewhere in the record, then it could be used to provide a better name (such as Ann Jenkins) for the wife.

Customer integration. As discussed earlier in this chapter, customer integration consists of reviewing the name and address information for two entries and determining whether or not these are likely to be for the same person. The approaches used for individuals and corporations differ. For individuals, one of the key components is the address. For corporations, we should recognize that the same company may have multiple offices, and therefore the tool also needs to consider companies with the same name yet having different addresses.

Use of external data. Information is commercially available to help cleanse and integrate customer data. Examples of these include valid address data and Dun & Bradstreet information on corporations.

Householding. Householding consists of recognizing that two or more individual customers are part of the same household. The tools available for this function look for common data in multiple records. Examples of common data to be reviewed include the surname, the address, the phone number, and the account number.

Summary

Top management must provide leadership to instill a quality mindset for the CRM initiative. It must adopt a philosophy that promotes quality and customer service, and it must then provide an environment that helps people succeed. The environment should document the relevant processes and ensure that each process contains appropriate measurements. These measurements are monitored as part of an ongoing quality improvement cycle, with actions taken based on root causes that contribute to unacceptable results. The measurements are inherent to the processes. Although some inspections may be performed after a product is produced, these inspections are merely additional measurement points, and their primary purpose is not to inspect quality into the product.

The CRM environment that people need to succeed includes an organizational culture and structure that promotes teamwork, a management attitude that helps people perform a good job, and a focus on providing quality for the customer.

The CRM program is heavily dependent on an integrated set of data that provides the people involved with an accurate and holistic view of the customer. This is often accomplished by building a data warehouse and ODS, and then providing the data to the business users through data marts and transactional interfaces. The data acquisition process is a critical part of building these databases. In this process, data is collected from appropriate sources; it is cleansed, integrated, and transformed; and then it is finally loaded into the data warehouse and ODS.

PART THREE

Implementing CRM

This last section of the book depicts the practical application of the concepts introduced in Parts 1 and 2. We start by looking at the key functions supported by CIF technology within business intelligence, business management, and business operations. Chapter 9 describes the business intelligence capabilities that are provided by the data warehouse, the data marts, and the decision support interface. Business intelligence provides information to support the marketing and analysis business strategies within the Customer Life Cycle. Chapter 10 describes the business management capabilities that are provided by the operational data store and transactional interface. Business management enables us to take action to provide personalized service based on our understanding of customers and customer segments. Additionally, the ODS enables us to have near–real-time consolidated customer information. In Chapter 11, we expand on the concept of consistent customer knowledge within the realm of business operations. The emphasis in this chapter is the technology that is needed to automate the integration of customer data from all customer touch points; sales force automation and customer contact center technologies are highlighted.

The next three chapters pay particular attention to the technologies that have become pervasive during the last few years. In Chapter 12, we explore e-commerce and conclude that companies must establish strategies that integrate e-commerce with its other channels. In Chapter 13 we recognize the importance of providing all employees with consolidated, integrated data sources and provide strategies for accomplishing this. Internet users don't automatically trust the companies whose Web sites they visit. Chapter 14 examines the role of privacy in creating and preserving customer trust and the importance of trust in building customer loyalty.

We close the book with a look into the future. Customers are demanding greater and greater control over the relationships they have with each other and with the selling organization. The successful CRM organization of the 21st century will need to address more than just one or two of the challenges presented throughout this book—they will need to address all of them.

Business Intelligence: Technologies for Understanding Your Customers

We have noted throughout this book various examples of how strategic or analytical information has helped the bank's relationship with both Bob and his parents. These examples abound, including offers of appropriate travel proposals (for Bob, a skiing trip of varying difficulty; for his parents, the Caribbean cruise offer), customized product mixes based on each customer's preferences and usage patterns (Bob likes to use the Internet; his parents prefer dealing with the local teller), and third-party offers such as investment advisors. Obviously, the bank has studied and analyzed the information about Bob and his parents to make these kinds of on-the-mark proposals to them.

A key success factor of any Customer Relationship Management (CRM) strategy is the ability to utilize the available information on customers to understand the characteristics of the customer base and to influence the ways in which customers and the organization interact. To accomplish this, data must be converted into information by adding context and facts to the data. Information becomes knowledge when decision makers are educated about the information and begin to use it. Finally, knowledge becomes corporate wisdom when the business community takes action by consistently using and enhancing this knowledge (see Figure 9.1).

The primary technology systems and processes within the Corporate Information Factory (CIF) that facilitate this conversion from data to wisdom are the business intelligence components. These components consist of the data warehouse, data marts, exploration warehouses, mining warehouses, and

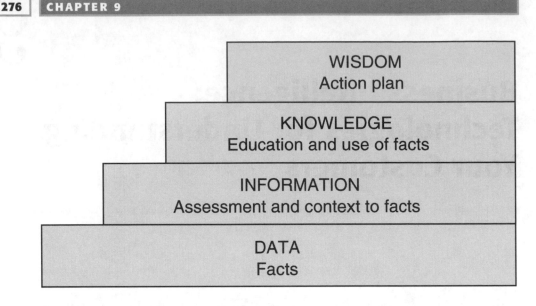

Figure 9.1 Moving from data to wisdom.

the decision support interface. They also consist of the processes to get information into the Corporate Information Factory and then out into the hands of the business community.

This chapter begins by describing the analytical components of strategic CRM. It will focus on the inherent differences among these components—the business intelligence components of the data warehouse and dependent data marts —and how these components are used to support the marketing and strategic analysis within the Customer Life Cycle. Next, the need for different data designs for potential data marts will be examined, focusing on multidimensional designs in particular. The differences between analytical applications and departmental data marts will also be described.

The chapter concludes with a discussion of the data delivery process and the decision support interface, two critical components that ensure the distribution and proper utilization of the business intelligence capabilities.

Defining the Strategic CRM Components

Chapter 2, "The Customer and the Corporate Information Factory (CIF)," provided a good overview of the various components of the Corporate Information

Factory and divided them into two groups: the tactical and strategic (see Figure 9.2). We explained in that chapter that the CIF creates an environment that supports not only the strategic analytical functions used to create corporate memory, but it also supports the tactical functions used to maintain the relationship with the customer. Strategic functions are based on historical records and consist of the analytical capabilities that determine trends in customer behaviors. These capabilities identify product costs or revenues, establish patterns of fraud or the risk of offering products to certain customers, and show whether an occurrence is an exception or a real trend that bears monitoring.

Tactical functions provide current or up-to-the-second views of our customers, products, finances, and other areas of business interest. These functions enable us to respond to situations like a customer complaint, a request for help, a payment of a vendor, a collection of monies due, or other day-to-day processes.

This chapter covers the strategic aspect of CRM, those static, historical components used to understand trends, patterns, and exceptions in our enterprises.

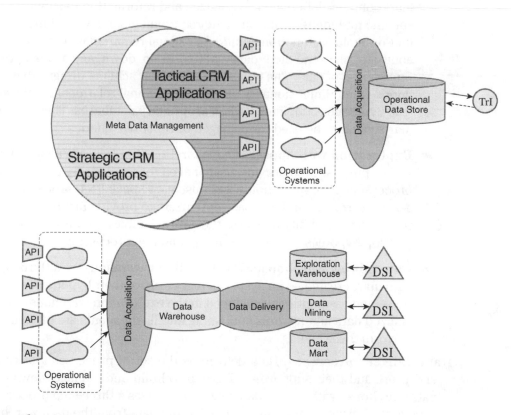

Figure 9.2 Tactical versus strategic CRM applications.

The following three chapters introduce the operational data store (ODS), sales force automation, and call center applications as the components that best support tactical CRM applications. For the strategic analysis in CRM, the components you will need are as follows:

Data warehouse. The data warehouse is the central point of data integration for business intelligence and the source of data for the data marts, delivering a common view of enterprise data. It is a subject-oriented, integrated, time-variant, and non-volatile collection of data for strategic analysis.

Data mart. The data mart is customized and/or summarized data that is derived from the data warehouse and tailored to support the specific analytical requirements of a given business unit or business function. It utilizes a common enterprise view of strategic data and provides business units with more flexibility, control, and responsibility. The data mart may or may not be on the same server or location as the data warehouse. The types of data marts available today are as follows:

- **Online analytical processing (OLAP) data mart.** The OLAP data mart contains data that is customized and reformatted to support the specific multidimensional analytic requirements of a given business unit or business function. Multidimensional requirements include the ability to "slice and dice" data and to drill up, down, and around predefined cubes of data. The cubes are either star schema designs that impose multidimensionality on two-dimensional relational databases or true hypercubes implemented on proprietary databases. These types of marts can also be used for managed or repetitive queries.

- **Exploration warehouse.** The exploration warehouse is a data mart whose purpose is to provide a safe haven for exploratory and ad hoc processing. An exploration warehouse uses specialized processing, server platforms, and database optimizers to provide fast response times with the ability to access the entire database. Analysts can develop hypotheses quickly from their ad hoc processing.

- **Data mining warehouse.** The data mining warehouse is a third type of data mart created so analysts can test or prove their hypotheses, assertions, and assumptions developed in the exploration warehouse. Specialized data mining tools containing intelligent agents are often used to perform these tasks.

Data delivery processes. Data delivery is the set of processes that enables end users and their supporting IT group to build and manage views of the data warehouse within their data marts. It involves a three-step process consisting of filtering, formatting, and delivering data from the data warehouse to the data marts.

Decision support interface (DSI). The DSI is an easy-to-use, intuitively simple tool for the end user to distill information from data. The DSI enables analytical activities and provides the flexibility to match the tool to the task. For example, if the business community would like to simply look at product profitability in many different ways (by market segment, by sales channel, or by customer types) and will run the same reports every week, then the appropriate tool would be a multidimensional one running against a star schema or multidimensional cube of data. DSI tools include those specific to data exploration and mining, OLAP, and query reporting.

This chapter discusses each of these components and provides examples of how they are used.

The Data Warehouse

Despite all of the books that have been written about data warehousing (see "Recommended Reading" section at the end of this book), a lot of confusion exists about what a data warehouse is and how it differs from a data mart or ODS, or even from an operational system. Without this understanding, we're less likely to use the right architecture for the right job.

The data warehouse is defined as a subject-oriented, integrated, time-variant, and non-volatile collection of data for strategic analysis. You can think of it as a big bucket of generic, detailed, enterprise-wide, static, and historical data. The data warehouse can serve as the source of data for data marts; it is not set up for a particular application or department.

Chapter 2 introduced the concept of the data warehouse by comparing it to a big box of Legos, those small plastic building blocks for children. Legos have a consistent interface, granularity, and form. You can build just about anything—a robot, a house, a bus, or an airplane—from their assortment of generic, standardized shapes. You are limited only by your imagination and the number of blocks at your disposal.

Data warehouses work the same way. The data warehouse consists of standardized, consistent pieces of data. By constructing the data warehouse in the most generic and flexible way possible, you can build just about any data mart (including exploration and data mining warehouses) you want from these pieces of data in your warehouse. You are only limited by your technology and the data that you can acquire from your operational systems. And the good news is that the pieces of data, unlike the Lego blocks, are reusable so you never run out of them.

The data warehouse is designed using relational technology, that is, a normalized entity relationship diagram (ERD) data model. As discussed in Chapter 6, "Developing an Integrated CRM Technology Environment," the data warehouse model is built from the enterprise data model, thereby inheriting the standards used in developing that model. Therefore, for the data warehouse to serve as a reliable and reusable source of data for the data marts, it is built with the following goals in mind:

- It reflects the enterprise's view of data in terms of business rules and strategic requirements. Because the data in the warehouse is to be used for multiple CRM analytical purposes spanning multiple departments, it must accommodate and reinforce the enterprise's vision of its CRM initiative.

- It is optimized for flexibility. The data must not display a bias or prejudice toward any one kind of analytical processing. For example, if the data warehouse is designed using a data model that is biased toward known data relationships or toward certain business processes, then analytical activities that search for unknown relationships are compromised or, in effect, eliminated. To avoid this, we recommend that the data warehouse data model follow the rules of normalization for ERDs.

- It is designed to promote optimal load performance. To improve the load performance, the data warehouse database should be designed with minimal redundancy and denormalization. For a low-latency data warehouse (one with rapid update cycles), a star schema design offers restrictions in update speed and insertion capabilities. Many of the mission-critical, large-volume data warehouses now appearing necessitate rapid insertion capabilities and therefore require a data model that supports this requirement. Again, our recommendation is for a mostly normalized ERD model.

- It is designed with ease of maintenance and the database stability in mind. The most stable model we can create is an ERD one (usually at least a third normal form). Business processes constantly change, but these types of changes rarely cause any significant changes to a normalized model that has no dependence on the processes. Therefore, the data warehouse data model is fairly normalized in the Date and Codd sense. As with any physical design, the model is adjusted, as described in Chapter 6, to best meet the requirements of a data warehouse.

- It is designed to promote optimal data delivery processing. To ease the delivery process, we may need to create subcomponents used by multiple data marts or separate types of data. Chapter 7, "Capturing Customer Information," discusses the necessity to create database partitions, standard summarized and derived fields, and conformed dimensions used by the data delivery process.

- It provides detailed data for subsequent use by the data marts. Because the data warehouse must be the source for data marts containing aggregated and summarized data, exploration warehouses containing detailed data, and data mining warehouses containing statistical samples of data, it must contain the proper level of detailed data to satisfy these very diverse requirements. The goal is for the data warehouse to have the "least common denominator" level of data for the data marts. That is, if one mart requires weekly summaries and another uses monthly summaries, then the data warehouse must contain daily snapshots that can be summarized to these mart levels.

This reusable collection of cleansed, integrated, stable data is an excellent source from which we can build other structures, namely the various types of data marts.

Data Marts

The data mart is the ultimate analytical resource for the enterprise. It is through this component that the business community garners its intelligence about its customers, products, resources, and other areas of interest to the corporation. Several types of data marts are needed to satisfy the analytical capabilities of the enterprise. Three types of data marts are available for our strategic CRM: OLAP data marts, exploration warehouses, and data mining warehouses. Similar to the data warehouse, much confusion exists about what constitutes a data mart. You may be asking how do you know if you have a data mart or some other structure. The following criteria can help you make that determination:

A data mart is based on a set of user requirements. Continuing with the Lego analogy, you could build things out of Legos based on known requirements. The house, robot, and airplane all have architectural stipulations that must be followed to construct them. The same can be said for the data mart. Each mart is meant to solve a particular business problem. For example, our bank may build a data mart to analyze customers, their purchases, and their usage history of the bank's products and services in order to determine its customers' lifetime value to the enterprise. Perhaps we build a mart to analyze the buying habits or product utilization patterns of our customers, or one that examines the success of our sales channels, or one to determine the effectiveness of our sales campaigns. Maybe we need to develop a data mart to study the demographics of our customers or to understand the cross-sell opportunities with our current set of customers. Chapter 2 defined the various types of data marts available for our analytical CRM activities. Each of these different data marts reflects a distinct business problem requiring distinct sets of data and that has distinct queries running against it. Focus is perhaps the most important characteristic of a data mart.

Size does not determine a data mart. Data marts come in all sizes, from a few megabytes of data to some real whoppers. For example, your first mart may contain limited history or you may have a small number of customers and need to answer only a few simple questions. Therefore, it may be a relatively small database. On the other hand, some customer demographic data marts are several hundred gigabytes in size and are rapidly approaching a terabyte or more. In all cases though, the data marts are still derived from the data contained in the data warehouse and so are generally smaller in size than the entire data warehouse.

A data mart can be co-located with the data warehouse. In order to be classified as a data mart, many people think that a mart must be physically separated from the warehouse—not so! You can build a set of star schemas or other database structures optimized for query analysis within the data warehouse environment. The key is that these structures are built *for a particular business purpose*. The functionality you just implemented in these schemas is the key determination of whether it is a mart or not. You may want to prepare for the eventual migration of these schemas into their own world, but there is nothing to stop you from testing out your mart wings within the warehouse world before shipping it out to another site.

No single technology or design technique is indicative of a data mart. Data marts come in all sorts of technological flavors, as has already been mentioned. Five years ago, the available technology was limited in the area of building data marts. It consisted of mostly relational, flat file, or proprietary hypercubes of limited size. Today a plethora of technologies support different types of data marts: relational (still the most popular), multidimensional databases, token-based databases, specialized and proprietary databases, bit-mapped databases, and even in-memory processing types of technologies. Each of these technologies is perfectly suitable for specific types of data marts.

Many different design techniques are also at our disposal. Again, the most popular design technique for data marts is the star schema, but other possible design techniques are available as well. For example, you may choose a statistical subset of data with a more normalized design (very useful for data mining). Flat file extracts of the warehouse also may be used. Perhaps your mart is a multidimensional online analytical processing (MOLAP) technology and you simply have hierarchies in your design.

Each of these technologies and design techniques has its place in the data mart world and supports different types of analyses: slice and dice or multidimensional processing, exploration, simple queries or reporting, and data mining or statistical analysis. It is important to remember that the user requirements should dictate which type of mart you are building. As always, the technology and design techniques should be based on these requirements, not the other way around.

Departmental versus Application-Specific Data Marts

If you've got a few tangible, documented business requirements to tackle, and you're reasonably sure that a new data mart will do the trick, you may be asking yourself how to strategically integrate the new data mart into your organization. Even though (as usual) the answer depends on the specifics of your situation, you'll probably end up with a data mart that resembles one of two proven types, and the integration that goes with it. Our nomenclature for these two classifications of data marts is departmental and application-specific. The following definitions may help you understand the differences between these two types of marts.

The definition of a departmental data mart is a decision support database that is built for a particular department or division within your organization. For example, the Sales Department may want to create a decision support database containing sales data specifically. These data marts are fairly generic in functionality and serve as repositories of historical data for use by that department's personnel only. The design must be fairly generic as well, that is, not focused on any particular functionality or process. An example of this type of mart would be one that was built for the Sales Department. It would answer questions about product sales, revenue by sales representatives, sales in geographic areas, products sold, and other sales-specific types of information. It would be set up for the users in the Sales Department only and may have sales-specific calculations in it (such as sales revenue calculations or commission amounts). Typically, these data marts are created from scratch within the enterprise. They are supported by either the line of business' information technology (IT) resources or resources from the department itself.

Application-specific data marts have a very different focus. They concentrate on a particular decision support process such as risk management, campaign analysis, and customer life time value analysis, rather than generic utilization. Because of their universal appeal in the company, they also are seen as enterprise resources. They can be used by anyone within the organization with a need for their particular analytical capability.

These data marts can be built from scratch within the enterprise using the line of business' IT resources or centralized IT resources. Also, a number of vendors offering "data marts in a box" have canned applications associated with them. The more popular CRM ones are Campaign Management and Call Center Statistics marts.

The form of mart you build, departmental or application-specific, results from the answers to three basic (and probably familiar) questions: What's it do, who's it for, and who's paying for it?

What Does the Data Mart Do?

First and foremost, the answer to this question should be that it efficiently solves the tangible, documented, business requirements. In addition, if the nature/scope of the requirement is clearly comprehensive and needed throughout the enterprise, then an application-specific data mart is in order. For example, a data mart to track product profitability would be useful to many people in different departments. If the nature/scope is limited, such as the mart discussed earlier that contains sales commission calculations, then a departmental data mart is probably better.

Tip 1: For departmental data marts, don't forget to determine whether other departments have the same requirement, that is, they would be interested in sharing the benefits and the costs. This may lead you to change the scope of the mart. This determination may cause you to rethink your direction from a department-specific mart to a more application-specific one.

Tip 2: For either data mart type, manage user expectations. Make sure that the users understand what the data mart will and won't do. Famous last words: "Our new data mart will answer all our questions."

Who Is It for?

Although the roster of users who access the data mart is important, this question goes to the politics of the situation and the desire to share data. The real question is who will ultimately benefit the most from the data mart's success. If the answer is the business analysts and executives of a single department, then the data mart should be departmental. The Sales Department will be the greatest beneficiary of the sales commission-tracking mart; therefore, that department will most likely be the sponsor for the mart. If the answer is the folks at many levels throughout the organization, then make it an application-specific data mart. Many people throughout the enterprise from finance to sales to marketing would like to have access to profitability mart.

Tip 3: Once you've identified who it is for, invite them to be the project sponsor(s). If you can't sell them on the role, then consider delaying the implementation until you can, because if they won't fight for the project at the start, they may fight against it later. Remember, the data mart is not being built for IT; it's being built for someone who perceives a business need.

Who Is Paying for It?

Although budgeting practices differ widely and IT departments often function under their own budgets, you should maximize the association between costs and benefits. So, if only one department is willing to cover the costs, a departmental data mart, such as the commission tracking one, is needed. If the budget sponsor(s) have overall or inclusive responsibilities or include many departments, then an application-specific data mart is the right one to build. The ramifications of this decision determine whether the data mart can be shared across departments or whether it will be set up exclusively for one department.

Tip 4: If the senior project sponsors don't have budget authority, consider whether the ultimate benefactor is actually higher up in the food chain.

Other Considerations

Once you've answered the preceding three questions, you should compare the answers to the inherent features of each type of data mart and evaluate which approach is needed. Keep in mind that there are pluses and minuses for each type of mart. Go into the project knowing the shortfalls of each type.

For departmental data marts, the pros can be summarized as follows:

- You have a good chance of delivering what the department wants. The users are usually very involved in the design and usage of this mart.

- You can get good funding because the department owns this mart.

- Most IT projects are funded this way—one department paying for its own system—so it is easy for the department to build a business case.

- The department controls the mart and therefore can make it perform almost all of the department's very proprietary analyses.

- Because only one department is involved, you have only a limited number of people to interview and ultimately satisfy.

The cons for departmental data marts are summarized in the following bullets:

- Performance issues occur because the data mart is not optimized for any set of queries or, worse, is optimized for some queries that cause performance problems for other queries.

- Redundant queries run on different data marts throughout the organization. The result sets from these redundant queries may not be consistent. This is somewhat mitigated by having the data warehouse feeding all marts, but it is certainly not guaranteed that two marts will produce the same numbers, and so on.

- Minimal sharing of findings takes place among departments.

- Little or no desire exists to support an enterprise view of the information.

- You may experience difficulty in getting funding for the data warehouse (an enterprise resource).

Application data marts have their own set of pros and cons. The pros for these data marts include the following:

- It is possible to create standard analyses and reports from these marts.

- An analytical functionality is created only once and is used by the business community in much the same fashion.

- The data mart is easy to tune and capacity is predictable.

- Many vendors today offer specific DSS applications that can plug into your data warehouse environment, thus speeding up the implementation of analytical applications.

The cons for application data marts are summarized in the following bullets:

- It may be difficult to customize the views or queries into the mart enough to satisfy the diverse set of users using it.

- Funding must come from an enterprise source, rather than a single department.

- It can be hard to get the business community to agree on the overall design of this application.

- Some of the analyses may be suboptimized due to the non-department specific nature of the mart. That is, the mart may satisfy only 80 to 90 percent of a department's needs because it is an application for the entire enterprise.

For the off-the-shelf applications you may purchase, you need to consider these additional factors:

- How will the purchased data mart fit into my strategic CRM architecture?

- How will it fit within my CIF?

- What will feed this application?

- How will this application share data with other areas of the enterprise?

- Which feeds must be generated from this application to support other strategic and tactical components?

Choosing the Best Data Mart Design

Without doubt, the most popular data mart designs are the star schema and its variations. There is good reason for this. The star schema is great for supporting multidimensional analyses in relational data marts that have known and stable requirements, fairly predictable queries with reasonable response times, recurring reports, and the ability to drill up, down, around, and through to more detail. Not surprisingly, multidimensional tools have earned a strong position in the entire analytical tool marketplace as well (see Figure 9.3).

The techniques for building star schemas are elegant, well explained, and well documented. These techniques include dimensions (the key business selection criteria such as product, market segment, customer, and time), facts (metrics of interest derived from our dimensions, such as revenue, units sold, usage amounts), and, when necessary, physical database schemas. Numerous projects have successfully applied these techniques and concepts. These models have the following goals:

- Star schemas reflect the business area's view of data. The model imitates the way the business community talks about its data. For example, a sales

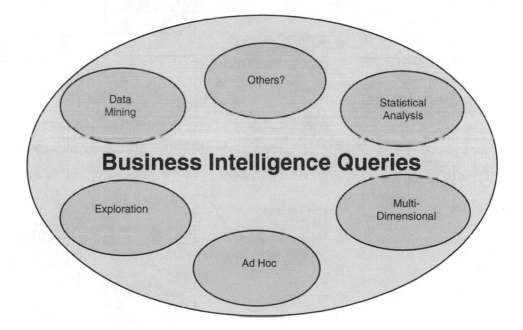

Figure 9.3   OLAP tools' position in the marketplace.

representative for the bank would want to see his or her sales revenue by customer, market segment, sales area, and product over the last six months. The star schema would satisfy these requirements precisely.

- Star schemas are optimized for legibility or understandability. The business analyst using them easily understands these models. They represent natural business constraints and measurements. Figure 9.4 is an example of a typical star schema for a sales revenue requirement.

- Star schemas are optimized for query response times. The model is a physical instantiation of the many table joins that would be necessary to answer the sales representative's questions. Because these have been pre-joined in the model, the queries run much faster than if the joins had to be done at run time. For example, to create the same sort of view of the data shown in Figure 9.4 using a third normal form (normalized) model, we would have to create a seven-table join using product, location, campaign, transaction, customer, channel, and program tables. With the star schema, the join has already been preformed for us, simplifying the overall process.

- Star schemas contain aggregated and summarized data. These aggregated and summarized fields speed up the query response time because no calcu-

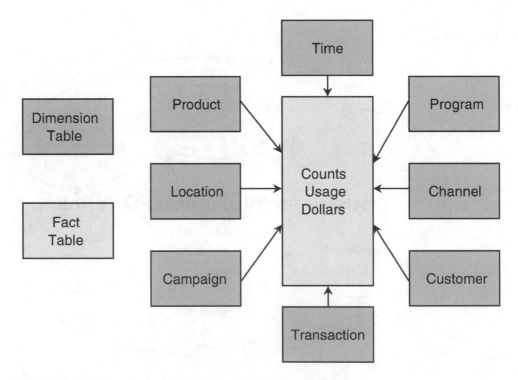

Figure 9.4 A simple star schema for sales revenue application.

lations must be performed at run time. They also help in the standardization of calculations and summarizations.

As powerful as these models are for multidimensional analyses, other issues make them less useful or even inappropriate for other forms of analysis:

- The size of some star schemas that try to answer all types of questions becomes prohibitive from a query performance standpoint. Generally, when this occurs, it is due to the designer not realizing that the business questions are not multidimensional in nature or that multiple sets of star schemas may be needed. Therefore, it may be significantly beneficial to split up this mart into two or more, one multidimensional and the other(s) using mining or exploration technologies. In other words, you may need an OLAP-type mart for known queries, such as that shown in Figure 9.4, and you may need a set of flat files for your mining requirements.

- Queries that do stock processes (for example, "Give me all dollar sales by location, product ID, and customer type over the past six months") may not open the data up for exploration and risk an environment that does not generate adequate return. That is, many of the real insights into customers and their behaviors are found in an analysis of unexpected or even unknown relationships. Because the star schema is based on known data relationships (that is, the dimensions and facts are predetermined by the design itself), it is impossible to find those "nuggets of gold" in these types of designs. For example, we would not be able to truly explore the relationship between Bob and his patterns of behavior (likes to ski, prefers to use the Internet for banking transactions, is a risk taker in his investment portfolio) with the star schema shown. These relationships would require very detailed transaction-level data in a format that does not predetermine any relationships (to location, to channel, to campaign, or any other dimension).

It seems reasonable to conclude that unique combinations of processing requirements and types of data require different structures. In other words, one structure isn't always best or optimal and may decrease the real value of your analytical CRM applications. Even though you can use a hammer to drive a screw into a piece of wood, it's not the best tool for the job. Similarly, even though a star schema can be used to perform an analytical analysis, it's not the best schema for all types of analysis.

The universe of analytical processing types is diverse and will only grow more so in the future. Today it includes data mining, statistical analysis, data exploration, and even true ad hoc queries where anything goes. The decision support users performing these types of business analyses often search for unexpected data relationships and gain the greatest value for the enterprise by understanding these surprising and unforeseen results.

Therefore, if your entire data warehouse environment consists of a single database design technique, then your ability to analyze your data is limited to the subset of analyses that the model best supports. To maximize your data warehousing return on investment (ROI), you need to embrace and implement analytical models that enable the full spectrum of analysis. Let's examine these alternative database designs.

Determining Alternative Database Designs

For many statistical, data mining, or exploratory analyses, no hint of bias or an arbitrary establishment of data relationships must exist. The star schema draws much of its strength from predefined relationships, and this prevents an analyst from being able to look for unknown or unexpected data relationships.

The truth is that database structures vary from normalized to denormalized to flat files of transactions, customers, products, and other interesting data subjects (see Figure 9.5.). The ideal situation is to craft the schemas *after* the

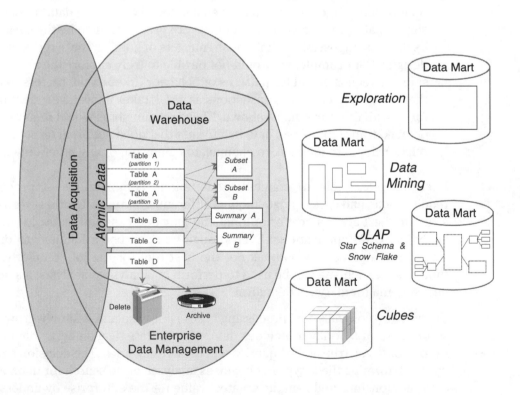

Figure 9.5   Different types of data marts.

requirements are established. Unfortunately, the database structure is often selected *before* the specific business needs are known. Those of us in the data warehouse consulting business have witnessed development teams debating star versus normalized data models long before even beginning the process of gathering the business analysis requirements. For whatever reason, architects and data modelers latch onto a particular design technique, perhaps through comfort with a particular technique or from ignorance of other techniques, and force all data marts to have that one type of design. This is similar to the person who is an expert with a hammer; everything he or she sees resembles a nail.

Database schemas should be based on the usage of the data and the type of information requested. No absolutes exist, of course. In examining data relationships, the best design may be one that does not preestablish or predetermine these relationships. Examples of such solutions would be flat files, floating point files used for data mining, or normalized files for low-latency data warehouses. On the other hand, multiple layer stars (such as multiple fact tables, elaborate snow flakes, or large summary tables) may work best for exotic financial reporting marts and the like. You must determine the type of mart that best satisfies the business requirements you received.

With that in mind, let's address when and where to use the various schema structures, and provide some guidelines for mapping them to the business requirements. This process includes several activities that you may find useful for selecting the database design that best fits the business problem at hand.

Start with the Business

During the requirements definition, you should avoid the tendency to jump ahead and start to create the data model in a star, third normal form, denormalized or other design structure that may seem evident. In truth, multiple schemas will be used throughout the data warehouse/data mart environment. The makeup of these components and their schemas must be based on performance criteria and business process requirements.

Once the business processes are identified, then the key business goals, or drivers (pain) must be documented, and the objectives for resolving these issues must be documented. Objectives are the quantifiable, measurable results of achieving goals. Each of the business processes associated with the business drivers (be they opportunity or pain) can then supply the goals and objectives that must be accomplished to address the opportunities.

Lastly, develop some scenarios, or conceptual prototypes, of how end users will react, assuming they have access to information to fulfill the objectives. Again, the business processes that have been identified participate in this process.

This provides a baseline model for further defining the presentation of the information and subsequent detailing of the requirements as we prototype our analytical capability.

Your business community member skills greatly impact the ultimate choice of database design. A user, who runs the same reports over and over performing the same analyses repetitively, is called a farmer. He or she will be very happy with an OLAP mart. A market researcher who jumps about from thought to thought, query to query, with unpredictable needs will find an exploration warehouse more to his or her liking. Table 9.1 should help you in determining which type of business intelligence community member you have for an end user, the form of analysis and database design most suitable for them, and examples of these types of users in your corporation.

Define the Measures

Next, the objectives from the first step are broken down into measures. For example, if the objective of the mart is to determine product profitability, then the calculation for profitability must be broken down into its component parts: total product revenue, total costs, and other items such as discounts or returns. Then the actual calculation for profitability needed in the mart must be defined and documented. Facilitated sessions, interviews, and studies of existing systems or reports are all required to obtain business-level measurement definitions. In turn, the measures provide the baseline for a list of information requirements needed in the data warehouse to be used in these calculations (the individual product revenues, individual costs, and other items that go into the calculations of totals).

To determine the level of detail or granularity and, eventually, the physical schema, determine the attributes for each measure needed in the marts and the specific information requirements using the criteria in Table 9.2.

Attributing the measurements generally results in the information required to accurately identify the level of granularity or detail needed for each mart. Many projects have grossly underestimated the granularity needed by assuming, or guessing what it should be. We strongly recommend usage of a formal process for determining granularity.[1] The completion of the measurement attributes provides the raw data used to determine information requirements needed for the data mart and data warehouse.

---

[1]*The Data Warehouse Lifecycle Toolkit* by Ralph Kimball, Laura Reeves, Margie Ross, and Warren Thornthwaite, John Wiley & Sons, is an excellent resource for such a process. In their book, they refer to granularity of data as "grain."

Table 9.1 Characteristics and Analytical Requirements of the Business Community Members

BUSINESS COMMUNITY	FORM OF ANALYSIS AND DATABASE SCHEMA PREFERRED	COMMUNITY MEMBER EXAMPLE
Farmers, who monitor the effects of tracking key performance metrics. They use predictable and routine queries.	Predominately use multi-dimensional data marts as well as star and hypercube schemas.	Marketing campaign managers, product managers, financial analysts, sales analysts
Explorers, who endeavor to understand how the business works by finding hidden meanings in data. They have unpredictable queries using massive amounts of detailed data.	May start with multi-dimensional data mart but soon require their own environment. Use star, hypercube, exploration technology.	Market researchers, process control engineers, fraud/risk analysts, workforce analysts
Miners, who scan large amounts of detailed data to confirm a hypothesis of suspected patterns. They have somewhat predictable queries and must have unbiased, unconditioned data.	May begin with multi-dimensional data marts but soon require their own environment. Use star, hypercube, flat files, data sets, and statistical samples.	Statisticians, actuaries, click stream analysts, and logistics specialists
Operators, who use the intelligence derived by explorers and farmers to improve business conditions. They use current, integrated data for tactical decision making.	Predominantly use operational systems or ODS (see Chapter 10). Predominantly third normal form schema for ODS.	Line managers, call center managers, CSRs, and inventory control managers
Tourists, who are aware of data produced by the business. They have unpredictable queries involving high-level summaries or aggregations of data.	Predominantly use multi-dimensional data marts or informal warehouses. Use star and hypercube.	Executives such as CEOs, COOs, CFOs, and senior managers

Table 9.2 Criteria for Data Mart Designs

DATA MART CHARACTERISTIC	DEFINITION OF CHARACTERISTIC	DATA MART DESIGN CONSIDERATION
Requirements	A list of information requirements based on measures, as would be manifested in decisional reports or operational reports	Is there a need for structured hierarchies (drill downs)? Will the users require access to the individual components used in the calculations? The more aggregated the data, the more star schema-oriented.
Periodicity	What is the time frame the requirement represents: ad hoc, real time, daily, or monthly.	The more unpredictable the queries (ad hoc), the more unstructured the data (flat files versus star schema).
Latency	How soon must the information be delivered?	A fast delivery time may require more normalization.
Volatility	How often does the data appearing in the requirement change?	Highly volatile data may require more normalization.
BI Community Member	Within the business functions, which types of BI users members will there be?	See Table 9.1

Select the Structure for Storing the Answer Data

Finally, plot the requirement against some type of structure option. Such options were presented in Chapter 6 and they are shown here again here (see Figure 9.6), or you can create one of your own. Such an option determination enables you to view where the overall requirements lie in terms of the physical database drivers, that is, the volatility, latency, periodicity, and the analytical vehicle that will supply the information (via the scenarios that were developed). These vehicles include repetitive delivery, ad hoc reports, production reports, and algorithmic analysis. This will ultimately feed into the choice of access tool for the DSI (refer to the section on the DSI).

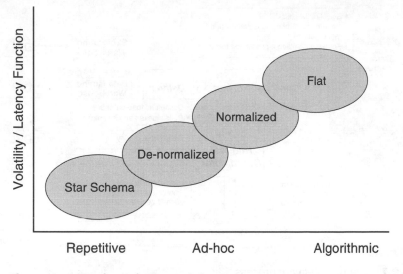

Figure 9.6 Database design options.

Source: "If the Star Fits," by Claudia Imhoff and John Landley. *DMReview.* April–May 2000.

Data Delivery

Data delivery is the set of processes that enables end users or their supporting IS groups to build and manage views of the data warehouse within their data marts. It is these processes that form the heart of the "getting information out" (GIO) part of the business intelligence components. In some respects, data delivery is similar to the data acquisition process described in Chapter 7. Both processes extract data and transform it for delivery to a target. The data delivery process is simpler because it is extracting data from the warehouse and does not need to deal with potentially archaic technologies of multiple sources, integration issues, and cleansing issues (see Figure 9.7).

The overall process of data delivery involves a three-step procedure consisting of filtering, formatting, and delivering data from the data warehouse to the data marts:

Filter. This step selects the desired data from the data warehouse by extracting it and putting it into a file ready for formatting. We recommend that you leverage the bulk unload utilities of your data warehouse environment where possible. Also, if you created conformed dimensions and/or standard calculated and derived fields, these should be used to ease the data delivery process.

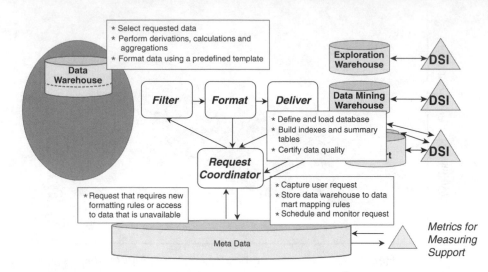

Figure 9.7 The data delivery process.

Format. This step configures the data based on the selected format (star schema, flat files, or normalized tables). These formats may be simple (if deploying an analytical capability to thousands of users) or quite complex (specialized analytics for fraud or risk management). We recommend that you perform the formatting on the source (data warehouse) environment because this platform is often more robust than the mart platform.

Deliver. This step transports the data to the desired location (if separated from the data warehouse platform). Tuning information (index requirements or partitioning schemes) is received from the template schema. The delivery step presents the data to the load utilities of your data mart database management system (DBMS) and prepares the data for usage by the business community. The step performs certification or data quality routines that ensure data completeness and accuracy and, as a final step, notifies the request coordinator that the process is complete.

The Request Coordinator is usually a piece of software similar to standard problem-tracking software except that it is used to submit, schedule and prioritize all requests involving new additions to the CIF such as a request for a new report, a new data element, or a new data mart functionality. The Request Coordinator is responsible for tracking and monitoring the progress of these requests and for reporting these findings back to the business community and team(s) responsible for delivery of the marts.

Data delivery may include customized summarizations or derivations for specialized data marts. For example, the determination of a customer's lifetime value is usually based on a complicated set of algorithms determined by the marketing or sales analysts. Recency, frequency, and monetary (RFM) analysis is another example of a complicated calculation.

The key to the success of the data delivery process comes from a close working relationship between the "getting data in" (GDI) resources and the getting information out (GIO) resources. You must ensure that these two sets of skill sets are synchronized and coordinated across all components of the CIF. For example, the GIO team must notify the GDI team of a new data requirement in time so that the GIO team has enough time to have the data extracted, cleansed, integrated, and loaded in time for the GIO team to use it. An end run around the GDI team is not an acceptable solution.

Decision Support Interface (DSI)

The decision support interface (DSI) is an easy-to-use, intuitively simple access tool used by the end user to distill information from data. The DSI enables the analytical activities and provides the business community with a powerful means of getting the intelligence it needs to understand its customers' needs and desires. It also provides the means to analyze the health and well-being of an enterprise.

The DSI provides the necessary flexibility to match the access tool to the analytical task at hand. For example, the DSI activities of data mining, OLAP or multidimensional processing, querying, and reporting on data may require a different type of data mart. The type of analysis required and the database design of the data mart will dictate the type of access tool needed. The order of selection then is to first determine the type of analysis your mart will be performing (OLAP, mining, or exploring) and then choose the appropriate tool from that category of tool.

Many criteria must be considered when choosing the right tool for your environment. The following are some criteria to consider when choosing your suite of access tools:[2]

---

[2]Two excellent articles on tool selection criteria are "Criteria for Evaluating Business Intelligence Tools" by Wayne Eckerson (*Data Warehousing Institute Journal*, Spring 1999, Page 27) and "The Decision Support Sweet Spot" by Wayne Eckerson (*Data Warehousing Institute*, Summer 1998, Page 2).

Technological considerations. These include considering the operating system and hard disk requirements, the minimum and actual amount of RAM needed, the network and DBMS connectivity speeds, and the optimum number and maximum number of users.

Vendor considerations. You should examine any different vendors' competitive advantages such as the overall product advantages, the technological or architectural advantages, the openness of the tool's architecture, the administrative ease, the standard reporting and ad hoc querying advantages, and the strategic partnerships with hardware and software vendors. Be careful though that you do not fall into the trap of chasing after the latest features.

Product considerations. Some aspects to consider when choosing the access tool include its multidimensional analysis capability; the number of dimensions possible; the user-defined parameter access by any dimension; its drill down, up, around, and through capabilities; its OLE (cut and paste) ease; data filtering capabilities (such as elimination of months, products, or customer types); graphical and data visualization capabilities; and predefined mathematical functions.

Other considerations. You should also examine whether other products are needed in addition to the access tool and what are the initial and maintenance costs of the tool (and any add-on tools needed) on a per-individual, per-volume, and per-upgrade basis. Also try to stay off of the tool selection merry-go-round. When you pick a tool, stick with for a while, rather than chasing after the next latest tool. You may eventually need a new tool, but wait until you determine what the current one lacks before going for the new one.

Summary

The data warehouse is the starting point for all analytical CRM capabilities. This component contains the detailed, static, enterprise-wide, and integrated sources of historical data for usage by all the data marts and is a significant contributor to the overall intelligence in your CRM initiative. It acts as the collection point for the detailed, historical data garnered from both the operational systems as well as the operational data store. Figure 9.8 demonstrates some of the collection points found in the Customer Life Cycle.

The data is extracted from the various systems, is run through the data acquisition processes, and is then loaded up into the data warehouse for usage by the data marts. Obviously, for CRM, the collection points and the quality of the data garnered from these points greatly influence the success of your initiative. Unlike the operational systems, the operational data store and the data marts,

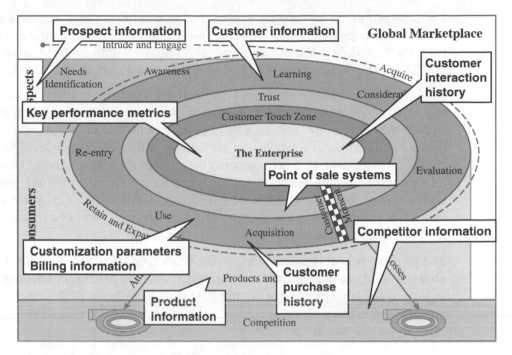

Figure 9.8 The Customer Life Cycle and the data warehouse.

the data warehouse is primarily mapped to the Customer Life Cycle in terms of information, not business functions:

- Prospect information is integrated with customer information so that correlations can be found in the downstream data marts.

- The customer interaction history is captured.

- Competitor information is collected and integrated.

- The point of sale information is stored.

- The product history is captured.

- Key performance indicators that reflect the health of customer relationships are retained.

From the data warehouse, we can build a variety of analytical capabilities such as OLAP data marts, exploration warehouses, and data mining warehouses. Each of these forms of analytical capabilities requires its own data, its own data design, and its own set of access tools specific for the business problem at hand. Choosing a physical database solution without first understanding the business problem may result in a mismatch. Star schemas best address a subset of the wide range of possible business needs, but like hammers, their use is limited. By including a variety of physical database solutions in your toolbox, you'll have the flexibility to efficiently satisfy a wider variety of business needs.

Data marts also have two different orientations. Departmental data marts usually satisfy departmental requirements for the departments who pay for them. Application data marts usually satisfy requirements for multiple departments or the organization as a whole and are funded within enterprise-level budgets. Neither type of data mart is necessarily better than the other, although each has its own ramifications. Each organization has its own unique cultural, political, technological, budgetary, and human resource issues. In practice, you may end up with a combination of both types of marts because you need to tailor your solution to your situation.

The primary role of the data marts in the Customer Life Cycle is as a source of strategic analysis that will arm the enterprise with the necessary information to influence consumer behavior. Figure 9.9 lists a sample set of the types of analytical capabilities your organization may need for its CRM initiative.

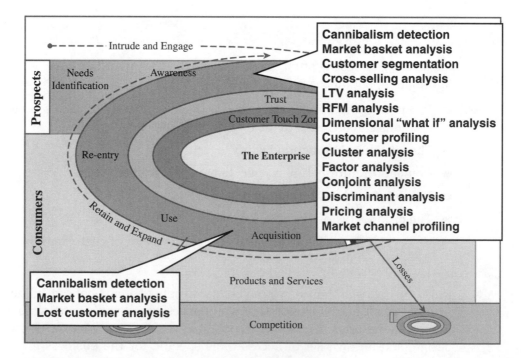

Figure 9.9 The Customer Life Cycle and the data marts.

Each data mart yields the information you will need to fully understand the history of your customers, their value to your organization, their preferences, and their patterns of behavior. Without this critical information, you will have little chance of successfully moving your organization toward a true CRM environment.

The data delivery process and DSI round out the business intelligence components you will need. Data delivery is responsible for ensuring the timely distribution of properly formatted data into the different data marts. The DSI is ultimately how we will be judged successful. If the users can easily and quickly get answers to their questions with minimal help and minimal hassles, then they will declare the business intelligence environment a success.

Chapter 10, "Facilitating Customer Touches with the Customer ODS," will continue describing the construction of the critical components of your CIF environment. In that chapter, the operational data store is the topic of discussion. We will cover its design, construction, and ultimate role in your Customer Life Cycle.

Facilitating Customer Touches with the Customer ODS

A s more organizations execute Customer Relationship Management (CRM) business strategies, customers themselves become more demanding about the treatment they receive when interacting with these organizations. Sophisticated consumers now demand a consistency of knowledge and treatment across all the points of contact within the Customer Life Cycle. At each touch point within the Customer Touch Zone, customers expect the organization to understand the breadth of products and services they already own, the customer's relationships with both employees and other customers (particularly family members), the value they bring to the organization, and the past contacts they have had with the organization. Further, they expect the organization to act on this knowledge, providing them with personalized service. Such personalized service will not only help ensure they stay with your organization, it may also be a key factor in the consumers' decision to enter into any relationship with you in the first place.

Let's look at this in more detail using our continuing saga of Bob, his parents, and their banking experiences. Chapter 1, "The Customer Becomes the Center of the Business Universe," introduced us to Bob and his parents and highlighted this new era of customer sophistication and increasing demand. Bob (a profitable banking customer) does most of his banking through the Internet and telephone banking center, while his parents (also profitable banking customers) prefer to conduct their transactions in the branch.

Figure 10.1 delves deeper into what satisfying Bob's expectations really means by illustrating just what the bank must do to provide Bob his preferred "how, where, and when" for interactions.

Bob has recently moved from a townhouse into a larger house. Because he does most of his banking using the Web, he logs onto the Internet banking site and changes his address, phone, and fax to reflect his new residence. Note that although he has multiple accounts, he submits the change only one time and approves it for all accounts, rather than changing the contact information on each individual account. Bob completes this transaction at 11:00 p.m., long after traditional banking hours have ended.

While on his customized banking Web page, Bob notices an icon for a guided hiking trip in the mountains of Switzerland. The bank's credit card division, having had past success in interesting Bob in adventure vacations offered by an affiliated travel service, has asked for and received his permission to notify him of other similar offers by placing banners on his Internet bank Web page. When

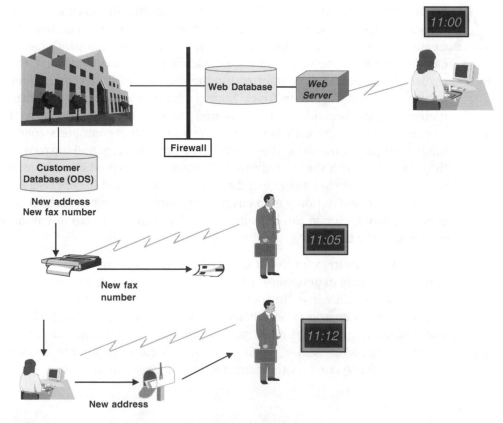

Figure 10.1 Coordinating service across channels.

he clicks on the banner, he discovers that the travel service offers several different trips, each catering to a variety of fitness levels and climbing skill sets.

While completing his banking transactions, Bob places a call to the fax-back service included in the travel information and requests a fax summarizing the details for each trip. As Figure 10.1 illustrates, the coordination of information across multiple customer touch points or channels plays a key role here. Five minutes prior to his request for the fax, Bob changes his contact information on the Web. His call to the fax-back service involves a completely independent channel (in this case, a channel run by an affiliated third party—the travel service) and is placed after hours (at 11:05 p.m.). If the fax is sent to the old (disconnected) fax number, the bank has clearly not met the how, where, and when conditions stipulated by Bob. The complexities involved in meeting these conditions will not ease his dissatisfaction if the bank fails. To Bob, the time of the transaction is irrelevant. It does not matter that the bank is operating on a skeleton staff at that time of night; it matters only that this is the time that is convenient for him. To Bob, the travel service is not an independent channel at all. The offer is coming through his bank, and the travel service is simply part of the extended enterprise (as described in Chapter 3, "Understanding the Customer Life Cycle"). It is imperative that the bank and the third-party fax-back service understand the change in fax number, and that the fax-back service initiates the requested fax immediately and to the correct number.

The story doesn't stop here, however. The bank, a CRM-savvy organization, is able to coordinate the Web and the fax-back service, issuing the fax to the correct number. Bob reads the fax immediately on receipt and determines that his brother and sisters may want to accompany him. (His parents may even go on the beginner trip!) He immediately calls the bank's 24-hour customer service department, requesting several glossy brochures mailed to his house. While making this call (approximately 12 minutes after he changed his address), Bob expects the customer service representative (CSR) to know about his change of address. This contact adds a third channel, telephone service, to the coordination effort required by the bank.

How does an organization facilitate this type of sharing of customer information across all the touch points? By using the customer operational data store (ODS). This chapter introduces the customer ODS as the primary vehicle to facilitate coordinated and consistent customer knowledge. We will look first at the characteristics of the ODS in general, and then examine the evolving functions of a customer ODS. We will highlight some of the decisions your organization must make when building a customer-centric ODS. Last, we will map the functions provided by the customer ODS to the Customer Life Cycle. Business representatives and technologists will both benefit from the explanation of the customer ODS that is provided in this chapter.

What Is an ODS?

The ODS is a subject-oriented, integrated, current, and volatile collection of data that provides a true enterprise view of information[1] (Each of these terms will be explained later in this chapter.)

Figure 10.2 portrays a logical view of the ODS. As you can see, the logical ODS is modeled to include all subjects of interest to the organization, such as customer, human resources, and product. Although we strongly recommend designing a logical ODS that includes the full scope of subjects (see Chapter 6, "Developing an Integrated CRM Technology Environment," for more details), it is entirely feasible that the physical implementation may represent only a subset of the logical ODS pictured in Figure 10.2. The customer ODS is just this: a subset of a complete logical ODS that focuses on the subject of primary interest to CRM, the customer. Maintaining the complete logical perspective ensures that relationships among all of the physical ODSs are preserved so that the enterprise has a consistent, integrated view of its tactical data. Although organizations implement ODS applications for subjects other than customers, the rest of this chapter will focus on the qualities found in the customer ODS.

Prior to examining the customer ODS, let's first look at the defining characteristics found in all operational data stores, including the customer ODS:

Subject-oriented. The ODS is organized around major subjects of interest to the enterprise. Its primary purposes are to collect, integrate, and distribute current information about its subject and to provide an enterprise view of this subject. For example, the customer ODS typically houses the most current information on a customer as well as information on all recent customer interactions with the organization including product ownership and summary usage statistics, statement information, summary-level contacts, and other related information.

Integrated. An ODS represents an integrated image of the subject. The information making up this image can be pulled from any system in the organization, both operational and informational. As the definitive record and the consolidation point for information about the subject, the ODS also feeds other systems in the organization with this valuable information. As an example, the customer ODS integrates all the different sources of tactical

---

[1]References for this section include *Building the Operational Data Store* by Inmon, Imhoff, and Battas, John Wiley & Sons, 1996 and "The Operational Data Store: Hammering Away" by Imhoff, *DMReview*, July 1998.

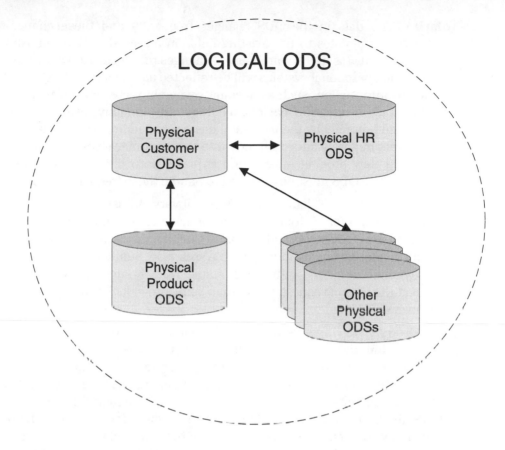

Figure 10.2   Logical and physical ODSs.

customer information into a consistent view, which is then used to interact with the customer across all contact points.

Current-valued. The ODS carries little or no history. Unlike a data warehouse, which is a series of snapshots of information used for strategic analysis, the ODS is a current picture of the subjects in question and is used for "action." Note that currency is relative and can be defined differently depending on the subject matter; the ODS used by Bob's bank may define "current" to include weekly account balance figures carried for one or two months. An ODS usually contains some recent historical information, such as the prior address, closed accounts, recent campaign and solicitations. The fine point to consider is that the ODS should have far less history than the data warehouse and should not be considered as a replacement for the warehouse. The ODS cannot facilitate the detailed analysis performed by business intelligence systems.

Volatile. The data in the ODS changes frequently and these changes are reflected as updates to the existing fields in a record, not as snapshots of whole records (as in the warehouse). Changes to information about the subject in the operational systems will be reflected as a change in the ODS. Some types of information, such as account ownership, customer touch records, and contact information, can change frequently. In many cases, the ODS can be updated directly by the users and customers, adding to its volatility. New customers might be added directly into the customer ODS at the same time that their new product information is placed into the business operations systems. The ODS must be designed to handle these frequent changes.

Detailed. The level of detail in the ODS will vary. A customer ODS may carry low-level detail for customer profiles but have only summarized information about customer contacts and accounts. Summary data in the ODS is different from summarized fields found in the warehouse. Summary fields in the ODS are dynamic in nature, rather than static. That is, summaries can be calculated at the time of request, rather than being pre-calculated and stored in the database.

Refreshed at varying speeds. An additional characteristic of an ODS is relevant to CRM: the speed at which the ODS is refreshed. Your organization has some choices in terms of the currency of information and the frequency with which that information is updated. In the banking world of Bob and his parents, the customer contact information must be updated in the customer ODS almost immediately, within a few seconds of its entry into the operational environment. This type of ODS is labeled as a class I. A class I ODS is used when the information must be very accurate and up-to-date at all times.

A class II ODS is a little more relaxed, using store and forward techniques for data updates, rather than performing synchronous updates. A class II ODS can receive updates every half-hour or hour. Bob's summary account balances may be updated into the customer ODS every 30 minutes. Because the service representative only uses this information to get a feel for Bob's financial picture, going instead to the product-centric account systems for his transaction details, class II updates are fine for account summaries. Some trade-off exists, however, in the update frequency and integration complexity. Because the information is not as current in a class II, integrating this type of ODS with other systems may be less difficult than for a class I.

A class III ODS is used when information currency requirements are not nearly as robust as those described earlier. A class III ODS is typically loaded in batches, most often on a daily basis. Bob's investment preferences can be updated into the ODS only once every day or so. Because investment preferences are used to understand cross-sell recommendations and do not change frequently, class III updates work well.

Multiple Update Types in a Single ODS

Note that a single ODS can have multiple classes of updates happening at the same time. This is frequently the case with the customer ODS. Some pieces of customer information are deemed to be more critical than others and can require a more frequent update. In the case of the bank serving Bob, the customer contact and account information is class I and must be updated immediately, whereas investment preferences and hobbies are updated only as class II or III, and the warehouse calculations such as loan pre-approvals are class IV.

The fourth type of ODS, class IV, is a special case where information to feed the ODS comes not only from the operational systems, but also from the warehouse. The information from the warehouse is loaded into the ODS only periodically, sometimes in an unscheduled fashion. Pre-approved loan amounts that are calculated in the warehouse data mart and loaded into the ODS on a monthly basis are an example of a class IV ODS update. Marketing uses the net worth and product usage information stored in the warehouse and data marts to determine these values. Service representatives dealing with Bob can use the pre-approval amounts to attempt to cross-sell credit products. Because the actual credit amount will be re-calculated if Bob applies for a loan, the monthly update frequency for this information is fine.

What Is a Customer ODS . . . and Why Do I Need One?

The customer ODS supports functions in the customer touch zone by supplying integrated customer data. Anyone who "touches" the customer should have access to this valuable information. Although the ODS concept is not new, many organizations are just beginning to realize its potential as a prime facilitator of CRM strategy. Confusion still reigns in some organizations as to just what constitutes a true ODS and which systems fall into the ODS classification. This distinction is quite important because systems that do not fit the characteristics of an ODS (particularly the subject orientation and integration) will have difficulty providing the enterprise view so necessary to CRM. The characteristics that make an ODS unique also enable it to provide this integrated, consistent enterprise view of customer information. Figure 10.3 distinguishes between a customer ODS and other, equally important but different applications required

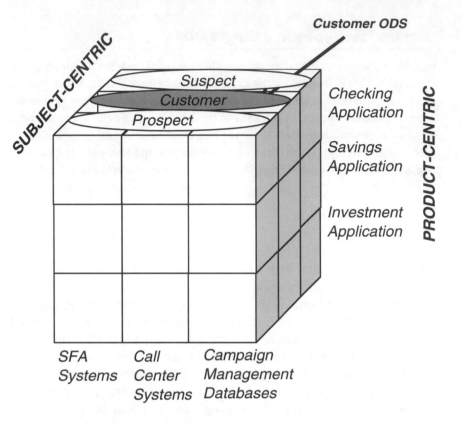

Figure 10.3 Product-, process-, and subject-centric CRM systems.

in a CRM technology environment. This discussion highlights the need for a customer ODS to facilitate CRM business strategies.

The cube in Figure 10.3 portrays three types of systems: product-centric, process-centric, and subject-centric. Each is designed with a different focus. Product-centric systems are designed to automate the accounting for specific products or services; process-centric systems are designed to automate the activities involved in completing a specific process; and subject-centric systems are designed to automate the collection, integration, and distribution of all information required for a specific subject. All may carry some amount of customer information. However, in a product- or process-centric system, a single subject, such as customer, is not the primary concern.

Let's look first at the product-centric systems, which fall on the right side of the cube. Some of the business operations systems within the Corporate Information Factory (CIF) fall into this category. These systems run the day-to-day business operations for a company and originate most of the data that feeds the remaining parts of the Corporate Information Factory. Legacy applications such as demand deposit (checking), savings, and investment are good examples of product-centric systems. These systems facilitate all transactions for a specific product or service. For example, when Bob has his paycheck automatically deposited in his checking account each month, the checking legacy application accepts the transaction and adjusts his account balance accordingly. In a robust CRM environment, many of these product-centric systems are linked to other systems in the organization. They may exchange information with the customer ODS, the warehouse, and the call center application. Bob's automatic deposit registers a transaction into the product-centric system, which in turn provides information to the summary account balance field in the customer ODS. An information exchange not withstanding, these systems are designed and organized with a primary focus on the product. The systems may contain some customer information, but this information will be duplicated for every account or product associated with the customer and thus is not the adequate or accurate source of customer information required by CRM.

The front face of the cube highlights the process-centric systems. These are a mix of operational systems and analytical applications or data marts. They are distinguished from product-centric systems because their focus is broader; they are designed to facilitate the completion of business processes, some of which can be quite complex. Examples of process-centric systems include call center systems (facilitating the customer service process), sales force automation (facilitating the sales process), and campaign management data marts (facilitating the campaign development process). These systems tend to have more customer information than their product-centric counterparts; some even have embedded customer components. Although customer information exists in these systems, their primary purpose is to automate a process and this is typically reflected in their design.

For example, consider customer service. Call center systems are designed to provide the call center with tools to assist in achieving outstanding customer service. All of the features required to monitor and enhance call center performance are included in these systems. Workflow management tools track the progress of a service issue through multiple calls and across multiple service representatives. Telephony features quickly and efficiently route the calls to appropriate operators and record and measure call statistics (call times and durations, call volumes, number of rings, dropped calls, and so on). Contact trackers record and share conversations with customers. The customer does play a significant role, but the design of the system is clearly oriented to support the function of customer service. Consequently, many of these systems look at the customer only from the service perspective. Broad-based customer definitions (such as the one discussed in Chapter 1) covering all functions in the organization may not be facilitated within this system. Referral sources, suppliers, and competitors may not be handled in the call center system because they are not required to service existing customers.

Additionally, as we saw in Chapter 4, "Are You Ready? Tuning the Organization for CRM," several different business units within an organization may perform the same process quite independently. Again, we will use customer service as our example. The communications company described in prior chapters has two diverse and independent business units: a cable company and a cellular company. The organization uses one call center and billing system for its cable business and a different system for its cellular group. The technical requirement for providing service in these two business lines is very different, and the company does not foresee running both call centers with a single system. Both call center systems house customer information, but this information is not shared across the two call centers, hampering the ability for the organization to obtain a complete view of its customers across both business units. Some vendors are integrating sales automation components with call center components, but few (if any) have taken the next step: tightly integrating these systems with the legacy applications or the warehouse and data mart components. These systems are an invaluable part of CRM technology, but they typically stop short of providing the functionality found in the customer-centric ODS.

Subject-centric databases, such as the customer ODS, are portrayed on the top of the cube in Figure 10.3. As defined in the prior section, a subject-oriented database is designed and organized around a major subject of high importance to an organization. Customer is clearly a subject area important to CRM, and the customer ODS represents business management at its most robust. As illustrated by the cube, each and every customer type included in the enterprise customer definition is also included in the customer-centric ODS. The customer ODS is not built around any single process or product, but it is designed instead to provide a non-partisan view of customer. Thus, it becomes the definitive record for all customer information. As the cube illustrates, the subject-centric customer ODS cuts across all process- and product-centric systems. This enables every system in the Corporate Information Factory (and every employee in the organization) to access customer information through the customer ODS. The ODS provides the consistent and comprehensive enterprise view of customer information to every contact point.

Overview of an Ideal Customer ODS

At its core, the customer ODS is simply a database that houses customer information. However, to get the most value from the customer ODS, companies need to take several additional steps:

- Integrate the ODS with other components of the Corporate Information Factory.

- Build intuitive and user-friendly access mechanisms to let select users view and modify the customer information.

- Combine these databases with toolkits, which enable the users to make the most of the information in the database.

- Pay close and ongoing attention to the quality of the information contained in the ODS itself.

This section focuses on the additional tools and capabilities that must be combined with the ODS itself to facilitate true CRM.

Figure 10.4 illustrates these tools and capabilities. The dotted circle represents all the capabilities that might be combined with the customer ODS. First, the database itself provides the definitive record for all profile information about the customers of an organization. The customer information within the customer ODS can be extensive, encompassing customer contacts, relationships, products and services owned and used, behaviors, preferences, and so on. It is the customer ODS that identifies and maintains the household relationship that exists between Bob's parents as well as the extended household relationship of Bob and his parents. This customer information provides the core of the customer ODS and facilitates all the capabilities discussed in the remainder of this chapter.

Second, as the definitive record for customer information, the customer ODS is integrated (loosely or tightly—for details, see the next section) to all systems that generate or use customer information. As illustrated by Figure 10.4, this facility is linked to all product applications across the organization. The two-headed arrow in Figure 10.4 illustrates that the ODS can receive information on the product applications and can send information to the product applications. The account balance summaries and product ownership information described in the previous section are examples of information received into the customer ODS from the product-centric legacy applications. The change of address information that originated in the ODS and was circulated to the other systems is an example of information pushed from the ODS into the other systems as required.

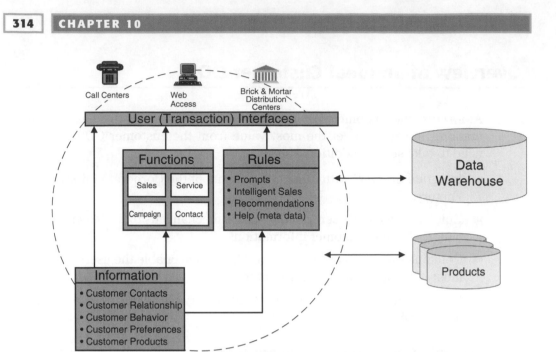

Figure 10.4 The ideal customer ODS.

The other link pictured in Figure 10.4 is the link from the customer ODS to the data warehouse and associated data marts. This link also has a two-headed arrow, which represents the capability to pass information to the warehouse and to receive information from the warehouse or data marts. Passing information from the customer ODS to the warehouse provides the marketing analysts with a consistent and complete picture of Bob's relationship with the bank, allowing an accurate analysis of Bob's profitability and lifetime value. Passing information from the warehouse to the customer ODS enables the bank to use the understanding of Bob, generated from data mart activities, to better manage all contacts with him. When the bank calculates Bob's lifetime value figure, assigns him a VIP profitability status, and places that status indicator on his profile in the customer ODS, it is acting on business intelligence from the analytical applications and is managing its touches with Bob accordingly. In this instance, all bank personnel that access Bob's profile will understand that he is a VIP customer and that they must treat him as such.

Third, the customer ODS must work with the user or transaction interfaces accessing the information in the customer ODS and providing it to all customer contact points (call centers, Web access, and brick and mortar distribution centers). This enables consistent service across all customer touch points and provides customers like Bob with visible proof that the organization places a high priority on serving them well. Without a consistent view of Bob's information across all touch points, the fax-back service and telephone banking representative would not have known that Bob had just used the Web to change his address and fax number. Failure to understand and act on this information could have cost the bank more than the sale of the travel services; it may have cost the bank its relationship with Bob and his parents.

The fourth feature illustrated by Figure 10.4 includes the tools pictured in the rules box. These tools work in conjunction with the ODS and the user interfaces to assist both individuals and systems to manage customer contacts in a way that benefits both the customer and the organization. The tools include rules-based personalization engines. These engines use the criteria developed from strategic analysis in the data marts in combination with current profile and product usage information to generate dynamic cross-sell recommendations. The banner ad placed on Bob's Web page is an illustration of this function. An analysis of his credit card usage highlights Bob as a candidate for the travel service. The personalization engine uses these analysis results to determine that the active travel ad would interest Bob and places it on his Web page when he logs on. If Bob had responded negatively to the advertisement, this same engine would have recorded the response and incorporated it onto his profile to ensure that the ad did not appear the next time he logged onto his Web page.

A second capability that can be combined with the data from customer ODS is a scripting tool. When a service representative talking to Bob determines that he has recently changed his address, the scripting tool can provide questions for the representative to ask (such as did his job change as well, is he familiar with the new area, what prompted the move?). This information can be used to improve service, to feed analysis for next best product opportunities, and to build the interaction and dialog with Bob. For example, the scripting tool may tell the service representative to ask if Bob is familiar with the bank ATM machines located near his new address. If not, the bank can mail or email a detailed list. Because Bob will be looking for this piece of correspondence, it is the ideal place to include a targeted product offer, such as home loan insurance or new mortgage interest rates.

A Detailed Look at the Ideal Customer ODS

So far, we have described the general characteristics of an ODS, distinguished this database from others in the Corporate Information Factory, provided an overview of the customer ODS, and introduced its role in a CRM environment.

For the remainder of this chapter, we will take a more detailed look at the functions described in Figure 10.4. We will look at both the customer ODS itself, as well as at the other capabilities that your organization can tie into the customer ODS to most effectively facilitate your CRM strategies. We will also highlight some of the decisions your organization will have to make when implementing the customer ODS and its associated capabilities.

Comprehensive Customer Definition

Chapter 1 introduced the need to adopt a comprehensive definition of customer that is understood and agreed upon across the enterprise. The customer ODS must accommodate this definition. To provide an enterprise view, the database must be founded on a customer definition that satisfies the needs of all business functions dealing with customers. Sales, Customer Service, Marketing, and Risk Management departments must all be represented. This broad perspective ensures the enterprise view of customer so necessary to CRM. Each organization will have its own enterprise customer definition, but a comprehensive definition typically includes numerous types of customers. Individuals, organizations, and small businesses are generally included. Customers who actually own and use products and services are included, as well as others who may be of interest, either to the actual customers or to the organization. Agents, beneficiaries, brokers, competitors, employees, guarantors, prospects, referral sources, and suppliers are a few of the common inclusions. Refer to Chapters 1 and 6 for a more detailed definition of customer and the included types.

Customer Relationships

Chapter 1 introduced the concept of the influence value gained by understanding and managing the various types of customer relationships. A robust customer ODS must facilitate the identification and storage of these relationships. The data structures in the customer ODS must be designed with a full understanding of the linkages necessary for CRM. Returning for a moment to our discussion of process-oriented systems versus subject-oriented systems, this is a function that is sometimes lacking (or only partially present) in a process-oriented system. We will look again at the call center packages. Because these are designed primarily to service the customer, they may not facilitate some of the more complex relationships required for enterprise CRM, such as managing supplier or competitor relationships. The relationships necessary for CRM range from basic to quite complex; all should be possible in the customer ODS. The following is a discussion of the types of relationships you should expect your customer ODS to handle.

Relationships between a Company and Its Customers

The most basic relationship is between the organization and the customer who owns products and services. This relationship can be business-to-customer (B2C) (in which the customer is an individual consumer) or business-to-business (B2B) (in which the customer is another organization). The relationship between Bob and his bank is a typical (or non-typical as Bob is more sophisticated and demanding than the average consumer) B2C relationship. Here Bob purchases and uses a number of the bank's products and services. The relationship between the systems integration firm and its business customer (introduced in Chapter 3) is an example of this basic association in the B2B world. The products and services sold by the systems integration firm are CRM applications and the manpower required to install these. Its customers are other businesses who want to implement this CRM technology but don't have the knowledge or resources to do it themselves.

In its most basic form, the relationship between an organization and its customers revolves around the products owned by those customers. This relationship is reflected in the ODS by simply establishing a link between the customers and the products and services they own and use. Each additional product or service purchased by the customer builds the relationship and requires an additional link from the customer to the new product information. These basic customer-to-product links provide the information necessary to enable all contact points to have a quick and accurate look at all the products and services owned by the customer. The bank uses these links to allow the telephone banking service representative, the fax-back service, and the Web system to view the same picture of Bob and all of his products and services. Note that some basic relationships exist in which the association between the customer and the product or service is not so straightforward as pure ownership (such as the user of a cell phone who does not actually pay the bill). These too should be accommodated.

A slightly more complicated flavor of the basic product ownership relationship must be facilitated within the customer ODS as well. The ODS must be able to link an organization's employees with the customers they manage. The relationship between Bob and his private banker is a good example. The bank must know which employee is responsible for managing Bob's overall relationship. Although this type of relationship between an organization and an individual consumer is usually fairly simple, it can get more complicated. In the B2B world, a team of employees may manage a single customer, and this team may change as the relationship evolves. The systems integration company has many people interfacing with its business customer. The account manager, the CRM expert consultant, and the project managers for each of the past projects all had relationships with the customer that should be identified and managed in a customer ODS.

Relationships within the Extended Enterprise

The next relationship that must be facilitated is also between an organization and its customers. The customers participating in this relationship, however, are not those that buy products and services. Instead, these customers are those individuals or organizations who have some business relationship with you that can affect the ultimate customer. The extended enterprise concept in the Customer Life Cycle provides several good examples: the supplier who manages the inventory in your retail stores, the competitor whose products are brokered through your sales force, and the third party whose products are sold by your organization as a value-add to your own products. The supplier, the competitor, and the third party each have the ability to influence your ultimate customers. If a popular product is not on the shelf in your store, the customer will be dissatisfied with you, not the supplier. If Bob's travel experience is less than ideal, he may not purchase any other non-banking services from the bank. And if your sales force brokers a competitive product that is not right for your customer, that customer may be unhappy with both the competitor and you. Each of these constitutes a relationship that can influence the satisfaction of your customers; each must be managed within the customer ODS.

Relationships that Your Customers Have with Each Other

The last relationship that must be handled by the customer ODS is potentially the most complex: the relationship between your customers, the C2C relationships. As we discussed in Chapter 1, your organization typically can't control these relationships, but understanding them and tailoring your customer interactions accordingly can strongly impact customer satisfaction (this impact can be positive or negative depending on your understanding or lack thereof). These relationships come in many different flavors: household (economic decision-making units), customers who share associations to products (joint bank account owners), individual customers who work for, or with, business customers (such as the plumber in Chapter 3), and customers who belong to groups that your organization sells to or that offer packages or discounts (such as the American Association of Retired Persons [AARP]). In each case, the more your organization understands about these relationships, the more you know about potential customer behavior. A robust customer ODS must handle all types of customer relationships.

Other Relationship Issues

It is not enough to simply build the data structures to store these relationships; the relationships must also be established, displayed, and maintained. Some of these relationships can be established by using commercially available software packages, such as householding tools for C2C relationships, or Dun & Bradstreet and other corporate matching software for B2B relationships (refer to Chapter 8, "Quality Relationships Start with Quality Customer Data," for more information on these tools). The tools can be applied in a batch mode to extract all customers from the database, identify potential relationships, review questionable relationships, and reload the accepted relationships into the database when the process is finished.

Although it is a good practice to run these batch processes periodically, an increasing requirement for up-to-date relationship information that cannot be obtained through the batch linking process also exists. The problem with the batch processes is illustrated with the following scenario.

Bob gets married and he and his wife form a new household. They notify the bank and open a joint checking account. Shortly thereafter, the Marketing Department personnel use the customer ODS to pull names for a direct marketing campaign. Bob and his wife both fit the campaign criteria and their names are included in the mailing. Because the next batch run of the householding software is not scheduled for another two weeks, the Marketing personnel do not realize that Bob and his wife are now one household. They send two mail pieces, exactly the same, one to Bob and one to his wife. This aggravates Bob because he has specifically notified the bank of the change in his marital status and the first bank literature he receives has ignored his notification. The situation is compounded when the telemarketing group calls Bob's wife to follow up on the offer and reads a sales prompt suggesting that she purchase a new product. This sales prompt was generated using her individual information, rather than the aggregated household information, and Bob already owns the product they have offered.

If the Marketing and Telephone Sales groups had been using current data about Bob and his wife, they would have sent one mailing, and the cross-sale product suggestions would have been generated based on the products of the entire household, rather than on the products of only one member. Updating this kind of relationship information only periodically does not work for more complex CRM strategies. To resolve this problem, many organizations now use some form of online linking capability in addition to the periodic batch tools. Building these automated online linking tools into the processes that add and update customers in the customer ODS enables new relationships to be identified at the time the information is entered, rather than forcing the organization to wait for the next batch process. This capability would have allowed the bank to recognize the new household link when Bob's wife changed her address and opened a joint account with him. Because the online tools are not quite as accurate as the batch tools, it is advisable for an organization to use both. Combining online and batch tools makes the previous example an exception rather than the norm.

Also, some types of relationships cannot be detected automatically (spouse relationships, company VIPs, and so on). Employees dealing with the customer must identify these relationships and the links must be manually input into the customer ODS. This requires that the customer ODS enable manually input relationship links, and that the business rules that govern the establishment and maintenance of these relationships are built into the customer addition and update processes. For example, many organizations do not allow a group like the AARP to be established unless an employee is actively managing the group. Requiring an active group manager makes someone accountable for the maintenance of the group and ensures that the customer ODS does not get cluttered with inactive groups. Embedding this business rule into the process to update the ODS causes the rejection of any group links where no accompanying employee relationship exists.

Extensive and Extensible Customer Models

Chapters 4 and 6 detail the requirements for comprehensive customer information standards that become the foundation for all CRM systems in the Corporate Information Factory. Standards can include accepted customer types, accepted abbreviations such as St for street, and business rules requiring an employee to be associated with every customer group. These standards are commonly documented in the form of data and process models and are used to build the customer component for all systems that carry any type of customer information. These models highlight the information required to support CRM business processes, provide a common point of communication between the technologists who build the customer systems and the business folks who use these systems, and ensure that all systems are built with the capability to share customer information. It is imperative that the customer ODS is built to follow the corporate standard for customer information as documented in these models. As the customer ODS will be the definitive record for all customer information and will be passing and receiving customer information to and from many other systems, it must incorporate an extensible design that can be shared with other applications.

This requirement does not preclude the purchase of vendor packages for the customer ODS. It simply asserts that any customer ODS (homegrown or purchased) must have an extensible data model and the associated database structures must be non-proprietary so that information can be shared with other systems. Applications with proprietary databases, or with limited capabilities to customize the customer component, must be considered very carefully. Chances are that these types of systems will not provide all the capabilities required of a true customer ODS. Organizations considering the purchase of process-oriented systems, such as call center packages or sales force automation packages, should look specifically at the customer model to ensure that the system will be able to share information with the customer ODS.

In addition, to provide a comprehensive view of customers to the enterprise, the customer ODS must have the capability to carry a great deal of information about those customers. As with the customer definition, the models and associated database must be developed from an enterprise perspective. At a minimum, Sales, Service, Marketing, and Risk Management must all participate in developing and validating the final data requirements. Figure 10.5 illustrates these requirements from a data model perspective. The example in Figure 10.5 is taken from Chapter 6 and has been expanded to include customer-level data elements.

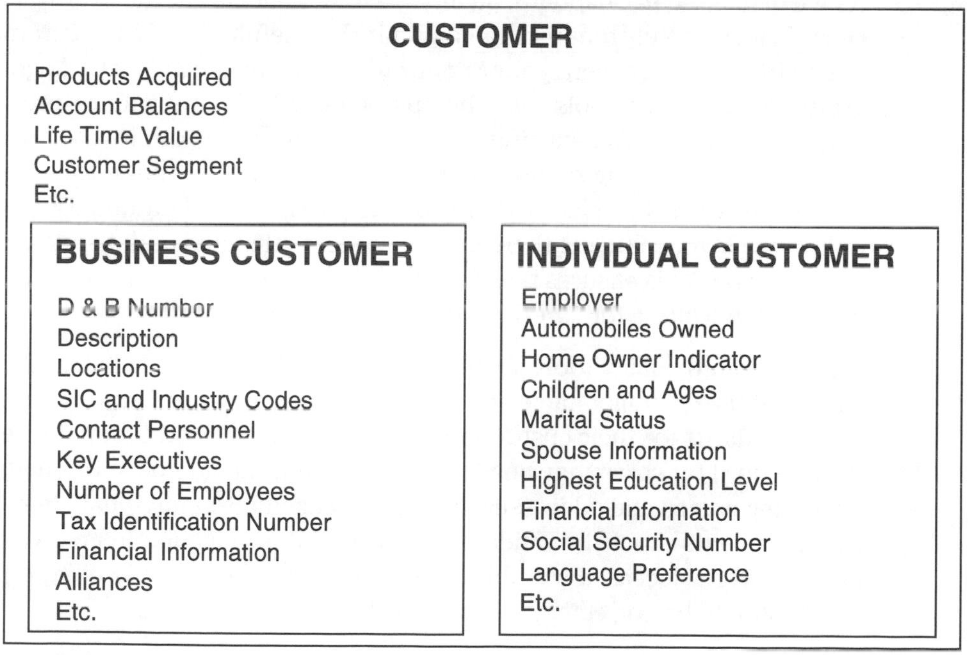

CUSTOMER

Products Acquired
Account Balances
Life Time Value
Customer Segment
Etc.

BUSINESS CUSTOMER

D & B Number
Description
Locations
SIC and Industry Codes
Contact Personnel
Key Executives
Number of Employees
Tax Identification Number
Financial Information
Alliances
Etc.

INDIVIDUAL CUSTOMER

Employer
Automobiles Owned
Home Owner Indicator
Children and Ages
Marital Status
Spouse Information
Highest Education Level
Financial Information
Social Security Number
Language Preference
Etc.

Figure 10.5 Extensible data model, customer example.

For individual customers, the ODS should have the following information: income, the make and model of automobile(s), the presence and ages of children, the highest education level, date of birth, gender, home owner or renter, employer, job title, marital status, spousal information, drivers license state and number, social security number, credit history, language and currency preferences, addresses(s), e-mail address, phone number(s), contact preference(s), purchased demographic information and basic census data, hobbies and interests, and preferences concerning your products if applicable.

Information on business customers should include the following: the number of locations and addresses, a business description, SIC and industry codes, contact personnel, key executives, the number of employees, Dun & Bradstreet numbers, and financial statements. The customer ODS should also carry the following for all customer types: the products owned and summary information about those products (such as daily account balances) with the ability to get to the detail in the product systems, profitability indicators and lifetime value indicators, risk indicators, segment codes, a summary of contact information with the ability to look at contact systems for details, and other types of business intelligence results.

Data Quality Tools

As we discussed in Chapter 8, quality customer data is another key to CRM success. Inaccurate customer data can limit the usefulness of the customer ODS, which in turn can prevent your organization from achieving its CRM goals. Integrating data quality tools into the customer ODS is one way to prevent this. Organizations are also starting to apply these tools in both a batch and online fashion, similar to the deployment of the relationship linking tools discussed earlier. As with the relationship tools, deploying the data quality tools in an online mode means using them in the processes that add and update customers into the ODS. This ensures that quality is enforced when information is entered, rather than waiting for a periodic batch run to clean up the data.

The integrated quality tools should perform validation, cleansing, and standardization of the customer name and address data. Many organizations develop specific standards for their customer name and address information. For example, the standard for street may be St, while North may always be shortened to N. All customer names and addresses should be parsed into individual elements, and these elements should be validated for correctness and completeness (for example, the word deceased should not appear in the name field). Where possible, errors should be corrected, and standards should be applied.

Quality tools should also perform name propagation. Many legacy product applications have little or no quality mechanisms built into them. Thus, more than one customer can be found on any given record, such as John and Mary Smith. We clearly do not want to let this continue in the customer ODS, so it is important to identify multiple customer names on one record and propagate the appropriate name elements to two separate customer records, such as John Smith and Mary Smith.

The integrated quality tools must also identify and merge duplicate customers. It is highly likely that a customer will exist more than once across the various product-centric legacy applications. These are typically organized by product or account and will have one record for each product or account. Bob exists many times in the bank's product systems: once for his mortgage, once for each investment product, once or more for the credit card and associated travel service purchases, and twice for his checking accounts (his and one he and his wife share). Because these operational systems are a major source of information for the customer ODS, duplicate customers can be a large problem. The integrated tools should be able to match name and address information, as well as some other user-defined elements, and identify potential duplicate customers. The merge component of these tools combines accepted duplicates into a single customer record within the customer ODS.

These matching capabilities have a second use as well, identifying the appropriate customer record to attach or overlay purchased information, such as demographics or Dun & Bradstreet files. In this case, the matching tool is run not to eliminate duplicates, but to find the customer in the database that matches the customer in the purchased information. When these matches are found, the purchased information is attached to the record in the customer ODS.

Similar to the relationship linking tools described previously, these quality tools are applied to the customer ODS using several methods. The online application of these tools is described earlier, but the tools can also be applied in a batch mode. This entails extracting the customer information from the database, running it through the data quality tool sets, correcting errors and validating matches, combining duplicate customer records, and loading the cleansed customer information back into the customer ODS.

The Transaction Interface

As indicated throughout this chapter, the customer ODS provides the enterprise view of customers. Any person or system that needs customer information will get it from the customer ODS. The transaction interface is the primary method for users to access the data stored in the customer ODS. Unlike the warehouse access tools discussed in Chapter 9, "Business Intelligence: Technologies for Understanding Your Customers," the primary purpose of the transaction interface is not to issue a query and bring back all the records fitting the characteristics specified therein. Instead, it is designed to pull one record at a time, such as one customer profile and all the associated information, and display this information in an easily readable format.

The searching mechanism described in the following section is an exception to this general characteristic. Good customer searches bring back any customer record that is a possible match to the search criteria. The user then examines the returned records and chooses the appropriate customer. Additionally, some other situations occur in which the users of the customer ODS have business questions that require the transaction interface to return a list of customers. One insurance company uses its ODS to return lists of insured properties to use in determining risk exposure in coastal areas during hurricane season. Also, unlike the data warehouse, users can directly update the customer ODS. Because the customer ODS provides an extensive customer profile, it is sometimes the best (or only) place an organization has to store new customer data elements, such as income, investment preferences, and so on. It is quite common for old product applications to keep a minimum amount of customer information, such as only what is needed to open the account or send the product.

In cases like these, the product applications are hard to modify, and the customer ODS becomes the only place to store the extensive customer information that the organization wants to begin collecting and using in its CRM strategies. In this case, the organization must build the transaction interface to enable users to directly update the customer ODS (rather than building the ODS as read-only, and forcing all information updates to be done through the data acquisition process detailed in Chapter 7, "Capturing Customer Information"). Use of the direct update capability means that the transaction interface must facilitate the addition, change, and (possibly) deletion of customer information, as well as its retrieval. Detailed process models similar to those described in Chapter 6 and the associated create, retrieve, update, and delete (CRUD) matrix, which specifies the business rules for each element of customer information, must be included with the development of the transaction interface.

WARNING

Opening the customer ODS and the associated transaction interface to a direct update facilitates a complete customer profile, and it enables the collection of new and useful customer data elements. However, a cautionary note is in order if your organization takes this route. Keep in mind that allowing a direct update will cause the transaction interface to become much more complex than if it facilitates only a retrieval of information. If the transaction interface updates information, it must deal with edit checks, referential integrity, and the reconciliation of information between the product and process systems and the customer ODS. The online data quality and relationship tools described throughout this chapter will have to be built into the transaction interface. The transaction interface will have to understand business rules, as it checks for referential integrity (no account summary information can be added unless an associated customer is included). If a change to a customer record happens in the product application at the same time that a user is attempting to change the customer directly in the customer ODS, the transaction interface must determine which change is correct, and it must understand which action to take. These issues are not insurmountable, just complex. Some organizations build the customer ODS as a read-only database at first and then gradually change the transaction interface to enable more complex update activities.

The transaction interface design is heavily dependent on the business processes that drive the use of the customer ODS. Customer Service may require a different interaction with the customer ODS than Sales or Marketing. The transaction interface may be required to provide different functions and views of data to different parts of the organization.

The transaction interface must also integrate with other applications. Many other systems will provide information to the ODS and receive information from the ODS. Middleware is an essential technology component that works in conjunction with the transaction interface to facilitate this transfer of information between applications. Middleware is software that connects different systems and enables them to share data. It acts as the go-between for diverse platforms and systems, providing a common link to many systems. In an environment where multiple systems exchange data, middleware can facilitate the process. Rather than writing an application interface from the customer ODS to each legacy system, an application interface from each legacy system to the ODS, and an application interface from each legacy system to the others, middleware requires only one application interface per system: to the middleware.

Middleware can help in the update process by keeping information until all databases that need it have completed their updates. More sophisticated middleware packages can even perform some of the data integration and transformation typically conducted in the data acquisition process. These emerging capabilities should not take the place of data acquisition. The authors strongly recommend that you include a robust data acquisition component in your CRM environment, as described in Chapter 7.

The combination of middleware and the transaction interface can be implemented in various levels of complexity depending on the required interaction of the customer ODS with the product applications. The simplest implementation occurs when the transaction interface updates only the ODS and not the product applications. Let's assume for this example that Bob calls the bank's phone service center to change his address. If the customer contact information is housed only in the ODS and not in the product applications, the service representative taking his change of address uses the transaction interface to change the information in the ODS. Because the information is housed only in the customer ODS, no product applications need to receive the change. The transaction interface and the associated middleware update only a single system. What happens if the address information resides in the customer ODS and in the product systems (a common occurrence)?

We have two options here: first, the interface can continue to access only the customer ODS, and the service representatives can make the update in two places, the customer ODS and the associated product systems. This is not very efficient and could lead to the service representative skipping the step of updating the customer ODS, which is very bad for data quality in the customer ODS.

A second alternative is to employ a more complex middleware and transaction interface implementation, one that accesses multiple databases. This is technically more difficult to implement but may provide more CRM functionality. Each organization must weigh the pros and cons of this decision and implement the transaction interface in the most suitable method for them. It is not unusual for organizations to use a phased approach to this problem: linking the most popular applications to the customer ODS first, and forcing a manual update of less used applications. As the resources become available, these organizations begin to convert the less used applications in subsequent projects. (See the previous warning on the complexities required of the transaction interface when changes come from both the product applications and the users themselves.)

The search mechanism mentioned at the beginning of this section also plays a key role in the quality of information in the customer ODS. If users have the ability to add and update customer information directly into the customer ODS, it is imperative that the search mechanism be accurate and fast.

Good search tools and algorithms can reduce the time it takes to service the customer, prevent duplicate customer entries, and reduce the need for a back office review and a correction of the data errors. If the searching mechanism does not return good matches, the service representative may enter a new customer record when one already exists in the database. If the search mechanism is too slow, the customer may have to wait an unacceptably long time while the Customer Service Representative also waits for the customer's profile to be returned. If the search mechanism brings back too many customers, the service representative may have to wade through too many records (such as 20 screens of Smiths) to get to the right customer profile.

Choosing the wrong profile can have severe consequences: adding information to the wrong customer profile or inadvertently giving one customer's information to another customer. Sophisticated customer searching mechanisms should be an integral part of the transaction interface. The search mechanism should enable user-defined search keys, and multiple keys should be accepted and utilized. Keys should be generated by parsing the customer name and address information into the same elements that are used for identifying duplicate customers, such as name elements (first, last, middle initial, suffix, and prefix) and address elements (street number, street name city, state, zip). In addition to direct indexing on key data elements (name, phone, and account number), keys should also include combinations of the elements generated from the parsing activity. Customers meeting the initial search criteria should be put through a customer-matching algorithm similar to the one described earlier, and the returned names should be ranked and displayed by degree of similarity to search criteria.

Summary

The customer ODS is a key component of the CRM technology environment. The customer ODS provides business management capabilities to the organization. It is the vehicle by which analysis performed in the warehouse and in data marts is made "actionable" and is distributed for use by the customer contact personnel. Figure 10.6 illustrates the role of business management and the customer ODS in the Customer Life Cycle.

A customer touch is any interaction between the organization and the customer. In the Customer Life Cycle, these interactions happen in the Customer Touch Zone. The customer ODS supports all activity in the Customer Touch Zone by supplying integrated customer data. Anyone who touches the customer should have access to this valuable information.

Although business management and the customer ODS facilitate all customer touches, they also play a predominant role in supporting processes that occur after the Customer Moment (the moment when a prospect decides to purchase the product or service from you, go to a competitor, or not make an acquisition). The product ownership information and cross-sales recommendations in the customer ODS facilitate the execution of marketing campaigns and cross-selling initiatives. Customer names and addresses for direct marketing campaigns often come directly from the customer ODS after the criteria for the campaigns are generated from the data marts. The product ownership information in the customer ODS is frequently used to measure marketing campaign performance, and also to tweak campaign execution based on interim results. Service representatives can use the customer ODS to see that a customer has received a marketing communication and use the service opportunity to follow up on the campaign. Contact and channel preferences and product usage statistics stored in the customer ODS can contribute to the organization's ability to

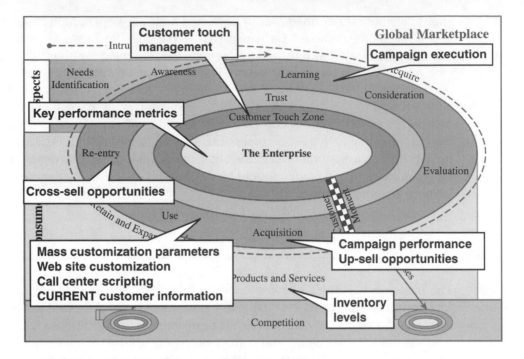

Figure 10.6 Business management and the Customer Life Cycle.

customize product and service packages. This information can also contribute to the organization's ability to customize Web access and provide customized advertisements and options based on customer preference.

The customer ODS works in conjunction with the product- and process-centric CRM systems to provide an integrated customer information environment. A robust customer ODS includes a comprehensive customer definition, extended customer relationships, extensible customer models, significant amounts of customer information, integrated data quality tools, and a strong transaction interface.

Chapter 11, "Automating the Sales and Service Process," focuses on two key process-centric CRM systems introduced in this chapter, the call center system and the sales force automation system.

Automating the Sales and Service Process

We opened the previous chapter with an example of Bob changing his address on the Web, initiating a fax-back service, and speaking to a telephone sales representative, all within the span of a few minutes. With these activities, Bob touched both the Sales and Service organizations of his bank. The bank, recognizing the importance of keeping its good customers happy, had already invested in the integrated technology required to make Bob's experience satisfactory.

Although Bob is a sophisticated (and demanding) individual, he is not that different from many of your own customers. Customers are increasingly requiring choices on how, where, and when they receive sales and service. Companies are scrambling to oblige for several reasons. First, competitive markets and technology advances are working together to change the dynamics of how organizations interact with their customers. Ten years ago, Bob could buy banking services only from a bank. Today he can purchase many of these same services from a bank, from an insurance company, from an investment company, or even from a non-traditional provider like GE Capital. Combining this competitive environment with today's sophisticated technology lets your customers access the competition with unprecedented ease.

Second, organizations are recognizing the growing importance of long-lasting and profitable customer relationships. Most organizations acknowledge that it costs more to gain a new customer than it does to sell an additional product to an existing customer. As a result, a higher importance is being placed on activities designed to retain and expand existing customers. Companies routinely develop specialized strategies for customers in the "acquire, use, and re-enter" stages of the Customer Life Cycle (refer to Chapter 3, "Understanding the Customer Life Cycle," for details on the Customer Life Cycle). Many of these strategies focus on cross-sell, up-sell, and customer satisfaction.

Third, products provided by competing organizations are frequently indistinguishable. A six-percent, two-year CD provides the same value regardless of the institution issuing it. When one company introduces a new product, most of the others follow suit shortly after. This "commoditization" of products and services is causing companies to search for other ways to differentiate themselves.

Enter the attempts to differentiate through sales and service. In addition to understanding the customer's demands for how, when, and where, companies are increasingly aware of the need to "know thy customer" and "apply this knowledge to all contacts." Many organizations are turning to systems in the business operations realm to assist them in these activities. This chapter discusses the automation of two business operations processes: sales and service. First, we look at why companies are automating these processes. We focus on both the myriad contact options that must be coordinated and the benefits that justify expenditures on these systems.

Next, we focus on the features required in an automated solution. First, we discuss the technology to automate customer service focusing on three primary components: workflow management, Computer Telephony Integration (CTI), and workbench capabilities. We also look at the difference between traditional service and help-desk support, and highlight additional automation requirements that are specific to each. Next, we highlight capabilities required for sales force automation. After covering the functionality of the individual components for sales and service, we examine the growing trend toward integrating these individual applications and functions, both with each other and with the rest of the Corporate Information Factory (CIF). Finally, we look at the role of these systems, and business operations in general, in the Customer Life Cycle.

A quick note on the role of the Internet in all of this: we consider the Internet to be simply another channel for customer communications. As with any other emerging channel, it comes complete with its own specific opportunities and challenges. As many companies are discovering, this is a channel that they have little choice but to adopt. Once adopted, it must be coordinated with all the other customer touch-points in the organization. Any discussion of the automation of sales and service processes must include the Internet as a possible contact point. The good news is that most technology solutions accommodate this contact point. For more detail on the role of the Internet and e-commerce in CRM, see the next chapter, Chapter 12, "Interacting with Customers Online."

Why Automate?

As Figure 11.1 illustrates, an organization must be able to touch its customers and prospects in a myriad of ways.

Sales or service activities happen through any of the following channels:

Internet. The Internet is clearly changing the way we interact with our customers. Take the hype away though, and the Internet is simply another customer touch-point. We will use Bob as our example. Throughout the course of this book, he has initiated and received service on the Internet (banking

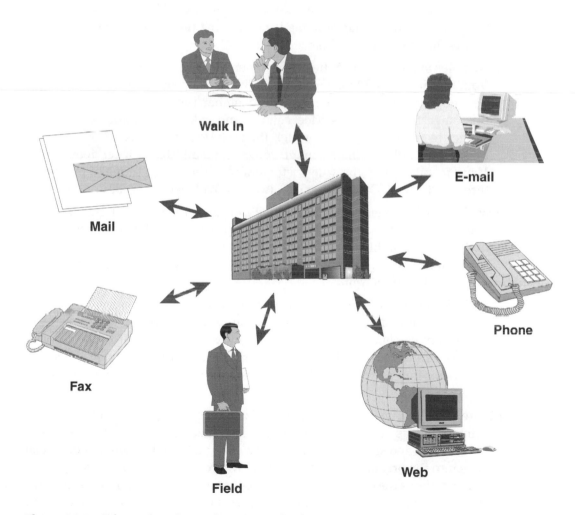

Figure 11.1 Sales and service environments of today.

transactions, change of address, and notification of new investment possibilities), he has been the target of marketing on the Internet (travel service promotions), and he has participated in sales on the Internet (the purchase of travel products and investment products). These are all examples of standard sales and service customer touches; they simply bypass more traditional media and use the Internet instead.

Walk-In. Despite the rhetoric of some of the dot-com companies, traditional brick-and-mortar sales and service facilities are not going away. Bob's parents use their local bank branch for most of their service transactions. In accordance with their stated preference, this is also the vehicle the bank uses to sell most new products to them.

Field. Field sales and service is common in some industries. Cable and phone line installations are good examples of field service. The investment advisor that visits Bob's parents at home is conducting field sales, as are insurance agents that come to your home.

Mail. Sales and service activities also happen through the mail. When you order from the Internet and the product is delivered to your home, you have experienced service through the mail. (Remember the acquisition stage in the Customer Life Cycle?) Service centers and sales organizations must also expect to receive requests through the mail. Product registration and warranty cards still routinely come through the mail; this is a service activity. Many manufacturers provide customers with the ability to make purchases through the mail. Catalogs almost always provide a mail-order option.

Fax. Fax-back services, such as the one Bob used to get vacation details, are common for both sales and service. Many product help facilities provide the option to fax problems or requests. Bob's travel service provides him with the option to fax in his travel requests, and to receive the resulting confirmations via the fax as well.

E-mail. E-mail is now a popular way to reach customers for both sales and service. Bob's investment advisor uses e-mail to notify him of new investment opportunities. Many retail organizations ask customers for their e-mail addresses and use these in sales and marketing. As with the fax, product help facilities often provide e-mail addresses as a way to submit questions and receive replies.

Phone. Call centers and telesales organizations still rely on the phone as the primary means of communication with customers and prospects. These telephone sales and service contacts can be either inbound, where the customer calls into the organization, or outbound, where the service or sales representative initiates the call. Bob uses the telephone banking system whenever the Web is not convenient for him. Although we may not like them, we all receive the occasional (or not-so-occasional) telesales call!

The number of touch-points available to the customer today has exponentially increased the complexity of providing sales and service. Organizations must be able to coordinate activities and information across all available touch-points. When Bob changed his contact information on the Web, he fully expected the telephone service representative and the fax-back service to know of this change. Had the bank not known this, Bob could have easily taken his business to an organization that would know. The good news is that technologies available to automate your sales and service processes accommodate all these contact points (including the Web). Along with the customer ODS (detailed in the previous chapter), these technologies provide the key to coordinating activities across all points in the customer touch zone.

Automating Customer Service and Sales

The technology for managing customer touches includes some components that are used exclusively for service, some that are used exclusively for sales, and some that are used for both functions. For clarity, in this chapter, we will look first at service, next at sales, and last at the integration of the two into a

Justifying CRM Automation

Many organizations invest in CRM technology, including sales and service automation, as a way to increase customer satisfaction, loyalty, and longevity, with the ultimate objective of increasing revenue. Table 11.1 highlights 12 justification factors identified as popular reasons for investing in CRM technology.[1] The justification factors are what investing organizations hope to achieve through the technology, while the impacts represent the expected effect on bottom-line profitability for each achievement.

Increasing satisfaction, improving loyalty, and increasing revenues by improving customer profitability are all goals of organizations that focus on activities in the retain and expand section of the Customer Life Cycle. Improvements in the sales and service business processes will assist in the achievement of these goals. As shown in Table 11.1, decreasing costs is also an important benefit of these CRM technologies. Improving productivity, decreasing transaction costs, reducing errors and support personnel requirements, and increasing speed to market are all other viable reasons to automate your sales and service processes.

[1] Justification factors taken from "Leadership Strategies in Customer Relationship Management," Meta Group, January 2000.

Table 11.1 CRM Technology Cost Justifications and Impacts

JUSTIFICATION FACTOR	IMPACT
Increase Customer Satisfaction	Increase Revenue
Increase Customer Loyalty/Retention	Increase Revenue
Improve Productivity	Decrease Cost
Increase Revenue from Existing Customers	Increase Revenue
Acquire New Customers	Increase Revenue
Develop New Products/Boost Market Share	Increase Revenue
Reduce Transaction Costs	Decrease Cost
Increase Speed to Market	Decrease Cost
Reduce Customer Contact/Support Requirements	Decrease Cost
Reduce Fulfillment/Customer Response Errors	Decrease Cost
Increase Brand Perceptions	Increase Revenue
Displace Costs	Decrease Cost

comprehensive operational CRM product suite. We will also discuss the role of these operational CRM suites in relation to the customer ODS and the Corporate Information Factory.

Automating Service

Not long ago, customer service was provided through two primary means. The customer walked into a brick-and-mortar facility (a bank branch, a retail store, or an agency) or they used the telephone to connect to a call center. As organizations realized the need to facilitate the multitude of contact options described in Figure 11.1, they adopted a new label for their call centers and brick-and-mortar facilities: customer care centers. The emergence of the Internet and self-service has yielded yet another term, customer contact centers. In the course of responding to a customer contact, a service request is generated. These requests can arrive in any media, from a phone call to an e-mail to a piece of paper.

Regardless of media, the key to a successful customer service experience lies in your ability to receive the request, route it to the appropriate provider, track the activity, update the correct databases, issue the necessary documentation, and, ultimately, to fulfill the service request to the customer's satisfaction. Automating this process requires the integration of several components: workflow management, CTI, and desktop management. Used together, these components can help your organization provide quality service at the time and place of the customer's choosing. Immediately following is a discussion of the functions you should look for in the technology you choose to automate your customer service environment.

A distinction is made in many organizations between traditional service and help-desk support. Traditional service focuses on the completion of transactions such as purchasing a product, while help-desk support exists to resolve problems and answer questions. Automating both traditional service and help-desk support requires the integration of workflow management, CTI, and desktop management. However, an additional requirement exists in help-desk support that is not typically needed in traditional service environments: the integration to problem resolution databases; while the traditional service organization requires a feature that is not needed in the help-desk environment: an integration to legacy product applications. This section ends with a description of the differences between traditional service and help-desk support and it highlights the additional technology functions required in each environment.

Workflow Management

The service requests described earlier are the basis of workflow management applications. A service request may be resolved with a single activity, or it can require a number of activities and involve several individuals or service teams.

Workflow management applies business process modeling and computer technology to automate specific business tasks or service request activities (such as transferring funds from Bob's savings account to his checking account). Workflow management applications aid in moving multiple requests through an organization and are particularly useful when the tasks touch many individuals or have multiple complex steps. In the example of Bob's funds transfer, the workflow application would bundle all the necessary steps to complete the transfer into a single work unit and forward it to the appropriate service representative(s). In some instances, the workflow application may simply enact the activities without ever requiring the intervention of a human being.

The workflow application engine contains all the business rules associated with the process and can perform tasks based on these rules: escalating the issue if not completed within a specified period of time, issuing reminders, tracking deadlines, and even generating letters or e-mail notices to customers. In creating and monitoring the service request from Bob (to transfer funds), the workflow engine understands the business rule that stipulates that the amount of funds to be transferred from an account cannot exceed the amount of funds available within that account. If this occurs, the workflow application can then generate a notification to a service representative to contact Bob prior to canceling the transaction.

Some workflow applications provide the capability to categorize requests into simple and complex customer interactions. Simple interactions require less functionality to automate. With these, the request may flow through multiple service representatives with varying levels of seniority or expertise, but the interaction is generally satisfied within the course of one contact. These can require the transfer of the contact information to multiple individuals but have no requirement to manage the interaction over time.

For example, Bob calls into the telephone-banking center with a request to transfer funds from one account to another. During the course of the call, he determines that he also wants to transfer funds into his brokerage account and purchase a stock. The service representative who takes the call can initiate the funds transfers but does not have the proper license to execute the stock trade. The representative completes those activities that he or she can and then transfers the call to another group for completion. Bob stays on the line until the request is complete. It takes several service representatives to process Bob's transactions, but the transactions are completed during the course of a single contact. The workflow application that is creating the tasks required to complete Bob's request has to create several tasks and associate each with a different service representative. It does not, however, have to monitor an outstanding task or check for ultimate completion at a future date, because the request will be completed (and the work unit closed out) when the call is terminated.

Complex requests can require that communication be initiated multiple times during the course of a request, either by the customer or by the service representative (or response mechanism in the case of an automated response). Status updates and problem escalations may take place, additional information may be required from the customer to satisfy the request, and several individuals may handle the request before it is completed.

Consider the following example. Bob's credit card is stolen and several fraudulent charges appear on his next bank statement. He calls the contact center and reports the charges to a service representative. The representative agrees to look into the matter and contact Bob with the results of the investigation. After Bob disconnects, the service representative uses the workflow application to initiate a process that includes the following steps:

- Retrieve the charge slips from the merchant.
- Compare the signatures to Bob's signature on file.
- Assess the validity of each disputed charge.
- Issue an e-mail notification to Bob informing him that his request is in-progress.

- Develop a recommendation to credit all disputed charges and drop the traditional $50 minimum charge to Bob based on his VIP status.

- Pass the recommendation to a supervisor for signoff.

- Finally issue a notification to Bob informing him of the good news.

Here the workflow application must monitor multiple tasks, each assigned to different individuals, over the course of several days. The workflow application must monitor the completion of each task and ensure the initiation of the next task in a timely fashion. The entire work unit cannot be completed and closed out until all tasks have been finished. The capability to satisfy complex requests takes longer to implement and requires more sophisticated functionality from the workflow management application.

If your workflow application will be used to facilitate complex interactions such as Bob's stolen credit card, it must contain robust functionality. A comprehensive workflow application should support all of the following activities:

- Create and relate entitlements to purchased products to help in the maintenance of service level agreements (SLAs). Entitlements represent the level of service or support the customer is entitled to receive based on customer value or the purchased service package. Bob, as a VIP customer, qualifies for an elevated level of service, one in which his requests take priority, and his entitlement is VIP.

- Receive new requests. The application must receive requests from all media including phone, e-mail, mail, Internet, Customer Service Representative, and so on.

- Validate new requests. This validation must include customer identification and validation of the entitlement of the customer, if appropriate.

- Receive and validate updates or changes to requests including entitlements.

- Issue automated responses to both customers and service representatives.

- Route the request to the next process step or activity when ready.

- Distribute the requests and workload across service teams. Also distribute activities to the appropriate resources based on workload and skill set.

- Submit and accept business documents to and from all media.

- Ensure the process step completion and ensure the overall work unit completion prior to closing the request.

- Notify the internal, responsible party of changes to the request.

- Issue notifications when a task is due or overdue for completion.

- Automatically escalate requests when service level agreements are missed.

- Submit or transfer requests to other systems of business partners to incorporate the extended enterprise.

- Return a completed request notification to the customer.

These workflow applications work together with the CTI functions to seamlessly handle a customer contact from the initiation of that contact to the completion of the resulting service request (CTI is described in the next section). Some workflow applications are industry-specific and are tailored to handle certain types of transactions, requiring only minor customization to make them specific to your company. Others come equipped only with basic tools and require that you build the work units from scratch. Determining which type of workflow application is best for your organization is a matter of measuring the complexity of your business processes against the functionality of existing industry or vertical applications.

Computer Telephony Integration (CTI)

In its simplest form, CTI is the seamless integration of telephone hardware with the computer. Complex CTI solutions provide the capability to link many different software applications, including workflow management, with various databases (customer, contact, and transaction information) and with other telephone hardware components. CTI, sometimes referred to as softphone, enables the service representatives to control the telephone using a computer. All the functions that can be performed on a regular telephone, including placing calls, answering calls, transferring calls, and hanging up, are enabled by CTI with the use of a keyboard, mouse, and headset. In addition, CTI enables calls to be routed to the appropriate service representatives, captures and maintains statistics on calls, and provides extensive call qualification and customer identification services.

A comprehensive CTI solution should contain the following functions or capabilities:

Automatic Number Identification (ANI). This technology enables the computer to recognize the number from which the call is being dialed (the customer's number). This number can then be compared to a database of customer information. Matching customer information can be retrieved and passed to the service representative's desktop at the same time the call is routed there. This capability enables the service representative to view basic customer information as the call is answered. When Bob calls the bank's telephone-banking center, the ANI feature can retrieve the number from where he is calling and use it to initiate a search in the customer database. If

Bob happens to be initiating the call from a number known to the bank, such as his home or office number, his customer information can be retrieved from the database and passed to the service representative along with the call. If Bob is calling from an unknown number, such as a hotel, he will be asked for some additional qualifying information prior to retrieving his customer information. This feature is also sometimes used as a security measure for activities such as activating new credit cards. Here you are asked to dial an activation number from your home phone, which the credit card company has on file. When you initiate the call, the ANI feature can read the number you are calling from. This number is matched against a database, and your account information is retrieved.

Dialed Number Identification Service (DNIS). This technology enables the recognition of the number that the caller has dialed. This is quite useful when a contact center services multiple products or provides various levels of service based on customer value, packages purchased, and so on. The number dialed can be compared against a database containing information on where to route the call based on the incoming number. The relevant information about the number called, (for instance, the call came in on the VIP preferred service number, rather than on the general help line) is passed to the service representative along with the call. This enables a single representative to service multiple lines while making it appear to the caller as if the service representative is dedicated to the particular type of service about which he or she has called. As a frequent traveler, Bob is given a special number to dial when seeking to make travel reservations. Within the call center is a group of representatives that is dedicated to serving the frequent travelers. When Bob's call comes in, the DNIS feature can retrieve the number he has called, compare that number to a database containing incoming lines and their characteristics, and route his call to the dedicated group of service representatives. The service representative answering the call knows that bob has called on the frequent traveler line and can answer the call accordingly.

Automatic Call Distribution (ACD). This technology works in conjunction with the ANI and DNIS services to qualify the call and route it from the telephone switch to the appropriate group of service representatives. It works with the telephone hardware to pick up the call, invokes ANI or DNIS, and chooses where to route the call based on the results. These technologies can be used to recognize when one group of representatives is utilized to capacity and can make intelligent decisions, based on skill sets and availability, on where to route an incoming call instead. If Bob calls the frequent traveler service line at a time when all the dedicated representatives are busy, the service center does not want him to wait on hold for very long. Instead, his call can be routed to a representative who only handles frequent traveler calls in an overload situation. The information about the number dialed will alert the representative that it is a frequent traveler calling, and the phone can be answered accordingly.

Predictive dialer. Predictive dialers read telephone numbers from input lists and automatically dial these numbers for outbound calling. They can recognize busy signals, no answers, and answering machines, and only pass the calls to a service representative if the calls are answered. They can also recognize signs that an ongoing call is about to be terminated and can initiate the next call while the representative is still on the phone closing out the current call. This ensures that the representatives are always busy and are not losing time waiting for the phone to be dialed. This technology is used frequently in outbound calling and telesales, as it frees the service representative from dealing with calls where no contact is made.

Interactive Voice Response (IVR)/Voice Response Unit (VRU). These technologies provide an automated interaction with the customer so that he or she can listen to menu choices and respond by pressing the appropriate keys on the telephone. Less complex service requests can be completed entirely with the VRU or IVR and never require the intervention of a service representative. The VRU can guide Bob through the transfer of funds from one account to another by simply providing him with the appropriate menu options and asking him to key his account numbers and other required information into the phone. Many contact centers route all incoming calls directly to the VRU/IVR systems as a first step, allowing the customer the choice of performing the transaction entirely through this technology, or keying out at various points to speak to a service representative. Although these applications can offload large volumes of work from the service representatives to the computer, it is important that the menus are easy to navigate and offer frequent options to transfer to a service representative. Listening to exhaustive lists of options, getting lost in a menu system and having to begin the call again, or never having the ability to talk to a human being can have a negative effect on customer satisfaction.

Speech recognition. This is an emerging technology that is being used frequently in contact centers today. It is commonly used in conjunction with a VRU/IVR and enables the computer to solicit spoken responses, rather than requiring the customer to key the information into the phone. Here the VRU/IVR can ask simple questions such as, "If you know your account number, say it now." The system can then recognize the spoken responses and take the appropriate action as if these responses had been keyed into the telephone. In more sophisticated applications, the systems can verify a caller's identity by mapping the spoken response against a database of past stored responses. If a match is found, the computer can identify the customer and retrieve customer information based on this identification. See the following sidebar for an example of an organization that is using this complex application of speech recognition technology to improve the customer ordering process.

Automated character recognition. This technology provides functionality similar to the VRU, including the capability to handle incoming customer contacts in an entirely automated fashion, except that it works with e-mail rather than with the telephone. The technology can read e-mail messages, identify key words or phrases, and compose and send a stock reply to the sender. It can also route the e-mail to the appropriate service representative if human intervention is needed.

Contact-specific repository. This function consists of the capability of the CTI components to access a common contact-specific repository that contains all the information about the contact. These contacts have traditionally been phone calls, but the growing need to deal with interactions on different media is expanding the uses of the contact repository. These repositories provide comprehensive information about the contact to any service representative who may deal with a customer request. At a minimum, the repository eliminates the need for the customer to repeat information, such as an account number, if the request is passed from one representative to another. At a maximum, the repository keeps the history and statistics on past contacts and provides a comprehensive view of all contacts with a particular customer, regardless of the type of contact mechanism. The customer ODS may also have contact information. If the contact information housed within the customer ODS is comprehensive enough, it may replace the need for a contact-specific repository. Some organizations use the customer ODS to house only summary contact information and keep detailed contact records in a repository, such as the one named here. Detailed contact information is key, regardless of where it is housed.

Customer information repository. Contact center solutions must also have the capability to interact with the database that contains information about the customer and all the products and services owned by that customer. This is where the customer information passed to the service representative is housed. Some of these applications provide their own integrated customer databases for this purpose. Others can be integrated to central databases such as the customer ODS. See the section entitled "Integrating Sales and Service Applications" for more details on the ideal integration options that provide a consistent and comprehensive customer view to all contact center personnel and applications.

Advanced Speech Recognition Technology in Use[2]

The Home Shopping Network has deployed sophisticated speech recognition technology for customers who call its contact centers to order products. The company had over five million repeat customers and was looking for ways to increase customer satisfaction, streamline the process of ordering merchandise, and collect additional customer and contact information for analysis. It had previously tried to give first-time callers a personal identification number (PIN) to use on subsequent orders, but customers had trouble remembering their PIN and this did not work as well as they had hoped.

The technology is employed by asking callers to speak their phone numbers. The application then matches the spoken number against a database of past callers. Matches are used to pull customer information, which is forwarded, along with the call, to a service representative. This technology enables the Home Shopping Network to recognize different callers from the same phone number or the same caller from different phone numbers and select the appropriate customer information. When receiving the call, the representative can simply verify customer identity from the information routed with the call. The representative can take the order without having to ask for all the customer information again. This has substantially speeded up the ordering process and contributes to increased satisfaction for repeat customers.

Desktop Management

The service representative desktop, also called a workbench, is the application that integrates the CTI functions with workflow management applications and displays the results on the desktop. The desktop provides a common front-end that enables the service representative to access all contact center components. The service representatives log into the desktop to initiate and perform all their assigned tasks. The contact and customer information is retrieved by CTI and Workflow and is displayed on the desktop through what is commonly referred to as a screen population or screen pop. If the sales and service components are integrated (see the following section) the desktop looks the same for each business area.

In addition to facilitating the request management and call management services, this application also provides other important capabilities such as name

---

[2] Peppers and Rogers Group. *Inside1to1*. August 5, 1999.

and address look-ups (access to the transaction interface for the customer ODS), calendar functions, access to online documentation, security, scripting services, access to internal corporate facilities such as an intranet, corporate directories, and so on. This is also where service representatives can access the contact center data marts for reporting and analysis capabilities. Many organizations provide updated lists containing relevant competitive offers, current promotions, and current product information through the workbench as well.

As organizations begin to share customer information across the organization, the need for a facility such as the desktop will become an important part of the integrated technology architecture. Enterprise Portals (EPs) are an emerging technology designed to tie together information and applications from all parts of the Corporate Information Factory into a single view. These Enterprise Portals will provide a service similar to the desktop described here, only the capabilities will be much more robust. As Enterprise Portals are developed, they may take the place of the desktop components currently used in automating services, or they may be used in conjunction with these components. See Chapter 13, "Putting It All Together," for a detailed discussion of Enterprise Portals.

Traditional Service versus Help-Desk Support

Most of the features discussed earlier are required regardless of whether you are providing traditional service or help-desk support in your customer contact centers. Help-desk support environments also require integration to a problem-resolution facility of some sort, and traditional service environments require integration to product or transaction systems. The rest of this section describes the differences in the two environments and explains the additional functionality you should look for when automating each type of service.

In a traditional service environment, the activities are typically focused on conducting a business transaction, purchasing a product or placing an order, lodging a complaint, or making some sort of non-product related request. Most of Bob's banking activities on the Internet fall into this category. He transfers money between accounts, pays bills, purchases investment and travel products, and occasionally voices customer complaints or compliments. In this environment, the goal of Bob's bank is to increase the quality of the interaction. Regardless of the mode of contact (phone, Internet, mail, or walk-in), the bank wants to ensure that the transaction is completed efficiently and effectively, that the interaction continues the dialog and furthers the relationship, and that Bob walks away highly satisfied.

Contrast this with the help-desk support environment. Help-desk support organizations exist to answer questions about products and services and to identify and resolve problems that customers encounter with these products. When Bob experiences difficulty logging on to the bank's Internet site, can't get a feature to work, or has a question about how to use the service, he calls the bank's help-desk support department. Rather than focusing on completing transactions, this environment focuses on answering questions and resolving problems.

In the support environment, the bank's goal is still to ensure that Bob has a quality interaction. However, this goal is augmented with several others: reduce the time it takes to resolve his problem (which will in turn increase his satisfaction level), increase the volume of problems that can be handled by the organization, and oftentimes ensure that the organization is generating revenue. Support is often charged back to the customer directly (through a maintenance contract) or indirectly (it is built into the product price).

Another important goal of the help-desk support environment is to learn from Bob and other customers and use that learning to improve the products and services offered. For example, many customers may call because they do not understand how to use an Internet transaction. The help-desk will collect statistics on these calls and, when the calls reach a certain volume, decide to rework the transaction.

In the traditional service environment, the number of transactions to be delivered (opening an account, transferring funds, or closing an account) is finite. A lot of complex transactions may take place, but most organizations have reference documentation on how to complete each possible transaction. Systems can be built around the business process documentation for each transaction, and service representatives can consult the documentation to learn the steps to follow. Help-desk support is a different story. The potential combinations of symptoms, problems, and solutions can be infinite. The ability to quickly resolve a customer's problem can depend largely on the subject matter expertise of the support representatives. The more products supported by the organization, the more knowledge the support representatives must have to function efficiently.

Effective help-desk support systems must address the issue of the knowledge required to provide comprehensive support, which is described earlier in the chapter. A key component of any automated solution for help-desk support (not typically required for traditional service) is the capability of the system to link into one or more problem resolution or knowledge management databases. A comprehensive knowledge management infrastructure can have a significant impact on the ability of the support organization to achieve its goals. Knowledge management can help the support representatives resolve problems without requiring them to be experts in all products supported. These problem resolution or knowledge management databases take several forms:

Question and answer databases: These are repositories of frequently asked questions (FAQs) and the answers to those questions. The questions, along with common variations, are loaded into a database. To resolve a problem, the support representative fashions the problem in the form of a question (How do I change my e-mail alias?) and submits this to the database. The search mechanism uses a combination of keyword and full-text search to return all similar entries, along with their associated answers. The representative can then guide the customer through the possible resolutions as returned by the database. Organizations sometimes post these databases on the Internet and let the customers access them directly as well.

Decision trees: Decision tree solutions consist of a series of questions pertaining to a particular problem. Each question in the tree is formed as an if-then-else scenario (Is option A turned on? If yes, check the next setting. If no, turn option A on and see if problem is resolved). These solutions are typically built by experts and entered into the database. Questions and answers can also be entered independently, and an inference engine tool can be used to lead the support representative from one question to the next. The inference engine tool can be programmed to understand which sets of questions and answers are related. This tool can then use the answer to one question to identify the next possible questions that should be asked. The answers to one question lead the representative to the next question, systematically eliminating possible solutions to the problem and ultimately arriving at the correct answer.

Solutions databases/case-based retrieval: In this instance, problems, symptoms, and solutions are loaded into the database. The data can be unstructured (text, documents, and so on) and the current problem or question does not have to match the cases or solutions exactly. The support representative simply searches for similar problems, reviews the closest results, and works with the customer to ascertain if any of the loaded cases match to his or her problem. Close matches can also be located and returned by an inference engine, which has the capability to search large numbers of solutions and return potential matches. As with the use of inference engines in the decision tree example, related problems are linked as they are entered into the database, and the inference engine understands how to find these matches.

Artificial intelligence: Most of the previous solutions rely on purchased knowledge databases or on databases that are built by tapping the expertise of existing support representatives as well as others who understand the products, such as product engineers, developers, and manufacturers. This knowledge is then applied to the appropriate format and is entered in the database. Additions to the knowledge base come only when someone formulates a new solution and enters it into the repository. Artificial intelligence solutions look at the steps required to arrive at existing solutions, compare them to new problems, and use a form of deductive reasoning to develop solutions to new problems. Support organizations are beginning to rely on these concepts to grow existing problem-resolution databases.

The second difference in the automation requirements for traditional service and help-desk support deals with the integration of product or legacy applications. These legacy systems are described in Chapter 1, "The Customer Becomes the Center of the Business Universe," and Chapter 2, "The Customer and the Corporate Information Factory (CIF)." This requirement is found in traditional service environments and is not typically required for help-desk support.

Take Bob's bank as an example. Verifying an account balance, transferring funds, depositing a check, or opening a new account all require immediate access to the systems that perform the day-to-day accounting for these bank products. When Bob deals with the telephone-banking center, the service representative starts with the customer service or customer care system but transitions frequently to the detail product applications. Automating the traditional service processes requires that the customer service application provide a single point of access to multiple, often different, product applications. Note that in organizations with a robust customer ODS, some of this integration may already exist and can be utilized for this purpose as well. See the section, "Integrating Sales and Service Applications," for more details.

Automating Sales

The push on CRM organizations to know their customers and apply that knowledge to each interaction applies to sales contacts as well as to service contacts. Sales force automation software provides a toolkit of capabilities that can ensure that your sales force is well informed, coordinated, and diligent in its lead management and sales follow-up activities. These applications facilitate the sharing of sales activity and prospect information across multiple sales individuals or teams within an organization. They also provide facilities to help your sales force interact with multiple prospects within a single customer organization. Although these packages are implemented in organizations where the selling is business to consumer (B2C), they are most frequently found in the business to business (B2B) world in which coordination of the selling effort is key to success. Figure 11.2 illustrates the typical distinctions in the B2B world that make sales force automation a necessity.

Organizations who sell to other businesses usually have fewer customers than their counterparts selling directly to consumers, and the volume of information about any single customer in the B2B world can be quite large. As we have men-

Differences	B2C	B2B
Number of customers	Many	Few
Decision makers	One	Multiple
Purchase consideration	Consumption	Value creation
Touchpoints/Channels	Many to one	Many to many
Transaction frequency	Occasional	Frequent, on-going
Transaction value	Low	High
Ultimate consumer	Customer	Customer's customer
Interaction	Periodic	On-going
Decision process	Informal	Formal

Figure 11.2 The selling process—B2C versus B2B.

tioned in other chapters, a number of providers, such as Dun and Bradstreet, sell information designed to augment your knowledge of these business customers and prospects. Sales to business customers are distinctly relationship-oriented, with ongoing and frequent contacts between sales personnel and customer contacts. Typically, multiple contacts exist within any single organization, and the chances are good that your organization will have multiple sales personnel calling on a given large company at the same time. It is essential to coordinate sales efforts across multiple individuals, and to ensure that the prospect is not receiving duplicate or conflicting offers from your organization. It is equally important to ensure that each person dealing with a prospect understands all the other offers or conversations that take place. More than one company has lost a sale (or worse, lost a customer) because two sales people called on the customer in the same day and did not realize the overlap in visits. These sales generally follow a formal decision-making process within the customer organization, and the decisions are frequently made by a committee of people or, at the very least, influenced by several individuals.

Bob's bank is a good example of the complexity of selling to businesses. The bank has approximately 10 million retail or individual customers as compared to about 400,000 corporate customers. A single service representative or branch teller can deal with most of the products sold to the retail base. The corporate products are much more complicated, requiring in some cases entirely different business units within the bank to sell and administer them. Cash management products are sold and administered by the bank's cash management group, credit products by the corporate lending group, and group investment products by the 401K business unit. Adding to the complexity, these products are often sold to entirely different areas within the customer organizations, requiring the bank to track contacts with many different individuals at each customer. Human Resources may buy the 401K products, while the CFO may obtain loans for expansion of the business. One thing is certain though, the business customers will understand exactly what they buy from the bank and, like Bob, will demand a level of sales and service that demonstrates the bank's understanding of them.

If you have a complex selling process, or a team sales approach, it is important to choose a sales force automation application that facilitates the type of coordination and consistency required to deal with the environment described previously and pictured in Figure 11.2.

A comprehensive sales force automation application package can include many components. Many of the package vendors offer the ability to pick and choose from a large variety of components to ensure that you purchase only the functionality you actually need to automate your sales process. For clarity, we will group the available functions into the following categories: desktop management, telesales and campaign management, sales configuration, and mobile access. The remainder of this section provides an overview of these categories and associated functionality.

Desktop Management

Sometimes called account or workflow management, these capabilities are similar to those described in the workflow and desktop sections discussed in service automation. As with the service workflow component, workflow in sales automation also focuses on automating a unit of work into a set of activities, which can then be routed to the appropriate sales individual for follow-up. Depending on the complexity of your sales processes, and the degree of repetition involved, you may not require the same level of formal workflow capabilities that you employ for service automation. Rather than defining specific steps, associating business rules to each step, and expecting the sales person to follow each predefined step exactly, many sales organizations use the desktop activity management capabilities in a less formal way. In this instance, sales professionals may have some predefined activities forwarded to them for action. They may also be expected to make their own entries into the workflow or activity management system for everything they do with a particular customer, including phone calls, letters and other correspondence, meetings, and presentations. This option enables other members of a sales team, including sales managers, to track activities for particular customers and for particular sales team members. These applications also contain contact management capabilities including the ability to view contact lists by salesperson, by customer, by product, and so on.

These desktops also have some or all of the following capabilities:

Calendar management. Calendar management enables sales professionals to schedule and track activities on a calendar in daily, weekly, and monthly views. Other customizable views, such as activity by customer or sales person, are sometimes available as well. The activities can be linked to customers and also to activities in the workflow management application. Calendars can be shared across sales teams, and the capability to view and schedule appointments on each other's calendars can be granted.

Contact management. The common contact repository described in service automation is also required for recording the details of all sales contacts with a customer. This enables the entire organization to view contacts with a particular customer during the life of the sales process and during the life of the relationship with the customer.

Customer information. As with service automation applications, the sales applications must have access to a common repository of customer information. Sales people must be able to access this information, modify it, and add new customers. Some packages contain their own customer component, while others enable integration into an enterprise customer file such as the customer ODS.

Sales reporting and analysis. This includes the capability to generate and distribute predefined reports that can be qualified by including selection criteria as a key to any sales automation effort. These reports can track sales activity and sales results by any number of criteria, including sales person or team, geography, customer, product, or campaign. The capability to create and customize the reports may also be provided to executives and sophisticated users.

Sales forecasting. Many applications also include forecasting components. Here leads can be entered and assigned an estimated probability to close, an estimated revenue figure and an estimated closure date. Typically, these components generate several types of reports from the entered forecast including the capability to track forecasted revenues by product, customer, sales person, geography, and opportunity.

Product catalogs/literature. Many of these applications also provide the capability for a sales organization to develop and maintain online catalogs of product features, competitive product feature and price comparisons, discount rates, and so on. The popularity of the Internet is also giving rise to a new feature in sales automation. This is the ability to use electronic engines that search the Internet for news of customer organizations, industry happenings, and items of interest to the sales personnel. The results of these daily or weekly searches are bundled into a Web page or downloadable newsletter and are distributed to the appropriate sales people. This capability enables sales professionals to keep in touch with what is happening in their customer base or industry without having to do the research themselves.

Telesales and Campaign Management

The telesales and campaign management category includes three basic functionalities: telesales, campaign management, and the automatic generation of e-mail, mail responses, and solicitations. Again, these can be implemented as needed or can be purchased as an entire package. Basic functionality is as follows:

Telesales. Many sales force automation packages facilitate inbound and outbound telesales activities. These are typically used for inside sales forces and for marketing organizations. Inside sales forces are those that conduct much of their activity on the telephone, as opposed to actually visiting customers. These groups are used to qualify new leads, to cross and upsell existing customers, and to do market research. Predictive dialer, automatic call distribution (ACD), and the capability to screen pop the associated customer information to the telesales representative while transferring the connected call are some of the common CTI functions found in the telesales components. The capability to create and easily modify call scripts for the telesales representatives to follow is another feature to look for as well.

Campaign management. Many of these applications provide the capability to create sales campaigns and track the results. Here you can generate lists of customers to receive a mailing or telemarketing call, tag the activity in the activity management component as part of a particular sales campaign, and schedule automatic or manual follow-up activities. Many of these components also provide rudimentary capabilities for campaign tracking and results analysis. Most do not, however, approach the robust functionality found in the data warehouse and data mart structures described in detail in Chapter 9, "Business Intelligence: Technologies for Understanding Your Customers."

Automated character recognition. This capability was described in the service automation section. The capability to create and distribute automated e-mail messages and regular mail pieces, both in response to incoming e-mails and from input lists of customers or prospects, is found in sales automation applications also.

Sales Configuration

A sales configuration consists of two related capabilities: the automatic generation of proposals and sales quotes, and the automatic configuration of technical product specifications for the customer's environment. Similar to the other component categories, these can be implemented singly or in an integrated fashion. The basic functions to look for follow.

Proposal generation. This capability enables you to automate the generation of sales proposals, sales quotes, and sales contracts. Typically, these contain revision history, past proposals, discount terms, and so on. Often, these applications integrate with proposal templates and with e-mail or letter generators to facilitate the automation of much of the proposal generation and delivery process.

Product configuration. Product configuration components work in conjunction with proposal or quote generators to ensure quality in complex product environments. These are useful in situations in which the products can be configured in various ways, and the customization of existing products to fit customer specifications is common. These systems assist in the three steps associated with product configuration. The first is to understand the customer needs and environment, and map these to the technical specifications of the products they are going to purchase. Next, the technical information of the products (programmed into the application) is used to determine if the suggested configuration is a technically viable solution (can the suggested machine work within the customer's existing factory configuration). The third step is to automatically calculate the final pricing structure for the configured solution. This component for technical sales environments eliminates the possibility of selling products that will not work together or within the customer's environment.

Mobile Access

If you have a mobile sales force, you will require the capabilities needed for mobile access. Remote users, third-party offices, virtual offices, and field sales personnel all require access to the functions and customer data within the sales automation package. A field sales person may visit many customers in the course of a day or week. This sales person will require the same access to components such as activity management, calendar management, and product catalogs as the sales people who are in the corporate offices. Most vendors facilitate remote access, using wide area networks (WANs) as well as the Internet.

Some important issues to evaluate when considering remote access include the data replication and data capabilities of the application. Remote users may need to have the system functions loaded on their mobile computer for continuous use, but they may be able to connect to the central site only periodically. When they establish this connection, however, they will be doing so to download data and to send their updates to the central application. The remote user must have a replicated copy of the database(s) loaded on his or her computer in order to facilitate this type of use. The application must be able to deal with the data issues if the mobile sales person can make changes to the data on his or her computer. If multiple users can change the same data, the application must be able to identify changes on the mobile computers, update those changes to the central application, and reconcile situations where the same data may have been changed in more than one location.

Several issues must be considered in a mobile computing environment. One is the length of time it takes to download and upload data. The more complex the issues, the longer the process can take. Data volumes and line speeds also affect the transfer time. Lengthy data transfer processes can discourage mobile use of the application. The second issue to consider is the data integrity of these systems once mobile computing is introduced. The synchronization process must be well thought out to ensure that data on the central site and data on the mobile computer is not corrupted. If a salesman enters customer information onto his or her mobile computer only to have it wiped out during the upload or download process, he or she will be reluctant to hook into the central site again.

Security is another issue to consider in mobile access decisions. Chapter 14, "Preserving Customer Trust—The Role of Privacy," talks about establishing security procedures as a method to safeguard the privacy of your customers. As you establish privacy and security measures, you must evaluate the security options available in these mobile access components to ensure that it adheres to your corporate policies.

Although laptop computers have been the traditional vehicles for empowering remote users with the sales automation capabilities, new highly mobile devices are becoming more popular. These devices are small, hand-held devices such as the Palm Pilots and newer pocket PCs that use the Windows CE operating system. As the capabilities of these devices to carry extended software increase, many organizations are beginning to equip their mobile users with these devices. Many vendors facilitate the same data synchronization and replication capabilities for these devices as they do for the laptops. Many also enable their application software components to run on these devices. If your organization is considering the use of these devices, it is advisable to look at the compatibility of your sales force automation software with the devices available.

Integrating Sales and Service Applications

The lines between sales and service are beginning to blur. As the myriad ways our customers can contact us (listed at the beginning of the chapter) demonstrates, it is harder to differentiate between sales and service customer touches than it used to be. Many touches that begin as a service opportunity end with an up-sell or cross-sell, and it is not uncommon for a sales person to receive a service request during the course of a pitch. When Bob's parents go to the branch to make their regular deposit and end up considering the purchase of a cruise from the travel company, a service customer touch has migrated into a sales opportunity. Likewise, when the investment advisor comes to their home to sell them a new investment product and departs with instructions to change the beneficiary on existing products to Bob's newborn son, the sales touch has resulted in a service request.

Although organizations generally use different applications to automate sales than they use for service, many also realize the benefit to be gained from integrating these technologies. Prior to calling on Bob to sell him anything new, his investment advisor always checks to see if he has any outstanding service requests or complaints. Thus, the advisor can determine if the timing is right to make the pitch or can inform Bob of the status of his request or complaint. Conversely, when fulfilling requests, the service representatives also know which marketing and sales promotions have been pitched to Bob. Armed with this knowledge, they can then remind Bob of the outstanding offers and possibly close a new sale.

Vendors of these automation products are responding to the need to share information between sales and service by offering integrated product suites in addition to the traditional stand-alone modules. The Meta Group predicts that through the end of 2001, these sales and service CRM products will have shifted into two distinct categories: stand-alone point solutions and integrated suite solutions.[3] The stand-alone solutions will focus on targeted, single-function applications with lots of functions and capabilities. The suites will focus less on extended functionality in each application and more on offering a pre-integrated interoperability and underlying architecture. The dynamics of the integrated suites are illustrated in Figure 11.3.

---

[3]"Leadership Strategies in Customer Relationship Management." Meta Group. January 2000.

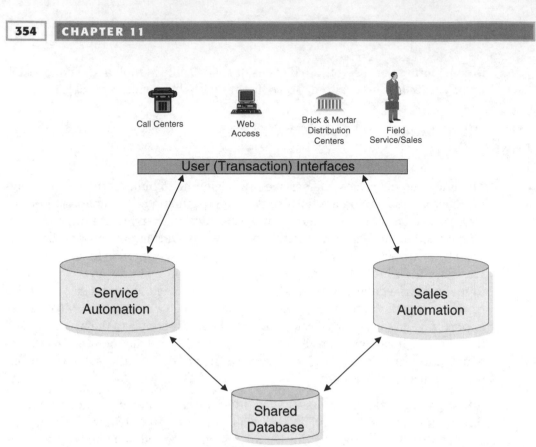

Figure 11.3 Integrated automation suites.

In Figure 11.3, the sales automation application and the service automation application share the same database of customer and contact information. This may not preclude each application from also containing its own database of application-specific information, but generally the information common to both is housed in a separate repository that can be accessed by all integrated applications. The sales and service applications can be accessed from various locations including the Internet, call centers, brick-and-mortar locations for walk-in sales or service, and from the field. Access to these systems can be controlled by a common set of user interfaces that are separate from the sales and service applications, as shown in Figure 11.3 (see sidebar for additional detail on access mechanisms).

In an integrated environment such as the one illustrated in Figure 11.3, sales personnel preparing for a call would view the customer contact information through the sales application prior to the call. Because the shared database contains common information, the sales people can view service contacts as

Access Mechanisms

The common access mechanism illustrated in Figure 11.3 is another form of the transaction interface described in Chapter 10, "Facilitating Customer Touches with the Customer ODS." As with the customer ODS, most users accessing the sales and service applications are interested in one customer record at a time and want to see all the details associated with that particular customer. Additionally, most users require this information to be provided very quickly, usually within a second of the request. The transaction interface is designed to provide this type of single customer access very quickly. As with the customer ODS, this single customer access need has some exceptions. Sales professionals routinely want to see lists of their customers for a simple analysis. The transaction interface can also handle these pre-defined list queries as well.

Note that many sales and service applications have their own user interfaces that can provide direct access. This can be useful if your organization does not have a common user interface layer or transaction interface. It can be expedient to bypass the common user interface layer completely and use only the access mechanism that comes with the application. This certainly shortens the installation time. However, a common user interface has distinct benefits. These include the provision of a common look and feel across many different applications and the capability to reuse the transaction interface when integrating other applications in the Corporate Information Factory (such as the customer ODS and the data warehouse and data marts). If you purchase one of these sales or service applications, you may want to consider implementing some combination of their canned access mechanisms with a common transaction interface.

well as sales contacts for the customer they are going to see. The service solutions operate in a similar way. For daily activities, service representatives use the service module, which provides access to sales and promotional contacts from the common database.

Integrating your sales and service applications is a clear step closer to facilitating CRM strategies. Your work does not stop here, however. Your organization must take another step: the integration of these modules to the rest of the Corporate Information Factory. Figure 11.4 illustrates this integration.

Integrating these applications into the customer ODS enables you to take advantage of the its substantial benefits. The customer ODS provides the integrated enterprise view of customers and is designed based on an extended customer definition that has been agreed on by all groups within the organization.

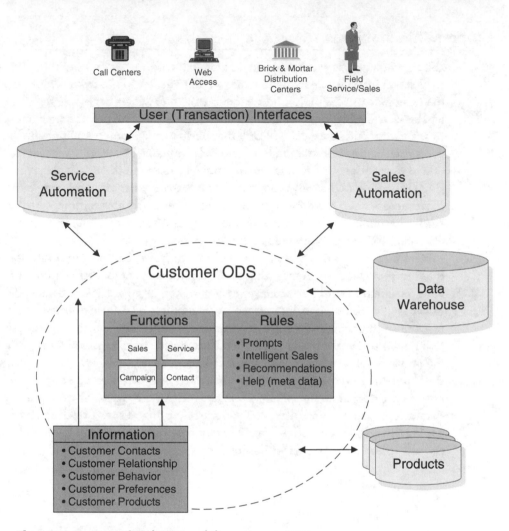

Figure 11.4 Operational CRM and the customer ODS.

Because the customer definition is embodied in the customer ODS, integrating these applications to the customer ODS ensures that your sales and service applications are using the same customer definition and associated information as the rest of the organization.

The customer ODS is the primary source of consolidated customer information for the data warehouse and data marts. It is also the primary recipient of strategic analysis results and is where these results are made actionable to the customer. Pointing your sales and service applications to the customer ODS ensures that your sales and service personnel benefit from this valuable information. Predictive engines, intelligent sales prompts, and meta data used in conjunction with the customer ODS can also yield high benefits to the sales and marketing applications. As we will see in Chapter 12, the customer ODS is the facilitator for implementing most types of Internet personalization technologies and strategies.

Again, let's use Bob as our example to demonstrate the role of the customer ODS in sales and service automation. Bob is a VIP customer for the bank, and information about him resides in various systems throughout the bank. He owns many products, so information about him exists in multiple legacy product applications. He belongs to one of the most profitable customer segments, and information about his profitability, and that of his customer segment, resides in several data marts. The bank also uses these data marts to develop customized Internet banner advertisements, which are housed in an Internet content server and displayed when he logs onto the Internet banking site. The customer ODS is the database that consolidates all information about Bob into a single profile. The ODS contains Bob's profitability figure and customer segment, which were calculated from the data marts. The ODS also contains Bob's customer identifier, which is used to point to the appropriate banner advertisements on the content server. The ODS links to all the legacy product systems where Bob has products or service transaction information. Finally, the ODS is where anyone who deals with Bob can add new information to his profile, thus increasing the bank's knowledge of Bob. Because this serves as the central repository of all information about Bob, directing your sales and service applications here ensures that your sales and service personnel are using the same comprehensive knowledge base on Bob as the rest of the organization.

These are several ways to achieve integration to the customer ODS. The most comprehensive way, shown in Figure 11.4, is to redirect the sales and service applications to use the ODS database, rather than using their own databases or the shared data pictured in Figure 11.3. This may require extensive customization to these applications but will also ensure that they benefit from all the data acquisition and data hygiene processes described in prior chapters. Some vendors, recognizing the need for enterprise integration, are designing these applications with independent customer components, which makes this redirection easier to accomplish.

A second alternative is to allow these applications to continue to use their own databases but develop a process to exchange information between the customer ODS and the sales and service applications. This can be done in a near real-time mode (for a class I or II ODS), or in a more relaxed mode (for a class III ODS). The decision you make depends on the nature of your ODS, the number of applications to integrate, and the existing transaction interface. Many organizations approach this integration in phases, starting first with a manageable project and progressively integrating the more complex pieces.

 One additional point of integration is emerging: the integration of sales and service applications to other operational solutions such as Enterprise Resource Planning (ERP) systems. Linking these disparate systems opens a window of information that starts with the customer and extends all the way back to the manufacturing source. This total view of both the supply and demand chain helps organizations to truly understand and manage the extended enterprise. Organizations can look backward to their suppliers, forward to their customers, establish tighter relationships on both sides based on better information, and in some cases recognize and eliminate unnecessary steps in the chain. Partnerships between ERP vendors and sales and service automation companies are frequent today. Soon, purchasing an integration component and plugging it into both systems might link these packages.

Summary

Many organizations are looking to their sales and service business areas to play a key role in the building and maintaining of long-lasting and profitable customer relationships. Automation is one way to facilitate increases in customer satisfaction, improvements in customer loyalty and retention, and increases in customer profitability. Automation can also help to reduce fulfillment and production errors, decrease the cost of providing service, and increase the efficiency of sales and service personnel, thus freeing them up to concentrate on the mechanics of relationship building.

Organizations typically focus on automating sales and service independently, although the benefits of implementing an integrated solution across these two business organizations are becoming increasingly apparent. Many vendors now offer integrated solutions that tie sales and service into a single software package, which enables the capability of selecting from a large variety of available functionality. The functions for automating your customer service processes typically come in the following categories: workflow management, CTI, and desktop management. The functions for automating your sales processes are categorized as follows: desktop management, telesales and campaign management, product configuration, and mobile access. The modularity of many of the most popular packages today affords a good deal of choice when selecting the combination of technology components and associated functionality that best fits your organization.

The systems required to automate your service and sales processes fall into the business operations section of the Corporate Information Factory. Business operations consist of those systems that perform most of the day-to-day operations of your business. In addition to service and sales automation packages, these systems include legacy product applications, billing systems, and accounting systems. Business operations systems play an important role in CRM. As Figure 11.5 illustrates, business operations systems work throughout the Customer Life Cycle.

In the retain and expand section of the Customer Life Cycle, these systems perform the following tasks:

- Facilitate the fulfillment of goods and services.
- Facilitate the billing and invoicing processes.
- Enable the product configuration and customization of mass-produced products and services.
- Provide the capability to collect and update customer information.
- Provide the capability to expand the share of wallet for existing customers.
- Provide opportunities to build the customer relationship.

In the intrude and engage, and acquire sections of the Customer Life Cycle, these systems perform the following tasks:

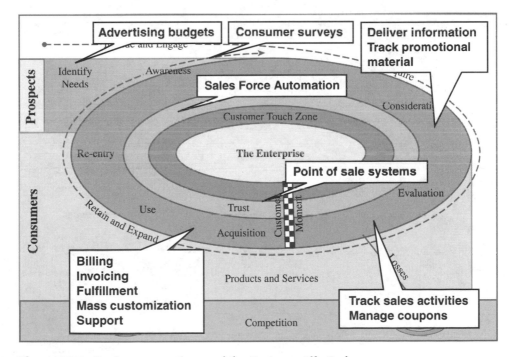

Figure 11.5 Business operations and the Customer Life Cycle.

- Provide the customer and prospect information required to perform sales activities.

- Provide the tracking and coordination essential to effective sales teams.

- Provide the capability to collect information on prospects and customers.

- Provide the capability to educate prospects and customers about the organization.

- Enable the tracking of sales campaigns, customer satisfaction surveys, and other promotions.

Facilitating customer choices for how, where, and when contacts occur is key to the successful CRM organization of the future. As organizations position themselves to provide this choice, while also providing consistent sales and service across all available channels, the automation of sales and service and the integration of these automated solutions into the rest of the Corporate Information Factory will become increasingly important. Chapter 12 examines the role of the Internet and e-commerce in CRM.

CHAPTER 12

Interacting with Customers Online

There is no question that the Internet is affecting the way we think, the way we communicate, and the way we do business. Virtually every industry is involved, and the landscape is continually changing. While presenting its second compilation of the e.biz 25—the men and women most influential in shaping e-commerce and the Web—*Business Week* notes that the members of this list have changed substantially from the first rendition, which was presented less than one year before.[1] The initial list was comprised predominately of e-tailers, which are business-to-consumer (B2C) organizations, and the companies that provided the supporting technical infrastructure. This time, over half the organizations included play in the business-to-business (B2B) market. What started as an electronic method of selling products and services has changed into something much more complex, touching the way organizations relate to their customers, their employees, and their business partners. Harvey Golab, Chief Executive Officer of American Express, said of the Internet:

> The Internet has the potential to bring not just change, but transformation. The Internet will certainly bring substantial change to our industry—changes that represent both opportunities and challenges. It offers a huge opportunity for payment vehicles, as it is a truly cashless society. But it also offers the challenge of disintermediation. And not only will the changes be dramatic, they will be fast. Adoption rates for the Internet are already faster than they were for the telephone or the television, and they are increasing daily. New sites, new companies, and new applications appear overnight. We have everything from online greeting cards to online garage sales—the difference

[1]"New Faces at the Party." *Business Week Magazine.* May 15, 2000.

being, of course, that, instead of pulling in your garage sale customers from a five-block radius, you can now go global in selling your Superman lunch box. It has already made the world a forever smaller place.[2]

Let's consider how the Web has changed our friend Bob, the typical sophisticated consumer:

- Most of his banking and investing is done on the Web. Bob relies on the Internet facility offered by his bank to do most of his bill-paying and money transfers. He receives investment advice electronically from his bank advisor, he researches potential stock purchases on the Web, and he conducts his own online stock trades as well.

- All of his family holiday and birthday gift purchases are done on the Web because Bob is a busy executive who travels constantly. His family is large and geographically dispersed, and his lifestyle leaves little time to go shopping, purchase gifts, and take them to the post office for mailing. Instead, he simply clicks onto his favorite online shopping sites, browses for the perfect items, and provides the payment information and delivery address as he completes the order. On sites in which he is a frequent shopper, he gets discounted prices, and his credit card information is provided once and stored for repeated use. Many times, he doesn't bother with pre-order payment information unless he wants to use a different card than the one he provided when he enrolled with the site.

- He uses the Web to pick all his hotels and vacation spots—Bob frequently uses the vacation options displayed on the Internet banking site and offered by the bank's affiliated travel service. When not choosing his vacations this way, he still uses the Web. He simply enters the city or location he is considering, reviews the tourist information contained on the Web site, and makes his decision based on what he reads. If the location's Web site is not sufficiently informative, he picks a different place for his vacation, one he can research on the Web. Once his destination is locked in, he uses the links from each city's Web site to investigate local accommodations. Not only can he learn about price, availability, and amenities, most times he can also take virtual tours and view photographs of the rooms and surroundings. If a hotel has not listed with the appropriate city or resort Web sites, Bob will not encounter it in his search for accommodations and thus will not consider it.

- When traveling on vacation or business, Bob uses his company Web site to monitor the activity of his employees and his customers. Bob manages the sales force in a distribution organization that sells books, movies, and

[2]This quote is from remarks made to the Faulkner & Grey Credit Card Forum on April 12, 1999, and can be accessed on the American Express Web site at http://americanexpress.com.

records to retail stores. Sales and inventory numbers are posted daily from the company operational systems into the data warehouse. The company Web site provides both employees and retail customers with the ability to access information in the data warehouse and associated data marts for reporting and analysis. Bob can create and view reports, generate e-mail lists for his staff and customers, and add activities into the sales workflow management system, all from the company Web site.

Bob's activities personify the remarks of Harvey Golab on the impact of the Internet. Bob does operate in a largely cashless (and paperless) society. His bank has radically transformed its service and selling options from the rigid immobile branch banking structure of years past into the flexible and dynamic world of the Internet. Bob benefits from the predicted disintermediation (that is, the appearance of non-traditional competitors who dilute an organization's customer base) by utilizing e-retail stores to shop for a variety of goods and services, at discounted prices, while bypassing brick-and-mortar stores altogether. Bob's ability to interact with his own customers and employees from wherever he (or they) happens to be located is reflective of the global nature of business today.

This chapter examines the role of e-commerce in Customer Relationship Management (CRM). We begin with an explanation of the impact of e-commerce. We then look at the three major e-commerce models that are employed today, along with the opportunities, and risks, they pose to effective CRM.

E-commerce technology is letting us engage our customers in a dialog and then use the knowledge we have about the customers to provide them with the desired services and products. The concepts of permission marketing (engaging the customer in the dialog) and personalization (customizing the way we deal with the customer) are the subject of the next section. None of this would be possible without a solid architecture. We close with an explanation of how the Corporate Information Factory (CIF) uses information obtained from the e-commerce activities to enable us to improve customer relationships to the mutual benefit of both the customers and our organizations.

The Impact of E-Commerce on CRM

E-commerce is an excellent example of a prime CRM tenet, one we espouse throughout this book: technology (including the Internet) is the key enabler of CRM strategies. E-commerce simply enables organizations to use the rapidly changing technology associated with the Internet to provide another point of contact. As we will see in this chapter, organizations are using the Internet to expand their sales, marketing, and service processes as well as to better manage their customer relationships. Consider what GE Capital President and Chief Executive Officer, Dennis Nayden, said about the Internet and GE in an interview with the Philadelphia Inquirer:

> Today we're in the midst of one of the most significant challenges and opportunities ever: e-business. E-business is nothing short of revolutionary. It's being led by customers, and when customers lead, the rest of us must follow, even 100-year old Fortune 500 companies like GE. If we're going to last another 100 years, we must respond on e-business terms, with e-speed. We recognize this need and are responding by creating direct links between our traditional business channels and the emerging new e-models. Traditional brick and mortar is quickly being transformed into what we call "click and mortar," powerful new offerings to existing and new customers.[3]

To GE, e-commerce is a customer-centric phenomenon that is driven by the recognition that successful organizations must let the customer choose how, when, and where interactions take place. It is, in effect, simply another channel to facilitate customer touches and build lasting relationships. Later in this chapter, we'll show you some examples of how GE is succeeding online.

The Internet Timeline

To understand the impact of the Internet on society in general and on CRM specifically, it is helpful to understand its origins and to recognize the extent of its rapid growth and acceptance. Figure 12.1 illustrates how rapidly the Internet has grown, as well as the extent that it has been accepted in various industries.

Early innovations in Internet technology originated from government research and within the scientific community as a means to share research and ideas across the globe. Today estimates on the number of people connected to the Internet run over 200 million. In less than 10 years, the Internet has transformed from a vehicle used by the government, the scientific community, and academia into a vehicle not only used, but also demanded, by most consumers, both businesses and individuals. The right-hand column of Figure 12.1 illustrates just a few of the uses of the Internet today. Almost all transactions in the financial services industry can be conducted online. Most major news sources and research facilities publish online, and travel can be planned and arranged online as well. This is just a sampling of the vast resources available to organizations and customers through the Internet.

[3]This quote is from an interview with the *Philadelphia Inquirer*, which is published on the General Electric Web site at www.ge.com.

The pace is staggering

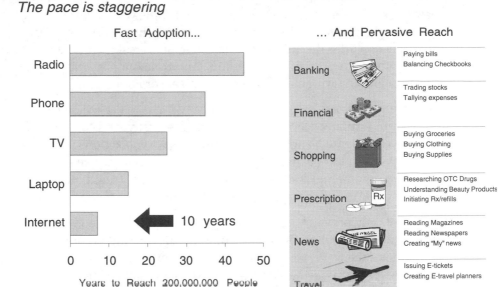

Figure 12.1 Internet timeline.

E-Commerce Models

Three primary e-commerce models are in existence today. Many organizations use a combination of these new business models in their CRM strategy.

E-Channel Only

In this model, the organization starts with the Internet as the primary interaction mechanism. The traditional definition of an e-channel-only business model is that no brick and mortar counterpart exists. Customers interact with the organization entirely through the Internet. Although many Internet organizations begin in this mode, not many end up here. This is because customers today are sophisticated, and they are demanding choices on how, when, and where they interact with their chosen business partners.

Bob is a good example of someone with these demands. When Bob moved his residence (discussed in Chapter 10, "Facilitating Customer Touches with the Customer ODS"), he informed his bank of this change over the Internet. However, within several minutes, he had also utilized a fax-back service and a telephone service center. The absence of any of these three options would have caused the bank to miss a sale.

Although this example may be fictitious, the concept portrayed is very real. Customers routinely switch channels when dealing with favored providers, and they increasingly demand the option to talk to a human being. Most organizations that consider the Internet to be their primary business are adapting to these demands by adding other options. Amazon.com has a large call center in operation already with plans to expand into several more.

These e-channel-only organizations typically focus in vertical markets and have appeared in virtually every industry within the past year. B2C and B2B transactions are represented, and in many cases, these organizations are in direct competition with traditional providers (retailers, financial service providers, and so on). The e-commerce challenges faced by traditional (multi-channel) organizations are described in greater detail later in this chapter.

E-channel-only organizations have originated one other unique business model that supports collaboration, not competition, among traditional providers. Companies such as Priceline.com, iWant.com, and Respond.com negotiate with businesses (such as airlines) to offer unsold merchandise (seats) at discounted prices. Rather than directly competing, these organizations are actually functioning as another distribution channel for traditional CRM organizations, albeit an independent one. Note that to the organizations utilizing these services, the dot-com businesses are sometimes considered to an expanded customer type, as discussed in Chapter 1, "The Customer Becomes the Center of the Business Universe."

Content and Community Businesses

The focus of these Internet businesses is cultural rather than commercial. Buying and selling products and services is not the primary purpose of a content or community business site. Instead, these sites are designed to serve the needs of groups of individuals or businesses with similar interests by providing information about those interests. CRMguru.com is one of many Internet sites focused on CRM issues, while iVillage.com is a site that serves as a focal point for issues pertaining to women.

The stated purpose of sites such as these is to provide customers with the ability to learn and to interact with others, some of whom may be experts and some of whom may be peers. These sites have lots of content relating to their stated themes, the ability to "ask the experts," and general conversation or chat sessions on topics suggested by visitors. Many of the CRM-related sites offer electronic libraries of information, including white papers, articles, summaries of past chat sessions, and Web-casts. These sites typically make heavy use of partners and affiliates. Banners and links that enable customers to click-through to traditional businesses are very common.

One CRM consultant we know found her last job while browsing on a CRM content site. She was simply visiting to keep her industry knowledge current during a period of unemployment and clicked-through to the Web site of a company she eventually joined. This type of click-through activity is how the majority of commerce happens from the content and community businesses. Advertisers and site supporters place banner advertisements on the content and community sites in hopes that customers like our consultant will click-through from the community site and purchase something from their more commerce-oriented sites.

Traditional Organizations with an E-Channel Presence

The most common business model for CRM companies is this model, in which a traditional brick-and-mortar company has developed an e-commerce channel to complement the other sales, service, and marketing channels it employs. Almost all major companies have some type of Internet presence today, stimulated either by competitive efforts or by customer demand. Organizations that are serious about adopting CRM, such as American Express and GE have paid special attention to their e-channel efforts and have worked hard to integrate these with all other channels. They have been rewarded for their efforts by increased sales, decreased costs, and increased customer satisfaction. Industry experts point to these efforts as "best in breed" and throughout this chapter, we highlight the CRM capabilities common to these and other successful sites. The remainder of this chapter focuses primarily on this e-commerce business model.

E-Commerce Opportunities and Challenges

What does the e-revolution mean to organizations adopting CRM? E-commerce not only provides opportunities to improve customer relationships, but it can also present challenges to how you compete and conduct business. Let's first look at the opportunities:

E-commerce helps your organization educate customers and prospects.
You can provide significant information about your products and services to any interested consumer or prospect who is willing to spend time browsing your Web site. This can be a key benefit.

In Chapter 3, "Understanding the Customer Life Cycle," we introduced the Customer Life Cycle and presented three stages that occur early in the decision process for most customers: needs identification, awareness, and learning. You have a good opportunity to influence a customer's thought process at this time. Using education to help the customer to redefine the problem, or to reshape the possible solutions, is not uncommon.

True to Mr. Nayden's words, GE is a good example of how to use this type of education to your benefit. A section on the GE Web site is labeled Learn, Shop, Buy. Clicking on this area yields 17 categories of GE products, including such diverse groupings as appliances, insurance, and power systems. Picking a group then enables consumers to explore product features and functions, prices, parts, warranties, and more. The site provides detailed comparisons on various models, contains frequently asked questions (FAQ) and answers, and facilitates mix and match build-your-own-solution options. It even provides consumers with the ability to submit e-mail questions or switch into a call center so that they can talk to a service representative.

The potential for education doesn't stop at products and services. White papers on relevant topics, company awards, community service activity, annual reports, press releases and speeches, and the location of brick-and-mortar facilities are just a sampling of the information contained on CRM-savvy Web sites. An educated consumer is an empowered consumer and the Internet provides a tremendous mechanism for education.

E-commerce assists your organization in disseminating information to the extended enterprise. Organizations who are adopting extended customer definitions are using their Web sites to integrate the supply chain, manage partner relationships, and disseminate information internally. In the extended enterprise, an organization may not own all components of the supply chain, but a CRM-savvy organization will manage these components as if it does own them.

In an earlier example, we discussed the supplier controlled inventory process that Wal-Mart employs in its retail stores. Wal-Mart uses its data warehouse to compare current and past sales and to make predictions on required inventory levels. It is the supplier's job to monitor actual inventory in the Wal-Mart stores against this warehouse application and to ship items when required. The suppliers access this information and the associated warehouse application using the Web.

Bob's employer, the entertainment company, illustrates another component of this e-commerce benefit. This organization uses its Web site to facilitate communications with its national sales force, its customers (the retail stores that sell the books, movies, and records), and its manufacturers (the record labels, publishers, and producers). Information on artists, authors, and actors is published to aid in the selling process. Analytic information such as billboard ratings (key sales predictors) and past performance information is made available to all groups through the Internet. The sales force uses this information to sell to the retailers. The retailers use it to ensure adequate inventory and to determine promotions, and the manufacturers use it to calculate production levels. In the future, the retail stores will also use the site to directly submit sales and transaction information and to digitally download music directly into their stores while preserving the publisher's copyright protection.

E-commerce enables organizations to cut costs. These cost-cutting measures come in several forms. First, the Web provides the opportunity to shift the load from overcrowded, higher cost service channels. In an effort to relieve pressure on call centers during high-volume periods, for example, many organizations that offer technical support (such as ISPs, software vendors, and hardware manufacturers) now promise responses in this priority: Web first, fax second, phone third. Financial service organizations have long recognized the savings associated with moving transactions from more expensive brick-and-mortar branches (tellers) to more efficient electronic banking facilities (telephone or ATM). For banks, the Internet simply provides a continuation of these savings. GE realizes similar savings from its Internet service and sales operations. Customer inquiries conducted over the Web are substantially cheaper, costing less than half as much as handling the inquiries in the GE call centers. Each customer phone call about one of GE's appliances costs around $5, as compared to the $0.20 cost of the same inquiry made over the Web.[4]

Organizations can also cut costs by using the Web to consolidate procurement activities. Large, geographically disperse organizations can create economies of scale by aggregating supply purchases to a central Web site, driving down costs and streamlining the procurement processes. By using the Web as the central procurement site, these companies can coordinate all procurement activities through particular vendors, thus opening the door for substantial volume discounts. They can also eliminate inefficiencies that may occur in uncoordinated procurement processes by implementing a standard procurement process that is designed for efficiency and for the elimination of redundancy. The Web also provides a forum for consistent and accurate reporting on all aspects of the procurement process.

Clearly, the CRM benefits of e-commerce can be great, but these benefits don't come without certain challenges:

E-commerce facilitates new types of competition. New marketplaces that drive down prices and intermediaries that compete for customer loyalty are two significant challenges stimulated by the Internet. B2B digital marketplaces enable companies and suppliers to trade more efficiently over the

---

[4]"Changing the Corporate DNA." *Forbes.com.* July 17, 2000

Internet. Companies such as Freemarkets, Commerce One, and many more are facilitating online auctions in which the purpose is to match buyers and sellers in the B2B world. These auctions come in various forms. A company looking to sell can invite multiple potential customers to view its wares. A buyer can invite multiple suppliers to bid and can select the best option (this is sometimes called a reverse auction, as the prices start high and are lowered in the bidding process). Companies can also visit ongoing vertical market auctions at any time to buy or sell on a one-time basis. These new market places not only drive down prices and affect the selling profit, but they also impact customer loyalty. If you have not put mechanisms in place to strengthen the loyalty of your customers and if you are not providing them with solid reasons to continue doing business with you, the new competitive environment could spell the erosion of your good customers. Managing customer relationships becomes much more important if you want your business customers to continue dealing directly with you, rather than switching to this impersonal but efficient mechanism.

Intermediaries such as Amazon.com and Autobytel.com present a similar challenge in the B2C marketplace. These organizations have the potential to displace distributors or to displace manufacturers from the distribution process. By collecting and selling books directly to consumers, Amazon.com presented sufficient threat to Borders, Barnes & Nobel, and others that these organizations launched e-retailing sites. Value America is an online retail store that sells a wide variety of consumer products at discounted prices. Autobytel.com provides services traditionally furnished by automotive dealers such as financing, extended warranties, and record keeping. These intermediaries can shift customer loyalty from the primary company to them in much the same way as the B2B digital marketplaces. Again, CRM-savvy organizations recognize the requirement to establish and maintain lasting relationships while protecting against the erosion of their customer bases in the electronic world.

E-commerce demands channel coordination. Today many organizations are under pressure to keep up with the Joneses by quickly developing or enhancing their Internet channels. If your organization falls into this category, beware. An Internet channel that is incomplete or not integrated with your other distribution facilities can be worse than none at all.

Retail organizations can be good examples of this downfall. Managing a large and dynamically changing inventory of products online is a significant challenge. In their rush to answer the competitive call of the e-channel-only e-retailers discussed earlier, many large retail stores have implemented Web sites that are far less than the equivalent of their brick-and-mortar facilities. A few of the common problems found on retail sites today include incomplete inventory, Web prices that are not coordinated with prices in the stores, the ability to see but not buy items, and poorly designed sites that are difficult to navigate and slow to respond. Companies that police consistency from store to store do not always look as closely at consistency from store to e-channel.

Consider the experience of a consultant we know who was (the keyword here is "was") a member of a large direct distribution entertainment company. The club routinely issued mailings containing current movie offerings, sale prices, and other offers. Members purchasing movies simply checked the appropriate box, sent the card back, and received the movies, and the bill, in the mail. While reading the latest movie offer sheet, this consultant found two movies she wanted that were on sale, and noticed the club's Web site address printed on the sheet. Curious, she logged onto the site and found that she could order her movies directly from the Internet, saving the effort of mailing the card back. She ordered the movies but couldn't find any prices listed on the site. She used both the comment facility on the site's order form and the e-mail facility offered elsewhere on the site to include her account number and request that she get the sale price. The movies did arrive, but the bill that arrived with them did not reflect the sale price listed on the original flier. Several e-mails and a phone call later, the consultant was able to receive the discount she deserved as a member of the club. She used that same phone call, however, to cancel her membership.

Contrast the entertainment company's Web site with the Learn, Shop, Buy concept embodied on the GE site. Potential customers have many options (we stopped counting after 50) in the appliances category alone. Although the number of options may seem a bit overwhelming, the site is clearly organized; prices, features and functions are easy to find; and the site is linked to the brick-and-mortar distribution locations. Customers are demanding e-channels that are rich in contextual information, contain detailed information about all the products and services, are easy to navigate, provide all the transactional functionality that other contact channels offer, and are available 24 hours a day, seven days a week. An example of a retailer whose e-channel is a CRM standout is shown in the following sidebar.

Permission Marketing and Personalization

When discussing the role of e-commerce in CRM, two new concepts deserve special attention: permission marketing and personalization.

E-Retail Channel Coordination Done Right

Circuit City introduced their Web presence with their e-superstore, www.Circuit-City.com. The organization was careful to coordinate this Web channel with their other distribution facilities. All 550 brick-and-mortar stores are fully integrated with the Web. Customers can browse the Web for all the merchandise offered in the stores, and they can order from the Web and take delivery at their homes. If they prefer to avoid the shipping and delivery charges, they can order from the Web and pick up the merchandise at the most convenient store. They can also return merchandise ordered from the Web at any store. Prices on the Web are automatically adjusted down to match in-store sales as these occur.[5]

Permission marketing is a new approach to marketing, recognized and nurtured by Seth Godin, formerly Vice President of Direct Marketing for Yahoo![6] Traditional marketing depends on your ability to divert the attention of the prospect or customer from whatever they are doing when they notice your marketing message. This is mass marketing: use marketing campaigns to get attention, and then use that attention to build brand recognition. In the Customer Life Cycle, this process begins with the needs identification stage and continues through the customer moment. Permission marketing acknowledges that this initial diversion (interruption marketing) is a necessary activity. It also emphasizes that brand awareness is still an important part of marketing.

Permission marketing states, however, that interruption marketing should never be the only technique employed. Instead, the attention gained by interruption should be used to initiate a dialog with your customers and prospects. Without this dialog, moving a customer through the early stages of the Customer Life Cycle to get them to the customer moment is entirely dependent on a series of interruptions, which can get lost among myriad other such interruptions the customer experiences in any given moment. Take a minute to count the number of billboards, corporate logos, and commercials, that you see in any given hour. You will be surprised at the totals.

Chapter 3 discussed the importance of engaging the customer in a dialog early in the Customer Life Cycle, and of maintaining that dialog (using it to learn about the customer) throughout the entire relationship. Trust and loyalty are

[5] Peppers and Rogers Group. *Inside 1to1*. July 29, 1999.
[6] Seth Godin. *Permission Marketing*. New York: Simon & Schuster, 1999.

built when you demonstrate that you know your customers and when you treat them as they have told you they want to be treated. Engaging your customer in an ongoing dialog is the foundation for permission marketing. Godin advocates that you use the initial communication (when you get a customer's attention) to solicit permission to begin the dialog. You may have to offer an incentive to the customer to begin this dialog, but that's OK. You may also have to reinforce that incentive at various points throughout the relationship. That's also OK. If you use the resulting dialog to gather the right information, you can tailor your communications and eventually modify behavior and stimulate a sale (more than one sale actually). Leveraging customer knowledge enables you to tailor customer interactions, generate interest, and stimulate anticipation for your communications. When you reach this stage with your customers, you are no longer interrupting them.

The relationship that Bob has with his bank is a good example of this anticipation. Bob knows that his bank understands him and he has given it permission to contact him with relevant offers (read on to Chapter 15, "The Future of CRM," to see the ultimate permission marketing: Bob and his bank in the CRM of the future!) The following sidebar summarizes the key steps to permission marketing.

Personalization

If permission marketing is the recognition that you should use marketing activities to engage your customers in an ongoing dialog, personalization is the utilization of what your customers have told you. Simply put, personalization is the ability to track and respond to customers in an individualized fashion based upon their past contacts and behavior. Personalization extends beyond the

---

The Five Steps to Dating Your Customer[7]

1. Offer the prospect an incentive to volunteer.
2. Use the attention to teach the customer about you over time.
3. Reinforce the incentive to maintain permission.
4. Offer additional incentives to get more (and different) permission from the customer.
5. Leverage the permission to change consumer behavior toward profits.

---

[7] From *Permission marketing* by Seth Godin, Simon & Schuster, 1999.

Internet to encompass all contacts within the Customer Touch Zone. Every contact with your customers should be a well-thought out, planned, and personalized approach.

The treatment Bob's parents receive at their bank branch is a simple example of personalization. They are greeted by name when they enter the bank. Bank personnel understand all the products and services they own, and, more importantly, they understand the types of things his parents like to do in the branch. The teller is always ready with a deposit slip (which the teller is happy to fill out) to receive the monthly social security check. Should they ever have insufficient funds to cover a check, the branch manager will call them prior to bouncing the check. Comfort is a definite aspect of personalization, and the branch employees go out of their way to make Bob's parents feel comfortable. Even more important, Bob's parents know that the bank recognizes their value and is willing to provide them with the personalized interactions that they desire.

Another important facet of personalization is differentiating your service offerings to provide something that your competitor does not. This is becoming more important as products become more commoditized and distinguishing features within products are harder to come by. Bed and breakfast hotels are a good example of differentiation. These hotels offer lodging, the same as the larger hotel chains. However, they also offer a much more personalized experience including more attention to details, a home environment, company, and local cuisine. The key to this differentiation is to cater to the right clientele for marketing that offering. The bed and breakfast hotels do not necessarily cater to the business traveler. Instead, they have developed their service to appeal to the leisure travelers who want to genuinely experience the area.

As you can see, differentiation does not require you to "one-up" your competition by offering everything they do *plus* something else. In many cases, the distinction will outweigh the competition's offerings. This is where knowing your customers becomes the most crucial leverage point in the success of personalization. A good bed and breakfast will actively solicit customer feedback and will continue communications after the initial stay.

In the e-CRM world, personalization is achieved through the following types of activities:

- Addressing your customers by name and remembering their preferences.

- Allowing visitors to customize content to suit their purposes.

- Showing customers specific content based on who they are and based on past behaviors.

- Using technologies and techniques for optimal customer understanding based on transaction history, demographic analysis, and collected information.

Personalization can take many formats, from simple to quite complex. Figure 12.2 illustrates some of the different types of personalization employed by CRM-savvy organizations today.

As illustrated by the figure, the type of personalization you can provide is dependent on the type and amount of information you have about the customer. You know very little about an anonymous visitor to your Web site, other that what you can pick up from the click stream data available from the visit. (For more detail on click stream data, see the next section). Thus, your goal is simply to personalize the site enough to stimulate a repeat visit. This can be done by matching the click stream characteristics to similar characteristics of known customers and applying a few simple personalization techniques (banner ads, navigation pointers, or some generated content) based on what those known customers have responded to in the past.

On the other hand, for customers with whom you have a lasting relationship, you have a wealth of information to draw from to personalize the interaction. You can draw on past transactions and past site visits, product ownership

Type of User	Known Attributes	Type of Personalization	Technology	Goal
Anonymous	Click-Stream Data: • IP Address • Referring Site • Browser Version • Date/Time • Page Requested	Dynamically generated content or ads based on click-stream data	Rules-based engine (e.g. BroadVision or Vignette)	Resonate with the user; foster a repeat visit
Known	Site Preferences	Customization, i.e., a user-configured Web site (like MyYahoo)	Web site subscription	Empower the user; foster repeat visits
Registered	Personal Preferences	Dynamic content based on personal preferences	Rules-based engine	Identify with the user; convert into a customer
First-Time Customer	Transaction: • Type of Product(s) • Ship/Bill Addresses • Credit Card • Credit Status • Other	Real-time recommendations based on purchase	Collaborative filter or rules-based engine	Anticipate the user's needs; cross-sell and/or up-sell based on purchase
Repeat Customer	Historical transactions, interactions, profile scores, and third-party demographics	Dynamic and proactive content and service based on a rich customer profile and statistical analysis	Real-time analytical engine and customer data warehouse	Know the user; foster loyalty, referrals, and greater share of wallet

Figure 12.2 Spectrum of personalization.[8]

[8]Patricia Seybold Group, 2000.

information, indicated preferences, and much more. At this point, your objectives with personalization are to foster continuing customer trust and loyalty, and to increase profitability and share the wallet. More sophisticated techniques can be applied, such as using a strong rules engine to determine which content to display and which products to offer based on the rich profile of analytics and customer information available.

All the techniques discussed in this section, and throughout the chapter, are dependent on the appropriate customer information and supporting technology. The next section covers the enabling information and discusses the role of the Corporate Information Factory in your e-commerce strategies.

Enabling E-Commerce

The concepts of personalization and permission marketing provide exciting possibilities to build relationships with your customers that will keep them coming back. Both strategies require substantial knowledge of your customers. Customer dialog is useless if the organization can't remember (and learn from) this dialog, and interactions can't be personalized without a strong foundation of customer knowledge to guide the personalization efforts.

In this aspect, e-commerce is no different than any other CRM business strategy. All successful CRM initiatives rely on an integrated technical architecture, such as the Corporate Information Factory, to provide integrated customer information. Robust e-commerce both generates customer information and requires it. In this section, we will look at the types of information used in personalized e-commerce and discuss the role of the CIF in facilitating personalization efforts.[9]

Customer Information for Click Stream Analysis

We've all heard or read about the new world of click stream analysis, which is the ability to examine all of one's Internet interactions, including which sites were visited, which products were considered, what was actually purchased, and so on. The difficulty for companies performing click stream analysis is making sense of the massive amount of information they collect and using that information on the current or next visit by the individual being tracked. Add the

---

[9]Portions of this section taken from "WhoAmI.com" by Claudia Imhoff and Joyce Norris-Montanari, *DMReview*, July 2000.

integration of customer information from sources other than the Internet (call center interactions, non-electronic purchases, and so on) and the complexity increases exponentially.

The ideal situation for personalization and permission marketing occurs when you can answer the following questions immediately upon arrival to a Web site:

- Who is the person entering the Web site?
- What sort of products and services should we offer him or her?
- What types of banner ads make sense to present to him or her?

Sounds simple, doesn't it? Unfortunately, it is not that easy. In fact, without a sound and proven architecture, it becomes not just difficult, but almost impossible. Let's examine what is needed to create the ideal situation, keeping in mind that all this has to happen in Internet time.

First, let's start with an understanding of Internet data. Though relatively simplistic in nature, click stream data is quite comprehensive and informative. It consists of the following pieces of information about the customer's identity, activities at the current Web site, activities at the immediately preceding Web site, and the following items:

Tracking information: This is the user's identification, consisting of a client IP address or proxy server identification. The customer or user identity and authorized user element are used when a secure logon is required. Customer profile information is a profile that is requested and provided (home address, e-mail address, phone numbers). This also includes the date and time that the Web server responded to the request.

Server request information about the URL: This includes the status of request (200 or OK is good) and number of bytes sent.

Current site information: This includes the referring Web site or page and the length of visit to the site. Note that this statistic is not always reliable (a customer could have been talking on the phone and happened to be visiting your site during this time). This information also includes the navigation path through the site, the content viewed, the advertising click-throughs used, the affiliate links used, the search parameters used, and the message boards or chat rooms viewed or used.

Transactions conducted on current site: This consists of the product purchased or account opened, the price of the product or the amount of the transaction, the time and date purchased, the form of payment, the form of shipment, the pick-up location, and whether it is a gift or not.

Prior site information: This includes the URL, the host name, the path followed while on the prior site, the documents viewed or downloaded, and the query string to get to the current site.

With this vast array of information, we can now answer basic questions about our customers visiting the site. Table 12.1 lists some of the basic questions we can answer with this invaluable asset, and it matches the available click stream data to each question. The answers to these basic questions provide the building blocks for our personalization efforts. They also provide the basis for many types of analytics associated with the Web and with marketing strategies. This analysis is used to tune the personalization campaign, it is used to gain a better understanding of Web-savvy customers, it is used to relate the recency and frequency of customer contacts with the monetary value of the customer, and it is used to determine appropriate marketing campaigns and product offers.

The questions in Table 12.1 focus on understanding the individual customer experience. A second category of questions (sometimes called the million dollar questions) is equally important to e-commerce. These questions focus not on individual customers, but on the collective experience of all visitors to your site. Among other things, these questions can be used to judge the quality of your site, focusing on content, usability, and effectiveness. A sampling of the million dollar questions follows:

- What is the correlation between referring site and customer value?

  - This question can be used to determine which external Web sites to maintain partnerships with. Partner sites include content and community sites, Internet service provider sites such as AOL, AT&T, or Yahoo!, and other company sites. For example, if the bank notices through its analysis that Bob and other profitable customers like him came to their site from one of the popular investment advice sites, it may target all customers coming from this site with special offers. It may also look for other similar partner sites and place more click-though options on these.

- Which type of content generates product sales?

  - This question is used to match content to sales. It will help determine how to organize the site, and it will help to determine what to put on the site. For GE, the volume of product characteristics, the feature comparisons, and the make-you're your-own-solution options are all examples of content that is key to increasing Internet sales of appliances.

- What are the characteristics of customers who browse but don't buy?

  - This helps the organization segment the customers so that it can begin to turn browsers into buyers. Browsers are placed in one segment, while buyers go in another segment. Common characteristics of the buyer segment can then be identified and used to help find those browsers who have similar characteristics. The identified browsers are

Table 12.1   Basic Customer Questions and Click Stream Data

QUESTION	CURRENT CLICK STREAM DATA	NON-CLICK STREAM DATA/CLICK STREAM HISTORY
1. Who is the customer?	Cookie and user identification information	Customer profile information from the ODS
2. Which products do they currently own of ours?	Current inventory of customer's purchases on the Web	Product ownership information from the ODS
3. What is the customer's frequency to this site?	Current visit information	Number of times the customer has visited the Web site, ODS, or warehouse
4. What is the recency of this customer?	Number of days (hours) since last visit	N/A
5. What are the past monetary purchases by this customer?	N/A	History of purchases from the ODS and warehouse
6. What are the buying habits of this customer?	Current purchase information from Web	History of purchases from the ODS and warehouse
7. Which Web marketing strategy works best for this customer?	Current Web navigation information	Prior campaign analyses for similar customers, banner ads that the customer responded to, and so on
8. What is the customer's navigational behavior (within this Web site and outside)?	Current Web navigation information	History of customer's Web visits from warehouse
9. Which banners, ads, promotions, and incentives should be presented to this customer and at what intervals?	Current responses on Web	History of customer plus demographic/psychographic analyses of similar customers (warehouse, banner ad content, content server)

likely candidates for conversion to buyer status and can be marketed accordingly. This segmentation also enables the organization to understand which navigational patterns should be used in making content and site organization decisions. The proper segmentation of customers ensures that the organization uses only buyers when making these important decisions.

- What are the characteristics of the customers that do buy?

  - This question can be used to understand buying customers. The organization can then develop a profile of the customers it would like to attract to its site and target its promotion efforts towards potential customers matching these characteristics. This profile is also used to conduct the browser to buyer activity described in the preceding bullet.

- Which areas on the site do the best customers frequent?

  - This is similar to the question about which content generates product sales. Here the organization is looking to understand which content is interesting to its best customers. When this is understood, the organization can ensure that it keeps these areas adequate and current.

- Which searches are not fulfilled, and what do the customers do when this happens?

  - Failed searches can yield valuable information. First, they can point to problems with site organization. They can also illustrate additional content that is being requested by searches. An organization may decide to add material or linked sites if multiple profitable customers are searching for (and not finding) the same things. Last, if customers are leaving the site immediately after a failed search, you may want to provide some incentive to stay after each failed search.

Before we look at the technologies necessary to use the information discussed previously, your organization should consider one additional point about click stream data. To answer the million dollar questions, you must analyze click stream information over time. The data warehouse with its various data marts is the appropriate environment for this type of heavy-duty analysis. Thus, this information must be stored in your business intelligence environment. The quality of the click stream data at this level can be questionable, with as much as 40 percent of the data incomplete or bad. The decision must be made whether to drop the data or keep it, knowing that the data may be unusable.

In addition to quality issues with the click stream information, the question of utility arises. As your organization analyzes the available data, it may decide that some of the available information may not yield much value. As an example, you may decide that the IP address of the site visitor is not reliable for customer identification, because the same customer can use several different computers to visit the site. In this case, you may decide not to capture and store IP addresses. One thing to remember with click stream data is that just because it's available doesn't mean it's valuable. Only you can make that determination as you begin to understand your own information.

Technology Architecture for E-Commerce

From the questions listed earlier and in Table 12.1, it is obvious that a need exists for access to both real-time current data as well as to historical analytical data. The e-commerce environment requires both tactical and strategic data structures and an architecture that supports both. The components of the Corporate Information Factory, discussed throughout this book, provide this architecture. Effective personalization requires click stream analysis, which requires that the Web channel be integrated to both the operational data store and the data warehouse. Reacting to the results of the personalization and click stream analysis requires that you change the Internet site accordingly when your customers visit. The following sections explain how to achieve the necessary integration between the technology needed for personalization and the components of the Corporate Information Factory required to put it all in place.

Technologies for Personalization and Dynamic Site Customization

To do a complete job of personalization, some additional technologies will be required to work in conjunction with your customer operational data store (ODS), data warehouse, and Web servers. These are the technologies that enable dynamic customization of the site based on available information and are summarized here:

Content management tools. These tools define what the customer sees when visiting your site. They are data repositories that store all forms of content that could be displayed on the site. They integrate with analytical engines and with the customer ODS to match the content to specific customer characteristics. The primary benefit is to enable dynamic decisions on what is displayed on a site based on the characteristics of the customer. These tools provide structure to the unstructured formats of information that can be displayed on the site. They also help in site performance by establishing content queues.

Rules engines. These tools enable the implementation of rules that control the interactions with customers. The rules are used to determine responses to specific customer actions. The tools can provide elementary guided selling experiences and can enable smart questionnaires to collect customer information. They can also integrate with click stream monitoring tools to determine the customer profile and select rules to apply based on that profile. The benefits of these tools include the capability to apply intelligence to the site and the capability to enable marketers to craft responses and employ them through the creation of appropriate rules.

Predictive engines. These tools go beyond the simple "if ... then ... else" logic typically found in the rules engine. They utilize heuristic techniques and decision trees to develop sophisticated recommendations that require a minimum of customization to implement. Because these tools do not require the predefinition of every rule, they are easy and quick to bring up and enable the personalization experience to continue with a minimum of human interaction. However, they also do not typically allow much customization of the process, relying instead on out-of-the-box implementations.

Collaborative filters. These tools perform recommendations based on groups of similar customers. The tool actually learns more about a customer (or customer group) by evaluating the success of prior recommendations. These tools learn from all customers, rather than from single individuals, and are typically employed in situations where large customer and product bases are required.

E-mail response. These tools automate the targeting and sending of mass e-mails and mass e-mail responses. The engines can parse the information from an incoming e-mail and craft a response with increasing accuracy. They are used to automate the handling of direct marketing campaigns and responses for order validation and for customer service follow-ups.

Role of the ODS and the Data Warehouse in E-Commerce

If the click stream analysis is required in a real-time or near real-time frequency, such as for questions 1 through 5 in Table 12.1, then the data structures supporting the Web must include a customer ODS. This requires programmatic processes to analyze current click stream data as well as customer information stored in the ODS. The ODS is used to pull current customer profile information such as product ownership, customers' home addresses, contact information, and so on. With the advent of the Class IV ODS, we now have real-time access to strategic analysis results, such as the best banner ad to offer or the appropriate incentive to offer.[10] The ODS simply stores the results of analyses. Now

---

[10]See *DM Review* article, "Teaching an Old Dog a New Trick" by Claudia Imhoff, July 2000.

we can answer the remaining questions in Table 12.1 and instantly produce the right information for our customer.

To accomplish the analysis to answer these questions in the necessary time frame (Internet time), we need the ODS, the warehouse, and its associated marts. Web server logs housing click stream data are usually collected throughout the day and accumulated for daily transmission to the data warehouse and data marts for analysis. This analysis is used to answer the earlier questions and to determine the appropriate actions to take with the customers as they return to your site. Marketing must continue to use the historical information in the warehouse and data marts to study this click stream data as well as the associated customer responses to its ads/banners/coupons.

Based on this analysis, we can better understand our customers: how they navigate through the Web site, where they paused, what they examined and passed over, when and where they left the Web site, and so on. This navigational information is invaluable feedback for future enhancements to the site to make it more usable. It is also used to dynamically change the site as repeat customers return. Figure 12.3 illustrates how the Internet technologies, the customer ODS, the data acquisition process, and the data warehouse work together to enable both instant and ongoing personalization.

Companies with little or no insight into their Web visitors simply slap up one of any number of predefined banner ads, hoping that one of these will catch a customer's eye and interest them. This is similar to the mass marketing or "spray and pray" techniques traditionally used by brick-and-mortar companies. However, companies using the integrated architecture portrayed in Figure 12.3 are truly able to answer the million dollar questions and personalize their sites accordingly.

How does this work? The answer is that the second group of companies likely has a sophisticated business intelligence environment that captures and analyzes customer click stream data and a customer ODS that provides instant access to the analysis results by customer. The trick is that they only have about a tenth of a second to recognize the customer, determine the appropriate banner ad, and then get it displayed on the customer's screen. Certainly, this cannot be done if this involves scouring and analyzing all previous click stream data to determine the appropriate ad. That could take several minutes or longer and customers will be long gone before the site even comes up.

Here is where the interplay between the ODS and the various analytical marts comes in. Figure 12.3 illustrates the role of these components in two different activities: the capture and data flow of click stream information, and the use of analysis results to dynamically personalize the Internet site (in this case, to display a targeted banner ad).

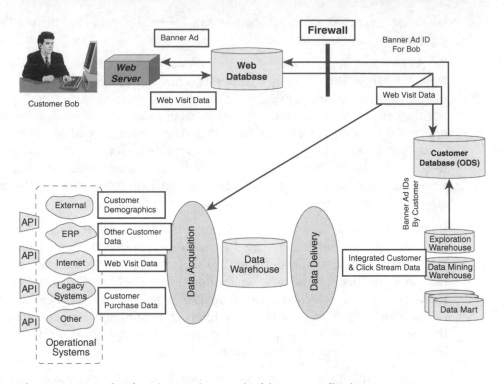

Figure 12.3 Technology integration required for personalization.

When Bob logs on to his Internet banking site, the click stream data about his Web visit is captured in a Web log or dynamically via a click stream data capture tool, and it is passed into the data acquisition process. The bank has built this capability into their data acquisition process using the techniques described in Chapter 7, "Capturing Customer Information." If your organization is integrating click stream data into the data acquisition process, Chapter 7 is a must read. In this situation, you simply treat the click stream data as an additional source.

As detailed in Chapter 7, you will complete the following steps with your click stream data source:

Mapping. This is the process of linking the data in the click stream data source to the database schemas for the operational data store and the data warehouse. It includes the logic for choosing the click stream data you want to keep and for analyzing the quality of this data.

Extraction, cleansing, and transformation. This is where you create the programs to capture the click stream data from the Web logs or from the click stream data capture tool. You then determine the necessary transformation rules for data integration into the warehouse and customer ODS, create the code to enforce transformation rules, and then clean the data as much as possible.

Loading. Here you define the process for delivering the click stream data to the appropriate target, either the data warehouse or the operational data store. For the data warehouse, this includes the processes to append or insert historical snapshots into the database. For the ODS, this includes the appropriate commit and rollback processes required to update records.

Audit and controls. Last, you define the processes that are necessary to permit comprehensive reconciliation and rationalization of the data entering the data warehouse or the ODS.

The data acquisition process for the bank transports the click stream data from Bob's Web site visit into the rest of the Corporate Information Factory. The bank uses several types of analytical applications (data mining, exploration, and traditional Online Analytical Processing [OLAP] types of marts) to perform the hard-core analytical functions on the massive click stream and customer data. These marts work in concert, the results of one perhaps feeding an analysis in another to determine Bob's preferences, buying history, or responses to different campaigns (banner ads, coupons, or other types of incentives).

Now that we understand how the click stream information gets into the business intelligence environment, and how it is used once it arrives, the next question is equally important. How does this analysis translate into instant action when Bob enters the Web site? Figure 12.3 illustrates this as well. The bank uses the analysis described earlier to answer the million dollar questions and determine which banner ad is appropriate for Bob. Note that although Figure 12.3 highlights banner ads, the same process is applied for all types of content changes. Once the banner ads and other content changes are identified for Bob (by warehouse analysis), the ID of each item is stored on Bob's profile on the customer ODS. When Bob enters the Web site, his identification is sent to the ODS and a process then looks up the banner ad ID (and other content specifics) for him specifically. These IDs are passed to the content server and, presto, the ad appears on his screen in subsecond time! Every time he logs on, the process picks the next ID in the listing and another appropriate ad appears.

Periodically, say, once a month, Bob's click stream and other data are analyzed again and a new set of banner ad IDs is loaded into the ODS for his next visit. This process enables the bank to continuously update its understanding of Bob, utilize each new insight in the ongoing analysis processes, and apply the resulting changes in content and personalization to each successive Web site visit.

Summary

E-commerce is becoming a driving force in the CRM world. As another channel for customer interaction, it is opening up myriad possibilities for how, where, and when we interact with our customers. This channel for customer communication provides many opportunities:

- E-commerce provides opportunities to educate customers and prospects on products and services, as well as on all other aspects of the organization.

- E-commerce provides the ability to disseminate information throughout the extended enterprise, enabling global access to information and providing for the management of all extended types of customers in an efficient and effective fashion.

- E-commerce provides a way to cut the cost of service transactions as well as procurement processes.

In order to succeed in the rapidly changing e-commerce world, your organization should follow a few basic guidelines:

- Provide your customers with the option to access Web-based sales, service, and marketing.

- Fully integrate all Web channels to existing brick-and-mortar facilities:

  - Ensure that common customer information is shared across all channels, Web and non-Web.

  - Coordinate product offerings, product pricing, and promotions across all channels.

  - Coordinate business processes and customer treatment across all channels.

  - Allow customers to easily transfer from the Web to any other available channel.

- Take full advantage of the Web's interactive nature to solicit and utilize permission from your customers and use that permission to build long and lasting relationships.

- Identify and use key customer data to personalize all customer contact experiences.

- Build the closed loop information environment personified by the Corporate Information Factory, and use the resulting information to continually enhance CRM activities.

The following chapter, "Putting It All Together," examines how you put all the pieces of the CIF into a cohesive, integrated process of workflow. The chapter will focus on the technology needed to accomplish linking together the appropriate components to accomplish a task. Enterprise portals are promising technologies that can be used to access the CIF components at the proper time, thus completing the full CRM environment.

CHAPTER 13

Putting It All Together with Enterprise Portals

Previous chapters in this book usually began with a continuation of the story of Bob, his family, and their relationship with the bank. This chapter looks at the example from a different viewpoint: the view that bank employees get when using the various systems, databases, and interfaces created for them. Consider the Customer Service Representative (CSR) interacting with Bob regarding a possible cross-sell opportunity. To properly perform this interaction, the CSR must know if

- The proposed product is appropriate for Bob and his lifestyle. To determine this, an analysis is performed in which customers like Bob are selected or targeted for this promotion.

- Bob is indeed interested or would be interested if he knew about the product. From his prior behavior or the behavior of others like him, the bank makes the determination that this is a good offering.

- He doesn't already have the product, or he didn't have it once and decided he no longer wanted it. Bob's historical and current product purchases are known and understood.

- The CSR is using the appropriate channel to contact Bob. The type of relationship that Bob wants with the bank is known and respected.

Think about how the CSR would garner all this information. Some of it resides in the day-to-day operational systems, some in the analytical applications of the data warehouse and marts, and some in the integrated current data residing in the operational data store (ODS). For the CSR to converse with Bob, rather than give him a cold call sales pitch, the CSR would have to have all this data at the ready, on the screen in a logical and easily accessible format. To present this type of picture means the development of a CRM technology infrastructure that fully leverages all of the enterprise's existing systems and available information assets, internal and external to the organization.

It is not possible to have a successful CRM implementation *without* the correct architecture in place to support it. The architecture must be flexible enough to accommodate ever-changing technologies, yet also be consistent and stable enough to provide a solid pathway for implementations. This architecture consists of the following components:

- **The Corporate Information Factory (CIF) roadmap.** A logical representation depicting the interaction and usage of the technological aspects of the CIF. These include a solid understanding of the roles of the data warehouse, data mart, operational data store, and meta data.

- **Administrative processes.** The processes used to update, maintain, and evolve the infrastructure as business utilization evolves.

- **Enterprise Portals (EP).** The mechanisms (many Web-based) to acquire, manage, and present customized information to the users of this environment.

A natural progression has been taking place in enterprises today as they move toward the full CIF environment. As enterprises mature in their information usage, they go through a series of predictable phases. Figure 13.1 demonstrates a typical progression where

- At first, unintegrated, chaotic operational systems are grown organically as the enterprise grows.

- The implementation of the data warehouse, data marts, and operational data store with their associated processes is a truly positive step in the evolution to an environment with a unified approach to an enterprise information infrastructure.

- Once the CIF is in place, the enterprise begins to build the final phase, the enterprise portal technology, to deliver the right amount of information to the people who need it, when they need it. This is a two-step evolution in which the first step is the development of a Toolbox and Library function, followed by the development of the Workbench. These three new components are discussed in detail in the following sections.

Chapter 9, "Business Intelligence: Technologies for Understanding Your Customers" and 10, "Facilitating Customer Touches with the Customer ODS" described the various components of the CIF in detail, and the administrative functions were described in Chapter 2, "The Customer and the Corporate Infor-

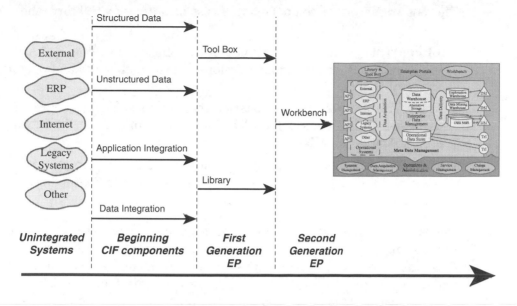

Figure 13.1 Enterprise information infrastructure maturity.

mation Factory (CIF)." This chapter will focus on the glue that knits the whole concept together, the enterprise portal technology. We begin by describing the components of a mature enterprise portal technology, and then cover the generations most enterprises go through in their evolution to the ultimate CIF architecture.

Enterprise Portals Defined

Enterprise portals are the user interface mechanisms that provide a single point of access for the enterprise user, including the publication, subscription, and notification of capabilities as well as single sign-on, query, and/or navigational interfaces into the data warehouse, data marts, and other CIF components. Essentially, enterprise portals give the user a seamless view of all of the capabilities and knowledge generated from the CIF in one easy-to-access mechanism. The key characteristic of enterprise portals is their integration of business people and processes with the capabilities and knowledge developed through the CIF. This requires a business model and nomenclature that represents the specific corporation using it—yours. The ideal situation is one in which the problems of too much or too little information, fondly known as information glut and information famine, are overcome.

The enterprise portal components consist of a Toolbox, Library, and Workbench:

Toolbox. This provides a mechanism for organizing, locating, and accessing the capabilities (the functions developed in the data marts and operational data store) of the CIF.

Library. This is a collection of materials that provides the information to effectively use and administer the CIF. This consists of technical, business, and administrative meta data.

Workbench. This consists of the technology used to automate the integration of capabilities and knowledge into the business process (marketing planning, customer care, research, and so on).

The enterprise portal can be thought of as a workshop where business capabilities (business intelligence and business management), administrative facilities (systems management, data acquisition management, services management, and enterprise data management) and knowledge (meta data, decision support results, unstructured data, problem resolution databases) are cataloged, combined, and integrated into the business processes via various workbenches. These workbenches automate the business processes and organize related capabilities to support the creation of such products as marketing plans, contact strategies, and product assessments. Chapter 11, "Automating the Sales and Service Process," gave us several examples of Workbenches, such as sales force automation and contact center coordination.

Why Enterprise Portals Are Needed

Most of us started building our CIF environments with the idea that the ultimate end products were data marts with nice front-end tools attached to them. From the success of the first mart, we began spinning out these point solution capabilities with little regard to how they fit into the over-all business processes. As a result, the interface into these capabilities and their associated meta data repositories began to resemble the well-known spider-web architecture that we see in the operational systems today (see Figure 13.2).

The users of this environment are given a confusing and complex set of tools, access methods, and pieces of knowledge that they must fit together into their process—and then remember the way they did it! Furthermore, these business people may not even know where the information came from, whether it is reliable, or understand its meaning or relevancy to their business problem. To compound the problem, they may need unstructured data (forecasts, business plans, strategic plans, e-mail messages, and so on) that may be registered in the environment but is not easily accessible or understandable.

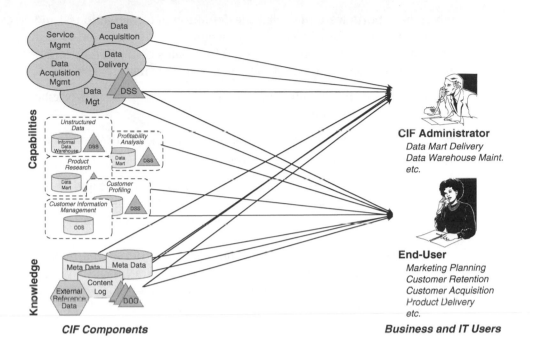

Figure 13.2 The beginning interface to the Corporate Information Factory.

A useful analogy can be made to a garage workshop. If your garage is similar to Bob's, there is little order to the location of tools and reference manuals. To perform a task such as building a bookshelf for his house requires a fair bit of organizing. First, Bob collects the reference manual (meta data), which in this case is the pamphlet he picked up at the hardware store on easy bookshelf making, and begins reading the instructions. Then he has to collect the various tools (capabilities) together by his workbench: hammer, saw, nails, wood, and measuring tape. After completion of the bookshelf, the tools and pamphlet are put back into the garage, willy-nilly. For the next project, fixing the leaking sink, the whole process starts all over again, this time using the tools and the reference books for plumbing.

This is similar to what business people face when they want to develop a new sales campaign. They too must first determine what tools they need, what meta data they need, and how to fit these into the process of developing and implementing the new campaign. They will need the capabilities we developed for them in the CIF such as access to the Campaign Analysis data mart, reports from Sales Channel Analysis and Product Profitability mart, as well as a current view of customers from the ODS. Then they will need the meta data stating when the reports were run, what the definition of a calculation is, and an explanation of the models used. If they decide to perform another process, say, developing a new demographic profile for a sales channel, they must start from scratch again, finding the tools and meta data for that process.

In contrast, a well-integrated information environment has a workshop (that is, enterprise portals) where the

- Capabilities and facilities are organized as tools into a Toolbox.
- Knowledge and meta data are organized into a Library.
- A Workbench is used to bring together the proper tools and knowledge to produce your bookshelf or fix the sink (or create the marketing plans or customer care strategies) by utilizing the Toolbox and Library.

It is this degree of integration into the business process that makes the CIF a truly strategic and integral part of the overall CRM business process. Figure 13.3 illustrates how the enterprise portal components align CIF capabilities, facilities, and knowledge to support the business community and the information technology (IT) staff.

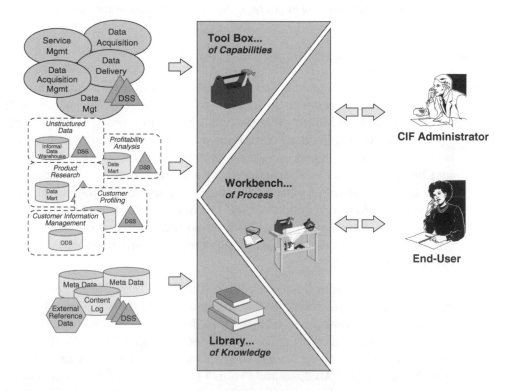

Figure 13.3 The component parts of Enterprise Portals.

Both the Library and Toolbox are available to the user or CIF administrator based upon the roles and responsibilities these individuals have either individually or as part of a specific team, project, or activity. Thus, their view of the Library and Toolbox is predetermined but customizable. Of course, the level of customization depends upon the individuals and their roles and responsibilities within their organization. Furthermore, the access to the Library and Toolbox can be considered boundless, in the sense that their access is just a different view of the same capabilities and knowledge.

The Workbench is established according to the particular business process at hand. Each Workbench is set up to perform a series of tasks defined as part of a workflow. For example, a Workbench could be created to manage campaigns or inventory, to detect and handle fraudulent claims, or to perform customer care functions. Refer to Chapter 11 for more examples of Workbenches for sales force automation and call center coordination.

Toolbox

The Toolbox provides a place to register business intelligence and business management capabilities as they evolve within the CIF. The organization of these capabilities into the Toolbox promotes reuse and so improves end-user productivity. In Bob's garage, we could simplify his search for tools by organizing them on a pegboard (with those nice white outlines of the tools to let him know which tool goes where). In the CIF, we need a form of business information directory that permits the registration of new or improved tools (applications), reports, and capabilities as they are developed. Then they are presented to the users in an easily accessible manner.

Some capabilities are common to most companies and belong in the Toolbox. The following capabilities are just a sample of these for both the business community and the CIF administrative staff supporting the environment:

Profitability analysis. This provides end users with the ability to measure customer profitability by time, location, market segment, product, demographics, and so on.

Pattern recognition. This provides end users with the ability to recognize trends in the data that may be indicative of market opportunities, fraud, and so on.

Customer view. This provides end users with access to detailed customer information. This information is generally used to support interaction with the customer and includes customer purchases, addresses, recent contact history, and other pieces of pertinent information.

Capacity planning. This provides the CIF administrator with information to determine how fast the data files are growing and when new disk space is needed to accurately determine capacity needs.

Performance tuning. This provides the CIF administrator with information on the usage of the environment (who is using the data, when they use it, how efficient the queries are) and any performance issues.

Resource management. This provides the CIF administrator with information on how the environment is being utilized and possible bottlenecks in the technology.

These tools can be organized in a similar fashion to the garage pegboard. For example, you can set up a Publish and Subscribe mechanism to distribute reports to the appropriate personnel. You can organize reports by particular capability (for example, all campaign analysis reports can be bundled under one heading in the Publish and Subscribe mechanism).

Library

The Library provides the business community and CIF administrators with valuable information that guides their use of tools and materials in the CIF. Again, in our garage, we can organize all the reference manuals and booklets into a bookshelf. For your CIF environment, you can begin by integrating business and technical meta data together. You can also collect and make available white papers on tool evaluations, strategic plans, and business cases for the CIF. Again, a mature business information directory provides the logical categorization of any informational object within a framework that is searchable and can be explored, queried, and modified as the business process or practice demands. The directory must evolve, as new and different pieces of meta data become available.

Most of this information is indigenous to the CIF (meta data or DSS results), but it may also be foreign, as in the case of a company directory or other informal information. Therefore, the directory must be able to handle both the structured data found within the classic CIF and the unstructured data such as that found in informal data warehouses (e-mails, notes, and other forms of important but unstructured data).

For example, in creating a new campaign, the Library would be used to:

- View the inventory of existing work done in this area (reports, capabilities, and results of previous campaigns).
- Assess existing data for its applicability in creating a new capability.

- Catalog new requirements, data, and capabilities.

The navigation of the library should be like surfing the Internet. The user enters a string such as "campaign analysis" and receives a list of references, reports, data marts to access, and other pieces of pertinent information on campaigns. These reference areas can be classified into the following components:

Dictionary. This provides a definition for campaign analysis. This definition includes a short and long description, an object type (data, a tool, or a report) and alias references where appropriate. It may also contain references to information outside of the dictionary (a See Also function), giving functional associations between items.

Encyclopedia. This is a compendium of business knowledge, either general or specialized, that combines all sources of meta data and content into a single repository. From here, users can gain great insight about the content of the CIF before performing any activities. The Encyclopedia is organized into several areas:

- **Data quality and metrics.** These are useful in understanding the quality of data within the CIF and the metrics used to measure it.

- **Data refreshment and use.** This is useful in understanding the currency of data in the CIF and the frequency of its use. This information will provide the business community with insights into what they should expect in their analyses (should I expect to see January billing data?) and CIF administrators with insights on how they can better tune the environment.

- **Capability requirements and use.** This is useful in helping the business community understand which business intelligence and business management capabilities are available, what they are positioned to support, and how to use them.

- **Reports.** These present published findings of previous analytical activities and observations on which to build. For example, you may want to publish key performance indicator reports, such as the fact that 20 percent of your customers generated 80 percent of your revenues last year and who made up those 20 percent.

News reports. These provide tips, techniques, and lessons learned so that everyone can work in the CIF environment more effectively. Newsletters are effective for this. In addition, this media can be used to quickly alert the CIF public about events that affect their ability to do business. For example, data quality problems or unscheduled down time can be broadcast through news flashes.

These materials contribute to the education process and promote new discoveries. As these discoveries are made, users can publish their findings through the Internet or perhaps via e-mail, thus increasing the base knowledge in the library.

Workbench

The Workbench fulfills a strategic role within the CIF architecture by presenting the library and toolbox in an easy-to-use fashion tailored to the needs of each business process (marketing planning, customer care, inventory management, or research). Again, going back to Bob's garage analogy, life would be wonderful if he only had to tell the garage that today he wanted to perform a wood working task, and presto! The garage would configure itself and present a fully functional workbench containing the right tools and the right reference materials so Bob could begin working immediately.

Then, once the task was finished, Bob could tell his virtual garage that he now wanted to perform a plumbing task. Voila! A newly configured workbench with the right plumbing tools and materials would appear.

So how might the process of delivering a product from the Workbench work in our CIF environment? The first step must be to document which business process will use the CIF capabilities and knowledge. For example, what are the steps to develop a new campaign? The marketing person may identify 20 clearly defined steps in this process, which would then be documented in the Workbench. Second, we would provide links into the relevant tools (the operational data store, one of the data marts created, or one of the operational systems) and library references. Third, we would train end users and deploy the Campaign Development Workbench. It can be that simple.

Generally, the implementation of the workbench should be uneventful, given the infrastructure is in place and the necessary tools and library references are available. The biggest challenge will be in defining the repeatable business processes and gaining the end-user commitment to follow it.

Developing Enterprise Portals

Just as with the creation of a mature Corporate Information Factory, enterprise portals should be developed in a step-wise fashion through two generations of the infrastructure. Most organizations evolve their CIF as they formalize their business processes and understand when and where the various applications and databases should be brought into play in support of these processes.

First Generation of Enterprise Portals

The first generation includes the infrastructure components needed to provide integration and the improved navigation of knowledge internal and external to the CIF: the Library. In addition, the navigation of end-user capabilities and administrator facilities are seen with the introduction of the toolbox. The enterprise portals provide for the registration of tools so that they can be quickly identified and used to support new business opportunities (see Figure 13.4). This is a critical step in the evolution of the CIF, as its usage begins to extend across the enterprise and beyond, and the strategic significance is increasingly realized.

To reach this stage of evolution, you must have a substantial business information directory (the corporate yellow pages) in place. It must be expandable to handle the new and evolving capabilities. It must be customizable in terms of the user's views to accommodate the specific needs of the individuals using this environment. Finally, it must have sufficient security measures while permitting access via multiple methods: intranet, Internet, extranet, local area networks (LANs), and wide area networks (WANs).

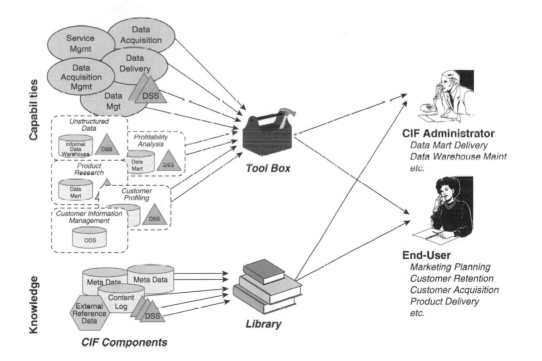

Figure 13.4   First generation of Enterprise Portals.

Second Generation of Enterprise Portals

The second generation is characterized by the strategic positioning of the various workbenches. This is accomplished when the business processes are defined and automated, and when the library and toolbox are seamlessly woven into this process via a series of workbenches (such as marketing planning and customer care). Figure 13.5 shows the logical architecture of a mature CIF environment.

Few technologies are available today that support this mature environment. Our advice is for you to look into forward-thinking companies and their portal strategies to find technologies supporting this last step. Look for companies that aspire to be portal ware vendors, providing an open business information directory solution that is independent of the content source, service component, or enterprise portal user interface. Promising technologies are XML, digital dashboards, and maturing portals.

Once you have process integration, then through strong collaboration, workflow, and knowledge management for the mass capabilities, you get process

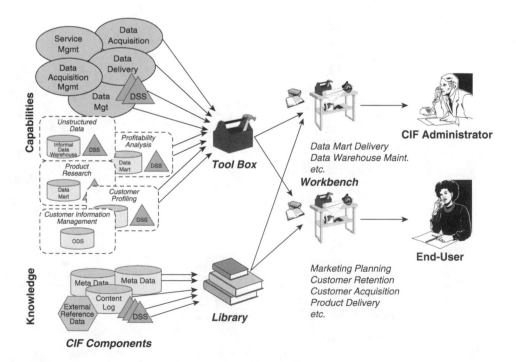

Figure 13.5 Second generation of Enterprise Portals.

automation. In the future, one could imagine the advent of intelligent agent technology that could remove the drudgery of certain tasks or act as a knowledge helper to provide your business community with context-sensitive information.

For example, your intelligent agent could contact you with the following information: "I noticed that you are interested in ABC's Web site. Do you want me to regularly monitor it for changes? Also, if they announce anything, do you want a copy of their press release and their stock price?" The enterprise portal here would not only perform the interaction, but would have all the windows you would need to act on this news open and ready for your usage, including the presentation of stock brokerage account, the stock purchase window, the stock quote window, and other pertinent information.

Clearly, the driving force behind enterprise portals is to overcome a number of some old and emerging enterprise computing and information retrieval issues. From a user perspective, the foremost value proposition is delivering the right amount of information to the right people at the right time. Enterprise portal technology is designed to overcome the overabundance of information sources that a consumer is expected to utilize during any one day.

In addition, the enterprise portal technology enables consumers to include information in their decision-making process that exists yet is inaccessible due to its infrastructure, such as the corporate intranet(s), file server(s), or client/server-based applications. Furthermore, enterprise portals empower the user, through personalization, to elect what to see and what not to see.

From an IT management perspective, these portals provide the promise of a thin client architecture that can be easily maintained. In addition, with suitable customization, the portals can be extended to meet the requirements of CRM, such as providing an environment for enhanced customer support. Again, from a maintainability standpoint, the requirement of a single point of access promotes the need for a consistent user interface, single sign-on capabilities to all applications, and accessibility from any network device. It also promotes the need for seamless integration between data, applications, and processes, and, lastly, to thwart the spread of rogue accessible intranet and Internet sites.

Enterprise portals are in the early adopter phase of the market. Today's technology is not a panacea. Many vendors have a slice of the entire picture. Furthermore, the user interface usually provides only a thin veneer over an incomplete infrastructure that may not scale or cope with the size and scope of the business's content requirements. Nevertheless, enterprise portals show great promise for the future, though they will require several generational iterations before they truly fulfill their promise.

The strength of the enterprise portal is not going to be measured solely by the glitz of the user interface. It will be measured by the extent the infrastructure underneath it delivers the value-add content and services that enable users to perform their jobs more successfully. Therefore, the role of the underlying enterprise portals is to build upon their personalization, publication, and notification mechanisms with the following capabilities:

- Access to business-level and technical enterprise meta data

- Strong security and customization linkages

- Enterprise-scale performance and platform support

- Support for multiple heterogeneous information sources, such as structured and unstructured data, as well as content repositories, such as electronic document management systems

- Application integration capabilities for enterprise applications

- A single semantically integrated corporate view, categorization, query, navigation, and personalization scheme—the corporate yellow pages taxonomy

- Sophisticated search and retrieval mechanisms

- Significant out-of-the-box content integration capabilities

- The capability to assimilate an emerging plethora of other enterprise portal solutions

Summary

For businesses to thrive, all employees must have access to the right data at the right time. Enterprise portals are the key ingredients for providing such access.

As we have seen, enterprise portals consist of three key components. The first component includes the data warehouse, data marts, operational data store, and the processes for their creation. These are the technological underpinnings of the Corporate Information Factory. The second component includes the administrative processes necessary to ensure smooth running of the technology. Enterprise portals make up the third component of the Corporate Information Factory architecture. This last part of the CIF provides the mechanism to integrate knowledge and tools into an intuitive, easy-to-use end-user and CIF administrator environment.

The components responsible for this environment are the Library and Toolbox. Building on these components, the Workbench integrates the Library and Toolbox into the business process to promote efficiency through ergonomics and repeatability. As each Workbench gets used, information is collected and circulated back through the enterprise, thus enriching its information content. Over time, this feedback loop will evolve into a knowledge fabric that enables corporations to better understand themselves and the markets they serve.

CHAPTER 14

Preserving Customer Trust — The Role of Privacy

In Chapter 1, we introduced Bob and his parents. Think about Bob's mother's reaction to the following phone call: "Hello, we understand that one of your jumbo CDs will be maturing soon, and we would like to meet with you to discuss your options." Do you think she would be pleased to get this call or not?

The answer is that it depends on who is making the call. Her bank has already established a track record of discussing investment options with her in these situations, and if her bank's investment advisor makes the call, she would be quite pleased to receive it. As a matter of fact, she expects to receive that call. But how would she feel if the call came from an independent investment advisor, one she did not know?

Receiving this call from anyone but her bank will cause her significant displeasure for several reasons. First, she has built up a relationship with her bank, likes its services, and is not looking for outsiders to replace these services. Second (and possibly more significant), the call indicates that a stranger has access to her private financial information. If she suspects that the bank provided that information, the bank's relationship with her, and with Bob, will be tainted at best and terminated at worst.

In this example, the distribution of confidential information to a third party, without the express consent of the customer, is a clear violation of the customer's trust in the organization. Let's revisit the role of trust in the Customer Life Cycle (introduced in Chapter 3, "Understanding the Customer Life Cycle").

Trust is established over time through positive interactions with an organization. These interactions take place with the extended enterprise, which is at the center of the Customer Life Cycle. Between the enterprise and the customer sits a key layer that is critical to ensuring that the customer stays in the Customer Life Cycle: trust. Trust embodies the customer's confidence in the enterprise's integrity. A customer who trusts your company is much more likely to provide you with information and to continue doing business with you than a customer who distrusts your company.

This chapter begins with a description of contemporary privacy issues and their importance within the context of CRM. Modern computing capabilities and the Internet have provided a more efficient, and potentially more threatening, way of collecting and using personal information, but the principles of privacy have been with us for decades. People do not like to provide personal information but are often willing to do so if they feel it will be beneficial for them.

After we explore the fundamental privacy issues, we examine the challenges encountered in preserving privacy and identify some of the external sources that are available to help companies maintain customer privacy and build customer trust. We then relate these issues to the enterprise's activities within the Customer Life Cycle: intrude and engage, acquire, and retain and expand.

The Importance of Protecting Privacy

According to *Webster's Unabridged Third New International Dictionary*, privacy is the "quality or state of being apart from the company or observation of others" and entails "freedom from unauthorized oversight or observation." The key word in the second part of the definition is "unauthorized." Privacy does not necessarily exclude oversight or observation, but it does require that such actions be properly authorized. Enterprises build loyalty when their customers trust them enough to give information that will enable the enterprise to provide personalized service.

The need for privacy begins with the exchange of confidential "individually identifiable information" between a customer and the enterprise, and it is not limited to e-business. Individually identifiable information includes anything that enables an organization to identify or contact an individual. Think about the last time you bought a car. If you paid cash for the car, the amount of personal information that you had to divulge was relatively small. It was limited to the information needed to legally transfer ownership of the vehicle, to register it in your name, and to prove (in some states) that you had insurance coverage. If, on the other hand, you leased the car or took out a car loan, the information required typically included data about your employment and financial worthiness (salary or assets) so that the lender could assess the risk associated with the loan. The employment and financial worthiness data are also examples of confidential individually identifiable information.

Definitions

The following are definitions of some terms that are often used in conjunction with privacy protection:

Cookie: A cookie is a block of text that is placed on a person's computer by a Web site. It is often used to recognize that person the next time he or she accesses that Web site. If the person provides individually identifiable information such as an e-mail address or credit card number at that Web site, the cookie can be linked to that information. By using the cookie, the Web site can connect previously discrete pieces of information about a person.

Harassment: Harassment is the receipt of unwanted contact or the unauthorized use of individually identifiable information by another party. Telemarketing calls, particularly if they are during dinner (aren't they always?) or to a cellular phone, are examples of harassment. In the first case, the call interrupts the customer at an inconvenient time, and in the second case, the customer may actually be charged by the cellular phone service provider for the intrusion.

Individually identifiable information: Individually identifiable information, sometimes called personally identifiable information, is any information that can be used to identify or contact a specific individual. This includes information such as the name, address, and social security number, and it can be linked to non-individually identifiable information.

Non-individually identifiable information: Non-individually (or personally) identifiable information is information about a person that is gleaned from that person's activity but that is not directly attributed to the individual. The bank knows that Bob's mother visits a teller at midday almost every Tuesday. It can use this information to initiate a call to his mother if she doesn't come in. Online bookstores may detect that a person has looked at several books on CRM and use that information to create a banner that promotes a new CRM book. (This can be done based purely on the navigation pattern, without actually knowing the customer's identity.)

Opt-in and opt-out: Opt-in is the option that provides a person with control over the collection and dissemination of his or her personal information, as well as control over the types of communications that he or she receives. With opt-in, the default assumption is that the authority is not granted. Opt-out is the option that provides a person with the ability to prevent individually identifiable information from being used by a particular enterprise or from being shared with third parties. With opt-out, the default assumption is that the authority is granted. In some states, people can place themselves on a list to be excluded from certain types of telemarketing calls. Many online merchants provide customers with the ability to opt-in or opt-out to uses of information collected about them. Opt-in and opt-out can be captured either manually (using a checkbox on a loan application, for example) or electronically (using a checkbox on a Web screen).

Privacy: Privacy is a person's right to understand how individually identifiable information about him or her is intended to be used, to have an option for permitting or prohibiting such use, and to have access and control over that information.

Privacy statement: A privacy statement is a notice, published by an enterprise, which declares its practices with respect to privacy protection.

Security: Security is the safeguarding of information so that only people authorized to access and modify it can do so.

Trust: Trust is the confidence a customer has that individually identifiable information about him or her will be appropriately secured and will only be used in an agreed upon manner by the recipient.

Why is privacy such a big issue? In his book *1984*, George Orwell wrote about Big Brother. As a society, we are still concerned about Big Brother watching us. Here are some reasons why individuals want to preserve their privacy:

People value their time. Most people do not appreciate receiving unwanted telemarketing calls, junk mail, junk faxes, or unsolicited e-mail. These are forms of harassment and are an invasion of privacy. In many cases, information about the individual is used to place that person on a list for an intrusive contact.

People don't want to be incorrectly grouped. Demographic information is often combined with individually identifiable information to include, or exclude, people in specific groups, and decisions about how the people will be treated may be based on the group in which they are placed. For example, a wealthy person may own a home in a depressed area. That person may be inappropriately grouped with others who live in that area and may be excluded from promotions and services aimed at wealthy people simply because of the mailing address. Similarly, a poor person may own a home in what has become a wealthy area. That person may be inappropriately grouped with wealthy people and receive promotions or services aimed at wealthy people, while being excluded from promotions for people sharing more appropriate characteristics.

People want to avoid embarrassment. They may do some things in private that they would not do in public. For example, many hotels that provide their guests with the opportunity to purchase a movie indicate that the name of the movie does not appear on the bill. This provides an illusion of privacy, and people may feel that their movie selection is private. In reality, the notice does *not* promise that information about the movies watched will not be divulged to third parties.

People want to prevent unauthorized use of their credit cards. Credit card information is provided for e-commerce transactions, and people are often hesitant to provide the information without proper assurances. Amazingly, most people don't hesitate to give their credit card to a waiter who disappears from sight for a few minutes. Precautions against unauthorized credit card use should not be limited to e-commerce.

People want to feel physically secure. People often go to great lengths to hide their true worth. Public knowledge of a person's wealth combined with information about their children's school could place the children in danger.

Privacy before E-Commerce

The car loan example introduced earlier demonstrates a few of the salient characteristics that are needed for an effective privacy policy, even without the introduction of electronic commerce. When the customer applies for the loan, the customer may exercise options on the information provided, may inquire about other information that will be used to evaluate the application, and may demand that use of the information be restricted to the evaluation of credit worthiness. In addition, if this is done at the car dealer, the customer gets to have eye contact with someone representing the lending institution.

The first characteristic is that the customer is in control of the information being provided. As a loan applicant, you can refuse to provide some of the information requested, recognizing that the absence of this information could jeopardize approval of your loan. We know of people who do not provide their salary on credit card applications, opting to leave it blank, and indicate "enough" or "over $25,000" (if that is the threshold above which a card would be granted). Often, the credit card or loan is granted, even without the requested information.

The second characteristic is that some of the information is obtained from other sources, with permission from the customer. The loan applicant typically must sign a consent form authorizing the lender to contact his or her employer and to obtain and use the customer's credit report. The customer also has the right to obtain a copy of the credit report.

The third characteristic is that the requested information needs to be relevant. The information requested on a car loan application should be limited to that needed for the lender to assess the loan request. The car dealer may also provide a form that requests other information, such as family size, recreational activities, and so on. This second request is not for information that is needed for the loan; it is for information to help the dealer target a future offering. The customer should have the right to provide only the information that is needed to assess the loan request.

The fourth characteristic is that the use of the information should be limited. The loan application should have a statement concerning the intended use of the information. If the customer feels that the proposed use is too broad, then he or she may attempt to modify the statement. Healthcare is another area in which there have been well-publicized abuses of privacy. Many people now read, and modify, statements concerning the intended use of medical information before submitting to medical tests or care.

The fifth characteristic is the ability to look into somebody's eyes. Even if the car dealer is not actually lending the money but is handling the loan for a third party, the customer has the opportunity to interact with a real person. With the human touch, the customer is expressing trust in that person as a representative of the lender.

The age of electronic commerce also has complicated the situation in the following ways:

- The customer may or may not be in control of the information being provided.

- The customer may or may not be aware of all of the information being provided.

- The customer may or may not have access to all of the information being provided.

- The customer may or may not be able to control how the information is used.

- The customer does not directly interact with a person.

Even though the applicant for the car loan expects that some of the information he or she provides will be placed on a computer, the human interaction and the submission of the information on paper provide a level of comfort. The reality can be different; the mere storage of the information on a computer provides a potential opportunity to breach a person's expectation that the information will be kept confidential. Any breach in this confidentiality can be very costly, and possibly fatal.

"Boca Company Sued for Giving Private Info to Killer"

This is the actual headline of the August 5, 2000, edition of the *Palm Beach Post*. The story describes how a person was able to obtain the social security number, birth date, and place of employment for a young woman with whom he was infatuated. He used this information to locate her and when he did, he killed both her and himself. The perpetrator was able to obtain the information using a few searches at an Internet site that charged him just over $200 for the service. The victim's family is suing the Internet company.

This example demonstrates that information, which we might consider confidential, is often publicly available, and that it can sometimes be used against us. In the electronic environment, the potential for combining previously discrete information about individuals increases, as does the potential for misuse of that information.

Although Congress is addressing the privacy issue, it is not illegal (as of the date of the article) to sell a person's social security number. Even though the social security number was not designed as a national identification number, it can be used to obtain a tremendous amount of information about a person.

Obviously, human interaction is missing from an e-commerce transaction in which the customer interacts only with a computer. To build the level of trust described in Chapter 3, the enterprise must replace the trust provided through the human interaction by trust generated through some other means.

Privacy with E-Commerce— Engendering Trust

To engender the trust needed to obtain information that enables a personalized online service without the human touch, companies must provide an environment in which their customers are comfortable with the way that information about them is obtained, maintained, disseminated, used, and secured. Any organization involved in electronic commerce needs to adopt, deploy, and disclose a policy to protect the privacy of confidential information. As mentioned in the previous definitions, this data is often called individually identifiable information or personally identifiable information. Adopting a privacy policy demonstrates the enterprise's understanding of the importance of privacy and its commitment to protect that privacy as described by the policy.

Enforcement

Commercial transactions are governed by a myriad of laws, and many of these pertain to the preservation of confidential information. The laws are particularly sensitive to information about children and to the widespread dissemination of medical and financial information about individuals. In many business transactions, the confidentiality is preserved through contractual terms. When this happens, the legal system merely plays a role in helping to enforce the contract.

The existing legislation cannot effectively enforce the respect of people's privacy in the Internet economy. Congress is addressing this issue and will probably continue to do so for several more years. Laws addressing some aspects of privacy protection will likely be passed, but these do not represent a comprehensive solution. One of the contemporary struggles is whether or not the e-commerce community can regulate itself.

Self-regulation is founded on the premise that the subject company plans to provide privacy protection and that it is willing to offer some type of guarantee. Participants generally consider self-regulation to be attractive because it limits the involvement of governmental agencies. Some companies belong to groups such as the Network Advertising Initiative. Membership in this organization requires that companies abide by a set of practices. Specifically, these companies agree not to use individually identifiable information about sensitive medical or financial data, information of a sexual nature, or social security numbers for online preference marketing. They also agree to provide a notice and choice on sites that collect non-individually identifiable information for online preference marketing, they provide consumers with a choice to opt-in for merging individually identifiable information with previously collected non-individually identifiable information, and they allow consumers to opt-out of providing individually identifiable information for subsequent merging in the future.

Some companies further demonstrate their commitment to enforcing their privacy policy by submitting to outside services such as TRUSTe or BBBOnLine. These services have minimum standards for the content of the privacy policy, periodically audit compliance with that policy, and provide a forum for consumers to lodge violation complaints.

A few key elements must be included in an effective self-regulated environment. Each participating company must have and follow a privacy policy that can be read by its customers, and that policy must satisfy a minimum set of criteria that may be imposed by the regulating body. The company must also be willing to permit an independent third party to monitor compliance with the stated policy, and it must provide customers with a reasonable forum for lodging and resolving complaints.

The problem with self-regulation is that the companies have the ability to discontinue adherence to the regulations. For example, Toysmart.com collected personal information, promising that it would never be shared with a third party. It subscribed to three privacy-protection seals, TRUSTe, BBB, and Certified Merchant. The company declared bankruptcy and initially considered its customer list to be a sellable asset. Existing bankruptcy laws did not address this type of asset, and varying opinions exist on the legal and ethical merits of Toysmart.com's position. The Federal Trade Commission sued Toyspart.com to protect the privacy of its customers. The basis of the suit was not the existing privacy legislation; the suit was based on Toysmart.com's violation of its privacy policy that effectively served as a contract between the company and its customers.

Developing and deploying a privacy policy is no easy task. It requires the involvement of employees throughout the company and entails a significant commitment of people and money. The required level of commitment may result in resistance. If this happens in your organization, you need to help the organization to recognize the value of the privacy policy. One of the major objectives of a privacy policy is to enhance your customer's trust in you. This helps attract customers and it also helps retain and expand their relationships.

As Figure 14.1 illustrates, the privacy policy requires the consideration of many departments, all of which need to understand the customer's perspective. Each

Figure 14.1 Privacy policy creation.

business unit with direct customer contact should participate in the development of your privacy policy. These business units typically include Sales, Marketing, Customer Service, Fulfillment, and any independent agents who sell or broker your products. Each has a unique perspective of the customers and the privacy requirements of these customers. These business units should identify the individually identifiable information that they will want to collect and use. They should also identify the importance of this information to their daily operations, because the collection and use of individually identifiable information may impact the complexity of the privacy policy.

The Human Resources Department needs to ensure that internal training and education programs are established to make sure people are aware of the policy and their role in executing it. The Human Resources Department also provides information about legal issues surrounding individually identifiable information. The Information Technology (IT) Department needs to plan and subsequently implement the technical architecture that will ensure the collection and use of the customer information. It should also help to ensure compliance with the privacy policy. The Legal Department needs to ensure that the privacy policy, as a public document, complies with all regulations and is properly worded. The Internal Auditing Department needs to ensure that the company can, and does, monitor compliance with the policy.

The development and implementation of a privacy policy should be approached as a project. Due to the resources and costs involved, people may resist creating such a policy. The project should have a business sponsor who can articulate the associated business benefits and who can muster the appropriate support and resources. Once the project is started, it should migrate through the typical phases of planning, analysis, design, construction, and deployment. The planning phase may result in a multi-phased approach so that something can be implemented quickly. Once the policy and the associated technology are implemented, both the policy and the technical components must be maintained. Companies should constantly review privacy policy guidelines issued by organizations such as the Online Privacy Alliance, the Network Advertising Initiative, TRUSTe, or BBBOnLine® to ensure that their policies do not become obsolete.

Privacy Policy Components

An effective privacy policy must be visible and clear. People completing a loan application at a car dealer should be able to obtain a copy of the company's privacy policy. Similarly, people logging onto a Web site should be able to immediately access the privacy policy. Because some Web sites create cookies, the

Privacy Protection Web Sites

The following is a listing of some Web sites that provide information related to privacy protection.

Americans for Computer Privacy:	www.computerprivacy.org
BBBOnLine®:	www.bbbonline.org
CPA WebTrust:	www.cpawebtrust.org
Direct Marketing Association, Inc.:	www.the-dma.org
Electronic Privacy Information Center:	www.epic.org
Federal Trade Commission:	www.ftc.gov
Individual Reference Services Group:	www.irsg.org
Network Advertising Initiative:	www.networkadvertising.org
Online Privacy Alliance:	www.privacyalliance.org
The Consumer Information Organization:	www.consumer.net
TRUSTe:	www.truste.org
U.S. Internet Industry Association:	www.usiia.org
Webwatchdog:	www.webwatchdog.com

consumer may want immediate assurances before doing any exploration on the Web site. The policy itself must be written in a way that the average consumer can understand. It should delineate the actual policy in plain language and should explain why certain approaches are being adopted. It should describe what information is collected, how it is collected, how it will be used, who is collecting the information, who is receiving the information, how the information is kept secure, how the accuracy of the information is assured, how the information can be corrected, and how the customer can complain and seek resolution of perceived violations. It is important to note that these attributes of the privacy policy are not dependent on the sales or service channel. They apply to face-to-face interactions, telephone calls, and e-commerce equally.

Information Collected

The privacy policy must clearly describe the type of information that is being collected about an individual. In traditional business transactions, the customer provides the information being collected and authorizes the collection of other information. The casual Web site user may feel very secure that things have not changed. It is the duty of the Web site hosting company to divulge information about other data that may be collected.

For example, if the Web site places a cookie on the user's computer, it is in a position to collect information about the person's migration through the Web site. In addition, the company can sometimes collect information about the Internet service provider (ISP) and the Internet protocol (IP) address of the user. The customer has the right to know what information is being collected about him or her. Amazon.com uses cookies to identify the person when they log in. The company is also aware of the customer's book purchases. This helps the company tailor the Web page based on that customer's preferences. Amazon.com's use of this information enhances customer loyalty and trust.

Problems arise, however, when information like this is abused. Imagine surfing the Web about information relating to a medical condition. You might not want others to know about your research, particularly if it is about a disease that you would like to keep confidential. With today's technology, however, you can be identified as the person doing the research, and without privacy protection, your employer and other acquaintances could be notified.

With caller-ID, for example, some information about you may immediately be available to the call recipient. Although technologically different than the cookie, this also represents information collected about you that you do not directly provide. Caller-ID provides the call recipient with your identity. One example of using this information to serve you better is the way new credit cards are sometimes activated. If you make the activation call from the phone number in your profile, the phone number is used to help validate you. If you use a different phone number, additional validation steps are often required.

The caller-ID is also used by call centers to improve customer service. The customer service representative may have your profile displayed on his or her computer screen simply by accepting the incoming call. Like the cookie, if the customer provides permission to use this piece of data, the opportunity exists to improve service.

Because technology enables companies to collect a tremendous amount of information about a customer, it is sometimes advisable to explicitly state what is not being collected. One particular area of sensitivity in e-commerce is the use of cookies. If a company does not use cookies, then it should explicitly state this in its privacy policy to further build the customer's confidence and trust in the company. For example, the Federal Trade Commission Privacy Policy specifically states that it does not use cookies.

Privacy issues about information collected go beyond that which is obtained directly from the customer or from that customer's activity. Once a customer is uniquely identified, companies have an opportunity to combine that information with other information it has about that customer. The additional information may be obtained internally, such as through a customer's transactions with the company, or it may be purchased externally, through services such as Dun & Bradstreet. Customers need to know what information is being collected about them directly; they also need to know what information is being combined to provide a more comprehensive view of their profiles and behaviors.

Amazon.com's privacy policy begins with a statement about the company's commitment to protecting the customer's privacy. It further explains that the reason for collecting personal information is to provide "a more personalized shopping experience." Over half of Amazon.com's privacy policy is devoted to explaining the type of information that is being collected, why it is being collected, and how it is being used. From a customer perspective, the opening remarks start to remove the barrier to providing information. Customers are generally willing to provide confidential information if they feel that it will help a vendor serve them better. Describing the information collected, the reasons for collecting it, and the way that it will be used further assure the customer that it is in his or her interest to provide individually identifiable information.

Information Collectors and Users

Your privacy policy is designed to bolster a customer's trust in your company. Just because you gain that customer's trust does not mean that the customer trusts all of your partners. The next area that needs to be addressed by the privacy policy is who. Relating this to the Customer Life Cycle, the question to ask is which other members of the extended enterprise are involved in collecting and using the customer data. If others are involved, then we must convey the reasons that we share individually identifiable information with them, and we should provide the customer with a choice on participation. (Choices are described in a following section.)

Introducing a third party into the privacy equation brings with it some complications. From our perspective as the supplier, we need to be careful about the information we share because it may lessen our competitive advantage. From the customer's perspective, we need to ensure that the customer has the same level of trust in the extended enterprise as he has in our company. At a minimum, if the information being shared might be considered confidential by the customer, we need to provide the customer with confidence that the third party is obligated to protect the customer's privacy. We are asking the customer to trust our judgment and to have confidence in our ability to properly negotiate and enforce agreements that protect privacy. Airline frequent flier programs, such as US Airways', provide good examples of the need to share customer information across partners and affiliates. US Airways' privacy policy actively discloses its practices with respect to third parties. It declares that the company does not "sell, trade, or rent personally identifiable information to others, except as outlined in the Dividend Miles program," and that members of that program may request to be removed from partner mailings. It further explains that it sometimes needs to divulge information to third parties to process the travel services request. It also indicates that it requires contractual obligations from third parties to safeguard the information they process for US Airways and that use of that information is strictly for the purposes of providing the required service. This policy demonstrates US Airways' commitment to protecting its customers' privacy and its recognition that this commitment needs to ensure that all third parties also protect that privacy.

Information Use

Information use is the reason that a customer is willing to provide individually identifiable information. The customer's hope is that the information will be used to improve the level of service. If the customer does not perceive that the information will be used to improve the level of service, he or she may not be willing to provide the information or to permit its collection on his or her behalf.

As a frequent flier, we have several ways we can purchase an airline ticket. We can go to a ticket counter, we can call the airline (or travel agency), or we can visit the airline (or travel agency's) Web site. When we deal directly with the airline, one of the first pieces of information we provide is our frequent flier number. This number provides the agent or Web site with information about us, such as our name, address, and seating preference. Remember, this is information we willingly provided to the airline. It also provides information about our status as a frequent flier. Also remember that when we signed up for the frequent flier program, we gave the airline permission to keep track of our flights. Regardless of the channel we use, the airline is in a position to better meet our needs because (1) it knows more about us and (2) it understands our value as a customer.

Amazon.com is very clear about its use of each type of information. Its policy explains, for example, that it needs a customer's name, e-mail address, mailing address, credit card number, and expiration date to be able to process and fulfill an order. The e-mail address is used to notify the customer of the order status. Few can argue with the necessity of this information. It also explains that the customer's traffic patterns through its Web site are used to personalize the shopping experience. Again, the customer is aware of the information being collected and how it is being used to improve service.

The length of time that information may be retained is also of interest to some customers. Customers may be willing to provide information for use in a particular transaction but may not be willing to have that information permanently stored. If information is only needed for a transaction, then alerting the customer to the retention policy may further the trust the customer has in your company.

Customer Choice

Some information is critical to a transaction, while other information is not. For example, if a customer wants to make a purchase online or by phone, a credit card number and expiration date must be provided. In a store, the customer physically provides the card. Although the customer may not need to divulge an e-mail address, the e-mail address may be requested to enable the company to provide a notification of the status of the order. If the customer does not want the notification, there should be an option to leave off the e-mail address. When a customer provides an e-mail address, he or she is opting-in; he or she is exercising an option and deciding to provide the information.

The e-mail address can also be used to send other notices to the customer, and the customer may not be interested in receiving these notices. Ideally, the customer should be provided with the ability to opt-in to each grouping of information for use or distribution. At a minimum, customers should be provided with the ability to opt-out of a particular use or distribution of the information provided. In our example of the request for an e-mail address, the customer could indicate that the only authorized use of the e-mail address is for notification of the order status.

The introduction of third parties, as described earlier, emphasizes the importance of customer choice. Customers should be able to limit the dissemination of their individually identifiable information to third parties that they trust, and for uses that they feel are to their advantage. Further, they should be able to limit third-party use of their information, even if the third party does not actually receive it. For example, an airline may have an alliance with a long distance telephone company and may want to help that company promote an offering. The airline has three fundamental choices: it can provide the telephone company with its frequent flier membership list, it can mail the promotional material without providing the list, or it can decide that its customers prefer not to receive the promotional literature. Its decision is extremely important because it impacts the customers' level of trust. The privacy policy should indicate how the information about the customer is being used, and it should provide the customer with the ability to opt-out of specific uses.

The privacy policy for Delta Airlines is a good example of a company that is providing its customers with an opt-out ability. This privacy policy indicates that Delta shares information with its SkyMiles partners to provide the product, service, and promotional materials the customer requests. Delta provides customers with a choice to opt-out of receiving the materials from the SkyMiles® partners. It further provides information to help customers avoid sharing personal information with Delta and to elect to refuse cookies. In this case, Delta is providing its customers with choices concerning both the collection and use of individually identifiable information, as well as the distribution of that information to third parties.

Providing choices to the customer makes execution of the privacy policy substantially more complex. It also improves the customer's trust in your company and promotes the recognition that your company is genuinely interested in protecting the right to privacy.

Ownership

Ownership of the customer's data is another area of sensitivity. When a customer makes an online purchase, the customer willingly provides the seller with information. Further, the transaction itself consists of mutually provided information. Regulations do not grant the customer ownership and, more importantly, exclusive ownership of the transaction information. If the seller is interested in building a long-term relationship with the customer, however, the seller may want to enable the customer to retain some level of control about how the information is used. For example, the seller may permit the customer to dictate whether or not the transaction can be made public knowledge.

Access and Quality Control

Customer data sometimes contains errors. These errors may be introduced by the customer (due to mistyping some of the information), by a third party, or by the company itself. Customers want the ability to ensure that information about them is accurate. Not only does information accuracy impact service levels, but to the extent that it is shared with third parties, the inaccurate information can have unpredictable consequences. Each of the airline privacy policies previously cited provides the customer with the ability to both access and update profile information.

Chapter 10, "Facilitating Customer Touches with the Customer ODS," describes the operational data store (ODS). This database can provide a means for consolidating and correcting the customer information. An ODS can enable a customer to initiate transactions that immediately update the critical information and can quickly make that information available to Customer Service Representatives and systems that support transactions with the customer.

Security

Even if the customer trusts your company with private information, he may not be confident of your ability to guard that information. This aspect of the privacy policy goes beyond a company's use of the information. It demonstrates the company's willingness and ability to implement safeguards that prevent access to the private information by unauthorized parties both inside and outside the company. Three critical elements must be considered here: physical security, procedures and education, and data distribution.

The physical security of the data entails safeguards such as user authentication and identification, firewalls, encryption, and computer room access restrictions that a company undertakes to guard its electronic data. These types of protection are not unique to CRM-related data. Companies with sophisticated computer systems, and particularly those that permit access by outside parties such as customers and suppliers, must implement very stringent physical security measures.

It's not enough to have physical safeguards. The best these safeguards can do is prevent unauthorized parties from viewing or changing the data. They provide limited protection against misuse by authorized parties such as employees. All employees must become familiar with the company's privacy policy and the company must make it clear that this policy is taken seriously. Employees must understand why the privacy policy is being implemented and the consequences to the company, and to the employee, of violating the policy and related procedures. Another aspect of the education program relates to data distribution. The education program must include information on how to safeguard individual computers that contain individually identifiable information.

Data distribution is another security exposure. Customer data is sometimes loaded onto individuals' computers, and people then travel with these computers. Companies must ensure that their security provisions address the loss or theft of computers with private or confidential information.

Privacy and the Customer Life Cycle

The Customer Life Cycle helps you view things from both the organization's perspective and the customer's perspective (see Figure 14.2). The customer enters the life cycle with a need and an awareness of your potential capability to satisfy that need. Your job during that point in the cycle is to draw the customer's attention (intrude) and begin a dialog with the customer (engage). The customer then learns more about your product or service, and considers and evaluates this (and potentially others) until the customer moment in which the

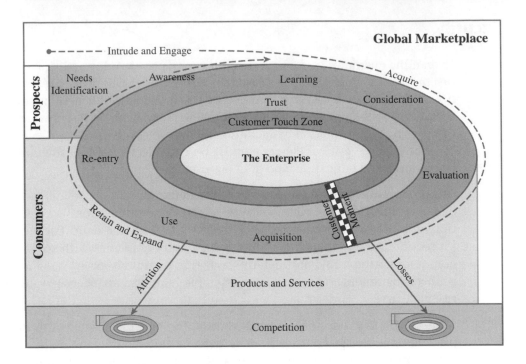

Figure 14.2 The Customer Life Cycle.

customer selects your product. Your job during this stage of the cycle is to acquire this customer. The customer then acquires and uses your product, and, you hope, re-enters the Customer Life Cycle. Product acquisition and use are where you perform the activities to retain and expand the relationship you have with the customer.

The way in which you handle individually identifiable information and the customer's perception of your privacy protection practices can significantly impact the customer's trust during each of the Customer Life Cycle stages.

Building Trust during Intrude and Engage

Our first contact with a customer—actually it's with a prospect that we hope will become a customer—occurs when the customer is identifying needs and becoming aware of options for satisfying these needs. This is our first opportunity to build trust; we will never again have another first opportunity. At this point, the customer has not directly provided us with any information. If we have information about the customer, we need to be very careful how we use it.

Think about the call Bob's mother received from the independent investment advisor. This call qualifies as an intrusion. That investment advisor was not an agent for a company with which Bob's mother did business. During the intrusion, the investment advisor alerted Bob's mother to his access to individually identifiable information about her. He knew that she owned a jumbo CD and that it was about to expire. By divulging his awareness of her financial situation, the investment advisor ruined any chance he had of building a trusting relationship and also ruined the trusting relationship she had previously enjoyed with the bank.

During the intrusion activities, companies must be careful with their use of individually identifiable information. Some of this information is publicly available. For example, information about mortgage loans and automobile purchases are often easily obtainable. This information can be used to develop a marketing campaign. In carving out the campaign steps, the company needs to determine the customer's potential reaction to the company's possession of this information. As an example, companies selling extended warranties often contact new car owners. The contact may take one of two forms:

- The company may send a general brochure to all new car owners. This approach is non-threatening, and does not divulge the detailed information that the company may have obtained.

- The company may send a personalized letter congratulating the customer as the new owner of a specific car model. This approach divulges that the company has some individually identifiable information, and it knows which car the customer purchased.

To determine the chosen approach, the company must project the effectiveness of each of these approaches. It must also project the potential ramifications to their customer relationships, if these customers realize that the company knows and uses information about the recent car purchase.

Once we have engaged the prospect, we have an opportunity to begin a dialog with that prospect. Our objective at this point is to increase the prospect's awareness of us and to bring the prospect into the Customer Life Cycle. We have entered the realm of permission marketing, introduced in Chapter 12, "Interacting with Customers Online." We want to have a role in helping the customer identify his or her needs. Our aim here is to learn more and more about the prospect so that we can target our offering and its presentation to the prospect's needs.

We also strive to continuously increase our prospect's confidence and trust in our company. We build this confidence and trust by appropriately using the information that the prospect provides us. We need to demonstrate our commitment to protecting the prospect's privacy. Posting the privacy policy is an important first step, but the prospect must also feel that we actually follow that policy. We need to be careful to ensure that all of the contacts the prospect receives from us or from third parties are consistent with the policy statements with respect to the use and dissemination of the prospect's information. If we fail to gain the prospect's trust, our chances of achieving the conversion from a prospect to a lasting customer are diminished.

Building Trust during Acquire

"Acquire" is the set of business processes leading up to the Customer Moment in which the customer makes a decision concerning the acquisition of our product or service. During the customer's first time through the cycle, we are just starting to build our relationship. During acquire, we continue the efforts we initiated during intrude and engage to maintain the dialog and further build the customer's trust. As in the previous stage, we need to be vigilant in our practices to ensure compliance with our privacy policy while we are helping the customer move through the stages of learning, consideration, and evaluation.

During the learning phase, the customer is getting specific information about our products and services and about our company. Our ability to preserve his privacy is often included in this learning experience. For some customers, this is the first exposure to our company. They may be contacting us directly without our having brought them through the intrude and engage stage. If the customer first becomes known to us during the acquire stage, we need to ensure that our dialog with that customer brings the customer to the appropriate level of awareness about our company and about our commitment to protect customer privacy, as part of the customer's learning experience.

As the customer moves into the consideration phase, he or she is solidifying his or her image of our brand and of our company. Emotions still play an active role here. Our company has not yet succeeded in being selected as a viable contender. We're just one of potentially many companies that the customer is considering. Our challenge during this phase is to strengthen our branding and to differentiate ourselves from the competition. We need to demonstrate that we truly use the information we have to provide them with a better level of service.

When the customer moves into evaluation, he is seriously considering our offering. We may be competing with others or we may be the only company being considered. If a request for proposal is involved, we have the opportunity to demonstrate that we can pull information from all sources—public records, customer's dialog with us, and third-party databases—to provide an offering tailored to that customer. We need to use the information the customer has opted-in (or at least not opted-out) for us to have to tailor the proposal. In this manner, we have an opportunity to further build the customer's trust in our ability both to deliver the offering that best meets the customer's needs and to protect the customer's privacy.

Building Trust during Retain and Expand

Once the customer has acquired his or her first product from us, any future business may be ours to lose versus ours to win. Bob's mother, due to her trusting relationship with the bank, isn't looking anywhere else. However, if she traces the investment advisor's information to the bank, she may very well start looking elsewhere.

The customer's activities during this stage are acquisition, use, and (we hope) re-entry. Our main challenge is to be sure that we deliver on our promises. The retain and expand stage is where we have the greatest exposure and also have the greatest potential payoff. We're in! If we want to build customer loyalty, we must be very careful to keep our promises about how we use the information we have about the customer. At this point, we're changing our attention from market share to wallet share. Having earned the customer's trust, we need to use the information we have to delivery consistently superior experiences so that they will continuously expand the business they are doing with us. A fine line exists between good customer service and customer stalking or harassment. As we get closer to the customer, we increase our potential for distinguishing the service we provide, but we also increase the potential for the customer to resent our contacts.

One of our peers recently received a call from his cellular phone company. The phone company was alerting him to the availability of a plan that it felt better met his needs. The company used individually identifiable information to draw its conclusion. Our peer did not object to this use of the information for the following reasons: (1) the company was using information directly derived from his business transactions with it, (2) the offer reflected a reasonable analysis of that information, and (3) the offer was designed to provide him with the same level of service at a lower cost. This is a good example of using the information to retain and expand the relationship.

Privacy and the Corporate Information Factory

The Corporate Information Factory (see Figure 14.3) was first introduced in Chapter 2, "The Customer and the Corporate Information Factory (CIF)." The architecture of the CIF enhances our ability to implement our privacy policy.

The operational systems provide the initial source of customer information. If these systems already exist, we may have little control over them. If we are building new ones, then we need to incorporate business rules that are consistent with our privacy policy. For example, if our policy tells our customers that we will not retain the credit card number that they provide us for a transaction, the operational system must include logic to remove the credit card number when it is no longer needed to ensure payment.

The data acquisition process captures, cleanses, transforms, integrates, and loads data from the source systems into the data warehouse or operational data store. Here, too, we need to ensure that the logic is consistent with the privacy

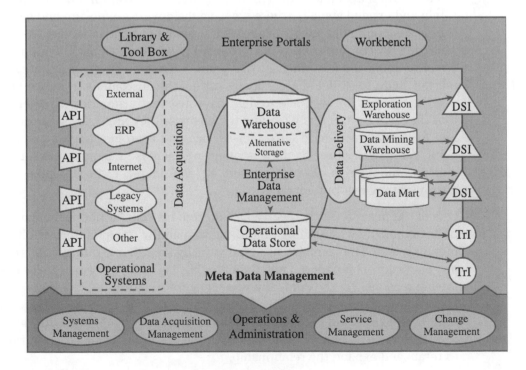

Figure 14.3 The Corporate Information Factory.

policy. For example, during data acquisition, we may merge our data with third-party data. If our privacy policy restricts this action in any way, then we must reflect those restrictions in the processing logic.

The data warehouse stores historical data. Again, our privacy policy may promise customers that we will delete certain data after a year. If this is the case, then the data warehouse needs to be constructed such that the data can be removed. Depending on the policy language, it may be permissible for us to retain summaries built on the data being removed.

The operational data store provides a great vehicle for ensuring the accuracy of the customer data in real time. By providing the customer access to the stored data and enabling him or her to generate transactions that update the operational data store through the transactional interface, we can make good on our promise of providing the customer with access and control over the data. If the customer is directly accessing the operational data store, we need to be sure that our security measures are such that (1) the customer can only access and update that customer's data, and (2) the customer cannot jeopardize the stability and integrity of our databases in any way.

The databases for the operational data store and data warehouse are managed in the enterprise data management layer. The creation of data mart subcomponents is of particular interest for privacy protection. One way of restricting the dissemination and use of selected information is to provide that information only through data marts, and to restrict the data marts only to parties authorized to have that information.

The enterprise data management layer manages the conforming dimensions. The objective of conforming dimensions is to provide a single source of data for data mart dimensions that are used in multiple data marts. The customer dimension may contain individually identifiable information. Rather than having a single conforming dimension with data about all customers, the enterprise data management layer could establish a master conforming dimension so that all data marts have consistent data, with filters applied in the data delivery process to restrict the data available in any single data mart to that which its users are authorized to access.

The data marts may contain either granular or aggregated information. When they contain only aggregated information, they do not present a privacy threat; when they contain granular data, they do present a privacy threat. (Protection for aggregated data may also be needed, but this is not a privacy issue.) This threat is compounded by the potential for the data mart, or an extract from a data mart, to be loaded onto a person's lap-top computer. Once on that computer, all the sophisticated protection provided within the company's facilities vanishes. As discussed in the security section, when data that is protected by the privacy policy is loaded onto lap-top computers, the software to protect it must be applied, and people must be educated on how to protect it.

The meta data layer is a great place to capture the business rules needed to carry out the privacy policy. For each data element, information about its confidentiality and protection can be captured in the meta data. This provides a convenient source of information about the privacy restrictions. Business users can access the meta data to understand the privacy restrictions. To understand how the meta data can be used to help deploy the privacy policy, let's examine a portion of the data model governing meta data.

Meta data management is actually a business activity. It is supported by a system for capturing, managing, and disseminating the meta data and a repository that contains the meta data. The repository itself is a database and should therefore be based on a business data model that identifies and defines each of the meta data entities and attributes. (Refer to Chapter 6, "Developing an Integrated CRM Technology Environment," for a more complete description of a business data model.)

In his book, *Building and Managing the Meta Data Repository* (John Wiley & Sons, 2000), David Marco provides a sample data model for the repository. Figure 14.4 identifies entities that support the deployment of the privacy policy and the attributes that should be added specifically for that purpose.

The new entities introduced in Figure 14.4 are Party Use Restriction Group and Use Restriction. New attributes are added to Attribute.

Party Use Restriction Group: This group is a set of parties (such as prospect, customer, and consumer) that shares a set of restrictions about the use of information concerning them. Examples of groups are children, elderly, and physically disabled.

Use Restriction: Use restriction is a standard set of constraints on the use of data collected at the attribute level. Examples of use restrictions include "may be used only to support billing activities," "no restrictions," and specific uses from which the data provider opts-out. The recursive relationship in the model indicates that a standard use restriction may consist of a grouping of other standard use descriptions.

Attribute: An attribute is a specific piece of information about an entity. For each attribute, two use restriction codes can be captured. One code is the default code. For example, if the attribute is annual salary, the default use restriction may be "use only for market segmentation." The second code provides the ability to override the default use restriction based on a party's participation in a party use restriction group. For example, if the attribute is address, the default use restriction may be "no restriction on use," but spe-

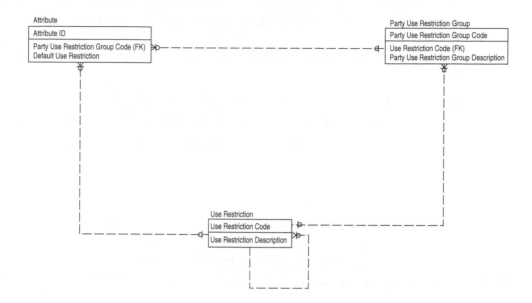

Figure 14.4   Privacy meta data.

cific parties may request that the address not be provided to any external company.

If this portion of the model is populated, then the enterprise has generic information about the use restrictions for each data element. This meta data can help it determine the information that can be used for each purpose. If an enterprise desires to keep information about use restrictions at the individual customer level, then it may be appropriate to add attributes to the data model for the operational data store.

Summary

CRM is built on trust. As we move customers through the Customer Life Cycle, we use that trust to strengthen the relationship and the customer's loyalty.

Privacy protection is no more an option now than it was 50 years ago; it's a necessity. Companies need to recognize the electronic age has brought with it improved ways of meeting the customer needs, and along with that, it has expanded the exposure to information use abuse. Customers are very concerned about this. As a supplier, you have a responsibility to protect your customers. The Corporate Information Factory provides a strong foundation for the infrastructure needed to protect privacy. Another key step in that protection is the establishment of a privacy policy that encompasses the following key areas:

- A description of information being collected and its use
- An identification of all parties who contribute or use that information
- Choices for the customer to opt-in or opt-out of specific information uses
- Customer control over the quality of the information
- Security

A policy encompassing these elements is a differentiating factor among some companies today. In the future, such a policy may become an entry ticket, something companies must have to even be considered as viable contenders. To succeed in any marketplace, companies must demonstrate that they value the relationships with their customers, that they only collect individually identifiable information that is relevant to providing personalized service, that they have and follow a clear privacy policy, and that information is used in a manner consistent with the principles of permission marketing. This is but one of the areas that is evolving in the world of CRM. Chapter 15, "The Future of CRM," explores the future of CRM and what companies must do to prepare for it.

CHAPTER 15

The Future of CRM

The title of the chapter presumes that CRM has a future. As you will see in this chapter, CRM as we know it today may not be viewed in the same light a few years from now. Consider the following scenario:

Bob and his wife are skiing in the Swiss Alps when Bob's watch (actually it's a wireless device with many capabilities including timekeeping) alerts him that he has a message. He looks at the watch face and sees that the message, which is from his bank, pertains to vacation plans. Bob has opted-in to such communication by giving his bank permission to contact him through his wireless watch for this and other selected alerts. He pushes a button and a friendly voice speaks to him. "Bob, we hope that you are enjoying your skiing trip. We have two important pieces of information for you. The new ski resort in Saas-Fee just opened and the surrounding ski slopes are suitable for both you and your wife. We have confirmed that a room in the chalet is available and can adjust your reservations if you wish. We recently acquired an interest in that chalet, and as a valued bank customer, we can provide you with a 50 percent discount. Would you like to take advantage of this opportunity?" Bob thinks for a few moments and orally responds "Please extend my trip by three days and make the arrangements."

He then says "next" to receive the second message. "Bob, your sister-in-law just booked a trip with us based on your recommendation and requested that we let you know that she and her husband will be vacationing 100 kilometers from your location in two days. We appreciate your confidence in our services and assure you that we won't let you or them down. We know of a fine restaurant midway between your two locations. Would you like us to make dinner reservations so you can all get together?" Again, Bob responds affirmatively, and also requests that the bank arrange for the dinner tab to be directly debited from his account so that he won't have to argue about who picks up the check.

Fifteen minutes go by and Bob receives another alert. "Bob, your chalet reservations and travel changes have been made, and your sister-in-law and her husband will be meeting you at the restaurant on Friday at 7:30 p.m. Your favorite wine will be at the table waiting for you and directions have been faxed to your hotel. There's also some movement on conglomerate.com, and we've executed the order you left with us to buy 1,000 shares. We'll send the usual flower arrangement to your parents tomorrow for their anniversary." Bob smiles and starts down the next slope.

Back at home, Bob's mother receives a call from the bank. She generally comes to the branch on Tuesday mornings but didn't show up Tuesday or Wednesday. After verifying that she had money to deposit and wasn't feeling well, the representative offered to pick up the funds and make the deposit for her. When he visited her home, he also brought brochures for summer cruises.

Taken individually, each of the interactions initiated by the bank are not too amazing. The remarkable aspect of this scenario is that the bank is engaged in all of these relationships with Bob. Further, based on the bank's understanding of Bob's and other customers' needs, it has expanded into other service lines that provide benefits to its customers and profit to the bank. In this scenario, we see that Bob's bank has expanded into other lines of business but still also manages his financial affairs. Further, the bank is serving as a focal point for businesses it doesn't own. The bank owns some travel lodges and is serving as the intermediary with a restaurant and florist. It also expanded its definition of Bob's household to include his sister-in-law, and even knows that Bob would like to have her join him on his vacation. (We discussed the importance of recognizing the expanded household in Chapter 1, "The Customer Becomes the Center of the Business Universe.") The bank is managing the relationship with Bob and knows quite a bit about him. It is respecting preferences established by both Bob and his parents and only alerts them to services for which they have opted-in, doing so in the manner they have prescribed, consistent with the privacy preservation practices we discussed in Chapter 14, "Preserving Customer Trust—The Role of Privacy." (Bob receives notices through his wireless watch, and his parents receive a phone call.) These are all activities that fit into the retain and expand section of the Customer Life Cycle. The extended enterprise (the bank and its affiliates) has encompassed more and more of the services that are important to Bob, and Bob need not be aware of the ownership of each of the participants.

We open the chapter with the current definition of CRM and describe how it will evolve. In our research, we found companies that excel at portions of the definition of CRM, but we had difficulty in identifying companies that excel in all aspects of CRM: business strategy alignment, organization structure and culture, and customer information and technology in support of mutually beneficial customer relationships. The successful CRM organization in the future will accomplish all aspects of this definition. The thrust of our initial definition remains constant; we must adapt our business strategy, organization structure and culture, and customer information technology (IT) to benefit both our customers and us. However, as we move into the future, the customer will be demanding greater and greater control over the relationship with our enterprise.

We then describe the characteristics of the successful CRM organization in the future. Attaining this future state is no easy job, and the challenges facing companies today are described in the next section, along with the actions these companies need to take. These sections bring together concepts introduced earlier in the book, based on what leaders in the field told us would be important for future success. It won't be enough to address just one or two of these; all the challenges must be addressed. We close the chapter with a discussion of the business imperatives facing modern corporations as they strive to better serve their customers.

The Evolving CRM Definition

As we look to the future, it's important to recognize our starting point. The definition of Customer Relationship Management that we provided in Chapter 1 is "aligning business strategy, organization structure and culture, and customer information and technology so that all customer interactions can be conducted to the long term satisfaction of the customer and to the benefit and profit of the organization."

The sidebar contains thoughts on what CRM means to a select group of key business and technology leaders. Most of these definitions of CRM are similar to the one presented in Chapter 1. They recognize the need to include a cross-functional view and to address the organizational structure and culture and the technology in establishing business strategy. They further recognize the importance of understanding more than just our transactions with the customer. The following two definitions reinforce these thoughts about the need to integrate strategy, organization, culture, and information technology, but they also suggest a shift in focus. These definitions emphasize that customer control is a natural outcome of the integration of all of the CRM pieces and an extension of the provisions for customer choice, permission marketing, and personalization:

- CRM is actually misnamed. It should be called CMR: Customer Managed Relationships. As we move forward, the customers will have more and more control over the relationships that they have with the company. The company still has a role—it must perform next-purchase analysis to help customers identify needs, and it must provide the interaction options demanded by the customers.

- CRM is the process of getting closer to the customer through a broad spectrum application of business processes and technology, with the customer having an increasing role in driving the business direction.

As we move into the future, the objectives embodied by the words in these definitions, and those illustrated in the sidebar will remain intact, but the focus of the enterprise's effort may shift to reflect an important change in control from the enterprise to the customer. CRM plans and actions must recognize this shift; the customer will be assuming a greater role in managing the relationship with the enterprise, and we must be well positioned to adjust our actions to address each customer's relationship need. The successful organization of the future will adjust its business strategy to reflect the customer's needs not just in terms of products, but also in terms of the customer requests. The organizational structure and culture cannot create a barrier to providing each profitable customer with the type of relationship that customer is demanding. Further, the information technology infrastructure needs to support whatever communication channel the customer wants: wireless, Internet, phone, e-mail, letter, or personal visit.

Variations on the Meaning of CRM

During our research on the future direction of leading CRM organizations, we asked key business and technology leaders for their definition. The comments we received represent variations of the definition we provided in Chapter 1, but all are consistent with the primary thrust of that definition. A representative set of these definitions is summarized in the following list:

- CRM is the set of systems, processes, and organizations that profitably drive customer loyalty.
- CRM is the strategic view that integrates how we want the business to relate to the customers, specifically seen through technologies available to support that view and make it come alive by integrating people, processes, culture, attitude, and so on.
- CRM is the management of the relationship so that the partnership with the customer grows, flourishes, and remains healthy over time.
- CRM is building customer loyalty, not merely relationship management, using a 360-degree view of the customer.
- CRM is the set of business processes and practices that directly addresses the relationships between key customers and the principal organization.
- CRM is the 360-degree view of the customers and their transactional activity with the company.

The Customer Life Cycle first introduced in Chapter 3, "Understanding the Customer Life Cycle," will continue to be important. Control, however, will shift to the wide band of customer activities. As the customer considers alternative options, greater demands will be placed on our organizations about the information needed and the way that the information must be provided. When the customer is acquiring the product, the customer will require greater control over the acquisition and delivery process. And when the customer is using the product, a variety of options for service and communications will be required.

Successful CRM Organizations of the Future

Throughout this book, we have pointed out actions that are needed for an effective CRM environment. The successful CRM organization of the future will have taken these actions so that it can realize the characteristics that follow. The most successful organizations will share all of these characteristics:

- The enterprise leader will have a consolidated 360-degree view of the customer, the customer's interactions with the enterprise, and the customer's relevant interactions with other customers.

- The enterprise will deploy a technology infrastructure that will enable it to focus on the customer. The customer does not care about the technology per se; the customer cares about his or her experiences with the organization.

- The enterprise will adjust to fulfill customer-managed relationships, recognizing that customers will control their own destiny.

- Successful companies will get their customers to invest in the relationship. As the differences between goods and services provided by companies decreases, investment by the customer in the relationship raises the cost of switching to another organization. The more the customer has invested in your organization, the higher the cost for a competitor to acquire that customer.

- The enterprise will be able to deal with information consistently across all channels and will be able to turn analysis into action.

- The enterprise will participate in managing relationships between customers and will use knowledge gained to improve its relationship with the customers.

- The enterprise will serve its customers with personnel and systems dictated by the customer's preferences and the customer's value.

- Customers will have a good feeling about the enterprise. The customers will have invested in the enterprise by willingly participating in increasing the company's knowledge about their habits, preferences, and relationships, and they will appreciate the superior service, which represents the return on that investment.

- Customers of successful CRM organizations will spread the word.

- CRM activities facilitated by a single view of the customer will become part of the business planning process and will be considered in the budgets and business plans. Business plans will be defined in terms of Customer Life Cycle management, and business decisions will be made based on customer lifetime value, not quarterly results.

This is a tall order, and to most companies today, this represents some significant challenges.

Challenges to CRM Implementation

Enterprises will still need to take internal and external actions that are in the best long-term interest of both the organization and its customers. The CRM challenge in the future, however, goes beyond managing just the organization's activities. We need to understand our customers as completely as possible; we need to make the customer part of our planning process through our interactions with the customer, the customer's investment in us, and the customer's interactions with other customers. We need to be able to absorb information about our customers in order to manage increasingly complex activities within our organizations, within organizations in our supply chain, and among our customers. The following are several areas in which companies face challenges as they strive to be successful in CRM or CMR.

Business Strategy Alignment

The business strategy must be focused towards the customer. CRM is more than call center operation, it's more than sales force automation, and it's more than marketing or customer analysis. It's the strategic view that integrates how we want the business to relate to our customers and how we want our customers to interact with each other. The customer actually controls the relationship, but the more we understand about the customer and his or her needs, the better positioned we are to influence this relationship. Call center operation, sales force automation, marketing, order fulfillment, and so on must all be approached with an understanding of how they interact to provide the customer with what he or she needs. This last word was chosen very carefully. It's more than just providing what the customer requests; it's more than just providing what the customer wants. It's understanding the customer well enough to anticipate what the customer needs and using that understanding to influence the customer to re-enter the Customer Life Cycle again and again. Further, it includes providing such a positive experience for our customers that they pass this experience on to others in their extended households and social networks, resulting in additional customers entering our Customer Life Cycle.

In the introductory scenario, the bank understood Bob's need to get together with his sister-in-law and her husband and combined this information with its knowledge about Bob's preferences in order to offer him a palatable solution. Its relationship with Bob and with his sister-in-law dictated the way their individually identifiable information (such as travel plans) could be used, and the bank respected these constraints. It understood Bob's vacation interests and provided him with an improvement to his existing plans.

The successful CRM organization of the future will not only focus its business strategy on the customer, it will involve the customer in creating that strategy. It will get the customer to invest time, energy, and intellect in the relationship. Buying a shirt at a custom clothing store such as the Custom Shop requires a fitting session. Assuming the customer is pleased with the initial shipment, the next time he needs shirts, this customer is more likely to simply place an additional order rather than spending the time to go through a fitting session at a competitor. With this investment, the company is more likely to meet the customer's expectations, and the customer is more likely to remain loyal.

Loyalty

Ultimately, the business strategy must address customer loyalty. In Chapter 14, we discussed the importance of trust in building customer loyalty. In the "retain and expand" portion of the Customer Life Cycle, our objective is to improve the loyalty of our most profitable customers. In order to do so, we must provide them with personalized positive experiences. Otherwise, why should they remain loyal? The link between customer loyalty and customer retention is pretty obvious; loyal customers come back. Loyal, well-treated customers can also help us in customer acquisition by spreading the word about their good experiences. Customer loyalty should be built using a repetitive five-step process, such as the one shown in Figure 15.1.

Identify Valuable Customers and Prospects

Identifying valuable customers and prospects helps enterprises focus their efforts. The intrude and engage activities within the Customer Life Cycle should

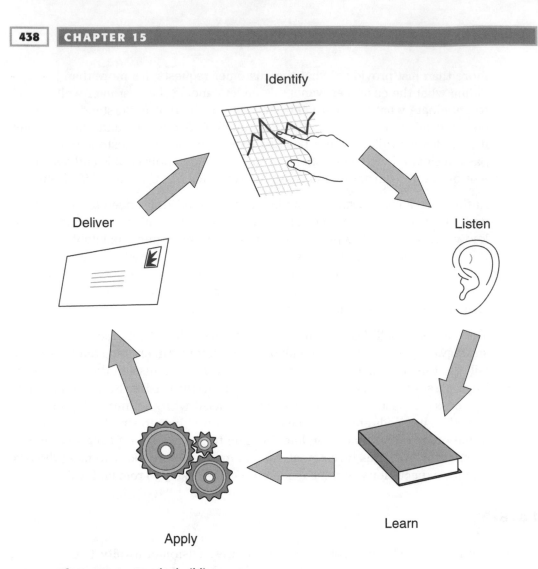

Figure 15.1 Loyalty-building process.

focus on the valuable prospects, the customer acquisition activities should be intensified for those customers that have the greatest potential to benefit the enterprise, and the retain and expand activities should try to preserve and enhance relationships with these customers.

Before building the relationship with customers and prospects, we must determine the ones with whom the relationship has the potential of being mutually beneficial. The section "Customer Selection," that follows describes ways of identifying the valuable customers. Once we identify these customers, as described in Chapter 3, we can use this information to qualify leads so that we pursue the ones that have the greatest potential to become valuable customers.

Listen to What the Customers Say

Be an active, sensitive listener. Gather information about the customer from all practical sources and integrate it with information from your customer touch points, regardless of who is representing the enterprise at the touch point. Some of the sources of information are point of sales, warranty claims, service appointments, demographics, publications, external databases such as Dun & Bradstreet and Polk, Internet activity, surveys, and personal calls.

The Corporate Information Factory (CIF) does an excellent job of capturing, managing, and dispensing electronic forms of customer information. This information enters through the operational systems, and some may be posted directly to the operational data store. Appropriate information is then loaded into the data warehouse and subsequently to the data marts. Other data such as paper, voice, and image, should also be cataloged so that it can be easily located.

Learn from What the Customers Tell You

Use the information provided by the customer to develop a deeper understanding of the customer's needs and wants. Recognize the important information that can be used to strengthen the customer relationship. The quality of this data is critical. The data acquisition process, as discussed in earlier chapters, helps us bring accurate data into the Corporate Information Factory. To be truly effective, however, the data needs to be more than just accurate; it also needs to be as complete as possible. We need to be innovative in ferreting out data sources, while still respecting our customers' right to privacy.

Apply the Understanding of the Customer across All Touch-Points

Combine knowledge of the customer with predictive and analytic techniques to enhance each succeeding customer interaction based on that customer's profile and past interactions. In many respects, this is more of an art than a science. It entails refining the knowledge we accumulate about the customer and making it actionable.

The data warehouse and data marts are used to help segment the customers and to understand the behaviors of customer segments. This data is combined with information about each customer's interactions to tailor the way we deal with that customer.

Deliver Meaningful Experiences to the Customers

Provide the customer with a meaningful dialog and a personalized, rewarding experience at each interaction. The dialog must have the right content and employ the right delivery method. Bob received data through his wireless device, whereas his parents received a phone call. Bob received information about adventurous vacations, whereas his parents received brochures on cruises.

View of the Customer

A common thread in the description of the successful CRM organization of the future is the view of the customer. These organizations will have a consolidated 360-degree view, and this view addresses more than just the person or company making the purchase. It also involves the customer's relevant interactions with other customers. It involves customers who become agents for the enterprise and spread the good word. The successful enterprises recognize that they need to listen and learn from interactions beyond the typical customer touch points. They're also aware that they must apply the knowledge they gain to further improve the delivery of positive experiences to the existing customer base and to the expanded customer base that is made possible through the satisfied customers initiating the intrude and engage activities of the Customer Life Cycle.

We will be seeing a significant evolution in the business-to-business (B2B) environment with respect to the view of the customer. The Internet has contributed to the shift of power to the ultimate consumer. This shift is rippling through the entire supply chain, and all companies in that chain, no matter how far removed from the actual consumer, must understand that consumer's values and tailor their products and services accordingly. The businesses in this environment will be expanding their customer view to include the ultimate customer, transforming that environment to business-to-business-to-customer (B2B2C).

Bob's bank understands that its customers do more than just financial transactions. It used its knowledge of its key customers to expand into the travel business through a combination of alliances and acquisitions. It has shifted its business strategy to consider the full supply chain so that it can better serve its ultimate customers. Bob's satisfaction with the bank's expanded services lead to his sister-in-law booking her vacation through the bank. The bank acquired another potentially profitable customer because of the way its service pleased Bob. The bank must now learn more about his sister-in-law so that it can expand the services provided to her and her husband.

Customer Selection

The business strategy also needs to address customer selection. Not all customers are profitable, and some customers are much more profitable than others. In the pharmaceutical industry, 29 percent of the physicians account for 80 percent of the prescriptions, as shown in Figure 15.2. The integrated prospect and customer information can be leveraged to ensure that customer acquisition and service activities and costs are commensurate with the lifetime value of the customers.

Patterns such as those in Figure 15.2 can be used in several ways. First, companies need to focus attention on the small number of customers that disproportionately contribute to their profitability. These are valuable customers, and they deserve to be treated as such. Analysis of this group may help identify opportunities to further increase their value either through cross-selling and up-selling, or by providing them with information they can use to promote our

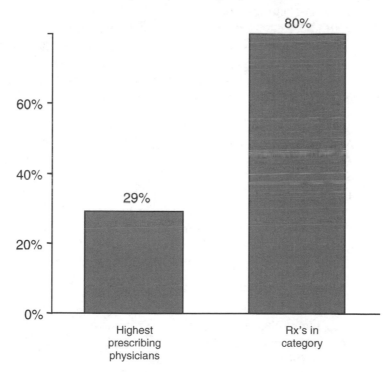

Figure 15.2 Customer value.

products. We should also involve some of these customers as we plan future products.

Second, companies need to understand the characteristics of these customers. What makes them different from other customers? Using the data warehouse and data marts, the customers can be analyzed, and we can then identify other customers with similar characteristics that are not contributing as much to our profitability. Armed with that information, we can tailor a marketing campaign for those customers and manage that campaign using our operational data store.

A critical piece of information needed to make all this possible is the profitability of each customer, not just the revenue the customer generates. The integration of information in the Corporate Information Factory is critical. Revenue data is usually readily available, but even this may not be at the required level of granularity. Further, we must know the cost to produce each product, the cost to provide service using each channel, and so on. The Corporate Information Factory architecture facilitates capturing this data, but many times, significant changes in the company's culture and strategy are needed along with the technological improvements. The company's cost and revenue capturing system must be based on accurate data accumulation and use, not on the politics that often result from a short-term, bottom-line focus.

Armed with quality information about customer profitability, companies are in a better position to make decisions about their products and their customers. For example, your company may discover that it has an unprofitable product. Your first reaction may be to discontinue that product. But what if your analysis reveals that your most profitable customers commonly acquire this product? How would that impact the action you take?

Similarly, you may discover that some customers are actually unprofitable, and these may be your largest customers (in terms of revenue). What do you do then? Armed with the information about customer profitability, you are in a position to take action. The action may be to increase the generated revenues (raise prices) or reduce costs (take actions to shift transactions to a less expensive channel). What's important here is that the successful CRM organization understands its customers and each customer's value and is positioned to take appropriate actions.

Acquisition Channel

Companies employ many channels to reach their customers. During the first few years of e-commerce, many retailers did not effectively merge their brick-and-mortar channel with their electronic distribution channel. We described the shortcomings of this approach in Chapter 12, "Interacting with Customers

Online." The retailers soon recognized the importance of providing the customer with a common view regardless of the channel. Customers could order something on the Web site and pick it up at the store; they could return an unwanted item to the store regardless of the channel used for the purchase.

The concepts presented in Figure 15.1 apply here as well. The retailers that adapted listened to their customer complaints and learned from the poor experiences. They applied this information to deliver a more consistent image of the company to the customer. Regardless of the channel used to contact the retailer or purchase a product, the customer received consistent information with the delivery mechanism tailored to take advantage of the channel selected by the customer. As we move into the future, the electronic channel should fade into being just one of several interchangeable ways of doing business. The successful CRM enterprise will recognize that the customer will be controlling the channel and that the enterprise must be prepared to provide the service using the channels of the customer's choice.

Extended Enterprise

Another channel challenge many organizations face is that the enterprise does not own the entire distribution channel and often does not deal directly with customers. Sometimes the distributor is serving as an exclusive agent of the manufacturer, but often, this is not the case. A retail store, for example, is the distribution channel for many consumer products. The product manufacturers may not interact with the customer directly, and the retailer also represents competitors. The automotive industry has a similar situation. The dealers provide the distribution channel for the automobiles and feel strongly that they "own" the customer. The situation is compounded by the fact that the same dealer can represent multiple manufacturers.

Companies faced with these types of distribution channels need to find innovative ways of building customer loyalty. Mass marketing is one method that is employed. Through marketing, the manufacturer is providing information to a prospective group of customers to make sure they are aware of the product and its features. The manufacturer is striving to create brand recognition that can overcome its lack of direct contact with its customers. With some products, companies also provide incentives for the owner to register the product, and they then obtain information about the individual customer.

Another approach is to provide a value proposition to the dealer or retailer so that it would be inclined to share customer information. In the automotive industry, the manufacturers buy databases about car owners, and these databases contain information that could help a dealer make another sale. By exchanging information, both the dealer and the manufacturer gain.

Sharing the sales channel can also be considered. This is beginning to happen in the automotive industry and will likely become pervasive in other industries during the coming years. The dealer's primary sales channel is the dealership itself, and some dealers are also providing entry points through the Web. The customer's perspective, however, is limited to the dealer's inventory. In the traditional environment, if a car the customer wants is not on the lot, the dealer has access to the inventory of other nearby dealers and can commit to delivering the car. With modern technology, the Web can be used to provide a view of the available cars. The manufacturer can facilitate sharing this information in a way that preserves the dealer's customer ownership. The customer can use the Web to identify the cars that can be available at the dealer within 24 hours. The customer need not know the location of the car.

The distribution channel challenge is compounded by another challenge, which is the topic of the next section. With the advent of modern computing capabilities and with common access to vast amounts of information, some differentiators among companies, particularly as they pertain to the manufacturing processes and products, are getting eliminated.

Commodity Business Environment

Consumers often treat the product itself as a commodity. As frequent travelers, we often rent vehicles. Our profile provides the renting agency with information about the type of car we want. Each of us invests time to provide the rental agency with our preferences, and through our usage pattern, the rental agency may have added more information to our profile. The product we are acquiring is a car for a set period of time.

The challenges faced by the rental agency are that (1) the same car is available at other agencies, and (2) we really don't care about the brand and manufacturer of the car. The car itself is a commodity; it does not impact our selection of the rental agency. Assuming the costs are reasonably close (we may be willing to pay a little more for better service), the differentiator is the personalized experience. Our initial selection of a rental agency is based on promises or other people's experiences. Once we start to use that agency, our decision to stay is based on the way we're treated: is the car ready when we get to the counter, can we avoid going to the counter, how quick is the check-in, do we get an upgrade on occasion?

The agency that is most likely to keep us as customers is the one that identifies us as valuable customers (based on our usage history), listens to us (uses the information from our profile to understand our needs), learns from us (expands the profile based on our actual business—maybe we asked for a newspaper when we arrive in the morning), applies that information (provides us with a *Wall Street Journal* in the car), and delivers the services we require. Our satisfaction level contributes to making us salespeople for the company. We are likely to share our positive experiences with fellow travelers, thereby helping the enterprise recruit additional valuable customers.

Not only are the products being treated as commodities, the differentiators in the production processes are also being reduced. Production processes are continuously being improved through technological advances and through the adoption of quality improvement measures such as those promoted by the Union of Japanese Scientists and Engineers (JUSE) that sponsors the Deming Prize and the United States Department of Commerce that sponsors the Malcolm Baldrige National Quality Award. The Enterprise Resource Planning (ERP) systems' initial promotional campaigns were aimed at the business leaders, not the technologists. They claimed that their packages would help companies improve their processes and gain a competitive advantage. When only one company acquires the package, it gains the advantage, but if other companies also acquire the package, the Enterprise Resource Planning system no longer provides it with a competitive advantage. It has helped raise the bar for all companies, and all of them are in a better position to improve their processes and thus improve their customers' experiences.

The successful CRM organization recognizes that competitors can catch up to even the most advanced production processes and the most refined products and services. Features such as cruise control and leather seats were considered luxury options in the past; now they're standard equipment even on some of the lower priced cars. These are no longer differentiators. The CRM organization recognizes that in order to retain customer loyalty, it must differentiate itself in the experience it provides its customers; products themselves will not be the differentiating factors for long. It must apply the cycle portrayed in Figure 15.1 to continuously improve its customers' experiences.

Organization Structure and Culture

In Chapter 4, "Are You Ready? Tuning the Organization for CRM," we proposed creating a Strategic Operations group to ensure that CRM is approached from an enterprise perspective. One approach to consider is creating a Chief Customer Officer (CCO) to head up this group. From a cultural perspective, the CCO concept places customers at the same level as some of the other corporate resources, such as those managed by the Chief Financial Officer and Chief Information Officer. The Chief Customer Officer is responsible for initiating the actions to address all of the customer-oriented challenges faced by companies striving to be successful in their CRM endeavors. Two major hurdles must be overcome for the CCO to be effective: authority and compensation.

Politically, the Chief Customer Officer of a customer-focused enterprise has a scope of responsibility that is almost the same as the CEO's. The expanded definition of the customer includes the traditional customer as well as the supplier, the agents, and so on. This covers virtually every area of the company. Further, one of the CCO's major responsibilities is to ensure that all of the organizational units work together to create the positive customer experiences. The CCO must have an appropriate authority level. If the CCO has a line responsibility, then he or she is in a reasonable position to carry out the mandates of the position. Sometimes, the CCO has only influence responsibility. The CCO may not have a staff and is therefore dependent on people borrowed from other groups. In these situations, the CCO may find himself or herself with a broad responsibility and limited authority. Any enterprise contemplating a CCO function needs to ensure that the authority is commensurate with the responsibility. This can be accomplished directly (perhaps through an organizational directive) or through having the CCO serve as the chairperson of a Steering Committee whose members have the required authority.

Compensation is another area that must be addressed. Most compensation systems are vertically oriented; they reward people for achieving a bottom-line result in a particular function. CRM requires a compensation system that also recognizes the importance of horizontal alignment. As described in Chapter 4, the reward system—the salaries and bonuses that individuals get—must emphasize the long-term benefits to be derived from an organization structure that is aligned with a customer-focused business strategy.

Very often, Sales or Marketing initiate CRM activities. Sometimes these are the broad initiatives that address the entire customer relationship, and other times these are initiatives aimed at a single function such as call center management or sales force automation. Similarly, the information technology group often identifies voids in customer information and initiates projects to consolidate customer data or to provide business intelligence capabilities. Independently, neither the lines of business nor the information technology group can effectively implement the combination of business and technology solutions needed for effective Customer Relationship Management. The problem is that neither organization contains all of the required skill sets and perspectives. The business units create the business strategy and are responsible for dealing with the customers, but do not have the experience needed to develop a CIF; the information technology group knows how to develop the various components of the CIF, but does not have the business perspective. They must find a way to work in concert with each other.

The traditional approach is to create a project within the information technology group with participation from the business areas. This approach places the burden of creating consensus on the information technology group, and this may be an unfair burden. Organizations contemplating or implementing a strategic operations group such as the one described in Chapter 4, or a matrixed Chief Customer Officer organization have another option. Responsibility for implementing the technology components can be brought into this group as well. Under the auspices of the CCO, a team consisting of information technology and business representatives can be formed to plan, develop, and deploy the needed infrastructure and systems. The information technology members of this team will continue to interact with their counterparts to ensure integration within the technological environment, and the business representatives will continue to interact with their counterparts to ensure that the needs of each of the business units are addressed.

The successful CRM enterprise of the future will recognize that a strong technological foundation is essential, but that its customers don't care about how the company meets their needs. The customers only care that their needs are met. These enterprises must tackle the organizational boundaries that create the traditional rivalry between information technology and the business units. They must find a way to meld the organizations to build and maintain the infrastructure needed for CRM.

Customer Information and Technology

The challenges described so far address the organizational structure and culture and the business strategy. A customer information architecture that provides a complete, integrated view of the customer is a prerequisite for meeting those challenges. As was presented in the beginning of this chapter, the application of technology is one of the distinguishing characteristics of the successful CRM organization of the future. Enterprises must be smart in order to recognize what the ultimate consumer perceives as being valuable, and they must be agile to be able to harvest the high value points defined by these consumers. Being smart and agile requires a commitment to integrate strategic thinking with their technological investments to ensure flexibility, and a commitment to the Corporate Information Factory approach to build and leverage knowledge assets. The Corporate Information Factory provides an architecture that can satisfy this need. It contains all of the essential components: a set of applications that run the day-to-day business, an operational data store that supports tactical analysis and also provides a means of integrating operational data, and a data warehouse and data marts to support the strategic analysis functions.

Operational Systems

Companies striving to become CRM leaders need to realistically assess their operational systems. The Corporate Information Factory provides an approach for integrating data from multiple sources. If the data is not available, the first step may be to substantially enhance or even replace the customer applications. The electric utility companies did just that in the 1980s and early 1990s. They realized that they were moving from a monopolistic environment to a competitive environment, and they also determined that the existing customer information systems would not serve them in that environment. They undertook projects, often costing tens of millions of dollars, to build customer information systems that would serve them well in a competitive environment.

The Corporate Information Factory provides an architecture to consolidate and cleanse existing data. If the point-of-sales systems do not capture information about the customers, the CIF will not solve the problem of missing data. If the operational systems do not provide the needed data once the customer focused business strategy is developed, then either these systems need to be improved or replaced or the needed functionality needs to be incorporated into the ODS.

Evolving Role of the Operational Data Store

In Chapter 7, "Capturing Customer Information," we described the operational data store, and explained how it can be used to integrate customer information without fully redesigning and rebuilding the legacy environment. Although the ODS is not designed to be the primary operational system, over time, the functionality of the ODS can increase to the point that it performs significant business operations activities, as shown in Figure 15.3. This is still not its primary purpose, and hence the figure shows that even though it does take on some business operations functions, its primary role is business management.

Initially, the ODS is used as a target for customer information that originates in the operational systems. If the operational systems do not provide an integrated view, the ODS can evolve to become the system of record for selected customer information. It is not intended to replace the functionality of the major customer operational systems such as the billing system and order processing system. It can, however, become the source of the basic customer data that these systems use, thereby streamlining the environment and providing a single source of data for customer data.

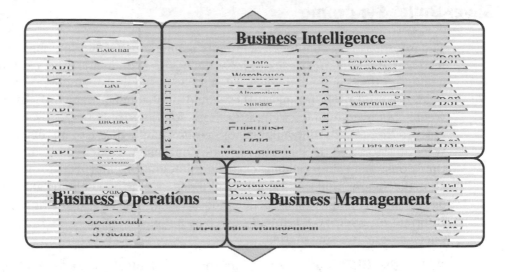

Figure 15.3 Evolving role of the ODS.

We focused our attention on the Customer ODS in Chapter 10, "Facilitating Customer Touches with the Customer ODS," and we pointed out that this was a subset of the conceptual operational data store. The expanded business strategy requires additional integrated information, and the ODS will need to expand in order to address other subject areas such as channels, products, external organizations, internal organizations, and locations. Inclusion of these subject areas within the ODS helps the enterprise better understand the customer, the customer's interaction with other customers, and the customer's interaction with other external organizations such as competitors, regulatory agencies, and alliances.

In Chapter 2, "The Customer and the Corporate Information Factory (CIF)," we emphasized the importance of developing the CIF in an iterative manner. We started with the customer ODS because it addressed the areas of immediate need. As the company expands its CRM program, so too should the ODS expand. The subject area model presented in Chapter 6 provides a good starting point for this expansion. Based on the company's business strategy, additional subjects from that model need to be developed further. As we discussed in that chapter, the business data model for the selected subjects gets developed, and then the system model for the operational data store is built.

Silver Bullet Syndrome

The information technology community is infamous for chasing the silver bullet. Over and over, our desire to meet the business demands drive us to pursue a solution that can be implemented quickly. In the mid-1990s, vendors of data mart oriented tools promised they could implement a data mart in 4 to 12 weeks. Many companies went after those solutions, only to discover that they entered the world of data mart chaos, as shown in Figure 15.4. In this world, we were able to build the data marts quickly because we skipped the difficult and time-consuming step of data cleansing, integration, and transformation. We soon discovered that these steps are still needed. Instead of being able to leverage them through the data acquisition process that is part of the Corporate Information Factory, we found ourselves manually trying to reconcile differences among the data marts.

Within the CRM world, some companies implement packages that address pieces of CRM, such as call center and sales force automation, and falsely conclude that they have implemented CRM. Each of these packages represents a project within a broader program. Successful CRM enterprises will adhere to an architecture such as the Corporate Information Factory and maintain a big-picture view of CRM so that each of the components is evaluated based on how it interacts with the other pieces.

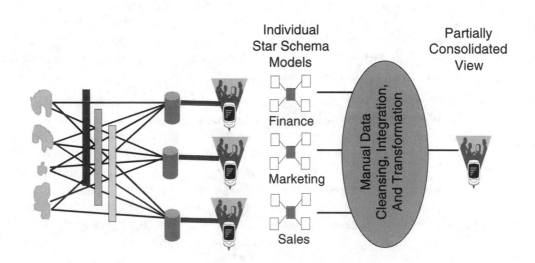

Figure 15.4 Data mart chaos.

Closed Loop Approach

Companies need to have an information infrastructure that provides a full perspective. The Corporate Information Factory provides the cornerstone of this infrastructure. Packaged solutions can fit within this architecture, with each of the packaged solutions being mapped into the appropriate portion of the CIF. Some are source systems, and some are decision support interfaces that provide analytic capabilities and are fed by transactional interfaces that enable personalized services. Progressive companies need to focus on closing the loop, as shown in Figure 15.5.

The closed loop approach creates an ecosystem. Within this ecosystem, all the parts interact with each other to provide a balanced environment. If any one part of the environment isn't working effectively, it affects the rest of the environment:

■ The left portion of the figure represents the various points at which customer interactions take place. These include point-of-sale, sales force automation, call center, direct mail, and so on. These interaction points provide the source of information for the ecosystem.

■ The data is transformed in the data acquisition process of the Corporate Information Factory. Some data is then moved into the data warehouse and data marts for business intelligence, such as multi-dimensional analysis,

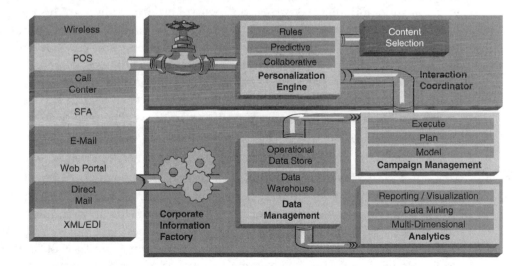

Figure 15.5 An ecosystem.
Courtesy of Braun Consulting, Inc.

data exploration and mining, and reporting and querying. This data is used to identify trends, affinities, and so on.

- Some data is moved into the operational data store for tactical analysis and management. The information about customer segments that is obtained from the business intelligence databases is combined with the customer-specific information available in the operational data store to design interactions best suited for each customer.

- The personalization engine reflects the assimilated information and controls the interactions with the customers on a channel basis. These interactions feed the operational systems, which close the loop by providing the data to feed the Corporate Information Factory.

Weighing the Costs and Benefits

The successful CRM enterprises that survive the next decade will need to overcome these challenges. They know that their long-term success depends on their ability to manage customer relationships. Customers are demanding this and they know some of what can be done. If your organization doesn't offer these types of services, they will look elsewhere.

Another challenge is the cost. Make no mistake, implementing an effective Customer Relationship Management program is expensive. Not only is the cost high, but not many, if any, generally accepted metrics for measuring success and for substantiating the return on investment are available. The return on investment for some specific projects within CRM, such as implementing sales force automation or improving a call center operation, can be calculated. CRM is a broad-reaching program, however, and many of the costs are associated with establishing the strategy, organization and culture changes, and the technological infrastructure to support the program. These represent investments in a foundation that enables the supporting projects. The progressive companies will recognize that these investments are essential for survival and will not resort to traditional cost-savings analysis.

Enterprises also need to evaluate the cost of being the leader in a new technology as well as considering the merits of being a fast follower. Being in front has its rewards, but sometimes the rewards are short-lived. Technologies can change and CRM leaders will refine the strategies they have pioneered. If your organization is not typically an early adopter, you may want to wait until some good role models are for the integrated approach we propose in this book. Fast following can lower the costs and risks, and the business benefits may be comparable. Organizations that adopt this approach will still strive to increase their customers' investment in the relationship. This investment will ensure that the customer is not as prone to switch to a competitor who may have a new product. If done correctly, the investment will also enable communication of the plan for transitioning to a full CRM strategy, replete with a focus on continuing to value the relationships of the best customers.

Summary

Enterprises need to manage their relationships with their customers and be sufficiently resilient to deal with changes in those relationships initiated by the customers. Customer loyalty will be a determining factor in the success of future organizations. Production efficiencies and even the products themselves will not be the differentiators; customer loyalty will be obtained through superior personalized service.

The successful future organization will involve its customers in its business planning process. It will have a 360-degree view of its customers, understand their value, and get them to invest in the customer relationship. It will recognize that with the investment comes control; the customers will control the relationship. The company's responsiveness to the customer's needs and its ability to personalize its services will engender increasing levels of customer loyalty. As a result, the satisfied customers, through their relationships with other customers, will influence others to do business with the enterprise.

Attaining this level of success is not an easy task. Companies face many challenges as they move in that direction:

- The business planning process needs to change. The single view of the customer must be considered in the business plans and budgets. These plans need to be defined in terms of Customer Life Cycle management, and the business decisions need to be made based on lifetime value, not short-term results.

- To enhance customer loyalty, enterprises need to identify valuable prospects and customers, listen to what they say, learn from what the customers tell the enterprise, apply that understanding of the customer across all touch points, and deliver meaningful experiences to them.

- To increase long-term profitability, enterprises need to gain an understanding of each customer's direct and indirect value. The direct value is the profit generated by each customer. The indirect value is the profit generated as a result of each customer. This includes the extended household and referrals. Armed with customer value information, enterprises can take actions to provide increasingly better experiences to the most profitable customers and to possibly provide increasingly poorer experiences to the least profitable customers in the hope that they will go to a competitor.

- To provide customers with a consistent view of the enterprise, companies will manage the sales and distribution channels so that they work in harmony with each other.

- The organization structure and culture also present significant hurdles. Customer focused organizations must ensure that they are appropriately organized. Two approaches cited in this book are the Strategic Operations Group and the Chief Customer Officer. Both are aimed at the same objective: to provide a centrally managed group of people who have authority and responsibility over the company's actions as they impact the customer.

- The consistent, 360-degree view of the customer is dependent on quality information. The Corporate Information Factory provides an architecture that fully supports CRM. CIF represents a logical architecture. Each company must evaluate its own environment and map a course of action that will deploy its technical infrastructure, based on the Corporate Information Factory. A critical element of this architecture is that all of the components interact with each other by design.

- The Corporate Information Factory is a component in an ecosystem that includes a personalization engine to ensure that customers enjoy positive experiences with the company. This personalized service will be the key differentiator in the future. Companies that are most successful in tailoring their actions to their customer's specific needs will best be positioned to acquire and retain valuable customers.

Improving customer relationships is not an option; it's critical to survival. Companies must take a holistic view to CRM. It can be implemented in increments, but each increment must consider its role within the bigger picture. It won't be easy, and you may never get completely there, but with each step you take, you will be getting closer to your customer. As you move forward on this journey, consider adhering to the following principles:

We have a plan and we're poised to deliver. We have a business strategy that provides a comprehensive roadmap, and the organization is moving along the road in unison.

We believe customer knowledge is the lifeblood of our business. We are aiming for a 360-degree view of our customers. We listen to our customers and take action to improve their experience based on what we learn.

Our strategic conversation is informed by new technology. We have defined an architecture such as the Corporate Information Factory and are deploying it iteratively to constantly improve the information about our customers and support the services they demand.

We recognize the differential value of our customers and invest accordingly. We use the information about our customers to understand their lifetime value and make decisions concerning products and services based on this value.

We won't forget to make money. Customer Relationship Management entails the alignment of business strategy, organization structure and culture, and customer information and technology so that all customer interactions can be conducted to the long-term satisfaction of the customer and to the benefit and profit of the organization. We will take the actions that provide our customers with long-term satisfaction and with the full expectation that we stand to benefit and profit as a result.

Acquire: Acquire is the set of business processes in the Customer Life Cycle leading up to the customer moment when consumers either become customers or do not. This includes needs development, awareness generation, knowledge transfer, consideration, pre-sales, and evaluation.

Acquisition: Acquisition is the process, within the Customer Life Cycle, by which the customer receives the products and services purchased. Many company processes are associated with the delivery of products and services ordered or acquired by the customer.

Administrative Meta Data: Administrative meta data is information for managing the Corporate Information Factory (CIF).

Agent: An agent is a party who controls the relationship with organizations and consumers who acquire the company's products and services.

Alternative Storage: Alternative storage is the set of devices used to cost-effectively store data warehouse and exploration warehouse data that is needed but not frequently accessed. These devices are less expensive than disks yet provide adequate performance when the data is needed.

Analytical Applications: Analytical applications are predesigned, ready-to-install, decision-support applications. They generally require some customization to fit the specific requirements of the enterprise. The source of data is the data warehouse. Some examples of these applications are risk analysis, database marketing (CRM) analyses, vertical industry "data marts in a box," and so on.

Architect: The architect is responsible for developing the conceptual architecture for the Corporate Information Factory (CIF) and for ensuring that the technical architecture is appropriate for the overall CRM effort.

Attrition: Attrition, within the Customer Life Cycle, is the erosion of customer loyalty, leading to the capture of some or all of the customer's business by a competitor.

Automated Character Recognition: Automated character recognition is a technology that can read e-mail messages, identify key words or phrases, and compose and send a stock reply to the sender. It can also route the e-mail to the appropriate service representative if human intervention is needed.

Automatic Call Distribution (ACD): ACD is a technology that works in conjunction with the Automatic Number Identification (ANI) and Dialed Number Identification Service (DNIS) services to qualify a call and route it from the telephone switch to the appropriate group of service representatives. ACD works with the telephone hardware to pick up the call, it invokes ANI or DNIS, and it chooses where to route the call based on the results.

Automatic Number Identification (ANI): ANI is the technology that enables the computer to recognize the number from which a call is being dialed (such as the customer's number). This technology is a component of the CTI environment.

Awareness: Awareness is the point in the Customer Life Cycle at which the consumers become cognizant of the enterprise and that the enterprise may be related to their needs, wants, and desires.

Bill Payer: The bill payer is the person responsible for actual payment of all charges incurred for the acquisition of the company's products and services.

Brick-and-Mortar: Brick-and-mortar is a term used to indicate a physical retail location offering a company's products and services.

Business Analyst: The business analyst is responsible for providing input concerning the CRM applicability, its content, quality, delivery, and human interface of the Corporate Information Factory (CIF).

Business Data Model: The business data model, sometimes known as the logical data model, describes the major things entities of interest to the company and the relationships between pairs of these entities.

Business Intelligence: Business intelligence is the set of processes and data structures used to analyze data and information used in strategic decision support. The components of business intelligence are the data warehouse, data marts, the DSS interface, and the processes to get data in to the data warehouse and to get information out.

Business Management: Business management is the set of systems and data structures that enable corporations to act, in a tactical fashion, upon the intelligence obtained from the strategic decision support systems. The components of business management are the operational data store (ODS), the transactional interfaces, and the processes to get data into the operational data store and to apply it.

Business Market: The business market consists of the organizations that buy products and services.

Business Meta Data: Business meta data is information that provides the business context for data in the Corporate Information Factory (CIF).

Business Operations: Business operations are the family of systems (operational, reporting, and so on) from which the rest of the Corporate Information Factory (CIF) inherits its characteristics.

Business Process Model: The business process model identifies and describes the major business functions and the processes within these functions.

Capability: A capability is an application created to perform a business operations, intelligence, or management function. Some examples are product profitability analysis, campaign execution, or inventory turn analysis.

Change Management: Change management is the set of processes for employing changes to tools, data, and software.

Click Stream: Click stream consists of the transaction(s) a person performs when visiting an Internet site. These include the selection of a product, the purchase of the product, requests for information, and the input of financial and contact information.

Competitor: A competitor is any enterprise that offers your customers products and services that rival your own.

Computer Telephony Integration (CTI): CTI is the seamless integration of telephone hardware with the computer. Complex CTI solutions provide the capability to link many different software applications, including workflow management, with various databases (customer, contact, and transaction information) and with other telephone hardware components. CTI, sometimes referred to as softphone, enables the service representatives to control the telephone using a computer.

Consideration: Consideration is the process, within the Customer Life Cycle, of narrowing the field of choices. It takes consumers to the point of contemplating how products and services will meet their needs and wants. Attitudes, feelings, and perceived match-to-needs strongly influence consideration.

Consumer: A consumer is the ultimate user of goods and services. All prospects and customers are consumers. In the business and government megamarkets, these consumers are often interim consumers who produce goods and services for the ultimate users.

Cookie: A cookie is a block of text that is placed on a person's computer by a Web site. It is often used to recognize that person the next time he or she accesses that Web site. If the person provides individually identifiable information such as an e-mail address or a credit card number at that Web site, the cookie can be linked to that information. By using the cookie, the Web site can connect previously discrete pieces of information about a person.

Corporate Information Factory (CIF): The Corporate Information Factory is a logical architecture and its purpose is to deliver business intelligence and business management capabilities driven by data provided from business operations.

Current: Current is a property of the operational data store (ODS) by which we provide it with data as up-to-the-second as we can technologically make it.

Customer: A customer is a party of interest to the organization who is involved with the acquisition of the company's goods and services.

Customer Life Cycle: The Customer Life Cycle is a generic model that facilitates communication about the way an enterprise interacts with its customers.

Customer Moment: The Customer Moment is the point of decision, the split second when a consumer decides to become a customer, to go to a competitor, or to not make an acquisition. The primary purpose of the Customer Life Cycle is to gain maximum influence at this moment.

Customer Relationship Management (CRM): Customer Relationship Management is the alignment of business strategy, organization structure and culture, and customer information and technology so that all customer interactions can be conducted to the long-term satisfaction of the customer and to the benefit and profit of the organization.

Customer Touch Zone: The Customer Touch Zone is the part of the Customer Life Cycle that represents the people, processes, and technology across all marketing, sales, and other communication paths between the customer and the enterprise. All customer touch points are in the zone.

Data Acquisition: Data acquisition is the set of processes that capture, integrate, transform, cleanse, reengineer, and load source data into the data warehouse and operational data store (ODS).

Data Acquisition Developer: The data acquisition developer is responsible for developing the applications to capture, cleanse, integrate, transform, and load data from the operational systems into the data warehouse and/or operational data store (ODS).

Data Acquisition Management: Data acquisition management is the set of processes that define, implement, and manage processes used to capture source data and its preparation for loading into the data warehouse or operational data store (ODS).

Data Analyst: The data analyst is responsible for developing data models for specific CRM systems and for ensuring that these models are synchronized with the enterprise data model.

Database Architect: The database architect is responsible for designing and tuning the CIF databases and for implementing security constraints.

Data Delivery: Data delivery is the set of processes that enables end users or their supporting IS groups to build and manage views of the data warehouse within their data marts. It involves a three-step process consisting of filtering, formatting, and delivering data from the data warehouse to the data marts. It may include customized summarizations or derivations.

Data Mart: The data mart is customized and/or summarized data that is derived from the data warehouse and tailored to support the specific analytical requirements of a given business unit or business function. It utilizes a common enterprise view of strategic data and provides business units with more flexibility, control, and responsibility. The data mart may or may not be on the same server or location as the data warehouse.

Data Mining Warehouse: The data mining warehouse is an environment created so analysts can test their hypotheses, assertions, and assumptions developed in the exploration warehouse. Specialized data mining tools containing intelligent agents are used to perform these tasks.

Data Reengineering: Data reengineering is the set of activities that investigates, standardizes, and provides clean consolidated data within the data acquisition process.

Data Stewardship: Data stewardship is the function that is largely responsible for managing data as an enterprise asset. The data steward is responsible for ensuring that the data provided by Corporate Information Factory (CIF) is based on an enterprise view. An individual, a committee, or both may perform data stewardship.

Data Warehouse (DW): The data warehouse is a subject-oriented, integrated, time-variant, non-volatile collection of data used to support the strategic decision-making process for the enterprise. It is the central point of data integration for business intelligence and is the source of data for the data marts, delivering a common view of enterprise data.

Decision Support Interface (DSI): The decision support interface is an easy-to-use, intuitively simple tool for the end user to distill information from data. The DSI enables analytical activities and provides the flexibility to match the tool to the task. DSI activities include data mining, online analytical processing (OLAP), query, and reporting.

Deployment: Deployment is the set of activities that migrate the data warehouse, operational data store (ODS), and data marts and the processes for migrating data through the Corporation Information Factory (CIF) into production.

Dialed Number Identification Service (DNIS): DNIS is the technology that enables the recognition of the number that a caller has dialed. It is a component of the Computer Telephony Integration (CTI) environment.

Dimensional Model: A dimensional model is a form of data modeling that packages data according to specific business queries and processes. The goals are business user understandability and multidimensional query performance.

E-Business: E-business is the set of business transactions conducted over the Internet. Also called e-commerce.

E-Channel: E-channel is the channel used for e-business. Typically, this is the Internet.

End-User Specialist: The end-user specialist is responsible for developing and configuring the end-user support environment and for providing appropriate training on the access tools. Their focus is on the ease of use and the appropriateness of the access for each data mart or operational data store (ODS).

Enterprise: The enterprise is the combination of the business and its agents that provide goods and services to consumers. The extended enterprise represents the complete value chain for goods and services.

Enterprise Data Management: Enterprise data management is the set of processes that manages data within and across the data warehouse and operational data store (ODS). It includes processes for backup and recovery, partitioning, creating standard summarizations and aggregations, and the archival and retrieval of data to and from alternative storage.

Enterprise Portals: Enterprise portals are the facilities that optimize use of the Corporate Information Factory (CIF) by organizing its capabilities and knowledge, and then assimilating them into the business process. Capabilities are organized into a tool box. Knowledge is organized into a library. The library and tool box are integrated into the business process via the workbench.

Evaluation: Evaluation, within the Customer Life Cycle, is the assessment by consumers of the suitability of a product or service before making an acquisition.

Expand: Expand, within the Customer Life Cycle, is the process for gaining the largest portion of acquisitions made by each individual customer in the global marketplace.

Exploration Warehouse: The exploration warehouse is a DSS architectural structure whose purpose is to provide a safe haven for exploratory and ad hoc processing. An exploration warehouse may utilize specialized technologies, in-memory processing, parallel processing, specialized server platforms, and specialized database optimizers to provide fast response times with the capability to access the entire database.

External Data: External data is any data outside the normal data collected through an enterprise's internal applications. There can be any number of sources of external data such as demographic, credit, competitor, and financial information. Generally, external data is purchased by the enterprise from a vendor of such information.

Frequently Asked Questions (FAQs): FAQs are frequently asked questions. These are often stored in a repository to assist customer service and support representatives in answering customer questions. Often, these questions and the associated answers will be placed on an Internet site and be provided to the customers as well.

Front Office: The front office is the direct customer facing processes in an enterprise. These include sales force automation, billing, order entry, and order fulfillment.

Getting Data In (GDI): Getting Data In is the set of activities that capture data from the operational systems and migrate it to the data warehouse and operational data store (ODS).

Getting Information Out: Getting Information Out is the set of activities that deliver information from the data warehouse or operational data store (ODS) and make it accessible to the end users.

Global Marketplace: The global marketplace is an international venue in which supply meets demand as consumers acquire goods and services from providers.

Government Market: The government market is the set of the government agencies that buy products and services.

Harassment: Harassment is the receipt of unwanted contact or unauthorized use of individually identifiable information by another party. Telemarketing calls, particularly if they are during dinner or to a cellular phone, are examples of harassment. In the first case, the call interrupts the customer at an inconvenient time, and in the second case, the cellular phone service provider may actually charge the customer for the intrusion.

Household: A household is an economic decision-making unit. The household is a customer type that is increasing in importance as organizations look more closely at customers and their interactions.

Individual Consumer Market: The individual consumer market is the set of individual consumers who buy products and services.

Individually Identifiable Information: Individually identifiable information, sometimes called personally identifiable information, is any information that can be used to identify or contact a specific individual. This includes information such as the name, address, and social security number, and it can be linked to non-individually identifiable information.

Information Delivery Developer: The information delivery developer is responsible for developing the processes for filtering, formatting, and delivering data from the data warehouse into the data marts and from the operational data store (ODS) into its transactional interface (TrI).

Integrated: Integrated is a property of the data warehouse and operational data store (ODS) that provides a common view of enterprise-wide data, leading to a single version of the truth. For CRM, this results in one and only one version of the customer.

Interactive Voice Response (IVR)/Voice Response Unit (VRU):   IVR and VRU are technologies that provide an automated interaction with the customer by which they can listen to menu choices and respond by pressing the appropriate keys on the telephone. These technologies are used in conjunction with the Computer Telephony Integration (CTI) environment.

Internet: The Internet is an infrastructure of servers permitting electronic transactions to occur throughout the world. Also known as the World Wide Web.

Intrude and Engage: Intrude and engage the set of activities in which the enterprise engages to build brand recognition and to gain and retain the prospect's attention.

Lead Management: Lead management is the process of identifying, qualifying, and informing prospective customers so that salespeople can efficiently convert these prospects into customers.

Learning: Learning within the Customer Life Cycle is the point at which consumers associate the enterprise with the ability to meet their needs, wants, and desires through products and services.

Library and Tool Box: The library and tool box are the collection of meta data that provides information to effectively use and administer the Corporate Information Factory (CIF). The library provides the medium from which knowledge is enriched. The tool box is a vehicle for organizing, locating, and accessing capabilities.

Loss: Loss, within the Customer Life Cycle, is the capture of a prospect by a competitor at or before the Customer Moment.

Management: Management (in the context of Customer Relationship Management [CRM]) is the ability to facilitate interactions between a party and the organization that are satisfactory to both the party and the organization.

Meta Data: Meta data is the glue that holds the Corporate Information Factory (CIF) together. It supplies definitions for data, the calculations used, information about where the data came from (what source systems), what was done to it (transformations, cleansing routines, integration algorithms, and so on), who is using it, when they use it, what the quality metrics are for various pieces of data, and so on. See also administrative meta data, business meta data, and technical meta data.

Meta Data Analyst: The meta data analyst on the Getting Data In (GDI) team is responsible for determining and satisfying the meta data acquisition, management, dissemination, and disposal requirements of the technical components of the CIF architecture. The meta data analyst on the Getting Information Out (GIO) team is responsible for determining and satisfying the meta data requirements for efficient usage by the business community.

Meta Data Management: Meta data management is the process for managing the information needed to promote data legibility, use, and administration. The contents are described in terms of data about data, activity, and knowledge.

Needs Identification: Needs identification is the process by which a consumer moves into the Customer Life Cycle. It consists of a developing perception of needs, wants, or desires that may be fulfilled by products or services. Savvy marketers can generate perceived needs, wants, or desires in the mind of the consumer.

Non-Individually Identifiable Information: Non-individually (or personally) identifiable information is information about a person that is gleaned from that person's activity, but that is not directly attributed to the individual.

Non-Volatile: Non-volatile is a property of the data warehouse that prohibits it from accepting transactional updates or changes. Instead, its tables are appended or inserted with new additions.

On Line Analytical Processing (OLAP): On Line Analytical Processing is the activity of querying and presenting data from multidimensional data marts.

Operational Data Store (ODS): The operational data store is a subject-oriented, integrated, current, volatile collection of data used to support the tactical decision-making process for the enterprise. It is the central point of data integration for business management, delivering a common view of enterprise data.

Operational Systems: Operational systems are the internal and external core systems that run the day-to-day business operations. They are accessed through application program interfaces (APIs) and are the source of data for the data warehouse and operational data store (ODS).

Operations and Administration: Operations and administration is the set of activities required to ensure smooth daily operations, to ensure that resources are optimized, and to ensure that growth is managed. It consists of enterprise data management, systems management, data acquisition management, service management, and change management.

Opt-In: Opt-in is the option that provides a person with control over the collection and dissemination of his or her personal information, as well as control over the types of communication that he or she receives. With opt-in, the default assumption is that the authority is not granted.

Opt-Out: Opt-out is the option that provides a person with the ability to prevent individually identifiable information from being used by a particular enterprise or from being shared with third parties. With opt-out, the default assumption is that the authority is granted.

Organization Change Agent: The organization change agent is the individual that helps the company understand the value and impact of the Corporate Information Factory (CIF) and deals with the organizational issues.

Permission Marketing: Permission marketing is a new marketing technique, first described by Seth Godin, in which the customer or potential customer gives the business permission to market to him or her.

Personalization: Personalization is the ability of a company to recognize and treat its customers as individuals through personal messaging, targeted banner ads, special offers on bills, or other personal transactions.

Predictive Dialer: A predictive dialer is the technology that reads telephone numbers from input lists and automatically dials these numbers for outbound calling. They can recognize busy signals, no answers, and answering machines, and only pass the calls to a service representative if the calls are answered. This is a component of the CTI environment.

Privacy: Privacy is a person's right to understand how individually identifiable information about him or her is intended to be used, a person's right to have an option for permitting or prohibiting such use, and a person's right to have access and control over that information.

Privacy Statement: A privacy statement is a notice, published by an enterprise, which declares its practices with respect to privacy protection.

Products and Services: Products and services are the deliverables provided by the enterprise to the customer.

Program Management: Program management is the set of activities that establishes the framework within which the data warehouse, operational data store (ODS), and data marts are developed and managed.

Program Manager: The program manager is responsible for overseeing the entire Customer Relationship Management (CRM) program and for managing day-to-day program activities within scope, budget, and schedule constraints.

Project Definition: Project definition is the set of activities that initiates the project and sets expectations.

Project Leader: The project leader is responsible for managing day-to-day project activities and for delivering the products according to scope, budget, and schedule.

Prospect: A prospect is a type of consumer identified by the enterprise as a likely customer candidate. It is the prospect that the enterprise targets to pull into the Customer Life Cycle.

Quality: Quality is conformance to requirements.

Re-entry: Re-entry is when the customer comes back through the Customer Life Cycle. It is usually easier, and less expensive for the company, after the first time around. Each trip through the life cycle should build trust and higher levels of familiarity.

Relational Model: The relational model is a form of the data model in which data is packaged according to business rules and data relationships, regardless of how the data will be used in processes, in as non-redundant a fashion as possible. Normalization rules are used to create this form of model.

Relationship: A relationship (in the context of Customer Relationship Management [CRM]) is the type of involvement a party has with the organization or with other customers.

Retain: Retain, within the Customer Life Cycle, is the process for keeping relationships with profitable customers once they have engaged the enterprise.

Security: Security is the safeguarding of information so that only people authorized to access and modify it can do so.

Service Management: Service management is the set of processes for promoting user satisfaction and productivity within the Corporate Information Factory (CIF). It includes processes to define, implement, and manage the creation and population of data marts.

Service Representative Desktop: The service representative desktop, also called a workbench, is the application that integrates CTI functions with workflow management applications and displays results on the desktop. The desktop provides a common front-end that enables the service representative to access all contact center components.

Speech Recognition: Speech recognition is an emerging technology that is being used frequently in contact centers today. It is commonly used in conjunction with Interactive Voice Response (IVR)/Voice Response Units (VRU) and enables the computer to solicit spoken responses, rather than requiring the customer to key the information into the phone.

Star Schema: A star schema is a dimensional data model implemented on a relational database.

Statistical Applications: Statistical applications are set up to perform complex, difficult statistical analyses such as exception, means, average, and pattern analyses. The data warehouse is the source of data for these analyses. These applications analyze massive amounts of detailed data and require a reasonably performing environment.

Steering Committee: The steering committee is responsible for establishing priorities for the efforts pursued within the Customer Relationship Management (CRM) program. It is often tasked with approving funding requests and resolving difficult integration issues.

Strategic Analysis: Strategic analysis consists of the study of historical records to determine trends, patterns, or exceptions in activities or functions. This form of analysis is used to anticipate or correct actions into the future.

Strategy: A strategy is a plan or method for achieving a specific goal.

Subject Area Model: The subject area model groups the major categories of data for the enterprise. It provides a valuable communication tool and also helps in organizing the business data model.

Subject-Oriented: Subject-oriented is a property of the data warehouse and operational data store (ODS) that orients data around major subjects such as customer, product, transaction, and so on.

System Data Model: The system data model is the technology-independent model of the data needed to support a particular system.

Systems Management: Systems management is the set of processes for maintaining the core technology on which the data, software, and tools operate.

Tactical Analysis: Tactical analysis consists of the ability to act upon strategic analyses in an immediate fashion. For example, the decision to stop a campaign in mid-execution is based on the intelligence garnered from past campaigns or the recent history of activities in the current campaign (cannibalism or incorrect audience targeted).

Technical Meta Data: Technical meta data is information that provides the details of how and where data was physically acquired, stored, and distributed in the Corporate Information Factory (CIF).

Technical Sponsor: The technical sponsor is responsible for garnering business support and for obtaining the needed technical personnel and funding.

Technology Data Model: The technology data model is the technology-dependent model of the data needed to support a particular system.

Thin Client Architecture: Thin client architecture is a technological topology in which the user's terminal requires minimal processing and storage capabilities. Most of these capabilities reside on a server.

Time Variant: The time variant is a property of the data warehouse that establishes it as a series of historical snapshots, each dated and accurate as of that point in time.

Transactional Interface (TrI): The transactional interface is an easy-to-use and intuitively simple interface for the end user to request and employ business management capabilities. It accesses and manipulates data from the operational data store (ODS).

Trust: Trust is the confidence a customer has that the recipient of the individually identifiable information about him or her will appropriately secure that information and only use it in an agreed-upon manner.

Use: Use, within the Customer Life Cycle, is when the customer receives services and can build a mutually beneficial relationship between the customer and the enterprise, leading to repeat purchases, up-sells, and cross-sells.

Volatile: Volatile is a property of the operational data store (ODS) that enables it to receive changes and updates to its data, thereby obliterating most or all of the history.

Workbench: The workbench is a strategic mechanism for automating the integration of capabilities and knowledge into the business process.

Workflow Management: Workflow management is the technology that applies business process modeling and computer technology to automate specific business tasks or service request activities. Workflow management applications aid in moving multiple requests through an organization and are particularly useful when the tasks touch many individuals or have multiple complex steps.

Zachman Framework: The Zachman Framework, named for its creator, John A. Zachman, provides an architected approach for viewing and communicating information about complex systems.

Berry, Michael J. A., and Gordon Linoff. 1997. *Data Mining Techniques*. John Wiley & Sons.

————. 2000. *Mastering Data Mining* John Wiley & Sons.

Dyche, Jill. 2000, *e-Data*. Addison-Wesley.

English, Larry P. 1999. *Improving Data Warehouse and Business Information Quality*. John Wiley & Sons.

Godin, Seth. 1999. *Permission Marketing*. Simon & Schuster.

Inmon, W. H. 1996. *Building the Data Warehouse, Second Edition*. John Wiley & Sons.

————. 1999. *Building the Operational Data Store, Second Edition*. John Wiley & Sons,

Inmon, W. H., Claudia Imhoff, and Robert Terdeman. 2000. *Exploration Warehousing*. John Wiley & Sons.

Inmon, W. H., Claudia Imhoff, and Ryan Sousa. 2000. *Corporate Information Factory, Second Edition*. John Wiley & Sons.

Inmon, W. H., J. D. Welch and Katherine L. Glassey. 1997. *Managing the Data Warehouse*. John Wiley & Sons.

Inmon, W. H., John A. Zachman, and Jonathan G. Geiger. 1997. *Data Stores Data Warehousing and the Zachman Framework: Managing Enterprise Knowledge*. McGraw-Hill.

Inmon, W. H., Ken Rudin, Christopher K. Buss, and Ryan Sousa. 1999. *Data Warehouse Performance*. John Wiley & Sons.

Kimball, Ralph, Laura Reeves, Margie Ross, and Warren Thornthwaite. 1998. *The Data Warehouse Lifecycle Toolkit*. John Wiley & Sons.

Marco, David. 2000. *Building and Managing the Meta Data Repository*. John Wiley & Sons.

Modahl, Mary. 2000. *Now or Never*. HarperCollins.

Moore, Geoffrey A. 1991. *Crossing the Chasm*. HarperCollins.

———. 1995. *Inside the Tornado*. HarperCollins.

———. 2000. *Living on the Fault Line*. HarperCollins.

Newell, Frederick. 2000. *Loyalty.com*. McGraw-Hill.

Peppers, Don, and Martha Rogers. 1993. *The One to One Future*. Doubleday.

———. 1997. *Enterprise One to One*. Doubleday.

———. 1999. *The One to One Manager*. Doubleday.

Peppers, Don, Martha Rogers, and Bob Dorf. 1999. *The One to One Fieldbook*. Doubleday.

Pine, B. Joseph, II, and James H. Gilmore. 1999. *The Experience Economy*. Harvard Business School Press.

Seybold, Patricia B. 1998. *Customers.com*. Random House.

Silverston, Len. 2001. *The Data Model Resource Book, Volumes 1 and 2*. John Wiley & Sons.

Walton, Mary. 1986. *The Deming Management Method*. Gamut Books.

A

abstractions, Zachman Framework, 159
accessibility
  data, 52
  database tools, 297
account management, 348
ACD (automatic call distribution), 339
acquisition channels, 442
acquisition stage, CLC, 65, 83, 88, 424
acting on improving production/service systems, 254
active group managers, customer ODS relationship maintenance, 320
adaptability of CIF system, 44
administrative functions, CIF, 54
adopting new quality philosophy, 248
agents, 11
alternative database designs, 289–291
analytical CRM applications, 38
ANI (automatic number identification), 338

APIs (application programming interfaces), business operations, 32
application specific data marts, 283, 286
appropriate sources for data acquisition, 209
architect, CRM development, 144
archived data, capturing data, 216
artificial intelligence support systems, 345
assessments
  data quality, 232
  operational systems, 448
asynchronous customer touch, 77
attributes
  defining for auditing, 231
  privacy, 428
  Zachman Framework naming/definition conventions, 177
attrition, 71
audit meta data, 234
auditing, 205, 228
  data warehouses, 229
  defining processes, 231
  methodology, 230
  ODSs, 229

authority and chief customer officers, 446
automated character recognition, 341, 350
automated customer service, 334
automated sales force, 330–331, 346
  account management, 348
  automated character recognition, 350
  B2B sales, 347
  calendar management, 349
  campaign management, 350
  contact management, 349
  customer data, 349
  forecasting, 349
  mobile access, 351–352
  product catalogs, 349
  sales reports, 349
  telesales, 350
awareness stage, CLC, 82

B

B2B (business-to-business)
  automated sales force, 347

customer ODS
relationships, 317
managing, 17
supplier relationships, 18
third-party vendors, 18
B2C (business-to-
customer), customer
ODS relationships,
17, 317
backups, loading data into
data warehouses, 224
batch processing,
customer ODS
relationship
maintenance, 319
beneficiaries, 12
bill payers, 12
branch marketing
campaigns, 99
branding, 80
budgeting data marts, 285
building trust stage, CLC,
81, 423–425
business analyst, CRM
development, 147
business community, CRM
development, 137, 153
business data model,
Zachman Framework,
173, 176, 180, 187
business intelligence,
33–34
business management, 35
business megamarket, 74
business models
e-commerce
content/community
Web sites, 366–367
e-channel only, 365–366
traditional businesses
with Internet
presence, 367

Zachman Framework,
development rules,
171, 175
business operations
APIs (Application
Programming
Interfaces), 32
CIF (Corporate
Information
Factory), 32
ERP (Enterprise
Resource
Planning), 33
business process model,
Zachman Framework,
174, 179–181
business requirements,
database design
planning, 291
business rules,
documentation, 265
business sponsor, CRM
development, 139
business strategy
alignment, 130,
436–437

C

C2C (customer-to-
customer), customer
ODS relationships,
19, 318
calendar management, 349
call center
automation, 334
campaigns
analysis, 38
CIF operations execution
example, 57
management, 350
capability of data to solve
business problems,

GIO team CRM
development, 136
capacity planning, EP
Toolboxes, 396
captive agents, 11
capturing data,
202–205, 213
appropriate sources, 209
archived data, 216
changed data, 217–218
data storage formats, 215
field integrity, 211–212
filtering, 219
in-use data, 217
logic problems, 213–214
mapping sources to
targets, 207
meta data, 236
quality issues, 263
sustainable identifiers,
207–209
update frequency, 211
case-based retrieval
systems, help
desk, 345
CCO (Chief Customer
Officer), 445–446
ceasing dependence on
mass inspection,
249–250
cell uniqueness, Zachman
Framework rules, 168
central campaign
coordination, 100
centralized
organizations, 105
challenges of e-commerce,
367–369
changed data, capturing
data, 217–218
characteristics
data marts, 281–282

data warehouses, 279
ODSs, 306
workflow
applications, 337
checking on improvement
of production/service
systems, 253
CIF (Corporate
Information Factory),
32, 37, 41
accessibility of data, 52
adaptability of system, 44
administrative
functions, 54
business operations, 32
call center needs, 39
capturing data, 213
consistency of data, 46
data acquisition
process, 47
data cleansing, 220–221
data integration, 221–222
key master tables, 222
data marts, 45
data reengineering, 47
data reliability, 46
data storage formats, 215
data warehouses, 46
data acquisition
process, 56
differences from
ODS, 48
reusability of data, 56
detailed query support,
54–55
DSI (decision support
interface), 52
exploration
warehouses, 45
filtering data, 51
formatting data, 51
goals of system, 49

intuitiveness of data
access tools, 52
level of detail
available, 56
marketing needs, 37
measuring data
quality, 232
meta data, 49
multi-functionality, 53
operational example,
57–58
operational functions, 54
privacy, 426–427
process-centric
ODSs, 311
product-centric
ODSs, 311
program management
teams, 129
business strategy
alignment, 130
funding, 131
GDI (Getting Data In),
132–134
GIO (Getting
Information
Out), 135
IT communications, 131
project
prioritization, 131
repeatable/reusable
processes, 131
quality of data, 48
sales force needs, 39
stability of system, 44
subject-centric ODSs, 312
timeliness of data
delivery, 50
CLC (Customer Life
Cycle), 62
acquisition stage,
65, 83, 88

awareness stage, 82
branding, 80
building trust, 81,
423–425
competition, 68–69
consideration stage, 84
customer moment,
64–65, 86
customer touch, 76–77
customer trust in
organization, 78–79
evaluation stage, 85
extended enterprise,
66–67
global marketplace
example, 67
identifying potential
customers, 72
intrude and engage stage,
65, 80
lead management, 73
magic moment, 86
megamarkets, 74–75
needs identification
stage, 64, 82
privacy, 421
products offered, 68
prospect stage, 63, 84
reentry stage, 65, 88
retain and expand
stage, 65, 86
tracking contacts, 74
usage stage, 65, 88
cleansing data, 205, 384
click stream analysis,
376–380
extraction/cleansing/
transforming
data, 384
loading data, 385
mapping data, 384
closed loop processing,
43, 451

collaborative filters, 382

collection policies, customer satisfaction, 100

column using meta model rule, Zachman Framework, 163

columns and perspective, Zachman Framework rules, 170

commodity business environments, 444

community Web sites, 366–367

compensation and chief customer officer, 446

competitors
as customers, 13
influence on CLC, 68–69

comprehensive customer definitions, ODSs, 316

consideration stage, CLC, 84

consistency of data, CIF, 46

constancy of purpose for improvement, 247

constraints, Zachman Framework perspectives, 159, 167

contact-specific repositories, 341

contacts, 24
management, 349
tracking, CLC process, 74

content management tools, personalizing Web sites, 381

content Web sites, 366–367

continuum of CRM interactions, 26–27

control meta data, 234

cookies, 407

cooperation ability in company, 107

coordination
marketing activities, 115–116
sales activities, 123
technology efforts, CRM development, 109

corporate self-regulation and privacy, 412–413

correcting data, 233

costs
CRM implementation, 452–454
data marts, 285

critical CRM success factors, 95–96
branch marketing campaigns, 99
central campaign coordination, 100
collection policies tailored to customer behavior and value, 100
cross-functional strategies, 99
customer-focused business strategies, 97
outbound call center telemarketing, 100

CRM (Customer Relationship Management), 3, 6
accessibility of data, 41
acquisition channels, 442
acting upon data, 43
analytical applications, 38
assessing corporate readiness, 8–9

changing definition, 433–434
CIF, 32
CLC, 81
closed loop processing, 43, 451
continuum of interactions, 26–27
costs of implementation, 452–454
critical success factors, 95–100
customer types, 9
data
reliability, 40
detail, 41
distribution channels, 443
e-commerce impact, 363–364
ease of data use, 41
examples of interactions, 25
expanding customer definitions, 93
flexibility of data, 41
goals of system, 49
implementation issues
business strategy alignment, 436–437
customer loyalty, 437
customer value, 441
how customers are viewed, 440
identifying valuable customers, 437
learning from customer feedback, 439
listening to customers, 439
lifetime value analyses, 43

managing interactions, 23–24

organizational cultural issues, 106–107

organizational structure, 101–103

partnerships, 18

questions to check CRM readiness, 7

relationships, 16–17

silver bullet syndrome, 450

specificity of data, 42

to functional needs, 40

strategic analysis components, 278

strategic components, 276

strategic functions, 277

strategy project teams, 128

successful future organization requirements, 435

system planning, 94

technology project teams, 128

timeliness of data delivery, 40

CRM development architect, 144

business analyst, 147

business community end users, 153

business sponsor, 139

coordination marketing activities, 115–116

technology efforts, 109

customer service coordinating activities, 119

integrating with other areas, 122

measures of success, 121

roadmaps, 119–120

data acquisition developer, 148

data analyst, 149

data steward, 140

database architect, 150

end user specialist, 151

executive level support, 112–114

GIO team, 151

implementing customer data standards, 111–112

information delivery developer, 152

integrated customer information environment, 108

marketing integrating with other areas, 118

measures of success, 117

plans, 116

roadmaps, 115

meta data analyst, 153

organization change agent, 141

organizational culture issues, 121

planning integrated customer information, 110

program manager, 142

project leader, 143

project management teams, 138

sales activity coordination, 123

sales integration with other areas, 124

sales roadmaps, 122–123

sales success measures, 124

steering committee, 145

technical meta data analyst, 150

technical sponsor, 145–146

cross-functional business strategies, 99

cross-functional cooperation, 103

CRUD matrix, Zachman Framework, 165

CTI (Computer Telephony Integration) ACD (automatic call distribution), 339

ANI (automatic number identification), 338

automated character recognition, 341

contact-specific repositories, 341

DNIS (dialed number identification service), 339

IVR (interactive voice response), 340

predictive dialers, 340

speech recognition, 340

VRU (voice response unit), 340

cultural issues in business and CRM development, 106–107, 445–446

currency of ODS data, 46

current view of subjects, ODSs, 307

customer care centers, 334

customer contact
    centers, 334
customer ODSs, 309
  active group
      managers, 320
  B2C/B2B
      relationships, 317
  C2C relationships, 318
  comprehensive customer
      definitions, 316
  customer data
      standards, 320
  customer profile
      data, 313
  customer relationships,
      316–317
  data acquisition
      middleware, 325
  data quality tools, 322
  data warehouse
      links, 314
  extended enterprise
      relationships, 318
  extensibility of
      design, 320
  indivual customer data
      requirements, 322
  maintaining
      relationships, 319
  manually inputting
      relationship
      links, 320
  personalization
      engines, 315
  product application
      links, 313
  scripting tools, 315
  search tools, 326
  transaction interfaces,
      323–325
  user interface links, 315
customer service
    automation, 334

coordinating
    activities, 119
  integrating with other
      areas, 122
  measures of success, 121
  roadmaps, 119–120
customer touch, 333
  intermediary channel, 76
  media channel, 76
  sales force
      automation, 331
  synchronous/
      asynchronous
      types, 77
customer touch zone, 76
customer value, CRM
    implementation
    issues, 441
customer views, EP
    Toolboxes, 395
customers, 12
  attrition, 71
  buying behavior, 38
  click stream analysis,
      377–380
  data quality tools, 270
  defining customers, 9–10
  demographic profiling, 38
  determining number,
      CRM assessment, 8
  identifying potentials,
      CLC, 72
  lifetime value analysis, 38
  loyalty, CRM
      implementation
      issues, 437
  managing interactions,
      24, 105
  managing
      relationships, 17
  moment, CLC, 64–65, 86
  online interactions, 363
  relationships, 17

retaining, 87
trust in organization,
    78–79

D

data
  accessibility, 52
  acting on, 43
  collection and privacy
      policies, 416
  establishing
      definitions, 264
  quality, 262
  security
      requirements, 265
  specificity, 42
  timeliness of delivery, 50
data acquisition, 47, 56,
    202–205
  appropriate sources, 209
  field integrity, 211–212
  mapping sources to
      targets, 207
  sustainable identifiers,
      207–209
  update frequency, 211
data acquisition developer,
    CRM development, 148
data analyst, CRM
    development, 149
data capture. *See*
    capturing data.
data cleansing, 220–221,
    266–267
data consistency, CIF, 46
data delivery, 50
  delivery processes, 278
  filtering, 295
  formatting, 296
data integration, 221
  key master tables, 222
  quality issues, 268
  resolving problems, 265

transformation
process, 222
data mart model, Zachman
Framework, 197–198
data marts, 34, 45
application specific,
283, 286
characteristics, 281–282
cost of production, 285
data delivery
processes, 278
data mining
warehouses, 278
departmental, 283, 285
designing, 287
DSI (decision support
interface), 279
exploration
warehouses, 278
OLAP, 278
operations, 284
star schema, 287–289
target audience, 284
data miners, CRM
development, 154
data mining warehouses,
34, 46, 278
data precedence, loading
data into data
warehouses, 224
data quality tools,
customer ODSs, 322
data reengineering, CIF, 47
data reliability, 10, 46
data requirements,
customer ODSs, 322
data steward
CRM development, 140
responsibilities, 264–265
data storage formats,
capturing data, 215
data transformation,
quality issues, 269

data visibility, CRM
development, 134
data warehouse
model, Zachman
Framework, 196
data warehouses, 34, 278
assessing data
quality, 232
auditing, 228–229
methodology, 230
characteristics, 279
correcting errors, 233
customer ODS links, 314
data acquisition
process, 56
differences from ODS, 48
e-commerce role,
382–383
goals of construction, 280
level of detail
available, 56
loading data, 223–225
reusability of data, 56
database architect, CRM
development, 150
database triggers,
capturing data
changes, 219
databases
access tools, 297
alternative designs,
289–291
comparing image
copies, 218
designing
business
requirements, 291
granularity, 292
structural issues, 294
DBMS logs, reading
to capture data
changes, 218

decentralized
organizations, 105
decision trees, 345
defining
customers, 9–10
processes for
auditing, 231
definition conventions,
Zachman Framework,
177, 183
delivery of data
filtering, 295
formatting, 296
Deming's 14 quality
points, 246
adopt the new
philosophy, 248
cease dependence on
mass inspection,
249–250
constancy of purpose for
improvement, 247
educational/retraining
programs, 261
improving
production/service
systems, 252–254
leadership, 256
life cycle cost, 251
removing fear, 257
removing numerical
quotas, 259–260
removing
sloganeering, 259
removing staff area
barriers, 258
taking action, 262
training, 255
departmental data marts,
283, 285
design extensibility,
customer ODSs, 320

designing
  data marts, 287
  databases
    alternate designs,
      289–291
    business
      requirements, 291
    granularity, 292
    structural issues, 294
desktop sales
  management, 348
desktop service
  management, 342
detail of ODS data, 308
detailed query support,
  CIF, 54–55
developing EPs, 399
development
  rules, Zachman
    Framework, 171
diagrams, Zachman
  Framework
  conventions, 179
dictionaries, EP
  Libraries, 397
dimensions, Zachman
  Framework, 159, 165
distribution channels, 443
DNIS (dialed number
  identification
  service), 339
documenting business
  rules, 265
DSI (decision support
  interface), 52, 279,
  297–298

E

e-channel only businesses,
  365–366
e-commerce
  business models
    content/community
      Web sites, 366–367

e-channel only, 365–366
    traditional businesses
      with Internet
      presence, 367
  challenges, 367–369
  channel
    coordination, 370
  click stream analysis,
    376–380
  cutting costs, 369
  data warehouse role,
    382–383
  impact on CRM, 363–364
  informing customers, 367
  new types of
    competition, 369
  ODS role, 382–383
  opportunities, 367–369
  permission
    marketing, 372
  personalization, 373–375,
    381–382
  privacy, building
    trust, 411
  replaying information
    to extended
    enterprise, 368
e-mail sales and
  service, 332
e-retail channel
  coordination, 372
employees as
  customers, 13
encyclopedias, EP
  Libraries, 397
end user specialist, CRM
  development, 151
end users, database design
  issues, 292
engage stage, building
  trust, 423
entities, Zachman
  Framework, 163, 176

naming/definition
    conventions, 177
  process
    relationships, 165
  starter model, 192
EPs (Enterprise Portals),
    343, 390
  developing, 399
  first generation, 399
  integrated information
    environment, 394
  libraries, 392, 396–397
  reasons for need, 392
  second generation,
    400–402
  single user access
    point, 391
  Toolboxes, 392, 395
  Workbenches, 392, 398
ERD data model
  (entity relationship
  diagram), 280
ERP (Enterprise Resource
  Planning), 33
ETL (extraction,
  transformation and
  loading), 205
evaluation stage, CLC, 85
examples
  banking customer
    needs, 4–5
  CIF operation, 57–58
  CRM interactions, 25
execution of campaigns,
    CIF operations
    example, 57
executive level support,
    CRM development,
    112–114
expand stage, building
    trust, 425
exploration warehouses,
    34, 45, 278

explorers, CRM
development, 154
extended enterprises
CLC, 66–67, 70
customer ODS
relationships, 318
extended households
CRM continuum of
interactions, 27
influence value, 21–22
extensibility of design,
customer ODSs, 320
extracting data, click
stream analysis,
205, 384

F
farmers, CRM
development, 154
fax back sales and
service, 332
fear, removing to
improving quality, 257
feedback loop, Zachman
Framework, 168
field accumulation,
loading ODSs, 227
field integrity, data
acquisition, 211–212
field replacement, loading
ODSs, 227
field sales and service, 332
filtering, 51, 219, 295
first-generation EPs, 399
forces impacting extended
enterprise, 70
forecasting sales, 349
formats for data storage,
capturing data, 215
formatting data, 51, 296
functions
data marts, 284
strategic, 277

tactical, 277
Zachman
Framework, 165
definitions, 182–183
naming
conventions, 179
subject area
relationships, 186
funding, CRM
development, 131

G
GDI team (Getting Data
In)
CIF program
management,
132–134
CRM development
role, 146
GIO team (Getting
Information Out)
CIF program
management, 135
CRM development
role, 151
global marketplace, CLC
example, 67
goals
CRM system, 49
data warehouse
construction, 280
government
megamarket, 74
granularity, database
design, 292
guarantors, 13

H
handling logic problems,
capturing data, 214
harassment, 407
help desk
automation, 335

databases, 345
decision trees, 345
differences from
traditional service,
343–344
inference engine
tools, 345
historical data, 42, 216
households
as customers, 14–15
CRM continuum
focus, 27
extended. *See* extended
households.
influence value, 19–21
managing interactions,
customer
contacts, 24

I
identifying potential
customers, CLC, 72
identifying valuable
customers, CRM
implementation issues,
437
implementing customer
data standards, CRM
development, 111–112
improving
production/service
systems, 252–254
in-use data, capturing data,
217
independent agents, 11
individual consumer
megamarket, 74
individually identifiable
information, 407
inference engine tools, 345
influence value in
households, 19–22

information delivery
developer, CRM
development, 152
integrated customer
information
environment, 108
integrated data, 221–222
data quality tools, 323
transforming, 222
integrated information
environment, EPs, 394
integration
data, CRM
development, 134
marketing with other
areas, 118
ODSs, 46
subjects, 306
sales and service,
353–358
intermediary channel,
customer touch, 76
Internet
click stream analysis, 377
customer touch
point, 332
interrogatories, Zachman
Framework, 161
intrude and engage stage,
CLC, 65, 80, 423
intuitiveness of data
access tools, 52
IT communications,
CRM program
management, 131
item singular model
appearance, Zachman
Framework rules, 180
IVR (interactive voice
response), 340

K–L
key master tables, data
integration, 222

knowledge management
databases, 345
lead management, CLC, 73
leadership, improving
quality, 256
learning from customer
feedback, CRM
implementation
issues, 439
learning stage, CLC, 83
libraries, EPs, 392,
396–397
life cycle cost, 251
lifetime value analyses, 43
listening to customers,
CRM implementation
issues, 439
loading data, 205
click stream analysis, 385
data warehouses,
223–225
ODSs, 226
quality issues, 270
locations, Zachman
Framework, 190–192
logic problems, capturing
data, 213–214
logic recursiveness,
Zachman Framework
rules, 171–173
logs, reading to capture
data changes, 218

M
mail sales and service, 332
maintaining meta data, 236
maintenance, customer
ODS relationships, 319
managing interactions,
23–24
manually inputting
relationship links,
customer ODSs, 320

mapping data, 205
click stream analysis, 384
sources to targets, 207
marketing
integrating with other
areas, 118
measures of success,
CRM development,
115–117
matrix, Zachman
Framework, 159
CRUD, 165
organizational unit-entity
relationships, 166
measuring quality of
data, 232
media channel, customer
touch, 76
megamarkets, 74
meta data, 49
audit and control, 234
capturing, 236
repositories,
auditing, 229
meta data analyst, CRM
development, 153
meta model uniqueness,
Zachman Framework
rules, 165
methodology for
auditing, 230
middleware, data
acquisition, 325
mobile access, sales force
automation, 351–352
models, Zachman
Framework, 168,
173–176
MOLAP (multidimensional
online analytical
processing), 282
monitoring campaigns,
CIF example, 58

multi-functionality, CIF, 53
myths about quality,
    240–244

N

naming conventions,
    Zachman Framework
    entities, 177
needs identification stage,
    CLC, 64, 82
negative aspects of
    data mart types,
    285–286, 289
non-individually
    identifiable
    information, 407
numerical quotas,
    removing to improving
    quality, 259–260

O

ODSs (Operational Data
    Stores), 36, 305
  assessing data
      quality, 232
  auditing, 228–230
  campaign execution, 57
  capturing data
    archived data, 216
    changed data, 217–218
    data storage
        formats, 215
    filtering, 219
    in-use data, 217
    logic problems, 213–214
  changing role, 448
  characteristics, 46, 306
  correcting data, 233
  current view of
      subjects, 307
  customer-centric,
      313–315
  data cleansing, 220–221

data integration, 221–222
detail of data, 308
e-commerce role,
    382–383
integration of
    subjects, 306
loading data, 223, 226
OLTP (online transaction
    processing), 36
process-centric, 311
product-centric, 310
referential integrity, 46
sales and service
    integration, 355–358
subject orientation, 306
subject-centric, 312
timely data
    acquisition, 51
TrI (transaction
    interface), 53
update frequency, 308
volatility, 308
OLAP data marts
    (online analytical
    processing), 278
OLTP (online transaction
    processing), 36
online customer
    interaction, 363
operational systems
  assessing, 448
  source application,
      capturing data
      changes, 218
  Zachman Framework
      model, 196
operations
  data marts, 284
  CIF, 57–58
  functions, 54
operators, CRM
    development, 154

opportunities in
    e-commerce, 367–369
Opt-in/Opt-out, 407
optimizing campaign
    performance, CIF
    example, 58
order of columns
    unimportant
    rule, Zachman
    Framework, 162
organization change agent,
    CRM development, 141
organizational culture and
    structure, 101–107,
    445–446
organizational
    units, Zachman
    Framework, 165
outbound call center
    telemarketing, 100

P

parties, Zachman
    Framework, 188–189
partitioning data, loading
    data into data
    warehouses, 225
partnerships, 18
party use restriction
    groups, 428
pattern recognition,
    EP Toolboxes, 395
performance tuning,
    EP Toolboxes, 396
permission marketing, 372
personalization
  collaborative filters, 382
  content management
      tools, 381
  e-commerce, 373–375
  e-mail response
      systems, 382

engines, customer
ODSs, 315
predictive engines, 382
rules engines, 381
Web sites, 381–382
personally identifiable
information, 407
perspective as unique view
rule, Zachman
Framework, 167
perspectives,
Zachman Framework,
158–159, 167
phone sales and
service, 332
physical security of
data, 421
pictorial function
representation,
Zachman
Framework, 183
planning
CRM system, 94–95, 110
improving
production/service
systems, 252
PMO (program
management
office), 156
positive aspects of data
marts, 285–286
precedence of data,
loading data
warehouses, 224
predictive dialers, 340
predictive engines, 382
prioritizing CRM
project, 131
privacy, 406–408
CIF, 427
CLC, 421
consent forms, 409

corporate self-regulation,
412–413
customer control of data
provided, 409
e-commerce, building
trust, 411
limited use of data
provided, 410
relevance of data
requested, 410
privacy policies, 415
accuracy of data, 420
customer choice to
reveal data, 419
ownership of data, 420
reasons for data
usage, 418
reasons for sharing
data, 417
privacy protection Web
sites, 415
problem resolution
databases, 345
process-centric ODSs, 311
processes
defining for auditing, 231
Zachman Framework,
entity relationships,
165
product applications,
customer ODS
links, 313
product catalogs, 349
product configuration
components, sales
configurations, 351
product focus, CRM
continuum, 27
product-centric ODSs, 310
product/service
profitability, 38
products
CLC impact, 68

determining number per
customer, CRM
assessment, 8
profile data, customer
ODSs, 313
profitability analyses, EP
Toolboxes, 395
program management
teams, CIF, 129
business strategy
alignment, 130
funding, 131
GDI (Getting Data In),
132–134
GIO (Getting Information
Out), 135
IT communications, 131
project prioritization, 131
repeatable/reusable
processes, 131
program manager, CRM
development, 142
project leader, CRM
development, 143
project prioritization, CRM
development, 131
project teams
program
management, 129
business strategy
alignment, 130
funding, 131
GDI (Getting Data In),
132–134
GIO (Getting
Information
Out), 135
IT communications, 131
project
prioritization, 131
repeatable/reusable
processes, 131

roles and
responsibilities, 138
strategy, 128
technology, 128
proposal generation, sales
configuration, 351
prospect stage, CLC, 63, 84
prospects, 16

Q
quality
data
assessing, 232
capturing, 263
CRM development, 135
integration, 268
transformation, 269
data cleansing
data acquisition, 267
operational
systems, 266
definition, 240–244
Deming's 14 quality
points, 246
adopt the new
philosophy, 248
ceasing dependence
on mass inspection,
249–250
constancy of
purpose for
improvement, 247
educational/retraining
programs, 261
improving
production/service
systems, 252–254
leadership, 256
life cycle cost, 251
removing fear, 257
removing numerical
quotas, 259–260

removing
sloganeering, 259
removing staff area
barriers, 258
taking action, 262
training, 255
establishing
expectations, 264
loading data, 270
tools and programs, 270
quality control, 228
quality customer data, 262
queries, detailed support,
54–55

R
records, ODSs, 227
recursive logic, Zachman
Framework rules, 171
reengineering data, CIF, 47
reentry stage, CLC, 65, 88
referential integrity,
ODSs, 46
referral sources, 16
refresh rates
data acquisition, 211
ODSs, 308
relationships, 16
B2B, 17
B2C, 17
C2C, 19
customer ODSs, 319
with customers, 46
repeatable processes,
CRM development, 131
required data, customer
ODSs, 322
resolving data integration
problems, 265
resource management, EP
Toolboxes, 396
responsibilities
data stewards, 264–265

project management
team, 138
retain and expand stage,
CLC, 65, 86, 425
retaining customers, 87
retraining programs,
improving quality, 261
reusability of data, 56
reusable processes, CRM
development, 131
right place, time and
product, CRM
readiness, 7–8
role of project
management team, 138
rules
engines, personalizing
Web sites, 381
Zachman Framework,
162–171, 180
rule 3 corollary, 181

S
sales
analysis, 38
forecasting, 349
service integration,
353–358
sales configurations, 351
sales force automation, 39,
330–331, 346
account
management, 348
automated character
recognition, 350
B2B, 347
calendar
management, 349
campaign
management, 350
contact management, 349
customer data, 349
forecasting, 349

mobile access, 351–352
product catalogs, 349
sales reports, 349
telesales, 350
sales reports, 349
sales roadmap, CRM
development, 122–123
schemas for database
design, 291
scripting tools, customer
ODSs, 315
search tools, customer
ODSs, 326
second generation EPs,
400–402
security, 406, 421
data, GIO team CRM
development, 137
See also privacy.
services
automation, 331
CLC perspective, 68
profitability, 38
sales integration, 353–358
shared systems areas, 105
silver bullet syndrome, 450
singular business model
rule, Zachman
Framework, 172
sloganeering, removing to
improve quality, 259
small business, influence
value, 22
snapshots, capturing data
changes, 218
social networks. *See*
extended households.
softphone, 338
solutions databases, help
desk, 345
source precedence,
loading data into data
warehouses, 224

source timestamps,
capturing data
changes, 218
specificity of data, 42
speech recognition, 340
stability of CIF system, 44
stages of CLC (Customer
Life Cycle), 63–65
staging areas, loading
data into data
warehouses, 224
standards for
customer data,
customer ODSs, 320
star schema data marts,
287–289
starter model, Zachman
Framework entity
definitions, 192
steering committee, CRM
development, 145
strategic components of
CRM, 276–278
strategic functions,
CRM, 277
strategic operations
groups, 105
strategy project teams, 128
structural issues, database
design, 294
structure of organizations,
445–446
subentities, Zachman
Framework, 190
subject area model,
Zachman Framework,
184–186
subject orientation, ODSs,
46, 306
subject-centric ODSs, 312
supplier relationships,
16–18

sustainable identifiers,
data acquisition,
207–209
synchronous customer
touch, 77
system data model,
Zachman
Framework, 193

T

tactical functions, 277
taking action to improve
quality, 262
target audience of data
marts, 284
teamwork, improving
quality, 258
technical meta data
analyst, CRM
development, 150
technical sponsor, CRM
development, 145–146
technological issues,
DSIs, 298
technology data
model, Zachman
Framework, 193
technology project teams,
CRM development, 128
telecommunications,
extended customer
relationships, 22
telesales, 350
third-party
partnerships, 18
timeliness of data
delivery, 50
timely data acquisition,
ODSs, 51
Toolboxes, EPs, 392, 395
tools, customer data
quality, 270

tourists, CRM
    development, 154
tracking contacts, CLC, 74
traditional businesses with
    Web sites, 367
traditional service
    environment,
    differences from help
    desk, 343–344
training as way to
    quality, 255
transaction interfaces,
    customer ODSs, 315,
    323–325
transforming data, 205
  click stream analysis, 384
  integrated data, 222
TrI (transaction interface),
    ODSs, 53, 323–325
trust
  building, 81
  e-commerce and
      privacy, 411
  in organization, 78–79
types of customers, 9
  agents, 11
  beneficiaries, 12
  bill payers, 12
  competitors, 13
  employees, 13
  guarantors, 13
  households, 14–15
  prospects, 16
  referral sources, 16
  suppliers, 16

U
Update frequency
  data acquisition, 211
  ODSs, 308

Usage stage, CLC, 65, 88
Use restrictions, 428
User interface links,
    customer ODSs, 315
Users, database design
    issues, 292

V–W
Vendor issues, DSIs, 298
Views, Zachman
    Framework, 158
Volatility of ODSs, 46, 308
VRU (voice response
    unit), 340
Walk-in customer
    service, 332
Web sites
  click stream analysis,
      377–380
  personalization, 381–382
Workbenches
  EPs, 392, 398
  management, 342
Workflow management,
    335–338

Z
Zachman Framework, 158
  attributes,
      naming/definition
      conventions, 177
  business data model, 173,
      176, 180, 187
    development rules, 171
  business process model,
      174, 179–181
  CRUD matrix, 165
  data mart model, 197–198
  data warehouse
      model, 196

diagrams,
    conventions, 179
  dimensions, 159
    relational matrix, 165
  entities, 163, 176
    naming/definition
        conventions, 177
    process
        relationships, 165
  feedback loop, 168
  functions, 165, 182
    definitions, 183
    naming
        conventions, 179
  interrogatories, 161
  locations, 190–192
  matrix, 159
  models, 168
  operational systems
      model, 196
  organizational units, 165
  parties, 188–189
  perspectives, 158
    constraints, 159, 167
  pictorial function
      representation, 183
  rules, 162–171, 180
    rule 3 corollary, 181
  starter model, entity
      definitions, 192
  subentities, 190
  subject area model,
      184–185
    function
        relationships, 186
  system data model, 193
  technology data
      model, 193